Silent But for the Word

Silent But for the Word

Tudor Women as Patrons, Translators, and Writers of Religious Works

Edited by Margaret Patterson Hannay

The Kent State University Press

Copyright © 1985 by The Kent State University Press, Kent, Ohio 44242
All rights reserved
Library of Congress Catalog Card Number 84-27802
Manufactured in the United States of America
ISBN: 0-87338-315-X

LIBRARY OF CONGRESS CATALOGING IN PUBLICATION DATA
Main entry under title:

Silent but for the word.

Includes index.
    1. Women—England—Religious life—Addresses, essays, lectures.   2. Women—
England—History—16th century—Addresses, essays, lectures.   3. Christian literature,
English—Women authors—History and criticism—Addresses, essays, lectures.   4. En-
glish literature—Early modern, 1500-1700—History and criticism—Addresses, essays,
lectures.   I. Hannay, Margaret P., 1944–
BV4527.S44   1985   809'.9352   84-27802
ISBN 0-87338-315-X

In Memoriam

DIANE BORNSTEIN

For as there is nothing more certaine then death, so is there nothing more uncertaine then the houre of death, knowen onlie to God, the onlie Author of life and death, to whom wee all ought endevour both to live and die.

The Countess of Pembroke's Translation of Philippe de Mornay's Discourse on Life and Death, edited by Diane Bornstein

Contents

Illustrations

MARGARET P. HANNAY

Introduction

T HE PROBLEM of the woman writer has traditionally been not the anxiety of influence but the anxiety of absence. Until recently, each woman—denied the knowledge of her predecessors—has been forced to devote much of her energy to self-justification, defending her right to be learned and articulate. As Margaret L. King notes, "The learned women of the Renaissance, in the eyes of their male contemporaries and friends, ceased, in becoming learned, to be women." Cassandra Fedele was called a "miracle," a male soul in a female body, and Isotta Nogarola was praised for overcoming her "own nature" by seeking "true virtue, which is essentially male." [1] Olimpia Morata recognized the necessity of denying her sex to be a scholar, a choice symbolized by giving up the traditional female implements:

> I, a woman, have dropped the symbols of my sex,
> Yarn, shuttle, basket, thread,
> I love but the flowered Parnassus with the choirs of joy
> Other women seek after what they choose
> These only are my pride and my delight.
> (King, p. 88n. 36)

This consciousness of defying a prescribed role prompts women to use the modesty topos with vivid intensity. As Virginia Woolf and many others have noted, the primary obstacle a woman writer (or speaker) must overcome is the societal norm which she has internalized. We may find a bitter irony in the way accomplished Renaissance women internalized the commands to silence that were so prevalent in their culture. Even Elena Lucrezia Cornaro Piscopia, the first woman to be granted a doctorate by the University of Padua (1677), a procedure which involved significant rhetorical accomplishment, declared that "the highest ornament of woman is silence." Even she lacked confidence in public speaking: "This I cannot do, because in the end I am a maiden." To overcome such internalized obstacles, a woman may search for a tradition in earlier women writers, as Woolf did when she began to explore the writings of Ann Finch, Margaret Cavendish, Aphra Behn, and Mary Wollstonecraft.[2]

The history of women's writings is often one of repeated loss and rediscovery. When a woman did write a significant work, it might be credited to a man. Laura Cereta was reportedly pleased when accused of presenting her father's works as her own since the accusation itself established her worth (King, p. 89n. 43). Sir John Harington credited Mary Sidney's *Psalmes* to her chaplain against overwhelming evidence of her own authorship simply because "it was more than a woman's skill to express the sense so right as she hath done in her verse." Marie de France was so conscious of this tendency to deprive a woman of her own work that the epilogue to her *Fables* reads:

> Marie is my name,
> I am from France.
> It may be that many clerks
> will take my labor on themselves—
> I do not want any of them to claim it.[3]

Marie's caution prevented the misattribution of her *Fables*, but the works of many other women writers have been repeatedly lost and rediscovered. For example, our own study of these women was anticipated in the early eighteenth century by an anonymous schoolgirl. A notebook preserved at the British Library contains a brief diary, some French exercises, and "A Catalogue of Ladies famous for their writings, or skill in the Learned Languages." Lacking the scholarly training and resources represented in this volume, the schoolgirl could only list the women with a few words of annotation, yet her catalog includes many of the women we discuss in the present work—Margaret More Roper, Catherine Parr, Queen

Elizabeth, Anne Askew, Lady Jane Grey, the Cooke sisters, Mary Sidney, Elizabeth Cary—along with others, to a total of some one hundred women. We do not know her sources, but she knew far more about her own tradition of English women writers than did Ann Finch, Countess of Winchilsea, who found her predecessors only in Scripture, as noted in the introduction to her poems published anonymously in 1713. The women who sang before the ark, those who sang for David's triumphs, and Deborah, the judge and poet of Israel, were apparently Finch's only known models. Ignorant of her countrywomen's past achievements, she still courageously rejected the idea that women were naturally inferior:

> How are we fal'n, fal'n by mistaken rules?
> And Education's, more then Nature's fools,
> Debarr'd from all improvements of the mind,
> And to be dull, expected and dessigned.[4]

Nevertheless, bowing to societal pressure, she gave up the "groves of Lawrell" to sing only "with contracted wing / To some few freinds."

Finch herself eventually became part of the tradition she sought: Virginia Woolf quoted from Finch in *A Room of One's Own,* a work conceived in indignation when Woolf was barred from the privileges of a Cambridge education because of her sex. Although Woolf analyzed the works of eighteenth- and nineteenth-century women writers available to her in print, she was denied the opportunity to recover earlier writers. Aware of no evidence to the contrary, she concluded that there were no Renaissance women writers and characteristically produced a witty explanation (frequently reprinted under the modern title "Shakespeare's Sister") of the conditions which prevented women from writing in the Tudor period.

Our knowledge of women writers prior to Finch's 1713 edition has dramatically increased in the twentieth century, particularly since 1970. Scholars poring through unpublished diaries, letters, and manuscripts, resurrecting books which have been out of print for several hundred years, following obscure leads through more obscure court cases and account books, have begun to reconstruct the works and lives of significant numbers of early women writers. Only those who have worked in this area fully understand how dearly bought are the facts summarized in a few sentences. As Meg Bogin says in her introduction to biographical sketches of the woman troubadours, "It is in the ardent hope of sparing others the travail required for the unearthing of each single fact that they are printed here".[5]

The best indication that studies of medieval and Renaissance women have come of age is the extensive bibliography of both primary and secondary sources now available. Since the general background for women's roles and education is now becoming well established, and since some of the major texts are now available in modern editions, the present study focuses on a specialized topic, the character of religious writing by and for Tudor women.

The essays in this collection argue that the policy of permitting English women only religious discourse had two primary results. The first, as those in authority no doubt intended, was that the wealth, energy, and learning of a substantial number of noblewomen made possible the rapid production of religious works, which were predominately Protestant. The second result, which they did not foresee, was that women occasionally subverted the text, even in translation, in order to insert personal and political statements.

This subversion of existing texts was a necessary strategy for women because silence was considered one of the primary feminine virtues throughout the Tudor period. As Thomas Becon admonished, " . . . let her kepe silence. For there is nothinge that doth so much commend, avaunce, set forthe, adourne, decke, trim, and garnish a maid, as silence."[6] Ominously, silence was said to be connected to that primary feminine virtue, chastity, as in the proverb "An eloquent woman is never chaste" (Labalme, p. 139). Thomas Bentley, in *The Monument of Matrones,* threatens utter ruin to a vocal woman: "There is nothing that becommeth a maid better than sobernes, silence, shamefastnes, and chastitie, both of bodie & mind. For these things being once lost, shee is no more a maid, but a strumpet in the sight of God" (Hull, p. 142). The fact that Bentley was writing clichés exemplifies the way in which a woman's desire for godliness was habitually used to silence her. Paradoxically, women were permitted to break the rule of silence only to demonstrate their religious devotion by using their wealth to encourage religious education and publication by men, by translating the religious works of other (usually male) writers, and, more rarely, by writing their own devotional meditations. Christine de Pizan justified her writing on such religious grounds: "He has truly placed language in women's mouths so that He might be thereby served." Young Anne Cooke used a similar explanation to justify her own study of Italian by dedicating to her mother her translation of sermons by Bernardino Ochino: "Wherein . . . it hath pleased you, often, to reprove my vaine studie in the Italian tonge, accompting the sede thereof, to have bene sowen in barayne, unfruitful grounde (sins God thereby is no whit magnified) . . . accepte this work as yelding some parte of the fruite of your Motherly admonicions."[7]

This one exception to the silence required of women means that the majority of extant works and translations by English women in the Middle Ages and Renaissance are on religious subjects. There are exceptions, of course—notably Mary Wroth's sonnet sequence, *Pamphilia to Amphilanthus,* and her pastoral epic *Urania,* both modeled on the work of her father, Robert Sidney, Earl of Leicester, and her more famous uncle, Sir Philip Sidney. However, Lord Edward Denny harshly castigated her for attempting this unfeminine work and admonished her to follow the "pious example of your vertuous and learned Aunt [Mary Sidney], who translated so many godly books and especially the holly psalmes of David."[8] Thus were women who ignored the limits of female discourse herded back within their proper boundaries. The strategy worked: Lady Mary Wroth gave a spirited reply to Denny, but published nothing further.

Although both Continental and English women were exhorted to silence, Continental women were generally better educated and given more opportunities for self-expression, particularly after the Anglo-Saxon period.[9] By 1500 Europe had an established tradition of secular writing by women. What is missing in the English tradition may be seen in the closely reasoned defense of women in Christine de Pizan's *Book of the City of Ladies,* in the passion for social justice in the laies of Marie de France, in the novella of Marguerite de Navarre, and in the love poems of the women troubadours. Unlike the male speaker in courtly love poems whose concern was with his own responses to the woman, the female troubadour was always concerned with "the beloved male at the center of her world," a male who was usually absent and often unfaithful. Her passive experience was presented as removed from the world of male activity; she was powerless to control her lover when he left for what he considered the "real world." These poems by female poets show significant differences in both form and content from those by their male counterparts. The twenty-three extant poems by the women troubadours are straightforward, with less emphasis on craft and no use of allegory. Perhaps this is because, as Meg Bogin suggests, "They do not idealize the relationships they write about."[10]

These women troubadours wrote in an intensely personal voice, as they sought not allegorical veneration but love, acknowledgment of themselves as persons, and a voice in determining their relationship (Bogin, p. 72). They asserted their right to an active role in love: "When a lady's mind / is set on love, she ought / to court the man, if he shows strength and chivalry" (Castelloza, in Bogin, p. 125). The songs also speak of what the men never mention—the pain of pregnancy and childbirth—concluding that "making babies I think is a huge penitence" for making love (Bogin, p. 145). These personal elements are largely absent from the writings of medieval and Renaissance English women, whose own voices were suppressed, but the twelfth-century Provençal troubadours do reflect the same bitter experience of love that Lady Mary Wroth recounted in *Pamphilia* before she was silenced.

In England, early writings by women were apparently exclusively religious, and even these are scarce. In the Anglo-Saxon period, learned nuns like Lioba, who later became Abbess of Bischofsheim, corresponded with St. Boniface and wrote saints' lives. Yet learning in English convents deteriorated rapidly after the Norman Conquest. Even in Benedictine nunneries, which required periods of study, "it was evidently considered altogether outside the scope of women to concern themselves with writing. While the monks composed chronicles, the nuns embroidered copes," according to Eileen Power (p. 238). There was in England no learned house to compare with Gandersheim, Hohenburg, or Helfta (p. 293), nor was there an English woman who produced a body of work comparable to the saints' legends, epics, and dramas by Hrothswitha of the Gandersheim monastery in Germany. English nunnery libraries apparently contained little besides a few service books (p. 241). After the thirteenth century, few nuns knew Latin, even enough to read their charters or understand the prayers they repeated; by the fourteenth century, few nuns knew French (p. 260). Although male clerics still relied solely on Latin, their solution to the ignorance of the nuns was to translate a few appropriate documents—

the rules of the order, the charter, passages of Scripture—rather than teaching women Latin. In the familiar double jeopardy of the powerless, the nuns were denied learning and then despised for their ignorance. In the fourteenth and fifteenth centuries, apparently few English nuns could write, even in their native tongue; they were completely dependent on clerks for their records and accounts (p. 245). A simple request for a certificate of the convent's mandate threw the Prioress of Langley into panic; according to the visitation records, "Because they are unversed in letters they cannot understand the writings" (p. 251). A better system for silencing women could not have been devised.

A few medieval English women did find voices, despite these restrictions. The mystic anchoress Julian of Norwich recorded sixteen visions in her *Revelations of Divine Love.* Her own ambivalence toward her position as woman and writer is evident: "But God forbid that you should say or take me for a teacher . . . for I am a woman, ignorant, weak, and frail." Nevertheless, she bases her right to speak on the will of God: "Since I am a woman, should I not therefore believe that I ought to tell you about the goodness of God, when I saw at the same time that it was His will for it to be known?" (Wilson, pp. 281–82). Margery Kempe, whose attempts to live like the Virgin Martyrs were much impeded by a husband and thirteen children, nevertheless persisted in wearing a hair shirt, praying aloud publicly, recounting visions, preaching, and taking pilgrimages to Jerusalem. Illiterate, eccentric as she was, she left us the first autobiography in English; better adjusted women did not record their lives. Her work remained unpublished and unknown until the twentieth century. Some few early Tudor women might have had access to manuscripts of the meditations of Julian of Norwich, or the Anglo-Norman life of St. Catherine, by Clemence, a nun of Barking. More would have known the legend that St. Catherine defeated fifty philosophers in debate and that St. Athanasius was converted by her preaching, thereby making St. Catherine a model of female speech and learning. Unfortunately, even this model was virtually discredited for most Englishwomen by the Protestant Reformation.

Although the Reformation has traditionally been hailed as a liberating force for women, the Protestant emphasis on the Word of God encouraged education for women so that they could read the Bible and the appropriate commentaries, not so that they could speak or write their own ideas. The

court replaced the convent as the milieu most likely to encourage scholarship for aristocratic women, but the enforced rhetorical ignorance of
women was maintained. In the sixteenth century, William Harrison declared that the ladies of the court were engaged in "continuall reading
either of the holie Scriptures, or histories of our owne or forren nations
about us . . . . And to saie how many gentlewomen and ladies there are,
that beside sound knowledge of the Greke and Latine toongs, are thereto
no lesse skilfull in the Spanish, Italian, and French, or in som one of them,
it resteth not in me."[11] But court ladies, learned though they may have
been, were commonly admonished to hold their tongue in all the tongues
they knew.

For other women, the ability to read did not necessarily imply even the
ability to form letters. David Cressy estimates that between 1580 and
1640, 90 percent of women in ecclesiastical court cases in London and 95
percent in the countryside were unable to sign their names; yet the number
of copies sold of books specifically written for women indicates a substantial literacy rate. Teaching women to read the words of men without
teaching them to write their own was one effective means of silencing
them. Even when they were encouraged to learn to write, as by Martin
Billingsley in *The pen's excellencie*, it was because they lacked good memories "especially concerning matters of moment," and could thereby
"commit many worthy and excellent things to writing, which may, occasionally, minister unto them matter of much solace." Although he thought
that women should learn to form their letters, Billingsley envisioned that
their writing would be only copying and their audience only themselves.
He offers no hint of an independent discourse.[12]

Mary Ellen Lamb argues in this volume that "the professed [public]
goals of a humanistic education were perverted when they were applied to
women." For men, learning was a means to serve the state, but for women
it became an end in itself, a way of "keeping them busy, much like . . .
sewing . . . in a fashion which did not threaten the established power
structure. Instead of a means to exert control, education was, for women, a
further means of being controlled." Denied the rhetorical training deemed
necessary for public office and for original writing, women were encouraged to translate suitable works by men because such activity "did not
threaten the male establishment as the expression of personal viewpoints

might"; translations are "defective" and therefore "all translations are reputed femalls," John Florio declared, apologizing for his own labor in this degraded activity.[13] How the women themselves felt about being restricted to such degraded activity can be inferred from the statement of Anne Locke, a friend of John Knox, in the preface to her translation of Taffin's *Markes of the Children of God:* "Because great things by reason of my sexe, I may not doe, and that which I may, I ought to doe, I have according to my duety, brought my poore basket of stones to the strengthening of the wals of that Jerusalem, whereof (by Grace) we are all both Citizens and members" (Labalme, p. 118). It is a remarkable statement, revealing her reluctant acceptance of the limits put upon her sex, her determination to achieve as much as was permitted, and her religious motivation for undertaking this particular work.

Religious motivation, which permitted women to translate, could be used to force them out of original discourse and into translation. We have already noted the way in which Lady Mary Wroth was condemned for her secular epic and told to translate "godly books" instead. Similarly, Gregorio Correr told Cecilia Gonzaga to give up her studies and her composition of original Latin works so that she might instead translate religious works into the vernacular for the instruction of "unlettered virgins." By this admonition, he cleverly doubled her guilt if she continued her independent composition (Labalme, p. 90n. 50). Not only would she be defying God by refusing to turn to religious translations, but also she would be depriving her unlearned sisters of matters necessary to their salvation.

Debarred from original discourse by the absence of rhetorical training, urged to translation for the greater glory of God, women did translate an extensive body of religious work, usually at the prompting of father, brother, or husband, and usually works which would be particularly useful to the state or to a political faction. When their work was published, it was often anonymous; if it was known to be by a woman, it was usually restricted to manuscripts in the family circle, as was most of the work of Margaret More Roper. Undoubtedly, many Tudor women writers and scholars will never be rediscovered, but more information is available than we had originally dared to hope, particularly on women connected with the court. The aristocratic bias of our selection is obvious: noble women were more likely to be educated, more likely to be surrounded by scholars who praised and encouraged their study in exchange for patronage, and more likely to have their work published or at least preserved in manuscript. In this study of works by aristocratic women, the first and final essays address theoretical concerns; the others discuss, in chronological order, the works of particular women.

The lives of these aristocratic women, although less restricted in many ways than those of women in the lower classes, were still tightly constrained by an emphasis on the virtues of chastity, silence, and obedience. Valerie Wayne provides a perspective on their situation by outlining Tudor expectations for the Christian woman, focusing on Juan Luis Vives as a humanist who did assume that "women can be virtuous and so are worthy of being instructed in how to be." Yet Vives, like other humanist advocates of education for women, assumed that the primary goal of that education was a chaste life: "A woman hath no charge to se to but her honestie and chastyte. Wherfore whan she is enfurmed of that she is sufficiently appoynted." A woman was not to teach, to write, or to speak; even her reading was carefully supervised. If she should brazenly read prohibited books or even read "good books with an ill will," she should be prevented from reading: "And so by disuse forgette lernynge if hit can be done." Vives outlined "an exceedingly narrow and confined" life for women, Wayne concludes, yet "the rigid life he prescribes . . . was not the worst alternative for them then: it was one of the best available."

The subsequent essays in this volume show individual women coping with these restrictions in their roles as patrons, translators, and writers of religious works. Rita Verbrugge argues that Margaret More Roper, whose scholarship was highly praised by early humanists but whose published work was carefully restricted to anonymous translation, demonstrates in her translation of Erasmus' *Precatio Dominica* "the care and concern for a responsible translation that belonged to the ideals of the early humanists." Yet by adding her personal perspective to the work, " 'the yong vertuous and well lerned gentylwoman' can and does speak with her own mind and voice."

Queen Catherine Parr, a more public figure, sponsored Protestant education and contributed her own devotional meditation, *The Lamentacion of a Sinner.* John King establishes that she and the women around her popularized "Protestant humanism through patronage of devotional manuals and theological translations for the edification of a mixed audience of elite and ordinary readers." Their piety and patronage served as the model for Elizabeth and the women of her court.

Through her examination of a translation presented by the young Elizabeth to Catherine Parr, Anne Prescott demonstrates that the princess subverted the text of Marguerite de Navarre's *Miroir,* toning down the religious fervor and altering the image of God as a loving father to a loving mother, a revealing personal statement from the reticent daughter of Henry VIII and Anne Boleyn. Silence for Princess Elizabeth was not only a feminine virtue but a diplomatic necessity; by holding her tongue, she kept her head.

Less fortunate were two women writers who came to prominence by martyrdom—Anne Askew under Henry VIII and Lady Jane Grey under Queen Mary. On the rack or in the Tower, these women broke the traditional silence to justify their actions; their faith gave them a message, a vocabulary, and a justification for writing. Elaine Beilin provides a rhetorical analysis of the *Examinations* of Anne Askew, a member of Catherine Parr's court, arguing that her "coreligionists found [in her] only a Protestant saint," but that later readers "might discover a remarkable woman creating a memorable self-portrait." Askew's works were written and preserved only because she was tried for heresy. Her courage on the rack dismayed her examiners but spared other women of the court from similar torture. John Bale declared that God chose Askew, a woman, as proof that He uses "the folysh of thys worlde to confounde the wyse, & the weake to deface the myghtye." Yet Askew presented herself as "a vanquisher of the papist foe, a learned, honest, God-fearing, Scripture-loving comrade in the faith." The qualities she values in herself are not the feminine virtues of silence and submission, but rather "piety, constancy, learning, and fortitude"—virtues which had been traditionally considered masculine.

Like Anne Askew, Lady Jane Grey, the "nine days queen," was noted for her political role rather than her writings, which were preserved in Foxe's *Actes and Monuments* (the *Book of Martyrs*) for propagandistic purposes. However, as Carole Levin establishes, she was forthright, determined, even strident in her self-justification, far from the image of the dutiful and submissive wife later imposed on her. By honoring her learning, her speech, and her courage, Foxe implicitly (and probably unintentionally) endorsed her as a Protestant model to replace St. Catherine. Lady Jane Grey's voice was amplified, not silenced, by beheading.

More fortunate women stayed within the boundaries prescribed for them. Mary Ellen Lamb examines the works of the Cooke sisters—Mildred, Anne, Elizabeth, and Katherine—who never violated societal norms by writing the works of which they were so obviously capable. Given their celebrated scholarship and their proven excellence in translation, why did they not write more than a handful of translations, personal letters, and a few epitaphs? Lamb suggests that silence was required of them except when they could quietly contribute to the good of the Church and the state. Their major efforts in translation, Anne's *Apologia Ecclesiae Anglicanae* and Elizabeth's *A Way of Reconciliation Touching the True Nature and Substance of the Body and Blood of Christ in the Sacrament,* are not only religious but also political, defining the doctrinal position of the Church of England in opposition both to Catholics and to schismatics. From their letters the sisters emerge as "vigorous, indomitable women energetically pursuing their affairs in a world not always sympathetic to their needs. . . . They exercise [their learning] often and without apology" in the limited spheres permitted to them.

Three essays focus on works by the most celebrated literary woman of the Tudor period, Mary Sidney, Countess of Pembroke. Diane Bornstein supplies a close stylistic analysis of Sidney's translation of Philippe de Mornay's *Discours de la vie et de la mort,* demonstrating that the countess is often more concise and yet more metaphorical than her original, avoiding a plodding literalism to capture the essence of Mornay's style. Compared to the contemporary translation of Edward Aggas, Sidney's is both more accurate and more lively. The skill of her translation makes us regret "that the countess limited herself to the silent art of translation and did not write her own meditations."

Nevertheless, Mary Sidney, like the Cooke sisters, managed to address public issues within the genres permitted her. After examining two original poems by Mary Sidney, poems in the appropriate feminine genres of epitaph and dedication, I conclude that the countess not only completed her brother's translation of the Psalms but also attempted to continue his involvement in Protestant politics. Giving Queen Elizabeth a psalter based on the Huguenot Psalms could have been interpreted as a political statement; when coupled with a lament for Sir Philip Sidney, acknowledged as a Protestant martyr, and a dedicatory poem which began with a reference to the Continent, the political intent of Mary Sidney's gift would have been unmistakable.

The personal and devotional aspect of Mary Sidney's verse translations of the Psalms is stressed by Beth Wynne Fisken who observes that what "began as an education in how to write poetry . . . ended in a search for wisdom." By identifying with the psalmist, the countess learned both "how to write poetry . . . [and] how to speak to God." She also speaks for herself in the expanded metaphors which reflect her own experiences as wife, mother, and lady-in-waiting.

Another avenue women were permitted was patronage. Mary Sidney's role as patron of both secular and religious writing is too well-documented to need rehearsal here.[14] Instead, Jon Quitslund considers the previously overlooked influence of the Russell sisters on Edmund Spenser's *Fowre Hymns,* one of whom had objected to Spenser's early hymns on "Love and beautie." In the *Fowre Hymns* "constancy to an ideal . . . is held up for admiration, while loss of everything but the immortal ideal is lamented," yet at least implicitly accepted.

In the early years of the seventeenth century, two women wrote religious works in genres usually reserved for men. Barbara Lewalski analyzes Aemilia Lanyer's *Salve Deus Rex Judaeorum,* a Passion poem which becomes "a comprehensive 'Book of Good Women,' fusing religious devotion and feminism"; Lanyer "presents Christ's Passion as the focus for all the forms of female goodness" in the poems. A second significant poem by Lanyer is "The Description of Cooke-ham," which may antedate Jonson's "To Penshurst" as the first English country-house poem. "Cooke-ham" laments the end of an Edenic state "in which women lived without mates, but found contentment and delight in nature, God, and female companionship."

The one Catholic writer discussed in this collection is Elizabeth Cary. Sandra Fischer observes that although Cary submitted to her husband's tyranny with outward patience and dissembled her learning, she wrote the first original extant English tragedy by a woman. In *The Tragedie of Mariam* the protagonist, like the author, faces domestic and religious tyranny. The impact of Mariam's death on the tyrant Herod was "perhaps more than

[Cary] could hope for personally, and she used the marginal genre as a forum for the philosophical investigation of the subject closest to her heart."

The essays conclude with Gary Waller's theoretical discussion, "Struggling into Discourse," which asks how the voices of silence can be heard, since female voices have so long been marginalized by the discourse of power. Confined to certain restricted areas of discourse, they speak through religious writing and translation; their sense of trespass when they attempt other genres is evident in "the uncanny intensity with which the traditional humility topos is incessantly used . . . to apologize for entering" any other, supposedly "male" domain. Waller challenges traditional critical methodologies: "Simply to acknowledge that there is relatively little material on which to work is to be limited by a positivism . . . imposed by a dominant intellectual paradigm that is suspiciously male-oriented." By addressing the theoretical and practical questions which underlie the current work on Renaissance women writers, Waller has followed Virginia Woolf's dictum that in considering women's writing, "it is necessary to leave oneself room to deal with other things besides their work, so much has that work been influenced by conditions that have nothing whatever to do with art."[15]

As we have seen, Tudor women rarely violated the boundaries set for them unless their very lives were at stake. In the sixteenth century, Anne Askew and Lady Jane Grey wrote only when they had little to lose by their spirited self-defense; Catherine Parr, Princess Elizabeth, the Cooke sisters, the Russell sisters, and Mary Sidney remained within the accepted confines. In the early seventeenth century, Lady Mary Wroth, from a family of writers, apparently had not sufficiently internalized the prohibition against original, secular writing by a woman and had to be silenced. Aemilia Lanyer and Elizabeth Cary were more wary, limiting their work to appropriately religious genres. Although these English women were relegated to the margins of discourse—to patronage, translation, dedications of translations, epitaphs, letters, and private devotional meditations—they did find their own voices through their proclamations of the Word of God.

VALERIE WAYNE

Some Sad Sentence: Vives' *Instruction of a Christian Woman*

WHY did Renaissance women write so little, and why did they so often treat religious subjects when they addressed an audience beyond their family circle? Since we are accustomed to think of the Renaissance as a time of great literary and artistic activity, the conscious or inadvertent exclusion of women from such work may seem especially puzzling to us. The causes of their silence surely extend beyond any rational explanation, but if I cannot fully answer the questions I have posed here—questions that are raised by this collection of essays—I hope I can at least identify certain assumptions and procedures for instructing women in Renaissance England that may have prevented those who did write, or those who could have written, from writing more. To this end, I will consider a text that few people know well and perhaps fewer still have any great desire to read: Juan Luis Vives' *De Institutione Foeminae Christianae*, which appeared in England about 1529 under the title, *The Instruction of a Christian Woman*.

The most popular conductbook for women during the Tudor period, Vives' work was commissioned by Catherine of Aragon for the instruction of her daughter Mary, and was issued in at least thirty-six English and Continental editions and in six modern languages by the end of the sixteenth century.[1] Richard Hyrde, who prepared the English translation, is often identified as an early advocate for women's education in England: he was a member of the household of Sir Thomas More, may have tutored

Margaret More Roper,[2] and wrote a strong defense of women's education
in his dedication to Margaret's translation of Erasmus' *Precatio Dominica*
(1523), called *A Devout Treatise Upon the Pater Noster*. In Hyrde's dedication to *The Instruction*, he says that More so appreciated Vives' work
that he even considered translating it himself and later agreed to correct
Hyrde's translation. Perhaps these associations help explain why *The Instruction* has so often been referred to by commentators as an educational
treatise.[3]

    It is an educational work if we consider the broadest meanings of that
term and their implications, particularly for Renaissance humanists, but
the word is misleading for a modern reader if it suggests a primary concern
with the formal course of study a Renaissance woman might have pursued:
The Instruction does not pretend to these latter concerns. Of its thirty-
eight chapters, only two are devoted to what a woman should study and
read, while Vives' stated purpose is that his book will give women "preceptes and rules howe to lyve."[4] He considers all aspects of their lives from
childhood to widowhood, and from apparel and walks abroad to private
meditations and sexual relations with their husbands. Since his book is
directed more toward women's conduct than to their formal education,
those who have called it a "conductbook" have, I think, represented it
most accurately,[5] although that term may suggest a separation between
action and motive, or between behavior and principle, that Christian
humanists would have questioned.

    Our confusion about its purpose also reflects our larger confusion about
what women were taught in the sixteenth century and why. Renaissance
humanists did advocate education for women who were apt for learning
and in a position to be tutored, but the aims in providing instruction for
those women usually differed from the aims for men. Vives makes his own
purposes plain in his preface: "As for a woman hath no charge to se to but
her honestie and chastyte. Wherfore whan she is enfurmed of that she is
sufficiently appoynted" (sig. B2r). In their educational programs, nearly all
humanists were concerned with the religious, philosophical, and moral
instruction of their students, and they turned to classical authors as en-
lightened teachers in those subjects. The emphasis was not so much on
acquiring knowledge as putting it into practice in an ethical and pious life:
hence the use of sententiae, or moral sayings, as a way of encouraging

moral action.[6] Yet when the same goals were applied to men and to women, they often produced different results. Of Vives' two long, instructional works now available in English, one is an educational treatise directed to boys and their tutors, called *De Tradendis Disciplinis,* and the other is a conductbook, *The Instruction,* for girls and women. He also wrote two formal plans of study, one for the Princess Mary and another for Charles Mountjoy, a pupil of Erasmus, but these more comparable works also show how differently he conceived of instruction for girls and for boys.[7]

While Vives was especially concerned about women's conduct, Richard Hyrde defends their academic instruction more strongly in his dedicatory letter to Catherine of Aragon, which appeared in three of the nine editions of *The Instruction* published in England through 1592.[8] He asks, "what is more frutefull than the good education and ordre of women, the one halfe of all mankynd" (sig. A2v), and expresses his wish that women were learned in Latin in every country or that *The Instruction* was translated into every tongue. Then Hyrde contrasts his own assessment of the worth of women's learning with those who ignored its influence or discouraged women from it:

. . . and moche I marvelled as I often do of the unreasonable oversyght of men whiche never ceace to complayne of womens conditions. And yet havyng the education and order of them in theyr owne handis nat only do litell diligence to teache them and bryng them up better, but also purposely with drawe them fro lernyng by whiche they myght have occasyons to waxe better by them selfe. (sigs. A2v–A3r)

Hyrde implies that learning will improve women's morals and lives so they may deny rather than confirm men's complaints about their behavior. He thereby affirms the value of the book he translates even as he shows he is more interested in women's academic education than its author.

Both Christian humanists, Vives and Hyrde, see as their opponents those men who do not believe that women can be virtuous at all. Vives also refers to them: "I pceyve that lerned women be suspected of many: as who sayth the subtyltie of lernynge shulde be a norishement for the malitiousnes of their nature" (sig. D2v). Those who complained about women or thought woman's nature malicious are generally identified as "antifeminists" (for lack of a better word)[9] in modern discussions of medieval and

Renaissance attitudes. The humanists, whether more liberal in their thinking as Hyrde, or more conservative as Vives, were nearly always women's defenders in the contemporary debate about them. In *The Instruction* Vives consistently assumes that women can be virtuous and so are worthy of being instructed in how to be. His preface also affirms the image of a good woman in his book. He says that Catherine of Aragon will find here a likeness of herself, "as if a peynter wolde brynge unto you your owne visage and image most counnyngly peynted. For lyke as in that purtrature you myght se your bodily similitude: so in these bokes shall you se the resemblaunce of your mynde and goodnes." Many good women like her are expressly named in the book, "but your selfe spoken of contynually though you be nat named." Catherine is, then, the exemplar of the work, the woman who exhibits all of the virtues it treats, while her daughter Mary is its intended, exemplary audience. Mary "shall rede these instructions of myne and folowe in lyvyng whiche she muste nedes do" (sig. B4r), finding here precepts for the ordering of her life just as she finds a living example of them in her mother. Similarly all women, Vives concludes, should be bound to Catherine for the example she provides and for the precepts Vives arrived at based upon her life, for "that hit hath ben thoccosion of my writyng" (sig. B4v).

So regardless of the positions humanists took on women's education, they were the best advocates women had during the early years of the Renaissance in England. Even their injunctions on women's conduct seem made to defend them from the criticism of antifeminists. Vives is certainly more conservative than some other humanists: William Woodward describes him as "typical of the somewhat severe, almost puritanic, cast of Spanish feeling which manifests itself in the writings of the first stage of the Renaissance in the Peninsula" (*Studies*, p. 209). But Sir Thomas More's interest in Vives' book, its publication throughout the sixteenth century in England, and the likelihood that Shakespeare used it for Kate's last speech in *The Taming of the Shrew*[10] all suggest that the views expressed by Vives strongly reflected and influenced some Tudor expectations for women.

An account of the relation between women's learning and their conduct which might have been widely accepted especially among humanists appears in *The Instruction* in a passage on More and his daughters, following a section on learned women from antiquity:

I wolde reken amonge this sorte the daughters of S.T.M.kn.M.E. and C. [Sir Thomas More, knight, Margaret, Emily, and Cecily] and with them theyr kyns woman, M.G. [Margaret Gigs]: whom theyr father nat content only to have them good and very chast wolde also they shulde be wel learned: supposyng that by that meane they shulde be more truely and surely chaste. (sigs. E1r-v)

While learned women were preferred over those who were virtuous but unlearned, their learning was valued primarily on the supposition attributed here to More, that it would increase their virtue. The end, therefore, for all instruction of a woman, whether for Vives, Hyrde, More, or other Christian humanists,[11] remained a woman's virtue—especially her chastity, which is why *The Instruction* is such an important book, far more important for its time than a treatise on women's education could ever have been.

The humanists' emphasis upon ethical conduct for women could, however, easily become yet another means of restricting their behavior and intellectual growth. As humanists defended women, they also prescribed specific roles for them, especially domestic roles, and they identified a limited function for their learning. The attention they gave to women's chastity also required restraints on other areas of development. After Vives takes up the education for a maid in his book, he explains what a woman should not do with her knowledge. She should learn "for her selfe alone and her yonge children or her sisters in our lord," not for anyone else. She should not rule a school or live among men or speak abroad or shake off her demureness and honesty. In company she should hold her tongue demurely, "and let fewe se her and none at al here her" (sig. E2v). The reasons he gives for these restrictions are biblical: he quotes Paul's requirements for women's behavior in Corinthians (14:34–35) and Timothy (2:11–14) almost verbatim. As he does so, Paul's first person injunctions merge with his own, so when Vives says, "I gyve no licence to a woman to be a teacher nor to have authorite of the man but to be in silence" (sig. E2v), the speaker might be of the first or of the sixteenth century. Then Vives restates Paul's reasons for those prohibitions in his own words:

Therfore bicause a woman is a fraile thynge and of weake discretion and that maye lightlye be disceyved: whiche thyng our fyrst mother Eve sheweth whom ye devyll caught with a lyght argument. Therfore a woman shulde nat teache leste whan she hath taken a false opinion and beleve of any thyng she spred hit into the

herars by the autorite of maistershyp and lightly bringe other into the same errour.
. . . (sigs. E2v–E3r)

The difference between the antifeminists' descriptions of women as malicious and Vives' description of them as "fraile," "weake," and easily
"disceyved," is the difference between strong evil and weak goodness.
Vives reflects typical humanist attitudes in what he says. Almost 150 years
after he wrote, Milton would make a similar distinction between Adam,
formed for "contemplation" and "valor," and Eve, for "softness and
sweet attractive Grace," and he would show how woman's weak reason
might be persuaded to evil action.[12] Humanists often conceived of women
as intellectually gullible—they were not stupid, but they might be easily
led. So it was all the more necessary to educate them. But they should not
lead others because they might lead them astray: "Womans thought is
swyfte and for the most parte unstable walkyng and wandrynge out from
home and soone wyl slyde by the reason of hit owne slypernes I wot nat
howe far. Therfore redyng were the best and therunto I gyve them coun-
saile specially" (sigs. C3v–C4r).

Reading therefore became a means of occupying women's weak and
wandering minds with wholesome thoughts. It was presented as an agent
of control more than of enlightenment and was identified with that other
occupation, the handling of wool and flax, as a craft, "whiche are two
craftes yet lefte of that olde innocent worlde both profitable and kepers of
temperance: whiche thynge specially women ought to have in price" (sig.
C3v). But the subject matter of women's reading had to be carefully controlled. Women should read the Gospels; the Acts and Epistles of the Apostles; the Old Testament; works by the fathers of the church such as
Cyprian, Augustine, Ambrose, Hilary, and Gregory; and others by Plato,
Cicero, and Seneca (sig. F2r). In his *Office and Duty of a Husband,* written
fifteen years later, Vives adds to this list Plutarch, and Christian poets such
as Prudentius, Aratus, Sedulius, and Juvencus.[13] Clearly, religious works
were supposed to constitute a large part of women's reading.

However, Vives also devotes almost an entire chapter—one of the two
chapters on education—to what a woman should *not* read. Plato cast
Homer and Hesiod out of the commonwealth, "and yet have they none yll
thyng in comparison unto Ovidis bokes of love: whiche we rede and cary
them in our handes and lerne them by harte: ye and some schole maisters

teche them to theyr scholers" (sig. F1v). Vives advises no such instruction
for women. They should not read the Spanish stories of *Amadis of Gaul,
Tristan and Isolde,* or the *Celestina,* that "baude mother of noughtyness";
the French stories of *Launcelot of the Lake* or *Paris and Vienne;* the Flemish
Pyramis and Thisbe, or the English *Parthenopex of Blois, Ipomedon, Guy
of Warwick, Bevis of Hampton,* or many others (sig. E4r). Ovid especially
should be banished, and "a woman shulde beware of all these bokes lykewise as of serpentes or snakes" (sig. F1v). If a woman takes such delight in
books of love that she cannot leave them, she should be kept from them;
and if the same woman reads good books with an ill will, she should be
kept from all reading. "And so by disuse forgette lernynge if hit can be
done. For hit is better to lacke a good thynge than to use hit yll" (sig. F2r).

Vives' chapter on what women should not read reflects the humanists'
strong disapproval of chivalrous romance. They also restricted men from
reading such books. At the same time the emphasis on such works suggests
how many men and women must have been reading those books and how
the humanists positioned themselves against some forms of secular literature. C. S. Lewis has referred to the humanists' educational approach as a
"new learning and new ignorance," adding that they "preserved from the
Middle Ages what least merited preservation" and "rejected (with con-
tumely) everything else."[14]

Although *The Instruction* treats most aspects of a woman's life, Vives
does not address the subject of women's writing or translating at all; he
seems not to have seen such work as a possibility for them. But he is
concerned with what women write when they practice handwriting. Here,
too, he prescribes the subject matter:

And whan she shall lerne to write, let nat her example be voyde verses nor wanton
or tryflyng songes: but some sad sentence prudent and chaste taken out of holy
scripture or the sayenges of philosophers: whiche by often writyng she may fasten
better in her memory. (sig. E2r)

The passage is interesting because it gives us an image of a Renaissance
woman writing. She is writing some sad, prudent, and chaste saying from
the Bible or a philosophical treatise, and she is writing it over and over
again. She copies the words of another, who is surely of another sex, and
she is told to make his words a part of her mind and memory. There is not a
hint in this passage of a woman imparting herself through her writing or

discovering through her writing who she is or what she can say. The purpose of her activity is not to communicate but to learn better her duty, and Vives does not suggest a larger purpose for handwriting elsewhere in his book.

In his plans of study for girls and boys, Vives makes his writing requirements for each sex more explicit. He advises the use of "paper-books," or books of blank paper, in which a girl is to write moral sayings of other authors. In a "large note-book (*librum vacuum*)," she is to jot down words, witty or graceful expressions, and *sententiae*, "from which she may seek example for her life." The notes she made would usually have been in Latin, so she would gain practice in that language as she wrote. Vives also advises girls to turn short speeches from English into Latin and gradually increase the difficulty of the passages they translate: "Let these partly be serious and religious, and in part joyful and courteous" (Watson, *Renascence Education*, pp. 144–46). The subject matter might be lightened, therefore, in works she was given to translate.

Boys, too, are instructed to make notes in their large notebooks, but they may include more categories—names, rare words, idioms, *sententiae*, joyous expressions, witty sayings, proverbs, difficult passages of authors, and other matters of interest. Vives also provides advice for boys on their Latin style. The words and sayings that they gathered are at first only collections from Latin authors, but "little by little you will mix your own composition until the time when your stage of erudition has developed, your writing can become all your own." As Vives discusses it, original writing for boys develops as an extension of copying other authors, who serve as models. "Speed and facility will be produced by exercise so that you will come to write at the same time with ease and excellence" (Watson, *Renascence Education*, pp. 243–45). In his larger work on education for boys, Vives sees such original composition as a natural extension of the learning process:

And since he who has acquired learning not only wishes to be of use to those who come into his company and to those with whom he lives, but also those who are distant from him, and to posterity, he will write down the thoughts of his mind in monumental literature to last for a long time to come. First he will know himself, and measure out his strength, in those things in which he is strong, on which he is fitted to write. The most suited of all the products of his thought for transmission to posterity are those which are endowed with study and strong judgment, and those which are best calculated to give inspiration. (Watson, *Vives*, p. 299)

The marginal gloss to this passage indicates its subject: "On Writing Books." A boy grew up to judge issues and inspire others through the writing of books and "monumental literature." A girl copied the words of others but was not instructed further in how to judge, write, or inspire. Her writing was supposed to be confined to her small paper-book and her *librum vacuum.*

These restrictions on women's writing are, once again, a function of Vives' purpose in providing them with any instruction at all. When asked what women should study, he replied: "I have tolde you. The study of wysedome: the whiche dothe enstruct their maners and enfurme theyr lyvyng and teacheth them the waye of good and holy lyfe. As for eloquence I have no great care, nor a woman nedeth it nat: but she nedeth goodnes and wysedome" (sigs. E1v–E2r). To ensure their goodness, Vives provides women with very practical advice on their conduct, telling them what they should wear (though it takes him twenty pages),[15] when they should walk abroad (rarely), how they should consider marriage a friendship and should not provoke the lust of their husbands, how they should mourn when their husbands die, and whether they should marry again. The book is divided into three sections, one each for the maid, the wife, and the widow, so it conceives of a woman in terms of her married status even while it advises that "it is nat comely for a mayde to desyre mariage and moche lesse to shewe her selfe to longe therfore" (sig. R4r). Unlike Xenophon and Aristotle who gave women rules for housekeeping, or Plato who made precepts for the ordering of a commonwealth, or the Saints Cyprian, Jerome, Ambrose, and Augustine who exhorted women to certain kinds of behavior and to "spende al theyr speche in the laudes and prayses of chastite" (sig. B1r), Vives tells women how they might actually lead chaste lives. His standards are not so different from those of other authors, but his purpose is more practical and more popular: he wishes to provide women with a comprehensive handbook—it is 320 pages long—that makes available the greatest Christian and classical teachings on their lives while it transforms those injunctions into simple rules for living accompanied by examples. But the rules are the same: "Fyrste let her understande that chastyte is the principall vertue of a woman and countrepeyseth with all

the reste: if she have that, no man wyll loke for any other: and if she lacke
that, no man wyll regarde other" (sig. L4v).

If we need to be convinced of the importance of chastity for English
Renaissance women, we may also consider the literature. Hero in *Much
Ado about Nothing,* Desdemona in *Othello,* Imogen in *Cymbeline,* and
Hermione in *The Winter's Tale*—all are good women whose very lives are
called into question when a man says they have not been chaste. For Brito-
mart in Spenser's *Faerie Queene* and the Lady in Milton's *Comus,* chastity
is what makes them most exemplary—it is their defining virtue. In Renaissance iconography, the figure of Lucrece holding a dagger toward herself
became the most popular exemplum for women: she was affirming her
chastity by committing suicide after she had been raped. Berthelet, "the
King's printer," who put out five editions of the English *Instruction,* had
his shop at the sign of Lucrece and used the figure as his printer's device.
The figure also appears opposite the first page of text in the 1541 edition
of *The Instruction.* All of Vives' restrictions on the lives of women are
given in the name of chastity, and the virtue was lauded and praised so
much during the Renaissance that it obscured the other virtues a woman
might exhibit or strive for. One good for women had become the only
good. If we are to understand Renaissance restrictions on women's behavior, we must question the application of that virtue in guiding their conduct. The more we see how it was applied, the more the figures of Lucrece
and Shakespeare's four heroines appear as ironic comments on the values
of the time, for women's lives do seem to have been sacrificed in the name
of that virtue.[16]

At the time Vives wrote *The Instruction,* virginity was still considered a
more virtuous state than marriage for men as well as women: even later
Protestants like Richard Hooker valued it more highly.[17] The emphasis
upon chastity as compared to virginity made sexual virtue more possible
for married persons by considering the spiritual state of one's being, not
just the physical state of one's body. Yet chastity is still more important
for a woman than a man, at least, says Vives, according to the laws of the
world. He discusses why a woman should not be jealous of her husband:

For the man is nat so moche bounde as the woman to kepe chastite at leaste wayes
by the lawes of the worlde, for by godis lawe both be bounde in lyke. Let her
consydre that the man lyveth more at libertie than the woman and hath more to
care fore. For she hath nothynge to se to but her honestye. (sig. f2v)

Man's greater secular freedom is used in this passage to require patience from his wife for his behavior, while her greater confinement gives her the opportunity to preserve her sexual virtue. Milton reasons on more religious grounds in his *Apology for Smectymnuus* when he says, "If unchastity in a woman, whom St. Paul terms the glory of man, be such a scandal and dishonor, then certainly in a man, who is both the image and glory of God, it must, though commonly not so thought, be much more deflowering and dishonorable" (p. 695). Both passages point to a difference between secular and religious standards for sexual behavior, but they also show the higher value placed at the time on women being chaste. That age was unwholesomely preoccupied with women's sexual goodness.[18] If women's weakness influenced their sexual behavior as Vives thought it did—for he describes them as "more disposed to pleasure and dalyance" (sig. C2v) than men—then women's lives needed to be controlled in order to ensure their sexual virtue. Vives' work prohibits dancing, singing, or even much talking with men for these reasons.[19]

Renaissance women who married could not emulate the Virgin Mary's virginity, but they might emulate her silence. Vives advises: "All maydes and all women folowe you her: for she was but of fewe wordes: but wonderous wise." He supports the injunction with secular authority too, for even a woman poet, Theano Metapontina, and Sophocles are of the same opinion: "Silence was the nobleste ornament of a woman" (sig. O3v). In the *Office and Duty of a Husband,* Vives addresses the husband as his wife's teacher and reminds him of advice from Juvenal: "Let not thy wife be overmuch eloquent, nor full of her short and quick arguments, nor have the knowledge of all histories, nor understand many things, which are written. She pleaseth not me that giveth herself to poetry, and observing the art and manner of the old eloquence, doth study to speak facundiously" (Watson, *Renascence Education,* p. 207).

Woodward observes that in excluding women from rhetorical training and valuing their silence, Vives' attitude "is the opposite of the doctrine of the high Renaissance in Italy." He adds that the learned women of England mentioned so often, such as Thomas More's daughters and the Cooke sisters, "were undoubtedly far rarer phenomena than learned women were in Italy" (*Studies,* pp. 206–08). If this is true, the Italian Bruni, who wrote what may be the earliest humanist tract on education for a woman, nonetheless said that "rhetoric in all its forms—public discus-

sion, forensic argument, logical fence, and the like—lies absolutely outside
the province of women." His countryman Bruto, whose conductbook for
women was published in England, also questioned the value of all learning
for a woman.[20] The tradition of discouraging women from eloquence was
at least a strong one among the English, and when they turned to the
Continent for models, they made most use of those humanists with conservative attitudes on women's education.

When we consider all of these injunctions on women's speech and writing, it may seem surprising that they wrote anything at all, but it is less
surprising that they often wrote on religious subjects. Those who instructed women were most often religious in their orientation, and the
books women were allowed to read were most often religious books.
Those women were also living in a century where almost half of the works
published dealt with religious concerns. Some women surely addressed
those subjects because they were seriously interested in the important religious matters of the day. It seems likely, too, that when they wrote, they
would take up the very concerns they had addressed in their paper-books.
Could they not appropriate the subjects Vives prescribed for their handwriting and their Latin annotations—that they copy "some sad sentence
prudent and chaste taken out of holy scripture or the sayenges of
philosophers"—to do more extended translation or writing of their own?
We need not assume that such an appropriation was always an active
choice. It might, instead, have seemed the only avenue not generally closed
to most of them. And if a woman doing such work was not thereby assum-
ing a chaste silence, she was at least affirming her chastity through her
choice of subject matter.

The more we consider it, the more remote this world of sad sentences
seems from the golden world of poetry that Sir Philip Sidney writes about.
In his *Apologie for Poetrie*, Sidney says that it is the business of the poet to
feign, to frame images of vice and virtue through a process which is, if not
dishonest, not entirely honest either. "The poet nothing affirmeth" is Sidney's way through this dilemma, but even that lack of affirmation might
have prevented a woman from entering his golden world through some
original writing of her own. "Verely I do nat alowe in a subtile and a crafty
woman suche lernyng as shulde teche her disceyt and teche her no good
maners and vertues" (sig. D2v): Vives will not approve of any sort of
intellectual deceit for a woman, regardless of how it might lead her and

others to a larger apprehension of truth. Of course, many religious writers also objected to men's imaginative writing during the period: Sidney's *Apologie* and Shakespeare's defense of play-acting in *Hamlet* arise from a context markedly suspicious of imaginative activity. The climate was even less hospitable when Puritan views became more influential. But if such work was difficult for men under those circumstances, how much more difficult was it for women, who were so often called to a more rigid performance of their duties in order to prove the goodness of their weaker natures?

Most Renaissance women were also excluded from what has been called the "Tudor play of mind," the rhetorical tradition, so important to humanist education, that posed abstract questions and argued answers on both sides of a topic. Joel Altman thinks that tradition "inspired and gave shape to a large body of Elizabethan drama." While More's daughters were permitted to dispute in philosophy before Henry VIII,[21] they could not, any more than other women, sharpen their wits through the disputative training provided men at the universities and the Inns of Court. Whether we see the generation of literature enabled more by an interplay of opposing argumentative positions, or by a knowledge of good arrived at through a knowledge of evil as a consequence of the Fall, or by the creation of imaginative worlds through poetic feigning, women were denied crucial elements for such literary activity. Their education was not primarily dialectic; they were not supposed to know evil; and they were not supposed to feign. To write a secular poem was to risk being thought a bad woman who knew about love and all the ambiguities entwined about the tree of the knowledge of good and evil. It was to put off, for a time, a sober sadness and a preoccupation with one's duty, to play with words, with literary forms, with complex ideas and contrary feelings. It was to be less, and more, than simply a good, chaste woman. Better to translate Erasmus' *Treatise Upon the Pater Noster*. Better still to do the embroidery.

In *The Nobility of Women*, a court dialogue by William Bercher (Barker) that survives in a manuscript of 1559, one character offers this opinion on all the rules men so often provided for women's conduct during the Renaissance:

The bryngynge upp and the traynenge off womans lyffe is so straight and kept as in pryson that all the good inclynacon which theye have of nature is utterly quenchyd. We se that by practyse men of small hope com to good proofe so that I maye affyrme the cawse of wymens weaknes in handlenge of matters to procede of the costome that men hathe appoynted in the maner of theyr lyffe . . . .[22]

The life that Vives' *Instruction* describes for women is an exceedingly narrow and confined one, and some women's good inclinations were surely quenched rather than encouraged through the kind of training that he advised. Yet his restrictions on women's learning and behavior seem at once sadder and more salutary if we consider them in light of their time, for Vives clearly thought of himself, and was thought by others to be, one of women's real advocates in the sixteenth century. His definition of women's nature as weak and his concern for their chastity were derivative, but in addressing the subject of their education and in guiding them to a moral and religious life, he was an innovator in the early years of the northern Renaissance. The rigid life he prescribes for women in his book was not the worst alternative for them then: it was one of the best available.

There are surely many reasons why women did not write more during the Renaissance, reasons that have nothing to do with conductbooks and literature. Many children and the dangers of childbirth, obligations of household and husband, poor living conditions for many, and scarcity of books for most—the reasons are legion. But the absence of any treatment of women's writing in Vives' comprehensive book suggests how unimportant that subject was for him and perhaps for others, and it also suggests that the women he thought were exemplary rarely wrote anything. The only image he gives us is of a woman practicing her handwriting, copying some sad, prudent, and chaste sentence over and over again. As she shapes her letters, she is being shaped by another's moral and religious precepts, but this process cannot be extended to original composition for she cannot, given her weak reason, be trusted to judge, write, or teach on her own. Yet it is likely that some women whose lives were shaped by those precepts eventually gave more credence to their own opinions. Catherine of Aragon certainly did when Henry tried to divorce her. And somewhere in those paper-books, a few women must have been writing words that showed more fully how they felt about their lives. When the Princess Elizabeth was imprisoned at Woodstock, she wrote a ten-line poem on a wall and scratched out a couplet on her window using a diamond. She also had with her there an English translation of St. Paul's Epistles, and in a blank space in the book, she wrote how she coped with her life in that place:

I walk many times into the pleasant fields of the holy Scriptures, where I pluck up the goodlisome herbs of sentences by pruning, eat them by reading, chew them by musing, and lay them up at length in the high seat of memory, by gathering them together. That so having tasted the sweetness, I may the less perceive the bitterness of this miserable life.[23]

RITA M. VERBRUGGE

Margaret More Roper's Personal Expression in the *Devout Treatise Upon the Pater Noster*

T HE title page of the English translation of Erasmus' *Precatio Dominica* shows a woodcut of a woman, seated at a desk, leafing through a large book.[1] Above the woodcut are the words:

A devout treatise upon the Pater Noster / made fyrst in latyn by the moost famous doctour mayster Erasmus Roterodamus / and tourned into englishe by a yong vertuous and well lerned gentylwoman of xix yere of age.

The "gentylwoman" is Margaret More Roper, who by the age of nineteen was a wife, mother, and acknowledged scholar within a small, elite circle of friends and acquaintances. Thomas Stapleton, in his 1588 biography of Margaret's father, Sir Thomas More, devotes a whole chapter to her, in order to prove that "in literature and other branches of study she attained a degree of excellence that would scarcely be believed in a woman." He mentions among other things "the admiring judgement passed by the most learned of English Bishops upon Margaret's learning and literary style."[2] Unfortunately, most of the records proving Margaret's excellence have been lost; of all her known works—Latin and Greek verse, "elegant and graceful" Latin speeches, a "clever" exercise in imitation of Quintilian's oratorical devices, meditations on *The Four Last Thynges*, and "eloquent" Latin and English letters—only a few letters and the above-mentioned translation are extant (Stapleton, pp. 103–09). Today the biographical information that places her most readily in time and history is not related to her own scholarship, but to the fact that she is the daughter of Sir Thomas More, renowned humanist and illustrious martyr.

How is it that in an age when critics seek to give belated recognition to competent women of the past, a learned female scholar such as Margaret More Roper has been overlooked?[3] The explanation for the general neglect endured by this historic woman may be that, as the daughter of the famous statesman, she frequently is included in the general comments about the More family and is occasionally indexed under her father's name. This factor, however, is not so much explanatory as indicative of the problem involved in drawing out the young scholar Margaret from the shadow of her more illustrious father. Almost everything we know about Margaret has come from Sir Thomas More's letters, through Thomas More's biographers, or by way of Thomas More's friends. Almost anything that can be said of her has to acknowledge her father's involvement at some level. Even the biographer Stapleton constantly measures Margaret's work up against her father's. While complimenting the elegant and graceful style of her Latin speeches, he adds "while in treatment they hardly yield to her father's compositions." At times More challenged his daughter to work on a similar treatise or translation, such as the meditative work, *Remember the Last Thynges,*[4] with the result, according to Stapleton, that More "affirmed most solemnly that the treatise of his daughter was in no way inferior to his own" (p. 103). As Retha M. Warnicke has pointed out, "Thomas' personality has so overshadowed hers [Margaret's] that it is difficult to resurrect her as a person in her own right."[5]

At best we see Margaret Roper as Robert Bolt portrays her in *A Man for All Seasons*—loved by her father and devoted to her father but still a secondary figure, intended by her relationship to her father to highlight More's "adamantine sense of his own self." Betty Travitsky, in her *Paradise of Women: Writings by Englishwomen of the Renaissance,* unconsciously falls into a similar pattern. Although Travitsky does mention Margaret More in the introduction, she quotes from one of Thomas More's letters; the editor does not even include an excerpt from Margaret's own letters in the anthology, although a sizable section of the work is devoted to "Letters and Diaries" of Renaissance women.[6]

Margaret's letters have not been completely ignored, however. A few of her letters have received special study, although the conclusions do little to bring out any sense of individuality for Margaret. Of Margaret's only extant letter to Erasmus, the Thomas More scholar Marc'hadour observes, "Like him [her father] she punctuates rather little."[7] And the letters exchanged between father and daughter during Sir Thomas More's imprisonment in the Tower of London, though moving and at times fascinating, ultimately provide nothing definite about Margaret.[8] The fact that her writing was like her father's, or as good as her father's (the ultimate compliment from a member of the More circle) has on at least one occasion created serious problems in identifying the true author of one important letter.

This interesting tower letter attracts attention to itself, first by its length, and second by the historical information that lists it as written by Margaret to her stepsister Alice Alington.[9] The circumstantial data reveal that in August 1534 Alice Alington wrote Margaret about a meeting she had managed to have with the new Lord Chancellor, Sir Thomas Audley. She repeats that Audley "merueyled that my father is so obstinate in his owne conceite."[10] All the other civil and ecclesiastical officers, she indicates, have given in and signed the Act of Succession (1534), except "the blynde Bisshopp [Fisher] and he."[11] Signing that act would in essence have indicated approval not only of Henry VIII's divorce from Catherine of Aragon and his marriage to the pregnant Anne Boleyn, but also of his break from papal authority. Margaret's letter is no simple response, explaining her father's conscientious stand. Although the letter begins with the seemingly artless reporting of her and her father's conversation which occurred as a response to Alice's letter, the major part of the letter is a carefully organized dialogue that in both structure and purpose is patterned after Plato's *Crito:* as Crito forces Socrates to consider every possible reason for making his escape while he still can, Margaret in her dialogue forces her father to consider every possible reason for taking the oath (No. 206, "Margaret Roper to Alice Alington," pp. 514–32). More's part of the dialogue discusses how that choice would be inconsistent with his principles. As in Plato's dialogue, so in Margaret's the speakers discuss the question of whether a wise man should follow the opinions and decisions of the many. That argument, the main one raised by Alice Alington for signing the act, is refuted not only on the literal level by More's part in the dialogue, but also by the inherent classical example of Socrates.

Margaret knew all the arguments raised by others for the signing of the oath. She had probably heard them all, both in and outside the home, from friends as well as relatives. One by one she raises each argument to challenge her father's steadfast position, from minimizing the oath, that it "wer in dede but a trifle," to the heavier attack of doing it for the sake of his kindred (No. 206, p. 520, l. 230). As in Plato's *Crito*, More, like Socrates, takes this part of the argument most seriously. More admits he had "full many restles nights" before he was imprisoned, admitting that this was the area that made him almost fainthearted. More's part of the dialogue affirms his original position: he must consider God's pleasure before the king's, and even before his beloved family's.

More's tone in the dialogue is different from that in his earlier arguments against the positions of Luther or Tyndale,[12] as Walter Gordon has pointed out:

More debates here not with a Tyndale or a Barnes but with his daughter, his last opponent whose strongest argument is her love for him. This tender relationship is put to a strain as the two take opposite sides in the dilemma confronting them. She would have him conform to save his life, and he cannot acquiesce where conscience prevents him. (p. 5)

But Margaret does not acquiesce either. Other classical or Renaissance dialogues may work toward a final resolution. This one does not: "Margaret does not yield in an illumined spirit of resignation as Crito does to Socrates. Disagreement persists to the end, if not in common sympathy, at least in desire and understanding" (p. 6).

Margaret's letter is obviously a carefully planned work of art and scholarship, but unfortunately as early as 1557, William Rastell, when preparing More's *English Works*, admitted he did not know for sure who the author was. The paragraph following Lady Alington's letter and preceding the response reads:

When maistres Roper had receiued this letter she at her next repayre to her father in the tower, shewed him this letter. And what communication was thereupon betweene her father and her, ye shall perceive by an aunswer here following (as written to the Ladye Alington). But whether thys aunswer was written by Syr Thomas More in his daughter Ropers name, or by her selfe, it is not certaynelye knowen.[13]

Consequently, several modern biographers and critics of Sir Thomas More have assumed More to be the author, pointing out that the letter has similarities to More's *Dialogue of Comfort Against Tribulation,* but forgetting that the critics who have studied both Margaret's and her father's writing have testified to the fact that Margaret's writing is virtually indistinguishable from her father's. A few critics conclude, "More and Margaret probably wrote the letter together." R. W. Chambers, in his essay "The Continuity of English Prose," discusses the question briefly, concluding, "And the letter remains a puzzle. The speeches of More are absolute More; and the speeches of Margaret are absolute Margaret. And we have to leave it at that."[14] But as long as the question of authorship remains unanswered, the sequential question whether Margaret's part in the dialogue reflects her true response to Henry's demands must of necessity remain unanswered.

Only one of Margaret's works exists, whereby we can view and study her abilities and scholarship independent from her father's pervasive presence—her *Devout Treatise Upon the Pater Noster,* the translation of Erasmus' *Precatio Dominica.* For the twentieth-century reader the inclination naturally exists to pass over this work with the attitude, that a translation is not an original work; the work belongs to Erasmus. However, the translation is as much Margaret's work as *Precatio Dominica* is Erasmus'. The translation and its source are well worth a closer study. To begin with, the Latin meditative work published as *Precatio Dominica Digesta in Septem Partes, Juxta Septem Dies* falls into the tradition of catechetical treatises on the Lord's Prayer, on the order of Tertullian's *De Oratione* and St. Cyprian's *De Dominica Oratione.* Whether Erasmus knew the earlier work is a matter of conjecture; he certainly knew the latter well, since he had in 1521 edited the works of St. Cyprian.[15] Margaret, too, was familiar with at least some of St. Cyprian's work. According to the biographer Stapleton (p. 104), she had helped to clarify a meaningless section of one of Cyprian's letters by proposing *nervos* for *nisi vos,* a correction that was incorporated by Erasmus in his edition of St. Cyprian's work.[16]

The publication in 1523 of the *Precatio Dominica* raises several questions. The seven meditations are very similar in content to the central section (chapters 9–27) of Cyprian's work.[17] Not only are many of the ideas and biblical references similar, but even the antisemitic bias, noted by DeMolen, can be matched to similar comments in St. Cyprian's work.[18] That Erasmus is not above such borrowing has, of course, been noted before in his use of Quintilian's *Institutio oratoria* for the content of his *De Copia* (1512),[19] and Erasmus was certainly not the only Renaissance scholar to publish in his own name works that leaned heavily on earlier sources.[20] More important at this point is what prompted Erasmus to publish this devotional work in 1523. Was it Martin Luther's extremely popular *Personal Prayer Book* of 1522 (which included meditations on the Lord's Prayer) that provoked Erasmus in a spirit of competition to publish a similar work?[21] Or was his publication evidence that he had similar concerns for good devotional works for the reading public—concerns heightened by the Lutheran book-burning demonstrations that were appearing in cities across Europe?[22] Was the lack of any acknowledgment an evidence that "he was pouring out works at such a rate that they showed signs of hastiness"? We know from Erasmus' own letters that until about 1520 he approved of Luther's ideas and concerns, but increasingly disapproved of Luther's unconcern for the ecclesiastical schism that was developing.[23] Did he find in St. Cyprian's work not only immediate, good devotional material, but also material that emphasized his concern for the unity, the oneness of mind and spirit that should be present in the Church, the body of Christ? Did Erasmus (directly or indirectly) initiate concern among his friends in England for the translation of such devotional works as the *Precatio Dominica* (1523), *De immensa dei misericordia* (1523), and possibly the *Enchiridion militis Christiani* (1503),[24] hoping to fill a void brought about by the English attack on Luther's works? How did Margaret come to translate the work so soon—within a year of its publication—while his other previous works had been left untranslated for years?[25] Many more related questions arise but most of them are unanswerable today since no mention is made of Margaret's translation either in the More correspondence or in the Erasmus correspondence.

We do know that Margaret More Roper was the "well lerned gentylwoman" responsible for the *Devout Treatise* even though her name does not appear anywhere on the translated work, not in the title page nor even in the dedicatory letter. It is possible that, although she may have been interested in having the meditations available in English, Margaret refused to allow her name to appear on the published work. Stapleton, in his discussion of her other works, maintains that she "fully deserved to be published and read by all," but either her "bashfulness" or "humility . . . never allowed her to consent to publication" (p. 106). If it had not been for the early efforts at censorship brought about by the Lutheran controversy in the 1520s, the translator for Erasmus' treatise might have remained anonymous.

As the first printed works pertaining to the teachings of Martin Luther reached London, the English clergy reacted quickly by reenacting the old regulations made more than a century before when John Wyclif had spread his ideas, and by uttering new proclamations aimed more directly at the growing printer's trade. At first, the old regulations found in *The Constitution of Archbishop Arundel* of 1406 were reenforced, particularly part 6 which stated that no book or tract relating to Wyclif or his followers shall be read at any school or hostel "unless it has first been examined . . . and approved" by the appropriate authorities; this became the basis for the new regulations.[26]

During these years Sir Thomas More was away from his home at Chelsea for long periods of time, and on occasion was thoroughly involved in the London antiheresy efforts. According to Alistair Fox's recent biography, "one must also concede that More did display lack of charity and an almost demoniac emotional violence towards his opponents" (p. 119). That More as Henry VIII's sole secretary (Guy, p. 16) during the first half of the 1520s had some part in the planning and revising of the *Assertio Septem Sacramentorum adversus Martinus Lutherus* has long been accepted.[27] In response to Luther's abusive reply to Henry, More prepared his *Responsio ad Lutherum*, which was printed in two different issues in 1523. But printed words were not sufficient for this controversy, and increasingly active measures were called for. When it became obvious that neither Pope Leo's bull of July 1520, with its command to seek out and burn all heretical books, nor Cardinal Wolsey's campaign, inaugurated in May 1521 with a book-burning ceremony at Paul's Cross (Reed, p. 161), nor the king's official stand as expressed in his or More's printed works, did anything to stem the steady stream of Lutheran literature, Bishop Tunstall called together the booksellers of London in October 1524 and warned them that they were not to sell or part with any imported books "unless first they showed them either to the Lord Cardinal, the Archbishop of Canterbury, the Bishop of London, or the Bishop of Rochester" (Reed, p. 163). One of More's biographers indicates that More

or his officials confiscated and destroyed Lutheran books on several occasions. In January, 1526, he directed a police foray into Steelyard, the German merchant community of London. As a result, some unauthorized Bibles and prayer books were confiscated and several merchants imprisoned.[28]

We may assume, then, that More was not directly involved in summoning the printer Thomas Berthelet (or Bartlett) for failure to comply with the new rules, but to what extent More was indirectly responsible is less certain. Evidently, Berthelet had neglected to obtain official approval for Erasmus' meditations on the *Pater Noster*. Records from the Vicar-General's Books[29] indicate that a "Thomas Bartlett" confessed "he had printed a certain work called *The Treatise of the Pater Noster* translated as he said by the wife of Mr. Roper in the vulgar tongue" (Reed, p. 166). Berthelet's revelation must have created some embarrassment for Thomas More, but we can only speculate on his public reaction as well as his private reactions to Margaret. We do know that at some time prior to the case in question, Margaret's husband, Will Roper, gave cause for concern and embarrassment by his heretical, Lutheran views which had caused him to be called before Cardinal Wolsey on the charge of heresy.[30]

Berthelet's case was obviously not one of heresy but of failure to comply with the new regulations related to works published abroad. The *Pater Noster* copy found in the British Museum, probably issued shortly after the recorded incident, shows every sign of having received official approval: on the reverse side of the title page is a large (13 cm. by 9.2 cm.) woodcut of Cardinal Wolsey's coat of arms, and at the end of the work is the statement:

Thus endeth the exposicion of the Pater noster. Imprinted at London in Fletestrete / in the house of Thomas Berthelet nere to the Cundite / at the signe of Lucrece.
Cum privilegio a rege indulto[31]

Thus the very machinery of censorship, aimed at suppressing the words of one person, in this situation helped to identify the words of another. There is not, and never has been, any doubt as to the identity of the "yong vertuous and well lerned gentylwoman of xix yere." Nor has there been any doubt as to Margaret's competence to take on the task of translating Erasmus' Latin meditatiòns into English.

Not only have Thomas More's biographers testified to his daughter's scholarly abilities, but Erasmus in letters to other leading humanists has testified to her attainments.[32] Erasmus was not one to use words carelessly; in his educational treatise *De Ratione Studii* (1511), he counsels for the careful choice of appropriate words and tropes to adorn a composition. When he refers to Margaret on two different occasions (1523/24? and 1529) as "the adornment of your British land," he uses the Latin word *decus,* a word that could mean all of glory, honor, moral dignity, virtue, and source of glory.[33] As a complimentary word of address, *decus* is not uncommon, but it is generally reserved for those who have shown themselves worthy in a literary sense. At the end of the letter of 1523/24? Erasmus refers to Margaret's successful achievement:

. . . there are in Germany families well-known which are trying, not without success, to achieve what you have already done with the utmost success. So fare-well, you who are not the least adornment of your British age and land. (Robin-eau, p. 35)

Regrettably, he was not more specific. When he said "what you have al-ready done with the utmost success," was he referring in general to the high level of scholarship she had attained? Or could he possibly have been refer-ring to her translation?

Erasmus is not clear as to what Margaret has done "with the utmost success," but Richard Hyrde, a young scholar described by his fellow dip-lomats as "singularly learned in physic, in the Greek and Latin tongues,"[34] who possibly was the one who saw the *Devout Treatise* through the press (Gee, "Margaret Roper's English Version," p. 260n), in the preface to the work is clear in his praise of her, both generally and specifically: although never mentioning Margaret by name, he lauds her attributes, offering them as "profe evydente ynough / what good lernynge dothe / where it is sure roted,"[35] and he speaks highly of "the goodnesse and perfectyon of the worke," suggesting:

that whoso lyst and well can conferre and examyne the translacyon with the originall / he shall not fayle to fynde that she hath shewed herselfe / nat onely erudite and elegant in eyther tong / But hath also vsed suche wysedom / suche dyscrete and substancyall iudgement in expressynge lyuely the latyn / as a man maye parauenture mysse in many thynges / translated and tourned by them that bare the name of right wise and very well lerned men. . . . (p. 103)

That Margaret did use discreet wisdom and substantial judgment in her choice of phrasing in the translation is obvious from a comparison of the translation with the original. Although Margaret often follows Erasmus' pattern of long and involved sentences, she goes well beyond a mere literal translation. She appears more concerned about presenting the sense of the phrase or clause with clarity than about providing a precise translation. An obvious example from the meditation on the first petition is her own additional comment after the assertion "the moost holy spyrite of thye sonne . . . boldely cryeth out in our hertes without cessyng / *Abba pater.*" Margaet adds, "which in Englysshe is as moche to saye / as, O father father."[36] Her own emphases are inserted on occasion by a personal interjected phrase, such as "I wolde to god" as in the sentence:

And I wolde to god that we also / whiche beare the name of thy children/ were nat dishonestie to thy glorie / amongest those that knowe the nat: for lyke as a good and wise sonne is the glorie and honour of his father / so a folisshe and vnthrifty childe / getteth his father dishonestie and shame / . . . (p. 108)

Margaret's work shows the care and concern for a responsible translation that belonged to the ideals of the early humanists. The only other English work in any way comparable is the Countess of Richmond Margaret Beaufort's *The mirroure of golde for the synfull soule* (1522), a mystical treatise originally written by the Carthusian, Denis de Leewis. *The mirroure* both in content and level of translation is definitely a medieval work. It would be tempting to digress into a history of the art and theory of translating and to discuss Margaret Roper's relative position to medieval and Renaissance translations, in an effort to prove that the competence exhibited in her translation places her well ahead of her time.[37] Suffice it here to say that much of what F. O. Mattheissen says in praise of prominent Elizabethan translators, beginning with Sir Thomas Hoby's translation in 1561, can be said of Margaret's work of 1524. She steers a middle course between an excessively free translation that characterizes medieval works and many Renaissance works as well, and the too nearly literal translation of many student foreign-language exercises which Flora Amos refers to as "translator's English" (p. 34).

Margaret's translation reads with a natural gentle rhythm using straightforward diction. The logical placing of the phrases and clauses, depending on their relationships to the other parts of the sentence, suggests an expertise in English composition that is not frequently found in the English prose of the early sixteenth century.[38] Hyrde's dedicatory letter, in comparison, has at times the awkward sense of an unsteady gait.

Particularly when compared to Hervet's 1526 English translation of Erasmus' sermon "of the excedynge great mercy of god," Margaret's choice of vocabulary in the *Devout Treatise* appears simple, straightforward, and unpretentious, as in the following typical passage from the meditation on the third petition, followed here by the same in the original Latin:

And that we may be able euery day more and more / to perfourme all this / helpe vs O father in heuen / that the flesshe may euer more and more be subiect to the spirite / and our spirite of one assent / and one mynde with thy spirite. And likewyse as nowe in dyuerse places thy children / whiche are obedient to the gospell / obey and do after thy wyll: so graunt they may do in all the worlde besyde / that euery man may know and vnderstande / that thou alone art the onely heed and ruler of althyng / and that in lykewyse as there are none in heuen / whiche mutter and rebell agaynst thy wyll / so let euery man here in erthe / with good mynde and gladde chere obey thy wyll and godly preceptes. (p. 116)

Hocut indies magis ac magis praestare valeamus, adjuva, Pater coelestis, ut indies caro minus reluctetur spiritui nostro, ut spiritus noster magis ac magis unanimis fiat Spiritui tuo. Et quemadmodum nunc multis in locis parent voluntati tuae, qui obediunt Euangelio Filii tui: ita idem fiat per universum terrarum orbem, ut omnes intelligant, te solum esse rerum omnium Monarcham, tuisque divinis legibus volentes ac lubentes obediant in terris quemadmodum in coelis nullus est qui tuae voluntati repugnet. (1224D)

Not only does the sentence indicate Margaret's sense of freedom in adding a phrase or two, and in reversing the order of several phrases and clauses, but it also provides an example of her tendency to double or couple the adjectives or verbs where Erasmus uses only one: "know and vnderstande" for "intelligant"; "heed and ruler" for "Monarcham"; and "mutter and rebell" for "repugnet." The training to do so probably came from Erasmus' own book *De Copia,* an extremely popular educational work on rhetoric that encouraged copiousness of words or amplification by such figures of speech as exempla and similes, not only for the writing of general compositions but also for the translation of foreign languages.[39]

In his comments on the general characteristics of the Elizabethan translator, Matthiessen states that "the structure of the sentence reveals the growing tendencies of the time—the passionate delight in fullness of expression, the free use of doublets and alliteration, and the building up of parallel constructions for the sake of rhythm," but he could have been speaking of Margaret's translation as well, since her work shows nearly all the same tendencies (p. 4). Her translation displays a mature independence in the rhetoric she chooses. Erasmus, in some of his lengthy sentences, may have several clauses in parallel form; Margaret in her translation keeps the idea of the sentence but at times alters the structure completely, building parallel structures of her own, sometimes combining the concepts of following sentences to do so.

In the meditation on the fifth petition "forgive us our debts as we forgive our debtors," Erasmus has structured his meditation into three closely related parts, each part relating to the word and concept "imbecillitatem."[40] Briefly summarized, the three parts are as follows: (1) Even though God's will requires that we be of one mind and spirit, we fail because of the "imbecillitatem" (inherent weakness) of our nature; (2) The Son, not ignorant of our "imbecillitatem," shows us a remedy and makes us capable of following a better way; and (3) Even as we acknowledge our inherent "imbecillitatem" we are encouraged by God's forgiveness to forgive and to live at peace with one another. Margaret translates the three "imbecillitatem's" as (1) "the weakenesse and frailte of nature"; (2) "the imbecilite and weakenesse of this membre"; and (3) "our owne imbecilite and feblenesse." By diffusing Erasmus' artful repetition, Margaret loses some of the rhetorical acuity of the original passage, but adds instead a gentler tone that enhances the theme of living in gentleness and concord with one another, as is evident in the passage from the middle section of the meditation:

. . . as often as we offende our brother / so often also we offende and displease the father / whiche commaundeddest we shulde loue our brother as our owne selfe / but thy sonne knowyng well inough the imbecilite and weakenesse of this membre / shewed vs a remedy therefore / gyuyng vs sure hope that thy goodnesse wolde remytte and forgyue vs all our offences / if we on the other side with all our hert wolde forgyue our brother. (pp. 119–20)

However, Margaret's translation does not always emphasize goodness and gentleness. In fact, even in the fifth meditation, it is only the example of

God's goodness and God's gentleness that she emphasizes. When she translates a simple attribute of Jesus, she at times adds an extra, loving phrase.
For example, she describes Jesus as "a very kynde and naturall childe" (p.
108), when Erasmus' word would suggest simply "natural" ("germanis-
simus," 1221B). But in discussing man's nature the emphasis often appears
to be in the opposite direction. When Erasmus provides the phrase "agnos-
cimus nostram humilitatem" (1219A), Margaret's translation of "we
aknowledge and confesse our owne vylesnesse" (p. 104) seems unnecessari-
ly harsh: "vylesnesse" is not a fair translation for "humilitatem." Similarly, when Erasmus states, "Nec auderemus te Patris vocabulo compel-
lare, indigni qui servi dicamur tui." (1219A), Margaret translates the last
phrase as, "which are farre unworthy to be thy bondemen" (p. 104), surely
an unnecessary emphasis on "unworthy." In the final meditation this negative tendency finds expression in a most interesting manner. In referring
to man's two choices for a master, God or the devil, Erasmus contrasts the
two by referring briefly to the devil as the devouring lion, and even more
briefly to God as shepherd by stating simply: "ovem erraticam reportas ad
ovile" (1228A). Margaret extends the metaphor to include a picture of the
sheep: "thou caryest home agayne to the flocke / the wandringe and
strayeng shepe: thou curest and makest hole the sicke and scabbe shepe
. . ." (p. 123). The comments and emphases indicate that not only does
she see man as "vyle" and "farre unworthy," but she also pictures him
metaphorically as a repulsive "scabbe shepe."

   Her independence of expression contributes to the work two opposing
emphases: a stress on the unworthiness of man, as well as an emphasis on
the loving kindness of God. These concepts themselves are not novel—they
prevail in the discussion of the day, in a world that is rapidly changing in
its religious perspective. Nevertheless, the fact that she chooses to add to
the work her personal perspective, not only by the occasional "I wolde to
God," but also by her particular emphases, indicates that in at least one
work Margaret Roper, the "yong vertuous and well lerned gentylwoman,"
can and does speak with her own mind and voice.

JOHN N. KING

Patronage and Piety:
The Influence of Catherine Parr

A T the very end of the reign of Henry VIII (1509–47), a circle of aristocratic women emerged who sponsored humanistic scholarship and patronized the translation and publication of religious works into the vernacular. Under the auspices of Catherine Parr, the king's last wife, this group of powerful women broke with traditional modes of patronage and devotion which had flourished at the Tudor court at the time of Lady Margaret Beaufort and Catherine of Aragon, respectively the grandmother and first wife of Henry VIII. In place of a long-standing commitment to the publication of medieval literature, works of monastic piety, and scholastic learning for an elite aristocratic readership, the younger women embarked on an ambitious program that fused Bible reading with private theological study. Their profound innovation was the popularization of Protestant humanism through patronage of devotional manuals and theological translations for the edification of a mixed audience of elite and ordinary readers. Many of these texts specifically addressed the requirements of a female readership, and all of these activities attest to the zealous Protestant faith of the women associated with Catherine Parr. Flourishing in particular during the radical Reformation under Edward VI (1547–53), these women transmitted their unique blend of patronage and piety to succeeding generations of aristocratic women who came of age during the reign of Queen Elizabeth.

Prior to the 1540s no tradition of educating women in a manner equal to men existed in England—not even the household of Thomas More furnished a precedent for the complete assimilation of humanistic learning and ethics with faith in the training of the daughters of Protestant aristocrats, notably those close to the line of succession to the throne of Henry VIII. Under the influence of Catherine Parr, however, Protestant humanists such as Roger Ascham, John Aylmer, John Foxe, and Thomas Wilson received appointments as tutors to the sons and daughters of royalty and nobility. Patronesses such as the Duchess of Suffolk (Catherine Brandon), the Duchess of Richmond (Mary Fitzroy), and the Duchess of Somerset (Anne Seymour) entrusted advanced Reformers with the training of Lady Jane Grey and Princess Elizabeth, both of whom succeeded to the throne, and the heirs of the dukedoms of Norfolk, Suffolk, Somerset, and other noble houses. Their patronage furnished an initial impetus for such writings as Ascham's *The Scholemaster*, Wilson's *Arte of Rhetorique* and *Rule of Reason*, and Foxe's *Acts and Monuments* (the *Book of Martyrs*). Members of Catherine Parr's circle also sponsored Protestant preachers and professional authors who turned out a stream of Reformist sermons, tracts, translations including the two massive volumes of Erasmus' *Paraphrases of the New Testament*, and even a play like Nicholas Udall's *Ralph Roister Doister*.[1]

During the years preceding Henry VIII's marriage to Catherine Parr in 1543, Anne Boleyn supplied the only English precedent for patronage by Protestant aristocratic women. John Foxe reports that the Lutheranism of "that godly queen" was well known both at court and throughout the land, and that she extended patronage to Protestant scholars and "professors of Christ's gospel." A tradition grew up that attributed the success or failure of religious reform to the influence at court of Henry VIII's Protestant wives—Anne Boleyn, Jane Seymour, Anne of Cleves, and Catherine Parr—all of whom Foxe eulogizes as agents of divine providence.[2] Although praise of Anne Boleyn as the divine instrument for Henry VIII's break with Rome became a conventional Reformist compliment to her daughter, Queen Elizabeth,[3] hindsight argument leads Foxe to exaggerate his account of Boleyn's influence. Only one printed book carries a dedication to her, and publication in translation of that evangelical tract seems to have been timed to coincide with Thomas Cromwell's campaign to dissolve the monasteries and eradicate Roman Catholicism in England.[4] Jane

Seymour died too early to wield influence consonant with the many eulogies whose praise centers on the role she played in the Tudor dynastic succession by bearing Henry VIII's long-anticipated male heir, Prince Edward. The king's German consort, Anne of Cleves, had negligible intellectual impact. Of the four Protestant wives, only Catherine Parr left a substantial record of documented sympathy for religious reform and encouragement of devotional publication.

Catherine Parr and her female associates developed a reputation for patronizing more extensive religious reform than that officially permitted by the Crown. When it became obvious that the king's death was imminent, the group of religious conservatives on the Privy Council led by Stephen Gardiner, Bishop of Winchester, and Thomas Howard, third Duke of Norfolk, attempted to block the ascendancy of the Protestant faction owing allegiance to Catherine Parr and Edward Seymour, uncle to Prince Edward. The conservative attack centered upon an attempt to implicate the queen and women of her privy chamber, as well as Catherine Brandon and Seymour's wife, Anne, in heresy accusations lodged against the Protestant gentlewoman, Anne Askew. Although she denied any connection to court circles, Askew's questioning in the Tower of London returned time after time to alleged contacts with high-ranking women. Askew's own testimony suggests the possibility that the charges lodged against her were simply part of a larger plot to destroy women at court by proving that they aided her during imprisonment:

I answered, that there was a man in a blewe coate, which delyvered me .v. shyllynges, and sayd that my ladye of Hertforde sent it me. And an other in a vyolet coate ded geve me viii. shyllinges, and sayd that my ladye Dennye sent it me. Whether it were true or no, I can not tell. For I am not sure who sent it me, but as the men ded saye.[5]

The traditional Christian belief in the intellectual inferiority of women buttressed conservative allegations, for the most damaging of Gardiner's charges was the accusation that Protestant women were violating the biblical admonition that men alone were ordained by God to serve as priests (1 Corinthians 14:33–35). Thus Anne Askew's disputes with clergymen over biblical interpretation were particularly controversial. Catherine Parr's aspirations to learning are praised by John Foxe, who reports that devotion to Bible study led her to retain as religious instructors and preachers learned Reformers whose sermons "ofttimes touched such abuses as in the church then were rife" (V, 553–54). Her daily schedule was known to include regular household worship and prayer; one confidant reports that she studied the Psalms and contemplative meditations day and night.[6] The king echoed Gardiner's strictures, according to Foxe, in voicing disapproval of his wife's willingness to enter into theological debate and support religious reform: " 'You are become a doctor, Kate, to instruct us . . . and not to be instructed or directed by us' " (V, 559). The success or failure of the plot against the queen's circle hinged upon Henry's response to his wife's theological learning. Unexpectedly shaping his sensational account of the hunt for heretical women in a comic mode, Foxe dramatizes the way in which the cleverness of his witty heroine enables her at the last minute to outwit her enemies through obedient submission to the king's authority as lord and husband (V, 553–61). One may only speculate upon the exact degree to which the macabre humor of this account reflects the lethal perils facing the wives of Henry VIII. James K. McConica, for example, hypothesizes that the conservatives' attack on women of the court was organized by the king in displeasure against the queen's advanced religious views. He argues further that her Protestant faith involved little more than the general patronage of such moderate reformers as Miles Coverdale (pp. 226–27).

Rumors linking aristocratic women to the authors of banned, heretical writings circulated freely. Gardiner's charges against the queen and her retinue included, for example, the accusation that "she had in her closet" copies of prohibited books (Foxe, V, 557). Promulgation of a proclamation banning Reformist books by favorite authors of the Protestant noblewomen coincided with the heresy hunt.[7] Coverdale's works were included even though he then served as almoner in the queen's privy chamber. Significantly his translation of the New Testament and the earlier banned version by William Tyndale were the focus of study and meditation by pious women. Anne Askew, for example, reports that she suffered for the sake of the free circulation of the gospels. John Bale's publication of the *Examinations of Anne Askew* served to vindicate posthumously the Protestant martyr and those aristocratic women thought to be her supporters. Soon after Henry VIII's death, Bale and another author of prohibited books, Thomas Becon, received appointments respectively in the households of Mary Fitzroy and Anne Seymour. The husband of the latter similarly extended patronage to another banned author, William Turner.

If a Protestant salon predated the rise to power of the Reformist faction during Edward VI's reign, its activities were inward-looking and private.[8] Almost the only published evidence of its leanings was the modest set of *Prayers Stirryng the Mynd unto Heavenlye Medytacions* (1545), which Catherine Parr "collected oute of holy workes." This text was fashionable at court where manuscript and, in all likelihood, printed versions circulated. It is quite important as the first evidence of a commitment by Protestant women to publication and popularization of courtly devotional works. The noncontroversial piety of this frequently republished text suggests that the devotional practices of women were in a state of transition. The heterogeneous meditations were abstracted from Book III (chapters 15–50) of Thomas à Kempis's *Imitation of Christ*, a work that had once appeared in print under Margaret Beaufort's sponsorship. Catherine Parr's haphazard selection destroys the methodical character and evocation of inward dialogue which characterize the original, offering instead loosely strung-out prayers such as the following:

O Jesu, King of everlasting glorie, the joie and comfort of all Christian people, that are wandering as Pilgrims in the wildernes of this world: my hart crieth to thee by still desires, and my silence speaketh unto thee, and saith: How long tarieth my Lord God to come to mee?

Come O Lord, and visit mee: for without thee I have no true joie, without thee my soule is heavie and sad.

I am in prison, and bounden with fetters of sorowe, till thou O Lord, with thy gratious presence vouchsafe to visit me, and to bring me againe to libertie and joie of spirit, and shew thy favourable countenance unto me.[9]

More importantly, publication of *Prayers or Medytacions* in inexpensive octavo format enabled a wide, popular readership to afford its purchase, in contrast to the larger and more expensive volumes favored by earlier patronesses.

Catherine's *Prayers or Medytacions* functioned as a supplement to Bible study. The queen's chamberlain, Sir Anthony Cope, gives some insight into the way aristocratic women might have used the text, for his *Godly Meditacion upon .XX. Psalmes* (1547) reduces Bible readings "to the kynde or fashion of prayers and contemplatife meditations.'' Based upon Psalms because it furnishes a "myrroure" of the image of Christ in one's soul, his selections should bring to mind events of Christ's life "as lyvely as they were set in colours forth before our eyes" (sig. ❊3r). Handwritten marginalia in one surviving copy (BL 697, g. 11) show how the volume was used in at least one household, for the glosses serve as a guide to daily prayer by assigning individual readings to specific days of the week. Cope's own emphasis on the Penitential Psalms and the handwritten annotations on grace, faith, penitence, and worldly vanity suggest that these pervasive concerns of Catherine Parr's writings were major themes of courtly piety. William Thomas's dedication of *The Vanitee of this World* (1549) to Catherine's sister, Lady Anne Herbert, embodies similar interests.

Devotion to Erasmian humanism and biblical studies led Catherine Parr to patronize the translation of the first volume of Erasmus' *Paraphrases of the New Testament*, an impetus acknowledged by the editor, Nicholas Udall, in his dedications. Princess Mary never completed the translation of the paraphrase of the Gospel of St. John requested by Catherine for this work (see McConica, pp. 231, 241), possibly out of disagreement with her stepmother's Reformist sympathies. Although Catherine conceived of the project as a work of courtly piety years before Henry VIII's death, its publication in 1548 under his more radically Protestant son converted the translation into a powerful public vehicle for the religious education of clergymen and commoners. The Royal Injunctions of Edward VI required every parish church to purchase the initial volume along with the Great Bible, and clergymen were ordered "diligentely [to] study the same, conferryng the one with the other" (sig. b4r). The translation project is an excellent example of the commitment of Protestant women to broadening the audience for devotional texts to include both aristocrats and commoners. Udall's preface to John includes the queen in the company of noble women who are able to write theological treatises and translate devotional works "for the use and commoditie of suche as are rude and ignoraunte of the sayd tounges," goals stemming from Erasmus' call in *Paraclesis* (1516) for the publication of vernacular translations of the Bible and popular religious literature. Udall argues that women's devotion to the Scriptures and pietistic writings supplanted secular literature and pastimes in noble households and at the royal court:

It is now no newes in Englande to see young damysels in nobles houses and in the
Courtes of princes, in stede of cardes and other instrumentes of idle trifleing, to
have continually in theyr handes eyther Psalmes, Omelies [homilies], and other
devoute meditacions, or els Paules epistles, or some booke of holy Scripture mati-
ers, and as familiarlye both to reade or reason therof in Greke, Latine, Frenche, or
Italian, as in Englishe. (sigs. AAa1r-v)

Hyperbole clouds his argument, however, for there is no evidence that
aristocratic daughters shunned secular entertainments.

Even before Catherine Parr's death in 1548, three of her female associates emerged as distinguished patronesses: Anne Seymour, Catherine
Brandon, and Mary Fitzroy. Anne Seymour's replacement of Parr as sponsor of the second volume of Erasmus' *Paraphrases* is a manifestation of this
development. John Olde credits Lady Seymour as its inspiration in his
preface to 1 and 2 Peter, even though the general editor, Miles Coverdale,
dedicates the volume as a whole to Edward VI.[10] Olde refers to the printer,
Edward Whitchurch, as her "graces humble servaunt" (sig. ∗ 1r). Although
the original courtly concern with humanistic piety survives, the open involvement of radical Reformers confers a more stridently Protestant edge
upon the text. Coverdale's additions to the original text—Tyndale's prologue to Romans and Leo Jud's commentary on Revelation—violently
attack the Church of Rome. The divided sponsorship of the separate volumes of Erasmus' *Paraphrases* typifies the explosion in Protestant patronage and propaganda after Henry VIII's death, when Edward Seymour, as
Lord Protector, presided over the removal of very nearly all restraints on
Reformist publication. The English could now openly read all of the previously banned books involved in the recent heresy hunt, and their authors
could write without restriction or could return from Continental exile.

Anne Seymour rivalled Catherine Parr as the leading lady in the land
after Henry VIII's death because of her husband's rise to a position of
authority at the court of a minor king. Accordingly Mildred Cecil's dedication of her manuscript translation of a sermon by St. Basil acknowledges
Lady Seymour's preeminent position at court (BL MS Royal 17 B. XVIII).
She and the two other Protestant duchesses, Mary Fitzroy and, especially,
Catherine Brandon, were wholly committed to the new Protestant ascen-
dency. Although they followed Catherine Parr's lead in appointing distinguished humanists as tutors in their households, they went beyond her

noncontroversial piety to encourage the radical activities of a tightly knit school of professional authors and translators, as well as the printers and publishers in the city of London who issued their works. In contrast to the complete silence concerning whatever patronage they may have extended under Henry VIII, they received during his son's reign an outpouring of dedications and acknowledgments (King, pp. 104–07).

The existence of this circle of aristocratic women is confirmed by publication of a second work by Catherine Parr, *The Lamentacion of a Sinner* (1547), for this text was "set furth and put in print at the instaunt desire of the righte gracious ladie Caterin Duchesse of Suffolke." Mildred Cecil's husband, William, edited the text on behalf of the duchess, in response to a request passed on by the author's brother, William Parr; the duchess is the likely source of the copy text. At least one manuscript of this work circulated in the courtly coterie, in addition to an anonymous translation into French verse based upon the printed text (BL MS Royal 16 E. XXVIII). McConica rightly concludes that Catherine Parr designed the work for use by noble women and that its affirmation of the doctrine of justification by faith alone lends a moderately Protestant tenor to the text (pp. 229–30). Nevertheless the marginal glosses to the Scriptures give the work the appearance of the evangelical works that poured out in defense of the new regime, and the text echoes polemical uses of biblical typology in attacking the Roman church. Catherine's praise of Henry VIII as a New Moses leading an Exodus out of the "captivitie and bondage" of papal Egypt implies that he initiated an on-going process of religious reform:

But our Moyses, a moste godly, wise governer and kyng hath delivered us oute of the captivitie and bondage of Pharao. I mene by this Moyses Kyng Henry the eight, my most soverayne favourable lorde and husband. One (If Moyses had figured any mo[re] then Christ) through the excellent grace of god, mete to be an other expressed veritie of Moses conqueste over Pharao. And I mene by this Pharao the bishop of Rome, who hath bene and is a greater persecutor of all true christians, then ever was Pharao, of the children of Israel. (sigs. E1r–v)

Such praise incorporates Protestant iconography descending from the title page for the 1539 Great Bible, which portrays Henry's reception of the Law from God as a latter-day Moses. When Coverdale transferred this conceit to Edward VI in his dedication to the second volume of *Paraphrases*, he combined it with a new biblical comparison to Josiah, the boy king who implemented religious reforms after a period of backsliding (2 Kings 22–23).

Catherine Parr's intellectual influence had its greatest impact on Princess Elizabeth, whose humanistic education paralleled the classical scholarship encouraged by her stepmother in the royal academy that she organized for the heir apparent, Prince Edward. The young princess acknowledged this influence by translating Marguerite de Navarre's *Le miroir de l'âme pécheresse* as a New Year's gift for her stepmother, entitled in English "The glasse of the synneful soule"; the manuscript provides a major link between the Erasmian pietism in fashion at the courts of England and Navarre.[11] Although no evidence supports John Bale's claim that the princess sent the translation to him for publication under the revised title, *A Godly medytacyon of the christen sowle* (Wesel, Cleves, 1548), no inherent improbability argues against Bale's claim that she sent him a copy written in her "owne hande" with appended translations of scriptural texts on virtuous women (Ecclesiasticus 7:19, 25:15 and 16, 26:3). Despite the pre-Reformist origins of the text, Bale uses it as a vehicle for exaggerated praise of Elizabeth's Protestant zeal with its biblicism and affirmation of justification by faith.

The patronage extended to Bale by Mary Fitzroy upon his return from exile suggests that a member of the aristocratic coterie might have sent Princess Elizabeth's translation to the Continent through the same German merchants who once delivered Anne Askew's manuscript account of her interrogation and torture to Bale. Bale and Foxe were both closely associated as radical Reformers with Mary Fitzroy, Duchess of Richmond. After Bale's return from exile, she protected and lodged him along with Foxe in her London house. The Protestant translator Nicholas Lesse reports that the duchess was known to have commissioned the publication of books designed to come "into the handes of the people" and that Bale served as her agent in making such arrangements.[12] It was during Foxe's continued service as tutor to the duchess's charge Thomas Howard, heir to the Norfolk dukedom, that the Protestant scholar began work on the historical projects that eventually led to *Acts and Monuments*.

Unlike her half sister Mary, Princess Elizabeth clearly had a reputation as a favorite of the Reformers. Convention alone should not account for Bale's choice of linguistic facility and religious zeal as topics in praise of

Elizabeth. Walter Lynne chooses the same subjects in dedicating his translation of an apocalyptic sermon by Martin Luther to the princess; similarly Joannes à Lasco (Jan Laski), in a compliment unique for this period, attributes the identical qualities to the princess in dedicating an edition of a Latin theological treatise by Johann Heinrich Bullinger, the Zurich theologian.[13] Lady Jane Grey's contemporary correspondence with Bullinger in Latin, Greek, and Hebrew shows that the learning of noble English women was well known in Continental circles.[14]

Underlying Bale's hyperbolic praise of Elizabeth in *A Godly medytacyon of the christen sowle* one may discern the influence of her tutor, Roger Ascham. His career furnishes a paradigm for rising in court circles by gaining the patronage of Catherine Parr and Catherine Brandon respectively, first as a tutor in the royal court and then in the household of the heirs of the Suffolk dukedom (see McConica, p. 217). Elizabeth's translation of *Godly medytacyon* epitomizes the method of double translation later advocated by Ascham in *The Scholemaster* (1570), for, according to Bale, she undertook the project primarily "for her owne exercyse in the french tunge"; she added translations of scriptural texts into Latin, Greek, French, and Italian as a final proof of learning (sigs. E8r, F1r–v).

Biblical paradigms such as the Woman Clothed with the Sun (Revelation 12), which were applied in praise of such reformist heroines as Anne Askew and Princess Elizabeth, contributed to the emergence of the Reformation iconographical tradition of the "true Christian woman." Formulaic praise of Anne Seymour as an example of the Protestant Woman of Faith is, for example, a recurrent theme in the many dedications addressed to her during the reign of Edward VI. The Archbishop of Canterbury's printer, Walter Lynne, in his *Briefe Collection* (1549) of scriptural readings for the consolation of the sick, praises her as "the most gracious patronesse & supportar both of good learnynge and also of godly men learned" (sigs. A4v–A5r). Her devotion to "daylye studye . . . in the holy Bible" makes her an appropriate patron for Lynne's 1550 translation of *A Briefe Concordaunce* ("The Zurich Concordance," sig. A2r), just as his edition in the same year of William Roy's translation of *The True Beliefe in Christ and his Sacramentes* (from Wolfgang Capito's *De pueris instituendis*) is said by Lynne to reflect her commitment "to se Goddes trueth both preached & set forth in writtinges" (sig. A2r). Although Lynne specialized as a translator in the writings of German reformers, he also published the translation of St. Augustine's defense of predestination that Nicholas Lesse addressed to the duchess. Lesse attempted to build his career as a translator on the patronage of noble women through dedicating a second predestinarian tract to Lady Seymour, in addition to another work by St. Augustine that he addressed to Mary Fitzroy. His links to eminent women may have led him to translate *The Censure and Judgement of Erasmus: Whyther dyvorsemente stondeth with the lawe of God* (c. 1550), which argues for the sexual equality of women, who should be free to marry whomever they please.

Anne Seymour granted positions in her household to three reformist authors: Thomas Becon, Nicolas Denisot, and William Samuel. Becon, who had once used the pseudonym Theodore Basille to conceal himself from heresy charges, wrote a Protestant nativity play and many other religious works under her protection. The strong appeal to aristocratic women of meditation on scriptural texts is documented by the collection of prayers that he prepared in gratitude for her generosity "sense [since] I came firste to youre servyce";[15] he reflects similar concerns in addressing another collection of biblical prayers, *The Castell of Comforte* (c. 1550), to Mary Fitzroy. The assumption that women are the intellectual equals of men underlies Becon's praise of Lord and Lady Seymour for providing both sons and daughters with identical instruction in the Bible and classics by humanistic tutors. In dedicating yet another collection of biblical prayers, *The Governaunce of Vertue* (1549) to one of these children, Jane, he argues that the goal of Protestant humanism is to produce "scholiers in the misteries of Christes scole" (sig. A2v).

Humanistic principles were put into practice in the education of the Seymour daughters. Their French tutor, Nicolas Denisot, complimented the linguistic abilities of Jane Seymour and her sisters, Anne and Margaret, by editing their Latin distichs on the death of Marguerite de Navarre.[16] Denisot's Parisian circle included intellectuals who were in the process of imitating classical and Italianate models in order to transform French poetry. Thus his edition of *Le Tombeau de Marguerite de Valois* (Paris, 1551), a translation of his students' Latin distichs into Greek, Italian, and French, also contained additional odes, hymns, songs, and epitaphs by such members of the Pléiade as Pierre de Ronsard and Jean Antoine de Baïf. The volume praises the three sisters for continuing the learned tradition established by Marguerite.

Aristocratic English women furthered the Reformation fashion for popular biblical poetry, however, rather than the neoclassical mode favored by Denisot and his Parisian colleagues. Thus another protégé of Anne Seymour, William Samuel, turned to the folk tradition of ballad song as the model for his paraphrase of the Pentateuch, *The Abridgemente of Goddes Statutes in Myter* (1551). Samuel and "gospelling" poets associated with him heeded Erasmus' call in *Paraclesis* for universal literacy, translation of the Bible into the vernacular, and the generation of popular biblical poetry so that "even the lowliest women" could understand the Scriptures.[17] Samuel echoes the Erasmian program in dedicating his *Abridgemente* to Anne Seymour as a text designed to "have my contray people able in smale some to syng the hole contents of the byble" (sigs. A2r–v). The gospelling movement as a whole came under the influence of the repetitive ballad versions of Psalms by Thomas Sternhold, who found favor with Henry VIII in a manner parallel to the contemporary vogue at the court of François I for the more sophisticated versifications of Psalms by Clément Marot. Sternhold, who served as a tutor to Prince Edward after Catherine Parr reorganized the royal nursery, pleased courtiers with verses like the following stanza from Psalm 6:

> Lord, in thy wrath reprove me not,
>   though I deserve thine ire:
> Ne yet correct me in thy rage,
>   O Lord, I thee desire.
> For I am weak, therefore, O Lord,
>   of mercy me forbear:
> And heal me, Lord; for why? thou know'st
>   my bones do quake for fear.
>
>   (vss. 1–2)

The standard of biblical poetry in fashion within the Seymour circle complements Catherine Parr's pietistic works in its eclectic appeal to a mixed audience of elite and ordinary readers. The wife of Seymour's close associate Sir Ralph Fane, for example, designed her versifications of 21 psalms of "godly meditation" and 102 aphorisms from the Book of Proverbs for use in the kinds of devotion practiced by Catherine Parr and her associates; this lost volume was entered as a collection of prayers in a contemporary book catalogue.[18] The support that Lady Elizabeth Fane granted to her publisher, Robert Crowley, suggests that the series of biblical poems and apocalyptic satires that he wrote or sold conformed to the taste in literature of aristocratic Protestant women. Crowley acknowledged her assistance by dedicating a millenarian poem entitled *Pleasure and Payne, Heaven and Hell* (1551) to Lady Fane "as to a ryght worthy Patrones of al such as laboure in the Lords harveste" (sig. A2v). In addition Crowley not only published biblical poetry by Lady Seymour's retainer, William Samuel, but he also produced the complete *Psalter* in ballad measure at the same time that Sternhold began to versify Psalms.

The eclecticism of Catherine Brandon typifies the emergence of a distinctive vein of Protestant humanism in England by the middle of the sixteenth century, for she is credited with sponsoring works of advanced learning as well as evangelical sermons and homely translations of theological texts. Works appearing under her auspices appealed to a complex audience ranging from Continental readers ignorant of the English language to native Protestants barely literate in their own vernacular tongue. The total of fourteen dedications to printed books that she received throughout her long life (1520–80) places her in the company of the twelve greatest patronesses of the English Renaissance; Franklin B. Williams remarks, in fact, that her achievement during the mid-Tudor period is more significant than the higher figures achieved by other women during the Stuart period when publication rates multiplied.[19]

Catherine Brandon's importance as a supporter of higher learning rests upon the appointment of Thomas Wilson as tutor to her sons, Charles and Henry, heirs to the Suffolk dukedom; surely their education put into practice principles that their instructor articulated in *The Rule of Reason* (1551), an introduction to logic, and in his handbook of classical oratory, *The Arte of Rhetorique* (1553). Wilson praises Lady Brandon in the latter work for her devotion to humanistic ideals and for being "especially to the learned, an earnest good patronesse, and moste helpyng Lady above all other" (sigs. b4r–c1r). He insists upon the existence of a direct connection between learning and faith, arguing that mastery of rhetoric, for example, is one means of salvation: "Eloquence first geven by God, after loste by man, and laste repayred by God agayne" (sig. A3r). Wilson's eventual rise to the office of secretary of state under Queen Elizabeth made him more

successful in the quest for patronage than his close associate, Roger
Ascham, whose *Scholemaster* joined Wilson's own writings on logic and
rhetoric as the fundamental Tudor handbooks concerned with the popularization of classical study as both the foundation of well-rounded education and the model for elegant simplicity in prose style.

Wilson's collection of a set of Latin panegyrics on the deaths of his
pupils may be read both as an anthology by successful Protestant humanist
careerists (most of whom went to the royal court from St. John's College,
Cambridge), and as an elaborate compliment to the Duchess of Suffolk.[20]
Contributors of epigrams and epitaphs included John Cheke, William
Cecil, and Nicholas Udall, all of whom had risen at court under Catherine
Parr's patronage; John Parkhurst, who served in succession as chaplain to
Catherine Brandon and Catherine Parr; as well as Laurence Humphrey and
Thomas Chaloner, whose many connections in Protestant circles included
Edward Seymour, Cecil, Foxe, and Bale. The coeditor, Walter Haddon,
also contributed commemorative poems in Latin to both *The Rule of Rea-
son* and *The Arte of Rhetorique,* and Udall added a companion poem to
the latter work.

The popularization of classical and biblical wisdom is the common
concern of every other book linked to Catherine Brandon. The gentleman-
poet John Harington addressed his translation of Cicero's *Booke of
Freendeship* (1550) out of French to her, for example, with the wish that
"how so ever it shalbe liked of the learned, I hope it shalbe allowed of the
unlatined" (sig. A3v). Having found consolation in the study and translation of French during a period of imprisonment in the Tower of London,
he dedicates the text in homage to the duchess as a "trew example" of
friendship (sig. A5r). The translator Nicholas Lesse looks to her as a patroness "at whose handes . . . the common people hath received already
many confortable & spirituall consolations, instructions, & techinges."[21]
John Day, who issued Lesse's translation, and his partner William Seres
acknowledged that they served Brandon as publishers by printing her coat
of arms prominently in six of their editions of biblical translations, commentaries, and sermons.

Catherine Brandon's chief protégé was Hugh Latimer, the most influential preacher during Edward VI's reign. Her insignia appeared in editions
of Latimer's sermons published by John Day: the extremely popular "Sermon of the Plough" preached at Paul's cross and a collection of seven

Lenten sermons preached at the royal court in 1549. Thomas Some dedicated his transcription of the court sermons to the duchess not only because of her reputation for piety and patronage of Christian learning, but "chiefly for the profyte which shall ensue through them unto the ignoraunte" (sig. A2v). Even before Latimer rose to become the most prominent pulpit spokesman for the Protestant lords who governed England during the minority of Edward VI, he had long served as a spiritual advisor to aristocratic Protestant women. After serving in Catherine Parr's household before her marriage to Henry VIII, his continuing access to the queen's privy chamber had implicated him in the heresy hunt. At that time Anne Askew had requested that he visit her in prison as a counselor: "Therfor I desyred to speake with Latymer [but] it wolde no be" (*Examinations*, II, sig. C7v). In praising Anne Seymour as a patron of learning, John Olde acknowledges Latimer for successfully recommending him to her preferment to the vicarage of Cobington in Warwickshire. After leaving the royal court, Latimer resided in Catherine Brandon's manor of Grimsthorpe in Lincolnshire, where he preached a series of private sermons before her in 1552.[22]

The succession to the throne of Mary Tudor (1553–58) upon the death of Edward VI effectively muzzled the Protestant patronesses and their protégés. The new queen had negligible standing as a patroness, for the many dedications that she received reflect her control of Crown offices and annuities rather than genuine sponsorship.[23] Although Anne Seymour and Mary Fitzroy remained in England along with such Erastians as William Cecil and Roger Ascham, Catherine Brandon was the highest ranking peer to join Reformers like John Foxe, Robert Crowley, and Thomas Becon in exile on the Continent. Hugh Latimer was burnt at the stake in Oxford, and Lady Jane Grey died at the headsman's block, not for her learning but as a pretender to the throne who was manipulated by Protestant lords who wished to remain in power. Princess Elizabeth, as Mary's legitimate heir, commented on similar suspicions directed against her during one of the imprisonments that left her for long periods under threat of death: "Much suspected by me /Nothing proved can be, /Quoth Elizabeth prisoner."[24] Like Catherine Parr, she turned toward meditation and prayer for consolation, expressing her uneasy disillusionment through translations of Boethius' *Consolation of Philosophy* and Petrarch's *Triumph of Eternity*.

Protestant patronesses were freed once again when Queen Elizabeth began her long reign (1558–1603), but they regained neither the power nor importance that they once enjoyed during the turbulent minority of Edward VI. Although their commitment to the popularization of Protestant theology and classical learning had changed little during the silence imposed by Queen Mary, their evangelical zeal often placed them at odds with Elizabeth's desire for compromise concerning controversial issues of ecclesiastical polity and ritual; instead they tended to support Puritan clergymen who agitated against episcopal authority. This was particularly true of the activities of three younger women whose father, Sir Anthony Cooke, came to court as a royal tutor under the patronage of Catherine Parr. The husbands of Mildred, Anne, and Elizabeth Cooke included two of the queen's chief ministers: William Cecil, Lord Burghley, and Sir Nicholas Bacon, the Keeper of the Seal. The advanced religious views of these sisters attest to the emergence of a cadre of powerful women who clearly considered themselves to be the equals of men in matters of faith and learning.

Catherine Brandon remained active as a sponsor of continuing ecclesiastical reform in contrast to Anne Seymour, who extended her retirement into Elizabeth's reign, perhaps as a consequence of the discrediting of the Seymour family through the attainder and execution of her husband and the efforts of their son, Edward, Earl of Hertford, to marry close to the line of royal succession. Catherine Brandon's flight from prosecution under Queen Mary gained her, on the other hand, an extravagant reputation as a Reformation heroine. In its praise for her exile and continuing devotion to the edification of the "ignoraunt & unlearned," Augustine Bernher's sober dedication of Latimer's *Seven Sermons* complements the romanticization inherent in Foxe's sensational narrative of the perils that the duchess encountered in England and on the Continent for her religious beliefs (Foxe, VIII, 569–76). In exile she settled in Poland at the invitation of Baron Joannes à Lasco, who had once praised the learning of Princess Elizabeth during his own exile in London. During the seventeenth century the ramification of the Foxe account into a popular legend resulted in a broadside ballad and a play that was "divers and sundry times acted, with good applause."[25]

Lady Brandon's survival as the senior member of a group of women who encouraged the dissent of Puritan clergymen and the publication of Calvinistic theology suggests that she was a major transmitter of pietistic methods once associated with the Catherine Parr circle. The translation of Calvin's *Sermons upon the Songe that Ezechias made after he had bene sicke* (1560) that her fellow exile, Anne Locke, dedicated to the duchess dowager provided a work suitable for use in private devotions. The translator was a member of the circle of Katherine Killigrew, one of the Cooke sisters; after the death of her husband, Henry Locke, Anne Locke married the prominent Puritan preacher Edward Dering. The meditative mode of the text is designed to provide a mechanism for protecting oneself against the vicissitudes of Fortune: "Yet having theyr myndes armed & fournished with prepared patience, and defence of inward understandyng, all these calamities can not so farre prevaile" (sig. A2r). Designed as a "meditation of a Penitent Sinner," the appended versification of Psalm 51 makes it clear that the translation expresses "the passioned minde of the penitent sinner." This psalm paraphrase came into Locke's hands in the form of a manuscript "delivered me by my frend" (sigs. 2A1r–2A2r), perhaps her spiritual counselor, John Knox. The Puritan John Field dedicated his 1583 edition of Knox's *Notable Exposition upon the Fourth of Mathew* to Locke after her third marriage to Richard Prowse.[26] Field suggests in yet another dedication that his 1580 translation of *The Other Parte of Christian Questions and Answeares,* a handbook on communion by Théodore de Bèze, may well serve Catherine Brandon during her dying days as a model for meditation intended to "set all thinges in order towardes that heavenly journey" (sig. ✻3v).

Roger Ascham's praise of Queen Elizabeth and Lady Jane Grey as paragons of classical learning in *The Scholemaster* captures a radical shift in the conduct of aristocratic women that took place during the middle of the sixteenth century, for until their time Thomas More's pioneering educational efforts had borne little fruit aside from the translation activity of his own daughter, Margaret Roper. The activities of Bible reading, religious zeal, and antipapal animus that Ascham advocates had received the approval of the circle of aristocratic women who actively patronized reformist authors, preachers, and translators, and who had control over the education of the descendents of many noble houses and almost every potential claimant to the throne of England. Under the influence of Catherine Parr women began to play an unprecedented role in the development of learning and institution of a Protestant religious settlement. Their synthesis of feminism and faith passed on a cultural legacy to such late Elizabethan successors as Mary Sidney, Countess of Pembroke, and the women to whom Edmund Spenser dedicated his poetic works, the Russell sisters. With its pervasive praise of Queen Elizabeth, Spenser's *Faerie Queene* is the most enduring compliment to the patronage and piety of the intellectual women of the English Reformation.

ANNE LAKE PRESCOTT

The Pearl of the Valois and Elizabeth I: Marguerite de Navarre's *Miroir* and Tudor England

WHEN in 1547 there appeared a collection of poems called *Les marguerites de la marguerite des princesses*—"the pearls of the pearl of princesses"—no reader was likely to miss the title's pun, for Marguerite d'Angoulême, Duchesse d'Alençon, Queen of Navarre, and sister to François I, was one of the most famous women in France. Charming, witty, and pious, she had been for many years not only close to the center of political power, but also, through patronage, correspondence, friendship, and diplomatic maneuverings, on good terms with figures so disparate as Erasmus, Melanchthon, Bucer, Lefèvre d'Étaples, Dolet, Calvin, and Pope Paul III.[1] Poets, especially those who, like Clément Marot, offended the reactionary theological faculty of the Sorbonne, had reason to love her; Rabelais dedicated his *Tiers livre* to her; and after her death in 1549 Ronsard wrote that she was "certes tout l'honneur / Des Princesses de nostre âge."[2] Many of those who crossed her path were English. She feasted at the Field of the Cloth of Gold, called herself Wolsey's adopted daughter, gossiped with the Duke of Norfolk, traded compliments with Anne Boleyn, expressed concern for Anne of Cleves (her son-in-law's sister), and corresponded with Henry VIII—in their early years there had even been talk of marriage.[3] There is no evidence she ever wrote to Catherine Parr, but many of those whom the English queen patronized knew Marguerite de Navarre at least by reputation or through mutual friends. It seems fitting, therefore, that on December 31, 1544, the

eleven-year-old Lady Elizabeth presented Catherine with her own beautifully bound and embroidered translation of Marguerite's long poem *Le
miroir de l'âme pécheresse*.[4]

   This episode and its aftermath are worth a sharper look than they have
yet received, in part because the translation offers precious if fragmentary
evidence about Elizabeth's childhood feelings, and in part because the *Miroir*'s career in mid-century England demonstrates tidily how questions of
reputation and influence are trickier than one would like. For instance,
Marguerite's patronage of learning and her posthumous fame as the author
of the *Heptaméron* have tempted some scholars to see her impact on England largely in terms of these roles and, because of her sex, to assume she
was particularly popular among women. She was, wrote Sidney Lee irri-
tatingly, "Adored by cultured ladies of Tudor England."[5] Perhaps so (he
offers no evidence), but Tudor men also had reason to pay attention to her.
They knew that she had more than charm, generosity, a flair for verse, and
a taste for reform. They—and presumably the cultured ladies as well—
also knew that she had power and influence.

   Marguerite probably composed the *Miroir* in 1530 to 1531; it was published at Alençon in 1531. Two years later there were several new editions
and then, for reasons still unclear, the Sorbonne condemned it.[6] Perhaps
the faculty sensed the poem's "Lutheran" emphasis on Scripture, its deval-
uation of good works, and its almost complete indifference to saints, pen-
ances, and purgatory; or perhaps the university leadership knew that the
king was out of town and therefore thought that Marguerite, who had
recently caused some reactionary professors to be removed and had long
been known as a protector of evangelical preachers—even, it was rumored,
of heretics—was now vulnerable. But François stuck by his sister and an
embarrassed university hastily undid its condemnation of the book, explaining with more desperation than tact that no one had actually read the
poem.

   Thus the *Miroir* was by 1544 a book with a past, further confirmation
that despite her warm relations with the papacy and her diplomatic caution Marguerite was at heart a Reformer. Had not the *Miroir*'s Paris printer, Antoine Augereau, been executed in late 1534 for "scandalous blasphemy"? (Jourda, p. 186). In truth more of a mystic than a theologian,
Marguerite seems to have remained an Erasmian and Gallican Catholic.[7]

Nevertheless, the text Elizabeth translated had angered the reactionaries and been protected by royal intervention, the sort of affair that raised hopes possible for many in 1533 (and for a few even in 1544) that François might, just as Henry was in the process of doing, take France into independence and reform, if not out of the Catholic faith.[8]

The *Miroir* has received a mixed press, denigrated especially by those who may not have read it but who refer to it in passing while describing Elizabeth's girlhood. J. E. Neale, whose comments remain the basis for later remarks in biographies of Elizabeth, thought it "an excessively dreary French poem" and found its "erotic mysticism" depressing.[9] Others have called it "self-flagellation," a "very long and very dull poem," and a "cheerless, spiritually anguished little book, full of Old Testament mournfulness and self-mortification."[10] Even the translation, says Paul Johnson, is "of visual rather than intrinsic interest." Some are kinder: the *Miroir* is "a classic of the French Erasmian movement" to McConica and "a classic of Erasmian pietism" to J. J. Scarisbrick.[11] But even Pierre Jourda complains in his magisterial biography of Marguerite that her poem lacks architecture, its couplets impelled by strong emotion undirected by any principle of construction (pp. 380–84).

Yet Marguerite's *Miroir* is, I think, a clever and touching work; even its repetitions can be pleasantly narcotic, a hypnotic litany.[12] The queen begins by stressing her own sinfulness (not pathologically; Marguerite never claims to be more sinful than others, and in any case if a mirror is to catch our reluctant eye and teach us reflection it must intensify its image). She is a Hell, an abyss with the tree of sin rooted in her and pushing its foliage into her nostrils, ears, and mouth. She deserves to die. Who can deliver her? God tries, but she betrays him. And yet, amazingly, he perseveres. Marguerite then accumulates meditations on the familial relationships through which mortals may understand this love. She views these connections with despair, for she knows that she has consistently violated and degraded them. But God does not give up on her. A betrayed husband, he forgives her adulteries, and a rejected father, he calls her home. So now she comprehends the paradoxes of life and death and now she accepts God as father, son, brother, and spouse, and herself as his daughter, mother, sister, wife. Such sweetness is annihilating. Now she can long for death so that dissolved she may live in Christ, absorbed into light. God will save her not through her merits but through the divine love that enters her and then works within her to love itself in return ("Il s'ayme donc en moy" [l. 1307]). Understanding fails her, but she praises the savior "Qui luy plaist faire de moy sa Marguerite" (l. 1430).

The poem thus has a definite direction: from self-loathing to joyful anticipation, from death in life to life in death, from dismay at her betrayal of God to faith in his steadfast love, and therefore to her acceptance of her own role as the beloved. It is structured not by argument but by the changing relationship of the speaker—the sin-sick soul—to herself and to the relentlessly merciful "other" who enters and in some sense becomes that self. The shift that reverses her feelings towards her ties to God is neatly conceived and the tone is often delicately controlled, as in the smiling but resonant line quoted above on becoming God's own margarite-pearl. Furthermore, the poem is an extended demonstration of the Bible's psychological power, all the more so because many lines cite or paraphrase Scripture (from memory or from Lefèvre's 1530 translation) and the margins often identify relevant texts.[13] Marguerite believed that God's Word, lovingly understood, works from within to enliven and redirect the soul, and in its reliance on that Word her *Miroir* is an evangelical argument by example.

Scholars sometimes assume that Elizabeth chose to translate this poem. In fact the schoolroom Catherine helped arrange for the royal children in 1544 (although her exact role remains unclear) included those like John Cheke who because of their awareness of Continental humanism if for no other reason must have known Marguerite by reputation. The queen herself, regent after Henry left for Boulogne in July and chief patron of evangelical humanism in England, doubtless sympathized with Marguerite as another beleaguered but powerful friend of reform and the new learning.[14] So one need not imagine Elizabeth searching the shelves for something with which to please Catherine. Someone older, possibly Catherine herself, would very likely have known of the book and pressed it on her. Recently welcomed by Catherine into something like a real family, newly restored to the succession if not to legitimacy, and probably sensing that she was now more noticeable and thus more exposed to danger, Elizabeth could hope that by obediently translating the *Miroir* she could please an influential and affectionate stepmother, and the latter could in turn reflect that such homage to Marguerite would yet further reinforce the Erasmian and Reformist tone of her particular circle.

There may also, however, have been diplomatic reasons for such an enterprise, for Marguerite had long been on good terms with Elizabeth's father. Renaissance diplomacy was a heartless business, but even so Marguerite's affection for Henry was perhaps genuine. He had supported her adored brother during his imprisonment in Spain; she had little cause to like Charles V, who refused to yield up Spanish Navarre; she shared at least some of Henry's quarrels with Rome; and she got on well with English diplomats, impressing them even in secret correspondence as "a wise and marvellous well-spoken woman."[15] The Duke of Norfolk, a Francophile and Elizabeth's great-uncle, wrote that Marguerite was "the most frank and wise woman he ever spake with" and called her his "mistress," one assumes in the chivalric sense.[16] Sir John Wallop reported to Henry in late 1540 that Marguerite "was, as usual, very gracious" and that he thought her sincere (*L&P*, XVI, 240, 306). Henry must have been particularly pleased to hear that she had defended his orthodoxy to the papal nuncio and reminded her brother what he owed the king of England (*L&P*, XV, 418; XVI, 1363). In sum, as one of her countrymen told Sir William Paget in 1542, she was "a right English woman" (*L&P*, XVII, 232). Such was Marguerite's at least apparent support for Henry (interrupted only by moments of exasperation) that in 1540 Wallop wrote Sir Thomas Cromwell that she had urged him not to send presents as this would reveal to the court the extent of her bias. She would, however, welcome a picture of Henry, the queen, and all three children (*L&P*, XV, 543).

Then there was her sympathy for reform, a sympathy with ambiguities the English seemed happy to overlook. Even in 1521 Cardinal Wolsey heard that she was criticizing the pope (*L&P*, III, 1456); Thomas Theabolde wrote Thomas Cranmer in 1538 that the papal legate, Reginald Pole, was disgruntled by her coolness (*L&P*, XIII, ii, 117); and in 1542 she so roundly attacked the pope ("the devil") and cardinals ("maskers in red caps") that one wonders if the usually astute Paget heard this friend of Paul III and Cardinal Jean du Bellay quite correctly. He thought so, for in 1545 he still hoped to "tempt" her to the "renunciation of the bishop of Rome."[17]

There is virtually nothing about Marguerite in surviving dispatches from January 1543 to the fall of 1544, probably because she was in semi-exile in Nérac. Late that spring, however, she returned to court and re-sumed much of her influence, so when Henry, stunned by the surprise treaty between Charles V and François I, put out peace feelers to the French he once more heard that Marguerite could be useful; that she, Cardinal du Bellay, and the king's mistress Madame d'Étampes formed an English party at the Valois court. (So du Bellay told the English; in his report Paget adds, "But as your Majesty warned me and the earl of Hertford [Edward Seymour] to beware of their subtlety, I said but yea and nay" [*L&P*, XIX, ii, 456].) Elizabeth, too, figured in these preliminary negotia-tions. Would the king like to marry her to a French prince, asked du Bellay? Maybe she could bring Boulogne as a dowery (*L&P*, XIX, ii, 470)? This plan came to nothing, but hopes for peace were at length fulfilled and Marguerite could write Paget of her pleasure at helping (*L&P*, XX, ii, 942).

Marguerite once more returned to Nérac, but in late 1546 Nicholas Wotton wrote Paget that "The Queen of Navarre is sent for, and therefore the Protestants' matter is likely to prosper" (*L&P*, XXI, ii, 638). He was wrong. Marguerite was too ill to come and her brother was soon to die, taking with him Marguerite's possible usefulness to the English and their new king, Edward. Before her death, however, she had helped her old friend Henry recover peace, and the first evidence of this aid appears in the diplomatic dispatches at just about the same time Elizabeth was working or starting work on her translation. It is tempting to think someone may have hoped such an effort, aside from its other purposes, would please a once more influential ally.

At some time the *Miroir* found its way to the royal household. There may have been more than one copy available to Elizabeth, but after exam-ining her translation I am fairly confident that she worked from the 1539 Geneva edition. Exactly how it arrived in England no one knows. There is, to be sure, evidence that Henry owned the *Miroir* before 1544. In February 1539 one Sydrac Hambert was trying to get to England, believing Henry "ordained by God to set forth his lively Word."[18] Hambert may have known that England was in the grip of considerable religious tension as the king tried to find his sometimes bloody way between reform and reaction. Maybe he even knew that the king had recently been irritated by news of criticism in France and by a fuss with the Sorbonne over an English Bible printed for him in Paris. Hoping to appeal to these anxieties, or simply a little deranged, Hambert attempted to peddle secret information to Cromwell in return, one assumes, for money and passage to England. Watch out for those men from Ferrara who claim to be bringing hawks to the king, he warned; they may be only trying to poison him, "as Italians are expert at that." And Cromwell should "beware of enemies of the gospel pretending to be friends," like the (unnamed) author of a book against the anabaptists that Hambert has sent Henry. He has also sent, he says, a "French book in rhyme composed by the Queen of Navarre called 'Le Miroir des Chrestiens.' " If he were not so broke he would come to England and tell Cromwell everything. Was this the copy Elizabeth used? Perhaps, but Hambert sent his strange communication so early in the year that we cannot be certain his volume was the 1539 edition.[19]

Neither do we know who, if anyone, helped Elizabeth with her translation. It seems unlikely that she was utterly on her own, yet her errors and omissions suggest inattention (or inadequate French) on someone's part. She opens with a letter to Catherine. She knows of the queen's "affectuous wille, and fervent zeale . . . towardes all godly lerning." So, to avoid idleness, she has turned "frenche ryme, in to englishe prose joyning the sentences together as well as the capacitie of my symple witte, and small lerning coulde extende themselves." Her effort is merely a beginning, so she hopes that Catherine will not show it to anyone "lesse my fauttes be knowen of many." Maybe Catherine can amend it. Happy New Year.

Although Elizabeth (or a helpful adult) often changed the scriptural references in the margins, omitting some and adding others, the translation itself is quite accurate, even dutiful. Here, for example, is the tree of sin:

> Si je cuyde regarder pour le mieulx,
> Une branche me vient fermer les yeulx;
> Et en my bouche tombe, quant vueil parler,
> Le fruict par trop amer à avaller.
> Si pour ouyr, mon esperit s'esveille,
> Force fueilles entrent en mon aureille;
> Aussi mon naiz est tout bousché de fleurs.
>
> (ll. 17–23)

If i thinke to loke for better, a braunche cometh and doth close myne eyes. and in my mouth doth fall when i wolde speake the frutte wich is so bytter to sualowe down. If my spirite be styrred for to karken [harken]: than a great multitude of leaffes doth entre in myne eares and my nose is all stoped whith flowres. (fol. 7)

Precisely because Elizabeth's translation is so literal, her departures from the original are suggestive. On the whole, she tones down Marguerite's fervor. Thus on several occasions (ll. 831, 955, 1072, and 1283) references to fire or burning drop in temperature: "brusler" becomes "styrre," "ardeur" is "goodness," and a couple of other hot words simply disappear. Sometimes Elizabeth limits the self-abasement. She omits Marguerite's claim to be "terre, cendre, et fange" (l. 370), ingnores the phrase "mon riens, et ma nichilité" (l. 863), and decides against calling herself "Chienne morte, pourriture de siens" (l. 1374). Even Marguerite's taste for repeated words evidently struck Elizabeth as wasteful or loud; typically, line 1109 beginning "O Mort, o Mort" now starts "O death."

Elizabeth's biographers have often remarked that we cannot know her reactions to the violence and betrayals of Henry's court. How did she respond to the executions of her mother, Anne Boleyn, and her stepmother, Catherine Howard? To the divorce of Anne of Cleves and the death of Jane Seymour? In public, as Paul Johnson puts it, she "kept her head down, her nose in her books, and said nothing" (p. 21). Yet some of her departures from Marguerite's text offer, I think, a tantalizing glimpse into her feelings in late 1544. Now, whoever asked or encouraged her to translate the *Miroir* forgot or did not know that it is more than a piece of piety by a famous and friendly patron of moderate reform. It also explores a set of analogies through which mortals can indicate otherwise incommunicable religious feelings, expressing them in terms of familial and erotic relationships. This powerful language is valuable, but it is also disconcerting, both because the analogies risk shaping a religious perception according to the anxieties and limitations of human relationships, and because to think about the Incarnation in this way runs rapidly into tangles of metaphor which if applied to other humans would suggest incest, gender confusion, and even loss of identity. Marguerite is thus deliberately playing with psychologically and semantically explosive material, although she has ample biblical precedent.[20]

Elizabeth had cause to feel within her very marrow the pain and ambiguity of family ties. Interestingly, poignantly, her relatively few errors and her somewhat more frequent omissions often concern this set of relationships. Some errors have no apparent importance, and because so much of what Marguerite says concerns family love, any errors are statistically likely to touch on that matter. Nevertheless, Elizabeth's at times startling deviations are worth noting and, unless much psychoanalytic thought is quite mistaken, cannot be without significance. To this English professor's untrained eye they indicate at best a confused anxiety and at worst a deep anger, particularly at her father. How much of this was conscious, of course, no one can know.

The first 145 lines have, so far as I can tell, no serious errors or omissions until, when Marguerite speaks of how Christ's love exceeds that of a father or brother, Elizabeth ignores the line "Tant fust il doulx, piteux, et debonnaire." Perhaps this means nothing, for she also omits line 512 on God as "Tresdebonnaire et tresdoux sans feintise"; could she have had trouble with "debonnaire"? Line 350 presents more of a problem. Marguerite writes, "Pere, fille, o bieneureux lignaige! / Que de doulceur, que de suavité / Me vient de tant doulce paternité!" (ll. 350–52). The word "paternité" shows clearly that the line refers to a father's love for a daughter, but Elizabeth translates "Pere" as "mother," although she keeps "paternity." This is, I believe, her first real mistranslation. Another omission comes when Marguerite reimagines the judgment of Solomon (God is also her king and judge); her "voisine," her own sensuality, has taken her living child and given her a dead one. But God restores the living baby, the new life, the redemptive offspring from within the self, because he can tell a real mother from a false one. Elizabeth's translation is accurate enough, but she omits Marguerite's line on her love for her child, "Pour qui voiez mon cueur tant travailler" (l. 468); maybe the topic troubled her. And about a hundred lines later Marguerite is astonished by divine mercy; mortals give us no such examples: "Si pere a eu de son enfant mercy, / Si mere a eu pour son filz du soulcy, / Si frere à soeur a couvert le peché, / Je n'ay point veu, ou il est bien caché . . ." (ll. 581–84). Elizabeth drops the line about a father's mercy to his child.

Then, almost immediately after, comes her most interesting if temporary departure from the text. At first glance Elizabeth's manuscript is neat and her handwriting pretty, but in fact the pages, especially in the second half, have some cancellations and corrections. This particular error, one of few in this part of the work, may preserve a moment when emotional pressure propelled her imagination in the wrong direction until her mind caught and redirected it to the sense of the passage. No mere mortal husband, says Marguerite, will pardon an adulterous wife; rather, there are plenty who from revenge have had them judged and put to death: "Assez en est, qui pour venger leur tort, / Par les juges les on faict mettre à mort" (ll. 587–88). Elizabeth wrote, "There be inoughe of them, wiche for to avenge their wronge, did cause the judges to condemne hym to dye." She then crossed out "hym" and wrote "them" above it. There is little doubt, I believe, that her "hym" means "him"; Elizabeth never uses the older "hem" (or the even rarer "hym") for "them" and she does elsewhere confuse genders. But who was "hym"? While forced by her text to think about husbands who execute errant wives, her pen at first brought the man, not the woman, to the block. Interestingly, a few lines later in a passage on husbands who lock up such wives she renders "tour" as "prison," not as "tower."

For a while Elizabeth's translation degenerates. There are more omissions, some looseness not like her usual method, and another moment of familial confusion. Whereas Marguerite refers to a child who will "son bon pere offenser" (l. 633), Elizabeth has "offende hys mother," and in the next line she writes of a sister who murmurs against "hys" brother. Then, for a time, the translation recovers its poise. True, line 717 refers to a king "plein de toute loyaulté" and Elizabeth to a king's "godlines," and there are other little changes of no great interest. For example, she omits line 740 on God's pity for his wife's weakness, but the translation is generally close (ll. 805–06 may be dropped because the French is confusing). Then, in a passage on how God's forgiveness makes of his spouse a new woman (the English softens this into "maketh me a godly and beautiefull creature"), Elizabeth omits the line "Sans y laisser renommee ne bruyt" (l. 836), in which Marguerite rejoices that even the echo of her sin, her exposure to scandal, is abolished. Shortly afterwards we are back to confusion over gender. Have I really recovered the place of your "espouse"? asks Marguerite (l. 842). Elizabeth renders this as "husbande," crosses it out and writes "wife."

Nearly a hundred lines later comes one of the poem's emotional peaks, when the soul can name God by all his family names, and this time Elizabeth has no error, although she drops the phrase in which Marguerite says she now names God thus "par amour hardiemment" (l. 931). Nevertheless, when after this passage of anaphoric addresses Marguerite then starts infolding the familial references more complexly into the verse, Elizabeth is once more nervous or confused, leaving out "frere" from the recitation of God's roles. Line 1083 may be omitted simply because Elizabeth was starting a new page and lost her place, but one can't help noting that another missing line, calling Peace the "soeur" of Justice (l. 1189), refers yet again to a family relationship. And, not surprisingly, Elizabeth drops the punning reference near the end to the author as God's own pearl. Indeed, nowhere does the manuscript refer to Marguerite.[21]

The absence of any reference to the Queen of Navarre is quite puzzling in a manuscript presented to the English queen while the French author was enjoying renewed importance. One would expect a compliment or two in the preface at least. Yet Elizabeth herself may not have felt much need, unless otherwise instructed, to praise a foreign monarch whose position she was not old enough fully to appreciate and who had only recently emerged from a period of semiretirement in which she had attracted diminished attention in England. Furthermore, if, as I suspect, Elizabeth's school exercise was begun with the hope (on someone's part) that a loving and appropriate gesture toward a stepmother might double as a diplomatic gesture towards the French king's sister, the translation must have come to seem not so useful after all. As New Year's Day approached it would be clear to whoever worked with her (or to Catherine, after she examined her present) that the manuscript was not a finished work, disfigured by corrections and by a few passages that needed clarification.

More important, it must have occurred to any adult who read beyond the first two hundred lines that this poem, with its impassioned evocation of God as a great king and judge who is kind to daughters and does not execute adulterous wives, was a most unsuitable means of displaying Elizabeth's talents at Henry's court. Nor could it be used even quasi-publicly to warm the hearts of England's sympathizers in France; Marguerite knew what Henry did to adulterous wives, although she wrote her poem before he took up that habit and although she tried to be understanding about the Catherine Howard affair (*L&P*, XVI, 1363). All this is speculative, of course. What is virtually certain is that no one in England who looked closely at this manuscript would feel comfortable about it while Henry lived. The poem's reputation as a once condemned work would bother him less (he too had had trouble with French reactionaries) than its appalling relevance to his family. Perhaps he cast a fatherly eye over the manuscript, but it is hard to believe he much liked the central section; this "mirror" would reflect him all too well.

Only after Henry was dead did Elizabeth's translation see print, and for reasons hardly literary. John Bale, once a pious monk and now a Protestant with views that landed his polemics on Henry's list of forbidden books and himself on the Continent in the safety of exile, was by 1548 arranging for his return to the England of Protector Somerset. Before he returned home, however, he published in April, at Wesel, *A Godly medytacyon of the christen sowle . . . compyled in frenche by Lady Margarete quene of Naver, and aptely translated into Englysh by the ryght vertuouse lady Elyzabeth doughter to our late soverayne Kynge Henri the viii.*[22] Bale does not say how he got the manuscript or who lightly edited it. Someone (Bale? Catherine? Elizabeth? Roger Ascham, Elizabeth's new tutor?) had at some point taken a look at the French text (by then reprinted in *Les Marguerites*), for several lines missing from Elizabeth's translation are restored (e.g., ll. 468, 481). But some errors, such as the turning of "Pere" to "mother" remain, so whoever checked the translation did so quickly or carelessly. The new version is, however, somewhat smoother and there are new biblical citations in the margins.

Marguerite's poem is a pious Erasmian meditation, an intensely private work. In his long introduction and afterword, Bale makes its presentation as polemical and politically significant as he can. Indeed he has doubts about the text itself, which he fears will bore us: "If the ofte repetynge of some one sentence, engendereth a tedyouse werynesse to the reader, lete hym wele peruse the holy workes of S. Johan the Evangelyst, and I doubt it not but he shall fynde there the same maner of writynge," for "a thynge twyse or thryse spoken, entereth moche more depely into the remembraunce . . ." (sig. E7v). These are not the words of a man moved by the poem he is publishing. Nor does Bale waste time praising its author, who had by now retired to Nérac. What interests him are the potential roles of the new king of England, his sister, and his stepmother. Bale admires Elizabeth with an extravagance anticipating her later elevation as England's Deborah or Astraea. Why, she composed her work at only fourteen (he is off by three years). What learning! And what charity in this unmonkish sharing of her labor's fruits! What may we hope from her "whan dyscressyon and yeares shall be more rype and auncyent" (sig. E8r)? As for her brother, Edward recalls those Old Testament kings who cast down idols and reformed worship—kings like Josiah, who cleaned out the "buggery chambers in the howse of the lorde" (sig. A5r). This is true nobility, beyond the reach of popish "blasphemouse bellybeastes, and most ydell wytted sorcerers" (sig. A4v).

In his afterword, Bale devotes considerable space to admirable women from his country's history. At first one might suppose this to be a contribution to the *querelle des femmes* or further indication of Bale's genuine gynophilia (after all, it was he who first promoted Anne Askew as a Protestant heroine). But Bale probably has something else in mind as well. Many of the women he cites—Locrine's widow Gwendolyn, Cordelia, Belyne's daughter Cambra, Martia—were queens who, as he points out, ruled in their own names or as regents until their sons were grown; another, the Saxon Hylda, disputed for the truth against the prelates. It would be hard to read such words in 1548 without thinking of the reliably Reformist Catherine Parr and suspecting that Bale was offering historical support for her continued or increased role in guiding the realm. In fact, Catherine's political influence had decreased since Henry's death and her marriage to the Protector's unruly brother; she died in childbed a few months after the *Godly medytacyon* was printed. (Bale was not lucky in his political flatteries and maneuverings, for he also managed to offend the government by an unwise attack on Paget, and his reception in England was at first cool, although the Duchess of Richmond took him in.)[23]

A year and a half after Bale's edition Marguerite died, on December 21, 1549. The following June there appeared in Paris a memorial volume of verse, *Annae, Margaritae, Janae, sororum virginum heroidum Anglarum, in mortem divae Margaritae Valesiae, Navarrorum reginae, Hecatodistichon*—104 Latin distichs by three daughters of Protector Somerset together with some learned poems by various hands.[24] The verse well captures the pious author of the *Miroir* if not the powerful and witty queen. The sisters praise her poetry ("carmina sacra canit," distich 25), her fame ("gloria, nomen honorque," 19), and her now heavenly mind ("mens coelum," 7), rejoicing that her imprisoned soul has escaped (23), its exile now over (71). Marguerite is the wise virgin with the ready lamp (13) who now lives dissolved (35), burning with the delicious kisses of Christ (55, 101) and the ecstasy of the divine bridal couch (100). She who had sought the stars (38) and studied how to die (39) now gains the aethereum (30). This fusion of Platonic and Pauline mysticism certainly befits Marguerite, and other lines recall the *Miroir* even more closely, particularly the many paradoxes about life and death. When Margaret Seymour praises the *Miroir*, then, one has some confidence that she has read it: "Quis speculum illius non admirabitur, in quo / Vera Dei effigies illa refracta datur?"[25] Furthermore, her reference to the now resolved dispute between flesh and spirit (59) suggests that she has also seen the *Discord*, published with the *Miroir*, and that she has therefore read Marguerite in French. And Jane says that Marguerite will now see her brother again (84), possibly showing the sisters' familiarity with the sad poems on François in *Les Marguerites*.

Now, the publication of this verse could not have been an exclusively personal homage, for daughters of so powerful a figure as Somerset were not free to act as private individuals. Someone must have inspired or encouraged them, or at the very least granted permission. One man who did encourage them was the French poet Nicolas Denisot, who had belonged briefly to Marguerite's household. He arrived in England shortly before Henry's death, singing the king's demise in abject Latin couplets that later influenced those of the Seymour sisters. In March 1547 he moved to Somerset House as tutor to the children. What caused his departure several years later is unclear. Somerset fell from power in October 1549 and by early December Denisot was back in France. Perhaps he left because his employer was in jail, but there is also evidence he was caught in some sort of espionage.[26] In any case, he kept on good terms with the Seymour household and it was he who arranged for the publication of the girls' verse. If he actually helped them write it, he must have done so by letter. In the meantime, Somerset had been released from the Tower in February and restored to the Privy Council in April.[27]

During this political drama, Paget and others had been in France negotiating a treaty which was signed in March. In early May there were parties and ceremonies in France and shortly afterwards parties and ceremonies in England (followed soon by a wedding between Anne Seymour and a son of her father's archrival, Warwick). Thus the volume Denisot published in June suited a number of people very well. Somerset could rejoice at another sign of his family's recovered prestige and its reputation as patrons of pious humanism; the French could feel complimented by this quasi-royal attention to their king's aunt; and Denisot could attract literary notice.

April of the following year saw a new edition, a full *Tombeau*. In his 1550 introduction Denisot had called upon France's poets to join the Seymours in mourning Marguerite, and now they responded handsomely. After a preface praising the "trois divines et doctes Soeurs vierges Angloises" and the defunct "Princesse tresillustre, perle et miroir de scavoir religion [*sic*]" comes a crowd of both long-famous and recently fashionable authors: Jean Salmon Macrin, Mellin de Saint-Gelais, Pierre de Ronsard, Jean Dorat, Jean-Antoine de Baïf, Joachim du Bellay, and others. Denisot reprints the Latin distichs, whose authors a prefatory epistle calls the "trois plus excellentes Princesses que oncques vostre Isle d'Albion sceut produire." After each distich there is at least one translation; du Bellay gives French quatrains for all of them, but other poets offer additional versions in various languages. To these polyglot exercises Denisot's contributors add a number of poems glowing with real or assumed admiration. One sonnet is by a woman, the "Damoiselle A.D.L.," whom I cannot identify. Playing with Marguerite's own devotional vocabulary, A.D.L. imagines her descending from Heaven to greet the girls who have so well sung her victory over the flesh and even thanked death for giving her repose; but the queen would remind them that their learned celebration has misplaced the credit, which should go to Christ:

> Dirois-tu pas oyant leur melodie
> Tant doctement celebrer ton grand bien,
> Mes Seurs, il fault que ce mot je vous die:
> Christ est mon Tout, sans luy je n'estois Rien.
> (sig. L7v).

The volume thus combines pious learning, elegance, courtly flattery, some passable verse, and the heady atmosphere that comes from knowing one's colleagues are people who count. This, in 1551, was the right crowd. Denisot had arrived. And yet once again there were good diplomatic reasons for an impressive literary show. The *Tombeau* appeared during negotiations for a marriage between Edward VI and a French princess and just before English envoys were to arrive in France for official ceremonies and celebrations (at one of which Henri II was made a Knight of the Garter). Ronsard was well aware that the volume to which he was contributing had political significance, for in his poem honoring the Seymours he refers to the recent peace:

Io, puis que les espris
D'Angleterre et de la France
Bandez d'une ligue ont pris
Le fer contre l'Ignorance,
Et que nos Rois se sont faits,
D'ennemis, amis parfaits,
Tuans la guerre cruelle
Par une paix mutuelle . . . .[28]

Marguerite would have been delighted. Living, she had been treated rather shabbily by Henri II, but dead she could once more help the cause of Anglo-French peace.

In this literary and diplomatic gathering, however, someone is missing. The *Tombeau*'s full title refers to the Seymour sisters as "Princesses en Angleterre," and, as the king's cousins, in a sense they were. Still, there is something about the title and about the absence of the *Miroir*'s English translator—England's chief Protestant princess had assumed the role of self-effacing scholarly sister but she was in no disgrace or exile—recalling the arrogance that had led Somerset's wife to quarrel with Catherine Parr and that would help bring Somerset himself, despite his real virtues, to a second and fatal fall later that year. In a few years his chief rival, now Duke of Northumberland, followed him to the block. But Elizabeth survived. In later years she must have thought of Marguerite from time to time (after all, she helped Marguerite's grandson, Henri de Navarre, gain his crown). Perhaps Elizabeth read the *Heptaméron* in French, published the year she came to the throne, or maybe she read some of its stories when on occasion they were translated into English. One of her prayers—devotions that touchingly stress God's fatherly love—asks Christ the Son to let her love him "for thy promises as my father."[29] A modern commentator on her prayers understandably finds this phrase "extraordinary," but not only is such generational confusion good trinitarianism, it is a rhetorical technique Elizabeth had met in Marguerite.[30] In any case, her own *Godly medytacyon* was reissued every now and then, so may one not hope she remembered the *Miroir* and its author with affection? It would have reminded her that although she had no father, brother, husband, or son, she had God as all of these—but then, perhaps equally important to Elizabeth, she also had England.

ELAINE V. BEILIN

Anne Askew's Self-Portrait
in the *Examinations*

I N 1545, Anne Askew, a member of the Reformed church, began to
write *The first examinacyon,* an account of her first imprisonment
and questioning by the Henrician reaction. Completed a year later,
just before she was burned as a heretic at Smithfield, *The first examinacyon* and *The lattre examinacyon,* the record of her second imprisonment,
document the climactic months in the life of an extraordinary woman who
became a popular Protestant martyr and a legend still current today.[1] Not
the least source of Askew's power in her own time was that she was a
woman, and her account of a woman's defying the authorities of the established church made her an important example for the early Reformers. In
her, John Bale saw how "the strength of God is here made perfyght by
weakenesse," and John Foxe called her "a singular example of Christen
constancie for all men to folowe."[2] Today, we might be more interested in
what we perceive as Askew's strength of character, revealed in her flight
from husband and home for the sake of religious belief, and in her courage
despite persistent persecution and torture. Then as now, the drama and
directness of Askew's writing fuels what the reader wishes to make of her,
but if her coreligionists found only a Protestant saint, other readers might
discover a remarkable woman creating a memorable self-portrait.

Askew was one of a small group of early sixteenth-century women educated on humanist principles.[3] Of these women, the few whose writings
were published took care that their lives and works observed societal stric-

tures on female virtue and domesticity. That they had ventured at all into the public sphere was masked by their supporters, whose prefaces lauded their chastity and piety, as well as their learning, and by the writers themselves, who, demurring against their own abilities, effaced themselves from their works and severely limited their literary endeavors. Against this background, Askew's experiences present an interesting series of complications. For her, virtuous domesticity was not possible, because her husband had thrown her out of his house and she herself sought a divorce. Then, the public nature of her questionings immediately assured the wide currency of her words. And her *Examinations* are the rarest form of sixteenth-century writing, the self-portrait. Until the late sixteenth and early seventeeth centuries, autobiography barely existed as an English genre, and the few examples of it are mere glimpses into the author's life and thought. *The Book of Margery Kempe,* (c. 1440), dictated to a scribe and written in the third person, is perhaps the first attempt at autobiography in England; Anne Askew may well be the next chronicler of her own experience, followed shortly by John Bale himself in *The vocacyon of John Bale* (1553).[4] What drew Askew to write her first-person narrative, to create herself, and why that creation had such power in her own time may be partly determined by looking closely at the text, its circumstances, and her biography.

To John Bale, the fiery Protestant propagandist, we owe the first publication of Askew's work, and through his interlinear "Elucydacyon," an insight into the conflict inherent in Askew's being both a woman—supposedly weak, silent, and domestic—and yet also a Reformist martyr—courageous, disputatious, and strong. Interested primarily in the propagandist value of Askew's text, Bale flattens and removes the problems by arguing that Askew's strength came wholly from God and was a sure sign of the truth of the Reformers' cause. Continually remarking on her inherent womanly weakness and daintiness, he can safely applaud the unwomanly or unnatural power in her words and deeds by attributing them to divine grace.[5] But to examine Askew's text without Bale's framework is to find Askew's depiction of herself a much less easy assimilation of the "weak vessel of the Lord" with the learned, argumentative, courageous woman who defied the male hierarchy of both church and state. By looking at the *Examinations* in their two different settings, with and without Bale's commentary, we have an interesting opportunity to compare the way a woman created herself and the way an admiring man adorned her.[6]

Whether Askew was, as Bale believed, the stereotypically weak woman made strong by God, or whether she was a strong woman made stronger by her faith is not the issue here. Although nothing in her earlier life suggests that she subscribed to the obedience and silence recommended for her sex, her assertiveness and loquacity do seem to have been motivated by a powerful conversion, and intense Christian belief informs all her writing. Her decision to set down her examinations in such detail (perhaps unique among the Reformist martyrs), to be responsible for her own record, whether inspired by the "good people" of her sect whom she addresses in her opening words, by the "dere frynde in the lorde" whom she wishes to persuade of the symbolic nature of communion, or by the need to clarify her own character and behavior, is in essence a decision to write her autobiography. As sparing as she is of references to her personal life and her past, those very details for which we read autobiography today, Askew does unfold her essential self, that is, her identity as a Christian woman. Though the *Examinations* covers only the period of her imprisonment and questionings, the years 1545 to 1546 were climactic, bringing the confrontation to which all her previous acts had been tending.

To write about the crisis of her life suggests that Askew possessed a reasonably developed sense of self; however, we must see this self motivated not by the individualism of modern autobiography, but by the desire to participate in a larger community, the Reformed church. By showing herself to be not a weak woman, but a vanquisher of the papist foe, a learned, honest, God-fearing, Scripture-loving comrade in the faith, Askew was seeking to disclose her true identity. Her sense of an audience eager to read her work engenders Askew's careful attention to the nuances of language and a style not of private revelation of self, but of a public celebration of the virtues she values: piety, constancy, learning, and fortitude. What should strike us here is that Askew presents herself in public as fully participant in the "gifts of the Lord," and as a teacher of doctrine and champion of her faith. If a Protestant woman no longer had the possibilities of Catholic mysticism to provide her an acceptable public role within the Church hierarchy, she now had another unmediated path to God.[7] By her own learning, she could read Scripture, and as a Reformer she trusted it to empower her words and deeds. Because Askew professed her faith in the years she did, without cloister, anchorage, or family to protect her, she ran headlong into a political and religious crossfire that gave her a new role, that of martyr. Her autobiography, then, is implicitly the making of a Protestant hero, and possesses the simultaneous self-effacement and self-centeredness that such a role might be expected to entail.

The Reformers, represented by John Bale, and the Henrician reaction, represented by Bishops Gardiner, Winchester, and Bonner, the Lord Chancellor Wriothsley, and various officials of city and church, both define Askew as "woman." Her inquistitors enunciate all the traditional dogma about a woman's not meddling in Scripture or speaking in church, and the Lord Chancellor seems particularly vindictive because so weak a vessel proves so immovable in her determination not to recant. But Bale seizes on this inherent weakness of woman and claims from it his most telling proof that God is with the Reformers: "2. Cor. 12. The strength of God is here made perfyght by weakenesse. Whan she semed most feble, than was she most stronge." Bale attributes to Askew herself this interpretation of her role: "And gladlye she rejoyced in that weakenesse, that Christes power myght strongelye dwell in her" (I, Preface, p. 9v). Bale's lesson for the faithful here is that the sixteenth-century Reformers fulfill Bede's prophecy that a renewal of the faith of the Apostles and prophets will be accompanied by "horryble persecucyon" and martyrdom (I, Preface, p. 2r). He therefore presents Askew, "a gentylwoman verye yonge, dayntye, and tender" (I, Preface p. 5r), as a latter-day version of the martyrs of the primitive church, particularly comparing her to a second-century martyr, Blandina, whom Eusebius had described as "small and weak and greatly despised, she had put on the great and invincible athlete Christ."[8] The title page of the 1546 edition clearly reflects this identification, for it pictures Askew in the loose flowing robes of the Roman world while yet standing on a Papist Beast, the common Reformist representation of the Catholic church as the horned monster from Revelation.

Bale examines the comparison to Blandina point by point, designing Askew's character and martyrdom to agree with the prototype in every way.

Blandina was yonge and tender. So was Anne Askewe also. But that whych was frayle of nature in them both, Christ made most strong by hys grace. . . .

Blandina never faynted in torment. No more ded Anne Askewe in sprete, whan she was so terrybly racked of Wrysleye the chaunceller and Ryche, that the strynges of her armes and eyes were peryshed. Blandina deryded the cruelte of the tyrauntes. So ded Anne Askewe the madnesse of the Byshoppes and their spechemen. . . . Christ wonderfullye tryumphed in Blandina. So ded he in Anne Askewe, whan she made no noyse on the racke, and so ernestlye afterwarde rejoyced in hym. . . . Blandina upon the scaffolde boldelye reprehended the pagane prestes of their er- rour. So ded Anne Askewe when she was fast tyed to the stake, with stomack rebuke that blasphemouse apostata Shaxton with the Byshoppes and prestes gene- racyon, for their manyfest mayntenaunce of ydolatrye.

Blandina at the stake shewed a vysage unterryfyed. So ded Anne Askewe a countenaunce stowte, myghtye and ernest. Infatygable was the sprete of Blandina. So was the sprete of Anne Askewe. The love of Jesus Christ, the gyft of the holye Ghost, and hope of the crowne of martyrdome, greatlye mytygated the payne in Blandina. So ded those iii worthye graces, the terrour of all tormentes in Anne Askewe. The stronge sprete of Christ gave stomack to Blandina, both to laugh and daunce. The same myghtye sprete (& not the popes desperate sprete) made Anne Askewe both to rejoyce and synge in the preson. So bolde was Blandina (sayth Eusebius) that with a presumpcyon of stomack she comoved with Christ unseane. I suppose Anne Askewes lattre examynacyon, wyll shewe her, not to do moche lesse. Gentyll was Blandina to the Christen belevers, & terryble to their adversaryes. So was Anne Askewe, verye lowlye to true teachers, but scornefull and hygh stomaked to the enemyes of truthe. Manye were converted by the suffer- aunce of Blandina. A farre greatter nombre by the burnynge of Anne Askewe. Though Blandina were yonge, yet was she called the mother of martyrs. Manye men have supposed Anne Askewe, for her Christen constancye, to be no lesse. (I, Preface , pp. 7v–9r)

In his account of Askew's ability to face her inquisitors and to with-stand "the terrour of all tormentes," Bale attributes to God all the strength given to a naturally feeble woman, and deduces that her courage must be proof that God is with her and that their mutual cause is divinely sanc-tioned. In his singularly unambiguous polemic, he defines woman's religious role in the words, "Thus choseth the lorde, the folysh of thys worlde to confounde the wyse, & the weake to deface the myghtye . . ." (I, Preface, p. 9v). When we come to the text of Askew herself, however, reading is considerably more complicated, because while Askew shared Bale's belief in God's strength and her own human weakness, by the very act of writing down her examinations, of self-conceptualizing, Askew creates a woman of faith, strength, and purpose. Askew did feel that God worked in her, but not because her female constitution was as inherently dainty as Bale wished to believe.

To compose this counterportrait of Anne Askew, we may consider how the events of her life influenced her authorial persona, her language, and her style. Her father, Sir William Askew, a Lincolnshire landowner and courtier to Henry VIII, educated his daughters, although he naturally believed that they were still wholly subject to their father where marriage was concerned. Askew found herself married off to Thomas Kyme, son of another big landholder, an uneducated, staunch Catholic, not at all sympathetic to his wife's faith. The priests of Lincoln were apparently responsible for urging Kyme to cast out his heretic wife, and Askew seems then to have seized the initiative by requesting a divorce. According to Bale, whose source also informed him that Askew had two children by Kyme, she justified her action, "by thys doctryne of S. Paule 1. Cor. 7. If a faythfull woman have an unbelevynge husbande, whych wyll not tarrye with her she may leave hym. For a brother or syster is not in subjeccyon to soch, specyallye where as the marryage afore is unlawfull." Her grounds for divorce, says Bale, were "bycause he so cruellye drove her out of hys howse in despyght of Christes veryte" (II, p. 15v), but neither at Lincoln nor later in the London courts did she succeed in ending her marriage.

Later, during her first trial in London, she records the antagonism of the priests of Lincoln, but pictures herself as already firm in her beliefs and sure of her ability to conduct a theological dispute. When Bishop Bonner rebuked her for saying that sixty priests of Lincoln were against her, she reports:

In dede (quoth I) I sayd so. For my fryndes tolde me, if I ded come to Lyncolne, the prestes wolde assault me and put me to great trouble, as therof they had made their boast. And whan I hearde it, I went thydre in dede, not beynge afrayed, because I knewe my matter to be good. More over I remayned there .vi. dayes, to se what wolde be sayd unto me. And as I was in the mynster, readynge upon the Byble, they resorted unto me by ii. and by ii. by v. & by vi. myndynge to have spoken to me, yet went they theyr wayes agayne with out wordes speakynge.

Then my lorde asked, if there were not one that ded speake unto me. I tolde him, yeas, that there was one of them at the last, whych ded speake to me in dede. And my lorde than asked me, what he sayd. And I tolde hym, hys wordes were of so small effecte, that I ded not now remembre them. (I, pp. 33r–34r)

Askew pictures herself as active and assured as she waits in the minster, ready for dispute, while the priests appear agitated, disorganized, and timid. In her anecdotal climax, she uses Bonner's questions to her own advantage, making him draw out her responses, so centering attention on herself. Her final sentence here is a two-edged slur, for Askew derides the substance of the priest's remarks by apparently forgetting them and puts Bonner in his place by not repeating for him what he knew already. Consistently Askew presents herself in control of her questioners by throwing their questions back, responding with another question, smiling, or reprimanding them for their poor judgment. She never plays the part of a weak woman, but assumes for herself intellect, assurance, and strength.

If such qualities in her persona reflect the real Anne Askew, they may explain her decision to leave Lincolnshire and Thomas Kyme. Her move to London, perhaps motivated by the divorce suit, or perhaps by a desire to join other Reformers, brought Askew completely out of the domestic sphere and directly into the public view. Associating with the Reformers who surrounded Catherine Parr—John Parkhurst, Anne Herbert, the Duchess of Suffolk, Lady Denny, Lady Fitzwilliam, the Countess of Sussex, John Lascelles—Askew came to the notice of Bishop Gardiner and Chancellor Wriothsley, both of whom saw in her a way to bring down the Reformist queen herself.[9] In March 1545 Askew was brought before the quest for heresy, so becoming the first gentlewoman to be judged by a London jury;[10] whatever she spoke there and recorded afterwards established her as a public figure.

In considering Askew's motives for writing down her two examinations, we may remember first how unusual such a step was. Many of the accused Reformers wrote letters, but these were almost entirely to clarify or declare points of doctrine for other Reformers.[11] No other contemporary autobiographical document remains that describes in such detail the questioning and suffering of a heresy trial, or gives so vivid a sense of the victim's personality. One hypothesis is that Askew was particularly driven by the need for self-justification. In a society in which all women of her class lived protected by their friends or family, and identified themselves solely within the family circle, Askew was cut off from paternal and marital protection (Sir William Askew died in March 1541; the eldest son, Francis, remained in Lincolnshire, and may indeed have betrayed his sister), and belonged only to a religious group whose ability to help her was restricted by fear of endangering itself. Although a gentlewoman of "verye auncyent and noble stock'' (I, Preface, p. 6v), her unrepentant defiance of the authorities of both church and state reduced the ability of her friends to aid her, and the power struggle at court between Catholics and Reformers made her more vulnerable to danger. Her record of her experience seeks to establish her firmly as a God-fearing, honest woman who consistently quotes Scripture and attempts to reveal only the truth. Her assertions in the *Examinations* are always positive, filled with a sense of her own rectitude, assured of her own virtue. At one point she is careful to record her wish ''that all men knewe my conversacyon & lyvyng in all poyntes, for I am so sure of my selfe thys houre, that there are non able to prove anye dyshonestie by me'' (I, p. 34v).

Writing may have offered Askew a way to create herself as she desired, rather than to be known either as a disobedient wife and heretic by one side, or as a distant figurehead by the other. By controlling the persona of Anne Askew and selecting and shaping the events of her imprisonment, Askew fulfills the role that she recognized she was to have for the Reformers, but she also becomes an autobiographer who composes the woman, Anne Askew. The work does begin, ''To satisfie your expectation, good people . . . ,'' and proceeds to bear witness to the strength of the reformed faith and the wickedness of its enemies, demanding of the writer that she subjugate herself to a concept: Anne Askew is one of the elect, a vessel filled with God's grace. But the crosscurrents of personality that consistently flow in the narrative do not support Askew's role as the weak woman made strong by God as described by Bale. Rather, the combination of her witty rejoinders and the very reticence with which she records her endurance on the rack are consistently self-conscious and stylized, portraying a woman who is neither dainty nor tender, but rather, tough in mind and body, learned, and tenacious. While the narrative concentrates mainly on recording conversation, it clearly highlights the occasions on which Askew outfoxes her questioners. Bale finds this as proof of God's presence; other readers will find a self-portrait of a woman who lived out an idea of herself as a teacher and a defender of the faith, the spiritual equal of any man.

In interpreting Askew's portrayal of herself, we will find some of the most striking points in the text to be those where Askew clearly asserts herself as a woman confronting the male hierarchy. At these stress points,

Askew represents how her clever responses allowed her to triumph over her questioners. In her first examination, she tells us:

Then the Byshoppes chaunceller rebuked me, & sayd, that I was moche to blame for utterynge the scriptures. For S. Paule (he sayd) forbode women to speak or to talke of the worde of God. I answered hym, that I knewe Paules meanynge so well as he, whych is, i Corinthiorum xiiii, that a woman ought not to speake in the congregacyon by the waye of teachynge. And then I asked hym, how manye women he had seane, go into the pulpett and preache. He sayde, he never sawe non. Then I sayd, he ought to fynde no faute in poore women, except they had offended the lawe. (I, pp. 10r–v)

Not only does Askew declare that she can understand Scripture as well as the bishop's chancellor, but she responds by questioning him, exacting an answer, and drawing an appropriate conclusion to discomfit the questioner. The style here is perfectly suited to Askew's aims, for it is unadorned, understated, and concise, thus allowing the climactic last sentence to exert its full force. The choice of "poore" to describe women is an example of Askew's controlled irony, for she has already shown herself to be anything but a poor unfortunate.

Here as elsewhere, Bale is silent on Askew's manner, applauding only her matter, and zealously associating her every thought with the earliest members of the Church. He comments extensively on the theme of women learned in Scripture who speak in public. Aware that the chancellor had expressed the prevailing view, Bale justifies Askew's knowledge by reference to the women at the tomb, to St. Jerome's correspondents, and to early English Christians like Helena, Ursula, and Hilda. By contrast, he infers that the chancellor's source is the old *Contra doctrices mulieres* "or els some other lyke blynde Romysh beggeryes" (I, p. 11r). Bale's strong language and unflaggingly vociferous style emphasize how restrained, witty, and subtle Askew is in her verbal defeat of her enemies; she seems more effective in underscoring their prejudices and injustices, and more in control. The accepted methods of rhetorical argument called for citing of past authorities and exempla, and certainly such means suited Bale's desire to justify the Reformers. But while Askew cites Scripture at every opportunity, she uses it not as Bale does, but in a directly pragmatic, situational way: "Paul says women should not preach in church. No woman has preached in church. Women have not defied Paul." And much of her effectiveness derives from her skilled presentation of the moment's drama, bringing to life through their own words the players and their parts.

Askew continually uses her dramatic abilities and plays upon her lack of formal training—her rhetorical "otherness"—in subsequent contests with her questioners. After the lord mayor sends Askew to the Compter, she records the visit of a priest who attempts to win her confidence and then exact a confession.

> Fortly he asked me, if the host shuld fall, and a beast ded eate it, whether the beast ded receyve God or no? I answered, Seynge ye have taken the paynes to aske thys questyon, I desyre yow also to take so moche payne more, as to assoyle it yourselfe. For I will not do it, bycause I perceyve ye come to tempt me. And he sayd it was agaynst the ordre of scoles, that he whych asked the questyon, shuld answere it. I tolde hym, I was but a woman, & knewe not the course of scoles. (I, pp. 13v–14r)

Again, Askew builds to her needle-jab destruction of the adversary's position. In the middle sentences, she takes the initiative away from the priest, offering two reasons why he should answer his own question: he asked it and he asked it with an ulterior motive, to trap Askew into admitting a derogatory view of the host commonly thought to be Reformist. Her ready wit listens for a cue, and once more she ironically plays upon the preconception of woman. "Scoles" belong to the male preserve of formal education—and also to hated Catholic scholasticism—and being "but a woman," Askew is excluded. Here, the "but" is as telling a choice as "poore" was earlier.

It is interesting to contrast Askew's emphasis here with Bale's response. Again, Bale does not remark on Askew's wit, but pounces eagerly on the priest's ignorance of doctrine, scorning his question as a blasphemous rejection of God's spiritual essence. While Askew is of course aware of the doctrinal crux at issue here, in *The first examinacyon* she is less concerned with elucidating her sacramentarian beliefs than with establishing her identity, with asserting her faith in Scripture, needling her inquisitors, and playing upon their preconceptions of woman's weakness and proper place.

For example, during Bishop Bonner's interrogation on the host, she reiterates emphatically, almost ritualistically, three times, "I believe as the Scripture doth teach me," and

> upon thys argument he tarryed a great whyle, to have dryven me to make him an answere to hys mynde. Howbeit, I wolde not, but concluded thus with hym, that I

beleved therin and in all other thynges, as Christ and hys holye apostles ded leave them. . . . Then he asked me, whye I had so fewe wordes. And I answered, God hath geven me the gyfte of knowlege, but not of utteraunce. And Salomon sayth, that a woman of fewe wordes, is a gyfte of God, Prover. 19. (I, pp. 27r–29r)

Touching Bonner's sore spot, for her words are few only in the sense that she does not speak the ones he wishes to hear, Askew ironically cites a text often used to support the dogma for woman's obedience and silence. She caps this retort a few sentences later when bidden to say her mind about her citation from Paul, Apostles 17, "God dwelleth not in temples made with hands." Askew tells us, "I answered, that it was agaynst saynt Paules lernynge, that I beynge a woman, shuld interprete the scriptures, specyallye where so many wyse lerned men were" (I, p. 31v). Underlining her own unsupported appearance before numerous questioners, Askew casts back the text previously used to accuse her, but alters its emphasis to disparage her enemies. Her tone mocks their wisdom and learning, and perhaps even their manhood, since all of them are lined up against one "poore" woman.

The linguistic games that Askew plays at these tense moments convey her as confident and self-possessed in the face of danger, certainly part of the character she wishes to create for her readers. Askew chooses to reveal her strength in *The first examinacyon* by using an ironic, witty style for herself, which she clearly contrasts with the style of her enemies, depicted as superficial, irascible, or insidious, but never righteous and never triumphant. She laughs at Christopher Dare for his ignorance, saying "I wolde not throwe pearles amonge swyne, for acornes were good ynough" (I, p. 2v). Like a mother reprimanding a child, she cautions Bishop Bonner's archdeacon who foolishly warned her not to read a book by John Frith:

Then I asked hym, if he were not ashamed for to judge of the boke before he sawe it within, or yet knew the truthe therof. I sayd also, that soche unadvysed & hastye judgement is a token apparent of a verye slendre wytt. Then I opened the boke & shewed it hym. He sayd, he thought it had bene an other, for he coulde fynde no faulte therin. Then I desyred hym, nomore to be so swyfte in judgement, tyll he throughlye knewe the truthe. And so he departed. (I, pp. 21r–v)

Skillfully, Askew molds her narrative to make herself the active, teaching voice, and the archdeacon becomes the abashed respondent; Askew gains the upper hand, the archdeacon is discomfitted and exits.

Askew's full awareness of style is vividly demonstrated by an exchange with Bishop Bonner:

Then brought he fourth thys unsaverye symylytude, That if a man had a
wounde, no wyse surgeon wolde mynystre helpe unto it, before he had seane it
uncovered. In lyke case (sayth he) can I geve yow no good counsell, unlesse I knowe
wherwith your conscyence is burdened. I answered, that my conscience was clere
in all thynges. And for to laye a playstre unto the whole skynne, it might apere
moche folye. (I, pp. 23v–24r)

Here she objects to the unpleasantness, both moral and figurative, of
Bonner's analogy, but resumes the linguistic upper hand by topping his
similitude. Normally her prose is devoid of figurative language, but she
uses it here to make two points: first, that she feels herself innocent and
strong before her enemies, and second, that anything Bonner can do, she
can do better.

In *The lattre examinacyon*, Askew's tone changes to a more uniformly
serious, earnest contemplation of her beliefs and her questioners. No doubt
she knew that this time the danger was greater. She presents her enemies as
doggedly evil, and repeats their reiterated questions as often as they are
asked, along with her own patient responses. When the Bishop of Winchester wishes to speak to her "famylyarlye," she responds, "So ded Judas
whan he unfryndelye betrayed Christ," and she demands two or three
witnesses to be always present. Bale is clearly delighted by her stand, gloat-
ing, "Ded she not (thynke you) hytt the nayle on the head, in thus taun-
tynge thys Bysshop? yeas" (II, pp. 18v–19r). Askew puts the bishop's next
remark, her own death sentence, simply and dramatically, "Then the Bysh-
oppe sayd, I shuld be brente." Not mourning for herself, always in control, nowhere in the Scriptures, says Askew, can she find that Christ or the
Apostles put anyone to death, another clear instance of the Romish con-
travening of God's word.

Much of *The lattre examinacyon* consists of scriptural quotations and
doctrinal statements about communion, once to a friend, once in confession of her belief, once to the Privy Council, and once to the king. Bale
accurately notes how even in danger, "Neyther lasheth thys woman out in
her extreme troubles, language of dispayre nor yet blasphemouse wordes
agaynst God with the unbelevynge, but uttereth the scriptures in wonder-
full habundaunce to hys lawde and prayse." Again Bale attributes such
constancy in a woman "frayle, tendre, yonge and most delycyouslye
brought up" to Christ's spirit in her (II, p. 27v). Wherever she derived her
strength, she convinces the reader of her power by a controlled, dignified,

assured style which portrays a woman humble before God, if never before the enemies she considers to be betrayers of God's Word.

Askew reveals the tremendous power of a story told without decoration and with restraint when she narrates her experiences in the Tower. Her captivity moved into its explicitly political phase when she was asked for the names of Reformers at court. Hoping to incriminate members of the nobility—the Duchesses of Suffolk, Sussex, and Hertford, Lady Denny, Lady Fitzwilliam, and by association, Queen Catherine—Sir Richard Rich and Lord Chancellor Wriothsley questioned and then tortured Askew for a confession. Their proceedings were cruel and vicious, as well as entirely illegal, since the law prohibited the racking of women, and Askew was a gentlewoman besides. Again, their actions probably mark how alone and unprotected she really was. But such considerations pale before the horror of their deeds described in Askew's dramatic, sparing account of her profound suffering:

Then they sayd, there were of the counsell that ded maynteyne me. And I sayd, no. Then they ded put me on the racke, bycause I confessed no ladyes nor gentyllwomen to be of my opynyon, and theron they kepte me a longe tyme. And bycause I laye styll and ded not crye, my lorde Chauncellour and mastre Ryche, toke peynes to racke me [with] their owne handes, tyll I was nygh dead.

Then the lyefetenaunt caused me to be loused from the racke. Incontynentlye I swounded, and then they recovered me agayne. After that I sate ii longe houres reasonynge with my lorde Chauncellour upon the bare floore, where as he with manye flatterynge wordes, persuaded me to leave my opynyon. But my lord God (I thanke hys everlastynge goodnesse) gave me grace to persever, and wyll do (I hope) to the verye ende. (II, pp. 44v–47r)

By understatement, Askew conveys both the silent virtue of her own remarkable fortitude and constancy—"I laye styll and ded not crye"—and by contrast, the vindictiveness of the two men, desperate to break her spirit. Like the devil's temptation, Wriothsley's words are "flatterynge," but this Eve pictures herself filled with God's grace and able to do God's will to the end.[12]

In his concluding remarks, Bale professes himself convinced that Anne Askew is now an "undoubted cytyzen of heaven" (II, p. 61r) and a "Saynt canonysed in Christes bloude" (II, p. 62v). Askew herself had written to her fellow sufferer, John Lascelles, "For I doubt it not, but God wyll perfourme hys worke in me, lyke as he hath begonne" (II, p. 49v). Bale

never swerves from his conviction that Askew's text demonstrates the
sanctification of the Reformers' cause. In her more personal statement,
Askew reveals how fundamental her faith was to her life, but her belief
that God was working through her did not proceed from any sense of
womanly weakness; for her, the source of human weakness before God did
not lie in male or female characteristics. In the scripturally based ballad
which she "made and sang when she was in Newgate," Askew wrote

> Lyke as the armed knyght
> Appoynted to the fielde
> With thys world wyll I fyght
> And fayth shall be my shielde.
>   (st. 1; II, p. 63r)[13]

. . . .

> Not oft use I to wryght
> In prose nor yet in ryme
> Yet wyll I shewe one syght
> That I sawe in my tyme.
>   (st. 10; II, p. 63v)

Conceiving of herself as a Christian soldier, she wrote her *Examinations*
as a record of how she bore witness to the evil she saw around her and how
she fought the good fight against it. She was sustained by the belief that she
was "bowne towardes heaven," and she triumphed morally and spiritually
over her accusers. Although her martyrdom tends to overshadow all else as
an ultimate expression of faith and courage, more accurately, it is the final
act of a whole life consistently guided by principle rather than by expe-
dience and personal safety. Askew's faith in the tenets of the Reformed
church catalyzed her rejection of the restrictions on a woman's thought,
will, and deed, so that consciousness of her sex as well as her religion
precipitated the crucial conflicts of her brief career. Confronting the priests
of Lincoln, seeking to divorce her husband, journeying alone to London,
and defying the male authorities of the Church and state were all acts by
which she defined herself as a true Christian woman, one who could not
accept her society's injunctions to be obedient and silent when she had been
called to stand firm and to bear witness to God's Word. It was also in the
role of the true Christian woman that Askew found her vocation as a
writer. As both author and protagonist of her *Examinations,* she could

bear witness to her faith and justify her actions as those of a godly, pious woman. Contradicting both her accusers and supporters who perceived feminine strength either as a threat or an impossibility, Askew created herself in the plain style as a godly preacher and teacher with a mission to perform. She thus joined the process of redefining women's role in the Church and in her society, a process which was to concern some sixteenth-century women and many of their heirs in succeeding centuries.

CAROLE LEVIN

Lady Jane Grey:
Protestant Queen and Martyr

JOHN DUDLEY, Duke of Northumberland, attempted to subvert the
Tudor succession and make his daughter-in-law, Jane Grey, queen
of England in 1553. The attempt failed, and Lady Jane was executed the following year at the age of sixteen. By the end of the sixteenth
century, the English people perceived Lady Jane Grey as the ideal young
victim: beautiful, modest, deferential, quiet, and passive. This image,
presented in 1599 by Thomas Decker and John Webster in their play, *The
Famous History of Thomas Wyatt*, was further developed by seventeenth-
century historians and passed into popular historical mythology, thus
making Lady Jane Grey so endearing, especially to the Victorians. Many
later historians, such as David Mathew and Barrett L. Beer, have continued
to accept the conventional notion of Lady Jane Grey as a weak, powerless
victim of political intrigue. But though the myth has clear historical roots,
Lady Jane Grey was actually a far stronger figure than this picture would
lead us to believe. One of the best educated women of the Tudor period,
she was in fact a Protestant queen and martyr of great courage and forthrightness whose life and writings represent a rigid and uncompromising
Protestantism that made her one of the best known women of her age.[1]

Lady Jane Grey's modern biographer Hester Chapman has presented
this alternative view: "She was . . . of the stuff of which the Puritan
martyr is made: self-examining, fanatical, bitterly courageous, and utterly
incapable of the art of compromise in which the Tudors specialized."[2]

David Mathew agrees with Chapman about the intensity of Lady Jane's religious conviction, but is less impressed with her intellectual abilities: "Lady Jane had one great quality, a burning religious zeal which lit up the character of a rather simple girl." Mathew also describes Jane Grey as passive, and adds that while she was "beautifully educated and very learned," he doubts that she was at all intelligent (p. 144). Beer characterizes Lady Jane as "easily manipulated . . . confused and bewildered" (p. 156). I would argue that Mathew and Beer are wrong in their summations of Jane Grey's character. To understand why Lady Jane Grey was more than simply a political pawn, it is necessary to examine carefully both her background and the uncompromising stance of piety she exhibits in her writing.

Most of Lady Jane Grey's works were written during the last six months of her life, while she was a prisoner in the Tower of London. The concerns she expressed in her prayers, letters, and dying speech demonstrate what constituted a religious life, how one could combat the temptations of despair and appropriately prepare for a tranquil death. These concerns link Jane Grey with other political and religious dissidents who sojourned in the Tower and also confronted these issues in their writings.

Lady Jane Grey, the granddaughter of Henry VIII's younger sister Mary, was born in October 1537. Since Henry VIII had only one son, Edward, it was a time of insecure succession. From the time of her childhood many people considered her an important pawn who might, with luck, even become a queen. Her education was appropriate to one of her position and her times. It not only reflected the Reformed church, but also the impact of humanism on attitudes toward women's education. In the first half of the sixteenth century the upper classes considered educating their daughters fashionable, and Lady Jane learned to read as a small child. By the time she was seven, her first tutor, Dr. Harding, had begun her instruction in Latin and Greek as well as a smattering of such modern languages as Spanish, Italian, and French.[3] Lady Jane Grey was also to spend a considerable amount of time in biblical and classical study.

Soon after the death of Henry VIII, Lady Jane Grey joined the household of his widow, Catherine Parr. Indeed, such an upbringing away from home was normal for persons of high station at the time, and since Jane Grey was a princess of the blood, the dowager queen's household would be

one of the few considered suitable for her. Within a few months of the
king's death, Catherine married her former suitor Thomas Seymour,
younger brother of the Lord Protector, Edward Seymour, Duke of
Somerset, and maternal uncle to the new king. Many people were scandal-
ized, but Thomas Seymour had plans for attaining power in his nephew's
reign, and marriage to the dowager queen could be quite useful. So could
control of Lady Jane Grey, and Seymour negotiated with her parents,
Henry and Frances Grey, accordingly, promising to arrange a marriage
between Jane and her cousin Edward VI. For her parents, having Jane in
the queen's household became potentially very important, since through
this marriage she would become queen of England.

For Jane Grey it may have been important for other reasons. The Protestant faith in which she had been raised would be further developed under
the influence of Catherine Parr, a humanist with Erasmian and Protestant
sympathies who had strong ties with Reformers. Parr's book, *Lamentacion of a Sinner* (1547), was "contemporaneous and controversial," argues
William Haugaard,[4] and clearly explicated Protestant attitudes toward
the old and new faiths. Roland Bainton describes *Lamentacion* as "one of
the gems of Tudor devotional literature" (p. 165). For Parr, reading the
Holy Scripture was of central importance to Christian devotion. Parr
argued in favor of justification by faith although she did not reject the
importance of good works growing out of faith, as when she claims, "This
dignitie of fayth is no derogation to good woorkes, for out of this fayth
springeth al good workes. Yet we may not impute to the worthynes of
fayth of workes, our justification before God" (in Haugaard, p. 358).
These doctrines, central to Protestant theology, will also be found in the
later writings of Lady Jane Grey. Undoubtedly, until her death in 1548,
Catherine Parr exercised some influence on Jane's development.

After his wife's death, Thomas Seymour dabbled with treason, and he
was executed as a traitor in March 1549. By then Lady Jane was back at
Bradgate with her parents, who were disappointed that she was not to
marry the king and instead had to settle for her betrothal to the son of the
Lord Protector, Edward Seymour. But while her political future seemed
less bright, she was becoming known both for her outstanding piety and
her learning. At this time, she corresponded with such Continental Protestant divines as Martin Bucer and Johann Heinrich Bullinger, and it may

have been their influence that gave Lady Jane's theology such a Calvinist tinge.

During this period Roger Ascham visited Bradgate and left a striking picture of this fourteen-year-old young woman in *The Scholemaster,* which was written for didactic purposes and published in 1570. That his account actually reflects his personal perception, however, is confirmed by letters written by Ascham at the time.[5] Ascham describes his encounter with Lady Jane Grey: "I found her in her chamber reading Phoedon Platonis in Greek, and that with as much delight as some gentlemen would read a merry tale in Boccaccio." Ascham asked Lady Jane why she was not enjoying herself with the others who were out hunting. She responded that those "good folk, they never felt what true pleasure meant." In answering the question as to how she learned the nature of this true pleasure, Jane replied candidly,

I will tell you . . . and tell you a truth which perchance you will marvel at. One of the greatest benefits that ever God gave me is that he sent me so sharp and severe parents and so gentle a schoolmaster. For when I am in presence either of father or mother, whether I speak, keep silence, sit, stand, or go, eat, drink, be merry or sad, be sewing, playing, dancing, or doing anything else, I must do it, as it were, in such weight, measure, and number, even so perfectly as God made the world, or else I am so sharply taunted, so cruelly threatened, yea, presently sometimes, with pinches, nips, and bobs, and other ways which I will not name for the honor I bear them, so without measure misordered, that I think myself in hell till time come that I must go to Master Aylmer, who teacheth me so gently, so pleasantly, with such fair allurements to learning, that I think all the time nothing whilst I am with him. And when I am called from him, I fall on weeping because whatsoever I do else but learning is full of grief, trouble, fear, and wholy misliking unto me. And thus my book hath been so much my pleasure, and bringeth daily to me more pleasure and more, that in respect of it all other pleasures in very deed be but trifles and troubles unto me.[6]

Her reply certainly contradicts the traditional picture of a meek and mild Lady Jane. Though mistreated by her parents, she claims to have compensated for this unkindness by exercising her mind and finding pleasure in study. She had enough insight to recognize that she was mistreated, and did not feel the necessity to hide that information from a sympathetic stranger. Unwilling to accept her parents' treatment of her unquestioningly and in silence, she had the courage and forthrightness to speak out.

Two other incidents occurred late in Edward VI's reign that Protestant hagiographers greatly emphasized in their discussions of Lady Jane Grey in the years after her death. Both of these incidents involved her Tudor cousin, the Lady Mary. One occurred when she was visiting Mary. In defiance of the law Mary had mass said in her household. While passing the chapel, Lady Jane saw Anne Wharton make a low curtsey to the sacrament on the altar. Jane asked Lady Wharton why she had curtsied, and whether the Lady Mary was in there. When Lady Wharton replied no, "that she made her curtsey to Him that made us all," Jane quipped, "Why . . . how can He be there, that made us all, and the baker make him?" Her satiric levity insulted Mary once it was reported to her, and she "did never love [Jane] after," John Foxe reports. Lady Jane demonstrated the same blunt integrity in another confrontation with Mary, this time over the issue of appropriate clothing. Mary had sent her cousin a richly elaborate dress as a gift, but, according to John Aylmer, Jane refused to wear it, saying "Nay that were a shame to follow my Lady Mary against God's word, and leave my Lady Elizabeth which followeth God's word."[7]

Of course most Tudor strategists considered Jane Grey to be more important for her position than for her great learning or her convictions. This concern for her political value became significant in 1553 when it was evident that Edward VI was dying. According to Henry VIII's will, should Edward die without heirs the crown would pass first to his Catholic daughter Mary, and only then to his Protestant daughter Elizabeth. Either of these choices, however, would have meant the end of his career to John Dudley, Duke of Northumberland and de facto ruler of England since the fall of the Duke of Somerset. Whether the decision to upset the succession and overturn Henry VIII's will began with the dying boy-king, who wanted to maintain England as a Protestant country, or with Northumberland, who wanted to maintain his power, is still disputed.[8] In any event, in May 1553 Lady Jane Grey was married to Dudley's youngest and only unmarried son, Guilford, an alliance that was pivotal in a whole series of marriages Northumberland arranged to augment his position. Though Lady Jane had strongly resisted the marriage on the grounds she was already precontracted to the late Duke of Somerset's son, her parents finally forced her to do their bidding. Edward VI produced a will that omitted both his sisters and made Lady Jane Grey his heir. This attempt to upset the succession failed miserably, and Mary was acclaimed queen without a battle. Jane, who had entered the Tower as queen, remained as prisoner. In February 1554, as an aftermath to the Wyatt rebellion against Mary's Spanish marriage, Jane was executed.

It was during her last months in the Tower that Jane accomplished the slender body of writings for which she is known. These include a letter to a friend newly fallen from the Reformed faith (probably her first tutor, Dr. Harding), a prayer composed within a few weeks of her death, letters to her father and sister Katherine written when she knew she was condemned to die, and her speech from the scaffold. A few days before she was executed, in the presence of Tower officials, Lady Jane Grey debated Dr. Feckenham, Mary I's confessor, about Christian doctrine. Feckenham had hoped to convert the sixteen-year-old prodigy, but the attempt proved fruitless. The debate was recorded and is also included in accounts of Jane Grey's works.[9]

While Lady Jane Grey was politically of little importance at the time of her execution in 1554 (Elton, pp. 380–81), once she died she immediately became a symbol of Protestant heroism and martyrdom. The publication of her work in 1554 was, considers John King, "the most powerful contemporary Protestant attack on the Marian regime."[10] In the decades, after her death Protestant writers told and retold the story of her patience, her courage, and her willingness to testify for the true church. Writing in 1555, John Bradford used the example of Lady Jane's death to demonstrate "that life and honour is not to be set by more than God's commandment" (in Foxe, VII, 238). An Italian residing in England during Mary's reign was also impressed; he described Jane's execution as causing "great sorrow of the people, especially when it became known to everybody that the girl, born to a misery beyond tears, had faced death with far greater gallantry than it might be expected from her sex and the natural weakness of her age." He added that at the actual moment of her death, she "submitted the neck to the axe with more than manly courage."[11]

Within a year of her death a doggeral poem purporting to be Lady Jane's last words, in which she laments her death in bad rhymes, was sold in London in broadside, and went through more than one edition. More significantly, there were immediate editions of her actual writings published by English Protestants abroad during Mary's reign, and her writings were also published in a variety of collections under Elizabeth. The most complete collection appears in Foxe's account of her life in his *Actes and Monuments*, popularly called the *Book of Martyrs*. This edition would, in fact, probably have reached the most people, since Foxe's work was one of the most widely read books in the Elizabethan period.[12] Foxe's edition may also have been the most accurate, given the sources that were available to him (King, p. 437).

Lady Jane Grey's writing, completed while she was in the Tower under sentence of death, are part of a larger genre of Tower writing that was accomplished in the early Tudor period. Such people as Sir Thomas Wyatt and Henry Howard, Earl of Surrey, were among those who wrote verse while in the Tower in the reign of Henry VIII. Perhaps the most famous writer to produce significant works while in the Tower was Sir Thomas More, who wrote *A Dialogue of Comfort* as well as a series of letters, mostly to his daughter, Margaret Roper, during his imprisonment. In *A Dialogue of Comfort* and the letters to Margaret, More expresses the concern over how a Christian ought to behave when his strength is tested by such adversity as he was experiencing. Another underlying theme to his work is More's preparation to meet his death appropriately, if his death was indeed what God willed. Though More was Catholic, and Lady Jane Grey was Protestant, Jane Grey's Tower writings reflect many of the same concerns.[13]

Lady Jane Grey's writings are a clear exposition of Protestant theology. She believed in salvation through faith alone, in the Bible as the sole authority, that the only two sacraments were baptism and the eucharist, and that the latter was taken as a memorial only. She writes in the tradition of early English Protestants who extravagantly denounce those who do not agree with their theology, yet who are also cognizant of their own unworthiness—aware that, despite any deeds they might do, they are still miserable sinners whose salvation will come only through faith in Christ.[14] Jane Grey expressed either contempt or pity for those who do not follow these precepts. Though some of her writings express a confidence that borders on arrogance, near her death she also revealed the temptations, especially to despair, with which she had to wrestle. Her writings suggest that this theology provided her great comfort as she faced her own death. One temptation never occurred to her apparently: born after the break with Rome, Jane Grey was raised her whole life as a Protestant. Since she knew no other way of worship, she did not feel any temptation to turn to Catholicism when Protestantism was under attack and personal danger was acute, and she scorned those less stalwart than herself.

Lady Jane demonstrates this perspective in the letter to a friend who had converted to Catholicism. In the second edition of the *Book of Martyrs* Foxe identifies the friend as Dr. Harding, Jane's first tutor, and this identification is for the most part accepted.[15] The letter is a vituperative condemnation of Harding for renouncing the Reformist faith. She filled it with biblical allusions of earlier apostates she knows her correspondent will also recognize. The tone and language of the letter appalled many Victorians, and they suggested, on no good authority, that the letter was actually the work of John Aylmer (Nicholas, p. lxxvii). Jane's contemporaries, however, had no trouble believing it to be her own work, and sixteenth-century Protestants applauded her forthrightness. Foxe in his introduction commends Lady Jane's "sharp and vehement" letter, since it came from "an earnest and zealous heart," and its purpose was "to reduce [Harding] to repentance, and take better hold again for the health and wealth of his own soul" (VI, 418).

In her letter Lady Jane does not spare Harding or show any sympathy for the political pressures he faced; rather, for betraying the true faith, she calls him "the deformed imp of the devil, . . . the unshamefaced paramour of Antichrist . . . a cowardly runaway." For Lady Jane, Harding's denial of the true faith is especially unforgivable because of his role as teacher: "Wherefore hast thou instructed others to be strong in Christ, when thou thyself dost now so shamefully shrink? . . . Why dost thou now show thyself most weak, when indeed thou oughtest to be most strong?" Reminding him of the fates of other apostates, Lady Jane adds, "Throw down yourself with the fear of his threatened vengeance, for this so great and heinous an offence of apostacy: and comfort yourself, on the other part, with the mercy, blood, and promise of him that is ready to turn unto you whensoever you turn unto him" (VI, 418, 419, 421).

That Lady Jane heartily believed the sentiments expressed in the letter to Harding can be further inferred by her markedly similar response when she heard Northumberland had recanted and accepted the Catholic faith. Jane had nothing but contempt for Northumberland, especially since she blamed him for the woes to her and to her house. These were all done in the name of retaining the Protestant faith, yet he apostated and hoped for mercy. Jane told visitors, "As his life was wicked and full of dissimulacion, so was his ende thereafter. I pray God, I, nor no frende of myne, dye so." Jane suspected that Northumberland's conversion was not sincere, but accomplished in the hopes of being pardoned. To her this rationale was unworthy of consideration. Even though she was so young, she would not consider apostacy as a means of prolonging life. "Shoulde I, who (am) yonge and in my (fewers) forsake my faythe for love of lyfe? Nay, God forbed!"[16]

The tone both of the letter and of this reported conversation castigating those who fall from the faith places Jane Grey squarely in the militant tradition of the early English Protestants.[17] Lady Jane clings strongly to this tradition in her theology as well. She explicated her religious beliefs clearly in her debate with Queen Mary's confessor, Dr. Feckenham, Dean of St. Paul's and Abbot of Westminster. After an initial conversation with her, Feckenham was convinced he might actually be able to bring Lady Jane to his beliefs. He arranged for them to have a public debate on disputed issues of theology. At first Lady Jane was reluctant since, she said, such debates should be for the living and not for the dying; Feckenham, however, finally brought her to agree. The debate was conducted in the presence of Tower officials, one of whom, presumably, recorded its principle points (Chapman, p. 197).

The debate began with Feckenham asking Jane what is required of a Christian man. Jane responded that faith alone justifies. She also recognized the importance of love, but added, however, that "Faith and love go both together, and yet love is comprehended in faith." Jane Grey did not deny the importance of good works—the necessity to "feed the hungry, to clothe the naked, and give drink to the thirsty, and to do to him as we would do to ourselves"—but she did not see such charity as a means to salvation. Despite any deed, "yet we be unprofitable servants." Good works were one way of honoring Christ and following his example: "I affirm that faith only saveth: but it is meet for a christian, in token that he followeth his master Christ, to do good works; yet may we not say that they profit to our salvation" (VI, 416).

As well as representing the two sides in the classic conflict about salvation through faith or through works, Lady Jane and Feckenham also expressed opposite views of the sacraments. Lady Jane, as a Protestant, accepted only baptism and the Lord's supper, rather than the entire seven sacraments. Using the Scriptures as her sole authority, Jane claimed she could find justification for only the two sacraments. Feckenham and Lady Jane also disagreed fundamentally on the nature of the eucharist. Jane did not believe that in taking the sacrament she received "the very body and blood of Christ." Rather, she said, she took the bread and wine to "put me in remembrance." Feckenham grilled Lady Jane, "Why, doth not Christ speak these words, 'Take, eat, this is my body?' Require you any plainer words? Doth he not say, it is his body?" Jane's response was clever but also passionately sincere. "I grant, he saith so, and so he saith, 'I am the vine, I am the door;' but he is never the more for that, the door or the vine." And Jane asked Feckenham in turn, "Where was Christ when he said, 'Take, eat, this is my body?' Was he not at the table, when he said so? He was at that time alive, and suffered not til the next day. What took he, but bread? What brake he, but bread? and what gave he, but bread?" Lady Jane was also upset that the Catholic church did not allow the laity to drink the wine of the Lord's supper: "Shall I give credit to the church that ta'-th away from me the half part of the Lord's Supper . . . which things if they deny to us, then they deny to us part of our salvation." Jane ended her discussion of the Catholic method of giving the eucharist with the same extravagant language that marked her letter to Dr. Harding. "And I say, that is an evil church . . . the spouse of the devil, that altereth the Lord's supper . . . . To that church, say I, God will add plagues." Yet Jane's farewell to Feckenham, once their debate ended with them both recognizing the futility of continuing, was gentler: "I pray God, in the bowels of his mercy, to send you his Holy Spirit, for he hath given you his great gift of utterance, if it pleased him also to open the eyes of your heart" (VI, 417).

The assurance in her faith that Jane expressed in the debate with Feckenham wavered in a prayer she wrote shortly before her death. Though still very stylized in the tone of early English Protestant writings, the prayer expresses her personal doubts and fears, giving us more of a hint of the woman behind the theology. In her prayer she described herself as a "poor and desolate woman." The exuberance of language, the piling on of image after image that is typical of Lady Jane Grey's other religious writings is very marked here. Passionately, she proclaimed, "I, being defiled with sin, encumbered with affliction, unquieted with troubles, wrapped in cares, overwhelmed with miseries, vexed with temptations, and grievously tormented with the long imprisonment of this mass of clay, my sinful body, do come unto thee, O merciful Saviour, craving thy mercy and help, without the which so little hope of deliverance is left, that I may utterly despair of any liberty." Jane, who had nothing left to her but her faith, begged God to "be merciful unto me now, a miserable wretch" (VI, 423).

The temptation that Jane wrestled with, that she most feared she would succumb to, was despair. She feared losing her faith in God's presence: "How long wilt thou be absent? for ever? O Lord, hast thou forgotten to be gracious? . . . Is thy mercy clean gone for ever? . . . Shall I despair of thy mercy, O God?" While she assured God she would not despair— "Far be that from me"—the possibility was so real for Jane that she had to pray for strength against it. "O merciful God, consider my misery, best known unto thee, and be thou now unto me a strong tower of defence. . . . Suffer me not to be tempted above my power." Jane felt she could not achieve such strength on her own, and that God knew better than she what would be the best for her: "Give me grace, therefore, to tarry thy leisure, and patiently bear thy works. . . . Only, in the mean time, arm me, I beseech thee, with thy armour, that I may stand fast" (VI, 423).

Apparently, Jane found that her prayer was answered; she was able to exhibit both an honest appreciation of her situation and a serenity to meet it. Both of these attitudes are expressed in the letters she wrote to her father and her sister Katherine the night before her execution. In her letter to her father, she did not gloss over the fact that it was his actions in joining Wyatt's rebellion that were bringing about her death. She began her letter, "Father, although it hath pleased God to hasten my death by you, by whom my life should rather have been lengthened," yet she also assured him that she gave God "more hearty thanks for shortening my woful days." Indeed, insisted Jane, "I may account myself blessed." In the matters of the attempted coup, Lady Jane had a clear conscience since she was "constrained, and, as you wot [know] well enough, continually assayed," but "mine enforced honour blended never with mine innocent heart." Jane had heard that her father was not only "bewailing" his "own woe," but "especially, as I hear, my unfortunate state." Thus while Jane clearly assigned to her father his share of responsibility for bringing on her death, she apparently did not want him to feel too despondent. She knew that both she and her father were soon to die, but "although to you perhaps it may seem right woful, to me there is nothing that can be more welcome, than from this vale of mesery to aspire to that heavenly throne of all joy and pleasure with Christ" (VI, 417–18).

The same resignation, even joy, at meeting her death is present in the letter she wrote her sister Katherine. Although it contains advice, the letter is also a statement about her own life and the way she regarded it as it was ending. The letter was written in some blank pages at the end of the New Testament, a book, she assured Katherine, that "shall teach you to live, and learn you to die." Knowing the Bible would give Katherine more than the possession of great lands, because with God's Word she will be the "inheritor of such riches, as neither the covetous shall withdraw from you, neither shall they steal" (VI, 422). Lady Jane Grey, about to be executed at sixteen, recognized that youth was no guarantee against the necessity of facing death: "And trust not that the tenderness of your age shall lengthen your life; for as soon (if God call) goeth the young as the old." As it turns out, this advice was pertinent to Katherine as well; she died at the age of twenty-eight after years of imprisonment for her imprudent marriage to Edward Seymour, Earl of Hertford.[18]

Though Lady Jane Grey believed herself innocent of the charge that led to her execution, she would also acknowledge in her scaffold speech guilt for loving the world too much and for forgetting God. She does not want Katherine to make the same mistake. "Defy the world, deny the devil, and despise the flesh, and delight yourself only in the Lord." Lady Jane also advises Katherine to do what she had evidently managed though with some difficulty herself: "Be penitent for your sins, and yet despair not: be strong in faith, and yet presume not. . . . Rejoice in Christ, as I do." Jane also alludes to the fact that, had she converted to Catholicism, she might have prolonged her life. She tells her sister, however, that such a choice would have been an unworthy one: "I pray God grant you, and send you of his grace to live in his fear, and to die in the true christian faith, from the which (in God's name), I exhort you, that you never swerve, neither for hope of life, nor fear of death" (VI, 422).

Lady Jane expressed recognition of both her innocence and her guilt, as of the precepts of her faith, in the final statement she made, her speech given upon the scaffold. Observers reported her calm demeanor as she spoke to the onlookers. Jane's avowal of innocence, which she expressed in her letter to her father, was reiterated, as was the guilt and unworthiness she expressed in her prayer. Lady Jane believed herself guiltless of the treason for which she was condemned, on the grounds that she had been coerced into these actions. "I am come hither to die, and by a law I am condemned to the same. The fact against the queen's highness was unlawful, and the consenting thereunto by me: but touching the procurement and desire thereof by me, or on my behalf, I do wash my hands thereof in innocency before God, and the face of you, good christian people." Yet she also admitted her sins as well: "I confess, that when I did know the word of God, I neglected the same, loved myself and the world." As a result, "this plague and punishment is happily and worthily happened unto me for my sins." While God had been just in so ordering her death, she was also aware of his mercy, "that of his goodness he hath thus given me a time and respite to repent."[19]

To the very last minutes of her life, Lady Jane stayed true to the Protestant precepts in which she had been brought up and from which she derived such comfort. She also believed to the end that faith alone, and nothing else, brought one to salvation. "I pray you all, good christian people, to bear me witness that I die a true christian woman, and that I do look to be saved by no other man, but only by the mercy of God, in the blood of his only Son Jesus Christ." Since, as a Protestant, she did not believe in purgatory and thus saw only blasphemy in prayers for the dead, she asked the people to pray for her only while she lived: "And now, good people, while I am alive, I pray you assist me with your prayers" (VI, 424).

To this decorous, probably well-rehearsed speech, Foxe added a description of Lady Jane Grey's last moments. After requesting the executioner to "dispatch me quickly," she tied a handkerchief around her eyes. She misjudged the space, however, and could not then find the block, saying, "What shall I do? Where is it? Where is it?" Those closest to Lady Jane may have been so appalled at seeing someone so young and courageous about to die, that they could not move to help her (Chapman, p. 207). This is the only time Lady Jane Grey ever faltered, and even then it was not her fault; she was blindfolded and literally could not find her way. Finally one of the bystanders guided her. She "laid her head down upon the block . . . and said, 'Lord into thy hands I commend my spirit,' and so finished her life" (VI, 424).

John King suggests that "there is no reason to doubt the authenticity" of the works Lady Jane Grey produced in the Tower or of her final speech. The authorities during Mary's reign were extremely lax in their attempts to stop prisoners' works from being sent out so that they might be published. Lady Jane, in writing her letters, prayers, and scaffold speech, would have been well aware of their potentially wide distribution, and shaped them accordingly; her private words were also public testimonials of her faith (pp. 421–22).

Though the year before the people of London had responded with sullen silence to the proclamation declaring her queen, in the years after her death Lady Jane Grey's writings were frequently published. Her courageous death at such an early age, in a period of such religious conflict and change, was worthy of note. Foxe's portrayal of Lady Jane Grey did much to make the Elizabethans aware of her, and the immensely popular *Holinshed's Chronicle* continued this picture of the indomitable Lady Jane Grey. Yet Lady Jane's brave death was not an example that her cousin and eventual successor, Queen Elizabeth, wished to acknowledge. As David Mathew states, "Her life and death was a subject on which neither Queen Elizabeth nor Cecil, her great minister, would ever dwell" (p. 160). After all, for the queen, trying to maintain the Anglican settlement, Jane's lack of compromise would hardly be a useful example.

Perhaps in part due to this need for conciliation, by the end of the sixteenth century this portrayal of Lady Jane Grey was beginning to change into the one with which we are more familiar. Though Lady Jane is the heroine of the aforementioned Decker and Webster play the authors de-emphasized the strengths of character noted in such previous accounts as Foxe. The Jane Grey of the play is quiet, modest, and deeply in love with her husband Guilford, who speaks far more articulately than she does. In the seventeenth century such historians as Bishop Burnet describe Jane as "so humble, so gentle, so pious" (II, 469). A woman of such tender age who could berate her parents, former tutor, and cousin Mary for not following the high ideals she set for herself may have been too uncomfortable a model by the end of the sixteenth century, as the belief in classical education for women and the need for even young women to battle papists both were lessening. The image of Lady Jane Grey was thus reworked to smooth away the harsh edges, but the resulting picture scarcely does her justice.

Lady Jane Grey, queen of England for only nine days, died on the executioner's block at the age of sixteen. The writings she left behind her are few: a prayer, some letters, a dying speech. Yet they provide us with a rare glimpse of a sustaining theology, and offer us some insight into the mind of one of the best educated women of her age. Elizabethans found in her devout life and brave death an exemplarly model of strength, educated conviction, and unfailing devotion. Though it is true, as many historians have argued, that Lady Jane Grey was a pawn in the political intrigue of 1553, she was also a strongly determined and articulate woman not afraid to speak out for what she believed, no matter what the consequences. Lady Jane Grey is worth noting not only for her political position, but also as an example of a sixteenth-century Protestant woman who died steadfast to her faith.

MARY ELLEN LAMB

The Cooke Sisters: Attitudes toward Learned Women in the Renaissance

DID women have a Renaissance?" a recent critic has asked. Her answer to her own question is a definitive no as she examines the social mores of Renaissance Italy, where it all supposedly started.[1] Looking at the male-dominated discourse of Renaissance England, another scholar, Gary Waller, points to the "marginalization and silence" imposed upon women by the very structure of their language. The books addressed to Englishwomen from 1475 to 1640 directed them to be chaste, silent, and obedient, as a recent title of a list and analysis of these works states succinctly.[2]

Yet the Renaissance seemed to have begun so well for women, at least in England. The education of women encouraged by the new attitudes toward marriage in the Reformation produced many impressively learned women: Margaret More Roper, who astounded kings and scholars with her fluency in Latin; the ill-fated Lady Jane Grey who, blessed with a kind tutor, preferred reading Plato's *Phaedo* in the original Greek to hunting in the park; Queen Elizabeth, whose extemporaneous speeches in Latin, Italian, and French were admiringly witnessed by foreign ambassadors; Mary Sidney, the Countess of Pembroke, who published her translations from French and Italian; and others. The celebrated daughters of Anthony Cooke—Mildred, Anne, Elizabeth, Katherine—were also educated at that time, described by Nicholas Udall, when the education of women was carried on with the greatest enthusiasm:

The great number of noble women at that time in England [were] given to the study of devout science and of strange tongues. It was a common thing to see young virgins so nouzled and trained in the study of letters, that they willingly set all other pastimes at noght for learnings sake.[3]

So where are the plays, the poems, the learned commentaries, the treatises that such a good beginning seemed to promise? By the end of the century, the combined works of these women amounted to a handful of translations, scattered poems, and a few epitaphs. The work of the Cooke sisters who were, with the exception of Queen Elizabeth and the Countess of Pembroke, the most prolific of women writers of this time, provide if not an absolute answer to this question, at least a place to start looking.

The daughters of Anthony Cooke, himself tutor to Edward VI, were educated well, and quite possibly their fine educations facilitated their good marriages. The eldest sister Mildred, wife of William Cecil, first Baron Burghley and Queen Elizabeth's principal secretary, was acclaimed by Roger Ascham as one of the most learned women in England. According to a contemporary biographer, she delighted in reading the early church fathers and translated "a peece" of St. Chrysostom's from Greek into English.[4] Anne, wife of Nicholas Bacon, Lord Keeper of the Great Seal, translated fourteen sermons by Bernadino Ochino, an Italian Calvinist, as well as the *Apologia Ecclesiae Anglicanae*, compiled by Bishop John Jewel and others. Elizabeth, who was first married to Sir Thomas Hoby, famous for his translation of Castiglione's *Courtier,* and then married to Lord John Russell, translated *A Way of Reconciliation Touching the True Nature and Substance of the Body and Blood of Christ in the Sacrament.* She was also acclaimed for the epitaphs written for her two husbands and other relatives. Katherine, wife to Sir Henry Killigrew, whom Queen Elizabeth employed on various diplomatic missions, was the author of an epitaph and a verse, requesting her elder sister Mildred to influence her husband to revoke a diplomatic task assigned to Killigrew. The epitaph and verse are recorded for posterity in Harington's translation of Ariosto's *Orlando Furioso.* A fifth daughter, Margaret, married less well and died fairly young, leaving us no recorded written work.[5]

A "peece" of St. Chrysostom, sermons by Bernadino Ochino, *The Apologie or Aunswer in Defence of the Church of England, A Way of Reconciliation Touching the True Nature and Substance of the Body and*

Blood of Christ in the Sacrament: the Cooke sisters' translations were confined to religious material, and in this their work was representative of that of other women of the Tudor period, for the majority of extant works by women were translations, and most of these from religious texts.[6] The reasons for this are various. The translation of scriptural passages, especially the Psalms, was a religious discipline among many English people, men as well as women. As an expression of private religious sentiment, most of these translations remained unpublished and have long since disappeared. A few such works found their way into print because of the status of their translators or for some other reason. Some translations, however, were more public in intent. If we can believe the many dedications of religious works, women formed the primary audience for the huge numbers of pious texts rolling off the presses in the sixteenth century. It would be only natural for women to wish to reply to some of the issues in these works, to express their own opinions about the religious questions of their day. Since the Church prohibited women from preaching, publishing their own ideas about religion was impossible, but translating the words of a male author was not. Making works originally expressed in Latin, French, or Italian conveniently accessible to an English audience was one of the few ways that they could contribute to a religious question of that time. The translations undertaken by Anne Cooke Bacon and her sister Elizabeth Cooke Hoby were among this latter type.

When Anne Cooke Bacon began the translation of the *Apologia Ecclesiae Anglicanae,* she undertook a difficult task, full of political import. It was the official document of the Church of England, to be placed "in all cathedral and collegiate churches, and also in private houses," as ordered by the Convocation of 1563.[7] Its task was no less than to prove that the Church of England was one church, to provide central tenets to unify its members, and to defend it against the Roman Catholic assertion that it was rife with sects and schisms. Defining Church of England policies against those of the Roman Catholic church, the impetus of the *Apologia* was anti–Roman Catholic, yet there were Protestants who took issue with the work, as well. Obviously, it was necessary that this critically important work be well translated in order to represent its positions clearly to the English congregations. A hasty and inaccurate translation published in 1562 was not adequate, and when Anne Cooke Bacon furnished an accurate translation in 1564, it was received gratefully as the standard translation used in all subsequent editions. Her translation was so precise and graceful that C. S. Lewis was later to say, "If quality without bulk were enough, Lady Bacon might be put forward as the best of all sixteenth-century translators."[8]

Elizabeth Cooke Hoby's translation also represents an attempt to further the solidity of the Church of England. Its title fully descriptive of its content, *A Way of Reconciliation Touching the True Nature and Substance of the Body and Blood of Christ in the Sacrament* treats the single most controversial issue in the *Apologie for the Church of England*: to what extent were the body and blood of Christ present in the bread and the wine of the mass? Elizabeth's translation replies to the outraged responses of the readers who disagreed with John Jewel's view that actual transubstantiation was superstitious heresy. *A Way of Reconciliation* is mollifying in tone: "Neither would wee strive so much about that terme of Transubstantiation . . . [it was] a sacramentall alteration" much like Baptism, a spiritual, not a carnal, eating of Christ's flesh. Lest this issue seem obscure or trivial to modern minds, it should be remembered that Henry VIII had sent people to the stake for rejecting the doctrine of transubstantiation.[9] It was precisely around issues like these that the Church defined itself.

We will, unfortunately, never know what "peece" of St. Chrysostom Mildred Cooke Cecil translated. According to the *Life of Burghley,* she took pleasure in reading the works of Basil the Great, Cyril, Chrysostom, Gregory Nazianzen, and others. This list implies a particular interest in the early church, especially the Eastern church. These fathers assumed special importance at that time because they represented for Protestants the period when the Church was pure before it was corrupted by the later practices of the Roman Catholic church. Thus, Chrysostom was quoted by both sides on the issue of transubstantiation: John Jewel interpreted material in Chrysostom's *Ad Caesarium* to mean that the bread of the mass remained bread in substance, while the anonymous author of *An Apologie of the Private Mass,* one of the works directed against the *Apologie for the Church of England,* interpreted a statement by Chrysostom to argue that Christ's body was actually present in the sacrament of mass (Booty, pp. 151–67). St. Cyril also wrote at length about transubstantiation. While we will never know if Mildred Cooke Cecil was engaged in this particular issue of the eucharist, it seems likely that her special interest in the early church fathers may have had doctrinal as well as devotional significance. Described by the Spanish ambassador as a "tiresome blue-stocking" and a "furious heretic" of great influence over her husband,[10] Mildred Cooke Cecil had at least the physical opportunity to forward the interests of her religious beliefs, which were sympathetic to Puritans, through discussions with her husband rather than through published translations.

The Spanish ambassador's account of Mildred Cooke Cecil's influence over her husband brings up an important context for the Cooke sisters' work: the interests of their close male relatives. Their father, Anthony Cooke, member of Parliament under Elizabeth, was active in discussion on the unity of the Church of England. It was he who brought the Act of Uniformity before the House of Lords. According to Jewel, Cooke argued vehemently for a scheme of his own.[11] Was Mildred Cooke Cecil's reading of Nazianzen influenced at all by a Latin translation of Nazianzen's *Theophania* attributed to Anthony Cooke? To what extent was the choice of translations by Anne and, especially, Elizabeth affected by their father's own edition of John Ponet's *Diallacticon de veritate natura atque substantia corporis et sanguinis Christi in Eucharista*, yet another discussion of transubstantiation? The husbands of Anne Cooke Bacon and Mildred Cooke Cecil provided a context of immense political importance. Both Nicholas Bacon and William Cecil were members of Elizabeth's Privy Council, as previously mentioned, Bacon as Lord Keeper of the Great Seal and Cecil as her principal secretary. Even more important, Bacon and Cecil were deeply involved in religious matters. According to Sidney Lee, "the Queen was content for many years following her accession to leave the ordering of church matters for the most part" in the hands of Bacon and Cecil, a privilege they used to further the interests of the reformed religion.[12] Finally, Cecil is thought to have been one of several authors of the *Apologia Ecclesiae Anglicanae*, attributed to Jewel as chief but not sole author. A work of this official importance required the involvement of several writers; at the least, Cecil's approval was necessary before it could become the official document of the Church of England (Booty, pp. 51–53). Was Anne Cooke Bacon at all influenced by her brother-in-law to translate this work? How important was her husband's approval to her? Did it motivate her?

Elizabeth Cooke Hoby's husband Thomas was himself a translator, and his translation of Martin Bucer's *Gratulacion of the mooste famous Clerke M. Martin Bucer . . . unto the Churche of England for the restitution of Christes Religion* demonstrates his interest in the Anglican church as set up under Queen Elizabeth. Bucer's views of transubstantiation are thought to have been especially influential for the authors of the *Apologia Ecclesiae Anglicanae;* their positions on that issue are virtually identical (Booty, p. 171). Hoby would certainly have been interested, then, in his wife's translation of *A Way of Reconciliation,* but how much did he discuss her translation with her? What form would his interest have taken—tolerance for the time she spent away from attending to his needs while she worked on the translation or active encouragement and praise? Was the translation his idea in the first place? The nature of the relationship between any of the husbands and their wives' translations is impossible to determine, but it seems likely that the male relatives of the Cooke sisters provided a supportive audience for their work. Certainly they were all heavily invested in the common goal of uniting the Church of England by clarifying and promulgating church policy. The father and husbands of the Cooke sisters must have welcomed their translations as contributions to a common cause.

There is another, broader social context for the Cooke sisters' translations, however, extending beyond their male relatives. Like many translations by women in the Renaissance, their translations were religious in subject matter. This choice of subject was undoubtedly motivated by various factors, such as personal piety and concern for the Church as an institution. An early translation by Anne Cooke Bacon, however, suggests an additional motive. In her dedication of her translation of Bernardino Ochino's sermons to her mother, the young Anne Cooke Bacon explicitly uses the religious content of her translation to justify her study of Italian:

Wherein among the rest it hath pleased you, often, to reprove my vaine studie in the Italian tongue, accompting the sede thereof, to have bene sowin in barayne, unfruitful grounde (sins God thereby is no whit magnified) . . . and for that I have wel knowen your chife delight, to rest in the destroying of man his glorie and exaltinge wholy the glory of God . . . accepte this work as yelding some parte of the fruite of your Motherly admonicions.[13]

Possibly other translations of religious materials were also motivated in part to defend the translator's education. Women's education was in serious need of defense at that time. "I haue herde many men put great dout whether it shulde be expedyent and requisite or nat / a woman to have lernyng in bokes of latyn and greke," Richard Hyrde wrote in his dedication of Margaret Roper's translation of Erasmus' *Devout Treatise Upon the Pater Noster*.[14] The objections to women's education were various, but the primary argument went this way: since the overwhelmingly important possession of a woman is her chastity, of what real use is her education? Thus, the bulk of defenses of women's education concerned themselves with showing how education furthered and protected, rather than hindered, a woman's chastity. "I never herde tell / nor read of any woman well lerned / that ever was . . . spotted or infamed as vicious," Hyrde asserts (sig. A4v).

Similarly, much of Vives' *Instruction of a Christian Woman* treats this issue, approving, for example, the example of the ancient Roman who shut up his wayward daughter with a starving horse until the beast killed and ate her. Compared with works on the education of young men like Ascham's *Scholemaster,* which discusses more conventional ideas about disciplining students as well as teaching them to translate from Latin, Vives' work is almost offhand about how women should actually be educated: let them read the "Gospelles, and the Actes, and the Epistles of the Apostles, and the old Testament, Saint Hierome, S. Ciprian, Augustine, Ambrose, Hilary, Gregory, Plato, Cicero, Senec, and such other" (sig. D5r). Women were, of course, strictly forbidden from reading romances, songs, and pagan authors of dubious morality like Ovid. In limiting women's reading so severely, even the defenders of women's education endorsed the assumption that women are morally frail. This assumption also pervades those very church fathers whom women were instructed to read.[15]

Thus, the controls humanism placed on women's education were severe. Lurking behind this fear of woman's moral frailty was no doubt a different fear: Education was power. For humanists, education was the means by which a learned man could gain the power to influence the ruler for the good of the state. Then, as at other times, education enabled the children of an elite to assume their expected places in their society.[16] Such an invitation was not, obviously, extended to women. A learned woman was, in fact, a threat. Might she not, ask the detractors of women's education described by Hyrde, use her newfound capacities to gain influence of some kind, to use "subtilyte and conveyaunce / to sette forwarde and accom-plysshe their frowarde entente and purpose" (sig. A2r)? The solution was simple: women were to avoid any public demonstration of their learning. According to Hyrde, their learning was to provide "especiall conforte / pleasure / and pastyme" (sig. A5r) to their husbands. Vives puts it even more succinctly:

Let her lerne for herself alone and her young children or her sisters in our Lord. For it neither becommeth a woman to rule a Schoole, nor to live amonge men, or speake abroade, and shake of her demureness and honesty, either al togeather or els a great part: which if shee be good, it were better to be at home within and unknowen to other folkes, and in company to hold her tongue demurely, and let few see her, and none al all heare her. (sig. C6r)

Elizabeth Jocelyn's prefatory letter to her *Mothers legacie* (1624) shows that some of these anxieties about learned women were shared by these women themselves. Educated from childhood by her grandfather, a master of Queens College and professor of divinity at Cambridge, Jocelyn was skilled at foreign languages, history, and poetry as well as Scripture.[17] Yet in this work expressing her dying wishes for her unborn child, she asks that her child, if a daughter, be denied the opportunity for learning she herself had experienced. Her daughter should be taught only the Bible, "good houswifery, writing, and good workes" because "other learning a woman needs not" (sig. B5v). She goes further, to describe the possible destructive effect of learning on a woman:

Though I admire it in those whom God hath blest with discretion, yet I desire not much in mine owne, having seene that sometimes women have greater portions of learning, than wisdome, which is no better use to them than a main saile to a flye-boat, which runs it underwater. (sig. B6r)

After praising a woman who balances her learning with wisdom as a "well-ballanced ship," she returns somewhat obsessively to the subject:

But, by deare, though she have all this in her, she will hardly make a poore mans wife; Yet I leave it to thy will. If thou desirest a learned daughter, I pray God give her a wise and religious heart, that she may use it to his glory, thy comfort, and her owne salvation. But howsoever thou disposest of her education I pray thee labour by all meanes to teach her true humility. (sig. B6v)

Jocelyn had apparently internalized these values of wisdom and humility in her own life and work so that any evidences of her learning were almost totally repressed. As her editor praises her, "Of all [her] knowledge shee was very sparing in her discourses, as possessing it rather to hide, than to boast of" (sig. a3v). Similarly, *The Mothers legacie* is praised for "scarce shewing one spark of the elementary fire of her secular learning" (sig. a1v).

Wisdom, discretion, a wise and religious heart, humility: in the name of these virtues, women were prevented from asserting their own intellectual competence in any secular and most religious spheres. To do so was to risk the charge, perhaps even by their own consciences, of being foolish, indiscrete, vain, and even irreligious, all attributes of "loose" women. No wonder educated women were on the defensive to show that their learning had accomplished no permanent damage to their character! And what better way than to translate Erasmus' *Paraphrase of the New Testament*, like Mary Tudor; or Marguerite de Navarre's *Godly medytacyon of the christen sowle*, like Princess Elizabeth; or Erasmus' *Devout Treatise Upon the Pater Noster*, like Margaret Roper? Margaret Tyler's translation of secular material, the Spanish romance *The Mirrour of Princely Deedes and Knighthood*, indicates the pressure women were under to translate religious subjects. Tyler repeatedly disavows her own responsibility for her choice of subject matter and promises a future translation more to the liking of readers critical of her for translating a romance; she describes detractors who "would enforce me necessarily either not to write or to write of divinitie."[18] No wonder no other woman published a translation of a romance in that century!

The misogyny that drove women to use translation as a way of justifying their education and character informs at least one person's concept of translation in general. In his dedication of his own translation of Montaigne's *Essayes* to the Countess of Bedford and her mother, John Florio uses metaphors suggesting the depth of the male anxieties at least partially responsible for preventing many women from writing original work. His remarks on translation read like a casebook study of latent as well as overt hostility toward women:

To my last Birth, which I held masculine (as are all mens conceipts that are their owne though but by their collecting; and this was to *Montaigne* like *Baechus,* closed in, or loosed from his great Jupiters thigh) I the indulgent father invited two right Honorable Godfathers, with the One of your Noble Ladyshippes to witnesse. So to this defective edition (since all translations are reputed femalls), delivered at second hand; and I in this to serve but as *Vulcan,* to hatchet this *Minerva* from that *Jupiters* bigge braine.[19]

This passage suggests the degree to which the misogyny directed against women engaged in intellectual endeavors dictated the form of those endeavors. Translations were "defective" and therefore appropriate to women; this low opinion of translating perhaps accounts for why women were allowed to translate at all. A man who labors in this degraded activity must justify himself, "since all translations are reputed femalls." Writing original ideas, or even collecting the original ideas of others, is "masculine" and deserving of male patronage. A mere translation, however, can be dedicated to women. The dynamics underlying this way of thinking are transparent. Translation, especially translation of works by males, was allowed to women because it did not threaten the male establishment as the expression of personal viewpoints might. Perhaps more importantly, however, translation did not threaten the male ego. By engaging in this supposedly defective form of literary activity, women did not threaten perceptions of male superiority; any competence they displayed could be dismissed by denigrating the task of translation itself.

But Florio's metaphors reveal even more fundamental anxieties. It is not uncommon for writers, male or female, to describe their works as "brain-children," so Florio's description of his work as a "birth" is not surprising. But he goes further: in this passage, women are deprived of that one creative act that would seem indisputably theirs. Giving birth is an exclusively male activity; Jupiter gives birth from his thigh and his brain. Jupiter himself is described in terms that suggest compensation for phallic insecurity; Bacchus and Minerva are born respectively from "his *great* Jupiters thigh" and "Jupiters *bigge* braine" (italics mine). These metaphors suggest anxieties based in the fundamental differences between the sexes, women's ability to bear children and men's role of getting and maintaining an erection. Surely Florio's wording of his efforts to "hatchet this Minerva"[20] from Jupiter's head implies considerable hostility directed toward this goddess of wisdom and the arts and, by implication, quite possibly to any women who, like her, profess competence in intellectual endeavors. Much of this material must have been subconscious. Florio is, after all, addressing this dedication to two women, one of whom was a major patron of his day, to obtain patronage in some form. One wonders how the intellectual Countess of Bedford and her mother reacted.

It would be easy to dismiss the implications of Florio's metaphors as one man's problem if it were not for the pervasiveness of the misogyny directed against intellectual women in that time. For a variety of reasons, some more deep-seated than others, intellectual Renaissance women had a thin line to toe. On the one hand, women like Margaret Roper, Lady Jane Grey, the Cooke sisters, and others were often praised for their education. Roper, at least, was expected to speak Latin on demand, for her fluency reflected glory on her father. But any public demonstration of learning initiated by women themselves was problematic, and strong psychological constraints were exerted against producing any actual written work displaying this learning. Of course, publishing by either sex was considered somewhat plebeian at this time, and editors often claimed to publish a work without the knowledge of the author. But for women, this modesty topos was especially acute. The editor of Anne Cooke Bacon's translation of Ochino's sermons, for example, stresses her "shamfastnes" which "would rather have supprest them, had not I to whose hands they were committed halfe against hir will put them fourth" (sig. A3r). He then goes on to express contempt for women who publish, a contempt which expands to include intellectual women in general, without any apparent sense of irony or contradiction in the immediate context for his remarks, a preface to a woman's translation of a religious text: "Speakyng in prynt lyke Parates with solemne countenaunces, [they] debate matters of importaunce, and grave weight, as though the ordre of Realmes appertained to them, or els warbling words of Scripture in all their doings, [they] deface the thing they most bable of" (sig. A3v).

Publishing even a needed translation like Anne Cooke Bacon's translation of the *Apologia Ecclesiae Anglicanae* was a delicate matter, and the editor of that work, too, stresses that publishing this document was his idea, not the translator's. He has published it without her consent or knowledge, "to prevent suche excuses as your modestie woulde have made in staye of publishinge it" (sig. A2v), he claims in his prefatory material.[21] That is, the editor would have the readers believe that she translated this highly technical and laborious work wholly for her own pleasure, and then submitted it to his judgement without any thought at all of publication, even though publication of this work was desperately needed. His emphasis is on her modesty, her deference to male judgement of her work, which she apparently values for its own sake: "You have used your accustomed modestie in submittinge it to judgement, but therin is your prayse doubled, sith it hath passed judgement without reproche" (sigs. A1r–v). This emphasis on her modesty masks an implied threat against women of learning who are not modest, who do not defer to male judgement. The prefatory material to Bacon's translation of the *Apologia Ecclesiae Anglicanae* makes it clear that this publication of a translation by a woman is exceptional, initiated by a male, and not meant in any way to provide encouragement to other women to publish their translations as well.

Bacon's act of translating itself, however (although not the publication of her translation) does provide an example for women to follow, according to the editor of the *Apologie for the Church of England*. Her learned industry sets a model for other gentlewomen who "shall (I trust) hereby be alured from vain delights to doinges of more perfect glory" (sig. A2v). In this sentiment, the editor is drawing on the most powerful argument presented for educating women in the Renaissance: learning occupies their minds. In Roper's translation, Hyrde's dedication to a young woman likewise presents the translator as a virtuous example for her to follow. In this context, learning is even better than sewing, Hyrde argues, for reading keeps women from "pevysshe fantasyes":

Redyng and stydyeing of bokes so occupieth the mynde / that it can have no leyser to muse or delyte in other fantasies / whan in all handy werkes / that men saye be more mete for a woman / the body may be busy in one place / and the mynde walkyng in another / while they syt sowing and spinnyng with their fyngers / maye caste and compasse many pevysshe fantasyes in theyr myndes. (sig. A4r)

This deflated view of a woman's education is specifically applied to translating later in the century in Nicholas Breton's "An Olde Mans Lesson," in which an old man advises a young husband in the finer points of matrimony: "If she be learned and studious, perswade her to translation, it will keepe her from Idlenes, & it is a cunninge kinde taske: if shee be unlearned, commend her huswifery."[22] The editor of young Anne Cooke Bacon's translation of Ochino's sermons also draws on this argument in his praise of her scholarly use of her time, as he condemns that average young women:

wast theyr tyme . . . in pricking & trymming to vayne hethennysh ostentation, and in devysing new fashions of apparell, to whome if in theyr glasse appeared the foule faultes of their filthy condicions as plainely as the defaultes of theyre fore-sayde faces, I doubt much whether they would delight to tool therin so often as they doe. (sig. A3r)

The misogyny of this editor, who had likewise condemned intellectual women who "debate matters of importaunce, and grave weight" as well as religious women, for "warbling words of Scripture," leaves very little space for women to move in without censure.

The narrowness of the intellectual boundaries within which educated women were allowed to exercise their learning undoubtedly accounts at least in part for the amount and nature of the Cooke sisters' translating. They fit their work neatly within the constraints of the time. They con-fined themselves to religious texts and they published only those transla-tions which were of some public benefit. These publications were almost against their will, if we can believe the male editors' prefatory comments containing the requisite praise of their modesty. It is not surprising, then, that Mildred Cooke Cecil evidently did not publish her translation from St. Chrysostom. It would have been more surprising if she had, under the circumstances. Interestingly enough, a translation of St. Chrysostom's commentary on Paul's Epistle to the Ephesians was dedicated to Mildred Cooke Cecil's daughter Anne in 1581. While I would like to believe that Mildred Cooke Cecil was the actual translator of this work, it is more likely that it was written by an anonymous scholar responding to a family interest in St. Chrysostom. In an indirect way, possibly Mildred's transla-tion encouraged or even elicited a translation by a male author while her own work remained unpublished. One wonders how many women pa-trons rewarded writers for work they themselves wished to accomplish, or work they had accomplished but which remained unrecognized in their private studies.

In addition to translation of a certain limited kind, there was another acceptable outlet for women's learning, an outlet which perhaps reveals even more clearly the force of the paternalistic power structure controlling women's learning. Women were allowed to write epitaphs, and they were especially praised for epitaphs for their husbands or other male relatives. Elizabeth Cooke Hoby is praised by no less a work than Harington's trans-lation of Ariosto's *Orlando Furioso* for her epitaphs in Latin, Greek, and English for both her husbands.[23] She also wrote epitaphs for her son, daughter, brother, sister, and a friend; several of these also showed her facility in ancient languages. Katherine Cooke Killegrew wrote a Latin epitaph on her own death, preserved on her funeral monument with a Greek verse of Elizabeth's (Ballard, pp. 144, 145). Mildred Cooke Cecil's daughter Anne wrote four epitaphs on the death of her son; these found their way into print in 1584. From the number of epitaphs written by the Cookes alone, it would seem that if we wish to assess the learning of Renaissance women, we should turn to funeral monuments. As emblems of sisterly, motherly, or wifely devotion, these epitaphs provided non-threatening outlets for their authors' learning and poetic skill.

One final outlet for learning allowed to educated women was the letter. In his commentary on Ariosto's *Orlando Furioso*, Harington also includes a Latin verse by Katherine Cooke Killigrew to Mildred Cooke Cecil. This verse is the only extant literary work by this author, and it appears to be drawn from a private communication with her sister:

> Si mihi quem cupio cures *Mildreda* remitti,
> Tu bona, tu melior, tu mihi sola soror:
> Sin malè cessando retines, & trans mare mittis,
> Tu mala, tu peior, tu mihi mulla soror.
> Is si Cornubiam, tibi pax sit & omnia laeta,
> Sin mare Ciciliae nuncio bella. Vale.

While it shows competence in Latin, Harington's praise of it as a verse "which I doubt if Cambridge or Oxford can mend" seems somewhat extravagant. "Englished" by an "ingenious friend" of the eighteenth-century scholar George Ballard, the final lines contain a forcefully expressed threat:

> His staye let Cornwall's shore engage;
>   and peace with Mildred dwell:
> Else war with Cecil's name I wage
>   Perpetual war.—farewell.[24]

Why did Katherine Killigrew take time and trouble to write her request to Mildred in Latin? Possibly the Latin verse implies a compliment, an understanding that Mildred, a Latinist herself, will understand and appreciate the education of the author. Even more likely, the Latin masks aggression, and Katherine is comfortable in making this threat in Latin in a way she would not be comfortable in English.

The force of the emotion expressed in this verse gives us some feeling of what Katherine was like: fiercely loyal to her husband, more than a little manipulative, capable of bitterness, somewhat impulsive. While all of these traits are not altogether positive, they are refreshing after all the descriptions of the modesty and virtue of the Cooke sisters. This verse reveals Katherine's humanity and individuality in a way that her sisters' translations did not, but in this respect the little Latin verse resembles the learning revealed in the letters of the other Cooke sisters. Instead of the modest, shy, bookish contemplatives conveyed by the prefaces to their translations, they emerge from their letters as vigorous, indomitable women energetically pursuing their affairs in a world not always sympathetic to their needs. Their letters reveal that their learning was truly second nature to them, as they exercise it often and without apology.

The learning demonstrated in the many letters of Elizabeth Cooke Hoby in the Cecil papers suggests a sharp legal mind. In a letter to her brother-in-law Lord Burghley, Elizabeth insists that the judges' opinions on a property dispute affecting her daughter be delivered to the queen *singulatim,* individually rather than together as a group, since some "being inferior be loth to oppose their opinions against their superiors." In pressing this suit to her nephew Robert Cecil, she even defends her view against an anticipated argument based on legal precedent: "Neither is this like Stafford's case in Henry VII's time, wherein the judges might deny to tell the King their judgements beforehand, for that was for treason and requisite to have been hanged in respect of the estate." Clearly, this is a woman who expects her intellect to be taken seriously by the major statesmen of England! She quotes Book I of Virgil's *Aeneid* to Cecil in warning him against various slanders circulating about him: "Ac veluti magno in populo cum saepe coorta est / Seditio, saevit que animis ignobile vulgus / Jamque faces et saxa volant: furor arma ministrat." In citing Virgil, she dignifies by implication the role of statesman to epic stature. Since this citation describes the ocean before it is absolutely calmed by Neptune, her choice of quotation anticipates his success in dealing with the rumors. Her skillful use of Latin is flattering to a man whom she will later call upon for political favors, alternatively instructing and pleading for aid in various legal and business matters. In her pursuit of a lease, for example, she is not above listing the gifts she had bought for Queen Elizabeth in order to obtain the lease: "It cost me truly, twelve years since, a gown and petticoat of such tissue as should have been for the Queen of Scots' wedding garment; but I got them for my Queen, full dearly bought, I well wot."[25]

The letters written by Anne Cooke Bacon convey similar forthrightness, although they reveal more religious zeal than legal or financial expertise. Through her life, Anne exerted much effort on behalf of Reformist preachers, some of whom she sheltered at her own estate. In a letter to her brother-in-law Lord Burghley, she pleads that Burghley might listen to two or three of them himself, for she had "profited more in the inward feeling knowledge of God his holy will . . . by such sincere and sound opening of the Scriptures by an ordinary preaching within this seven or eight years, than I did by hearing odd sermons at Paul's wellnigh twenty years together." Her letters to her sons show anxiety about the state of their souls and bodies. Her Latin phrases seem to be fully integrated into her own language, and I suspect that she was prone to using them in her speech as well as her writing, as she exhorts her son Anthony to testify for the true religion of Christ: "In hoc noli adhibere fratrem tuum ad consilium aut exemplum. Sed plus dehinc. If you will be wavering (which God forbid, God forbid), you shall have examples and ill encouragers too many in these days." From this point in her letter she writes in Greek to the effect that the Archbishop Whitgift has a destructive preference for his own glory over Christ's. Her Greek is her own translation from her own English, not a citation from an ancient source. Evidently she uses it here as a protection against overly curious servants and associates, for she accuses a Mr. Fant, whom she praises elsewhere in the letter, of being likely to open the letter even though it is sealed, for "he will pry and prattle." Often her letters reveal a mind ill at ease, suspicious, hostile, and sure that *sub omni lapide latet anguis,* as she warns her son.[26]

Mildred Cooke Cecil has left us fewer letters than her sisters, perhaps because of the probable directness of her communication with her powerful husband; instead of writing a letter, she could, if he were receptive to her ideas, mention a problem over the dinner table. She was evidently an active supporter of the Puritan cause early in Elizabeth's reign, but later withdrew somewhat. Letters to her show her activity in the lucrative business of wards. Cecil was master of the court of wards, and so several wards were educated in her household; others were awarded, sometimes to persons who offered her bribes to speak in their behalf to her husband. One letter from her that does survive, however, is written entirely in Latin. Addressed to a cousin Sir William Fitzwilliam, Lord Deputy of Ireland, it shows the confidence with which she offers political advice to this important official under attack and desirous of leaving his post:

And therefore I think it best this storm were overblown, and after some service done, a better time may be found to seek your departure. For otherwise, besides further discredit, you shall hardly get recompense for your former service, which would grieve me most of all. For when, upon your misliking, others are sought to be placed, it seemeth that the preferring of another is the disgracing of you.[27]

This is the advice of a shrewd political mind, accustomed to the tides and eddies of favor in the Elizabethan court, fully aware of the importance of appearances in this public context. Why did she write in Latin? Any very educated person could have read it, if that person wanted to take the trouble. Possibly she feared that a hostile party, unable or unwilling to translate Latin, might be spying on him, for she adds in a postscript: "Keep close your friends' letters, for craft and malice never reigned more." Unlike the slightly paranoid tone of her sister Anne's postscript, accusing an otherwise trusted servant of being likely to "prattle and pry," this postscript advises caution appropriate to one in a sensitive public position.

It would be inaccurate and presumptive to claim that we know the Cooke sisters from their letters. What they convey about themselves rises in part out of the context of their audience and their situations. Beset by property settlements and other financial arrangements, it behooved Elizabeth Cooke Hoby to understand English law. The more personal tone of Anne Cooke Bacon's religious and maternal fervors is natural in a letter to a son. The shrewdness expressed in Mildred Cooke Cecil's letter is appropriate to the kind of letter she was writing; if a personal letter to a son of hers had survived, perhaps she might have sounded a bit more like her sister Anne. Yet, even taking these differences in context into account, it is striking how different each of them sounds from the other; and it is equally striking how individually each makes use of her learning. Katherine's poem masks a threat of hostility; Elizabeth plunges through the complications of the law and the court with straightforwardness and energy; Anne's language with its "God forbid, God forbid" conveys emotion in its rhythms; Mildred sounds the most shrewd and the most cautious of the group. There is a great family resemblance, however, beyond their obvious learning. They are all forceful and resolute women, dealing competently with their society in whatever situation they are placed.

These individual and energetic voices contrast strangely with the image conveyed by their literary works and the editors' prefaces attached to them. The Cooke sisters revealed in their letters do not seem particularly demure or modest, shyly presenting themselves and their work to the judgment of men. The discrepancy between these projections becomes all the more significant because it seems representative of the learned works by other women in the period. Impressive, active, vigorous women sound very much the same in print. The translations by Renaissance women are different from the translations of Renaissance men in being exceedingly literal. Absent are the magnificent and occasionally quirky expansions of Harington's *Orlando Furioso* and Chapman's *Homer*; instead we find line-by-line transliteration. The explanation of the difference lies to some extent in the nature of the task itself. Jewel's *Apologie for the Church of England*, for example, carried too much official weight to allow tampering. At that time, many religious texts had by their very nature to be translated literally. The formal conventions of epitaph writing did not allow for individuality of expression, either.

But there must be another explanation, as well. Renaissance women could, at least theoretically, have chosen vehicles which permitted their self-expression; but they did not. The explanation lies primarily, I maintain, in the attitudes toward educated women at that time. The professed goals of a humanistic education were perverted when they were applied to women. According to the tenets of humanism, learning was supposed to enable an educated person to benefit the state, to influence the ruler toward the good. But for women, education was merely a way of keeping them busy, much like the sewing which occupied their less learned sisters, in a fashion which did not threaten the established power structure. Instead of a means to exert control, education was, for women, a further means of being controlled. Their new education did not reflect any change in the old misogyny. Learned women were continually praised, but their works were not. They were urged to read church fathers and to translate sermons, but the measure of their worth was still their chastity, their modesty, their demureness, the extent to which they submitted themselves to the control of men.

There is no doubt that women were silenced and marginalized in the Renaissance. Attitudes toward learned women deprived them of all but a few limited outlets for their intellectual abilities. The primary outlet, translation, deprived them of any original voice. It is sad to speculate about what poems, plays, commentaries, or treatises we have lost because women had to invest so much energy into showing humility and obedience to men. But the tragedy extends farther. What effect did this repression have on the women themselves? Did they merely shrug off this propaganda and live their lives as best they could, accomplishing whatever tasks were allowed to them? Or, like Elizabeth Jocelyn, did they internalize these values? Did they laugh with each other about the ways they appeared humble and modest that day, or did they censure each other for any act of intellectual assertiveness? Did they make up poetry to share with each other, or did they regard their own stirrings of creativity as wrong somehow? When Jocelyn begged that her daughter be spared the learning she herself had had, was it truly because she feared it would make her daughter proud? Or was it because she did not want her daughter to feel the pain of self-repression she herself had felt, if she were to be mocked or even impoverished, by not being considered suitable for marriage, for daring to show herself, without apology or humility, as a learned woman?

DIANE BORNSTEIN

The Style of the Countess of Pembroke's Translation of Philippe de Mornay's *Discours de la vie et de la mort*

S INCE Tudor women were encouraged to read and to translate religious works, the reasons for the Countess of Pembroke's decision to translate Philippe de Mornay's *Discours de la vie et de la
mort* may appear obvious. However, by this translation the countess identified herself with the intellectual avant garde of her day, demonstrated her
interest in classical Stoicism, and voiced personal concerns.

Mornay, a controversial Huguenot leader, writer, and soldier, was
greatly admired by the more intensely Protestant courtiers of Elizabeth's
court, particularly those of the Dudley/Sidney alliance. However, Mornay's *Discours* is not simply an exercise in Christian piety in the *ars mo-
riendi* genre, but a treatise on Stoic philosophy. He first published this
work together with a translation of some of the letters of Seneca, and the
Senecan influence in it is very strong. Stoic death literature advises that
philosophical insight will teach one the true significance of life and death;
the cultivation of the virtues will free one from slavery to fortune; and
dying well involves living well and accepting one's destiny.[1] All three kinds
of advice appear in Mornay's work. In fact, the emphasis is so much on
Stoic themes such as the miseries of this life, the deceits of fortune, the
inevitability of death, the necessity to face death with courage and honor,
and death as peace and rest, that when the author briefly speaks of Christian immortality, it almost strikes a jarring note. Thus, although the
Christian features of the *Discours* make it appear a characteristic choice for
a woman translator, this Stoic emphasis renders it unusual.

The *Discours* also would have appealed to Mary Sidney for personal reasons. First, and most important, it would have reminded her of her brother, since Sir Philip Sidney and Mornay had been close friends. They first met when Sidney was in Paris in 1572 at the time of the St. Bartholomew massacre, and they renewed their acquaintance when Mornay came to England in 1577 to 1578 on a diplomatic mission for the king of Navarre. In her memoirs, Madame de Mornay identifies Sidney as one of her husband's chief friends in England. When the Mornays' daughter Elizabeth was born in June 1578 they asked Sidney to be one of her godfathers (C. Mornay, p. 170). During this visit, Mornay probably gave Sidney a copy of his *Discours de la vie et de la mort,* published at Geneva in 1576. This may have been the copy used by the countess, for her translation agrees with this edition in most of its details. In one or two particulars, she favors a later edition, so she may have had a copy hand-corrected by the author, or she may have seen a later edition. Sidney had been interested in introducing his friend's writings to a larger English public and had started translating *De la verité de la réligion chrétienne,* completed by Arthur Golding in 1587, after Sidney's death. [2] Thus in translating the *Discours de la vie et de la mort,* the countess was carrying on Philip's legacy, as she later did in completing his Psalm translation and in editing his work for publication.

Secondly, this particular work by Mornay, written at the request of his wife Charlotte (C. Mornay, p. 145), would have appealed to the countess because of its topic, Christian and Stoical meditations on the theme of death. She completed the translation on May 13, 1590, so she must have been working on it not long after the death of her three-year-old daughter Katherine in 1584, and the deaths of her father, mother, and brother in 1586 (Waller, p. 19). The interest of both Madame de Mornay and the countess in this topic points to the interest of Renaissance women in personal devotional treatises, and perhaps more particularly, in works on death (Beaty, p. 54); the high rate of child mortality, the statistical odds that a woman would die in childbirth, and the many foreign and civil wars of the period, meant that women had to be constantly prepared to face their own deaths or those of the people they loved.

Mornay's *Discours* went through twelve French editions between 1576 and 1600. In 1576 Edward Aggas, a London printer and bookseller, made the first English translation, entitled *The Defence of Death.* Following her usual method as a translator, referring to earlier translations when they existed but improving on them, the countess evidently made use of Aggas' work. An examination of the two translations makes it clear that although she has some of the same errors as Aggas, her work is nevertheless an independent—and superior—translation. On occasion, she made minor errors that do not appear in Aggas, but she corrected most of the errors or inaccuracies that plague his version. Despite the fact that both works are close translations, their additions and omissions are not parallel. The countess' version is more concise (Aggas' work is about one-sixth longer), more accurate, more faithful to the original, more metaphorical, smoother in syntax, and far superior in style. The contrast between the translations of Aggas and the countess reveals her skill as a translator even in this early work, completed almost ten years before her *Psalmes*.

The countess followed the meaning and the graceful, balanced prose style of the original. There is a great deal of parallelism in the French work, and the countess retained it but sometimes had to change the structure of the sentences to create the same effect in idiomatic English. She is often more concise than even the original, compressing the same semantic content into less wordy syntactic structures, or using a single term for a doublet. Similarly, she is often more metaphorical, using a concrete image instead of an abstract term or extending a metaphor that appears in the original.

The opening paragraph provides a typical example of her style:

It seemes to mee strange, and a thing much to be marveiled, that the laborer to repose himselfe hasteneth as it were the course of the Sunne: that the Mariner rowes with all force to attayne the porte, and with a joyfull crye salutes the descryed land: that the traveiler is never quiet nor content till he be at the ende of his voyage: and that wee in the meane while tied in this world to a perpetuall taske, tossed with continuall tempest, tyred with a rough and combersome way, cannot yet see the ende of our labour but with griefe, nor behold our porte but with teares, nor approch our home and quiet abode but with horrour and trembling. This life is but a Penelopes web, wherein we are alwayes doing and undoing: a sea open to all windes, which sometime within, sometime without never cease to torment us: a weary jorney through extreame heates, and coldes, over high mountaynes, steepe rockes, and theevish deserts. And so we terme it in weaving at this web, in rowing at this oare, in passing this miserable way. Yet loe when death comes to ende our worke, when she stretcheth out her armes to pull us into the porte, when after so many dangerous passages, and lothsome lodgings she would conduct us to our true home and resting place: in steede of rejoycing at the ende of our labour, of taking comfort at the sight of our land, of singing at the approch of our happie mansion, we would faine, (who would beleeve it?) retake our worke in hand, we would againe hoise saile to the winde, and willinglie undertake our journey anew.[3]

Here is the French for comparison:

C'est un cas estrange, et dont je ne me puis assez esmerveiller, que les manou-vriers pour se reposer, hastent par maniere de dire le cours du Soleil: que les marin-iers voguent à toute force pour arriver au port, et de si loin qu'ils descouvrent la coste, jettent cris d'allegresse: que les pellerins n'ont bien ni aise, tant qu'ils soient au bout de leur voyage: et que nous cependant qui sommes en ce monde attachez et liez à un perpetuel ouvrage, agitez de continuelles tempestes, harassez d'un si scabreux et mal-aisé chemin, ne voyons toutes fois la fin et le bout de nostre tasche qu'à regret, ne regardons nostre vrai port qu'avec larmes, n'approchons de nostre giste et paisible sejour qu'avec horreur et tremblement.

Ceste vie n'est qu'une toile de Penelopé, où tousjours y a à tistre et à retistre, une mer abandonnée à tous vents, qui ores dedans, ores dehors nous tourmentent sans cesse: un voyage facheux, par gelées et par chaleurs extremes, par roides montagnes et par precipices, par deserts et par brigandages. Ainsi en devisons nous en faisant nostre besongne, en tirant à cest aviron, en passant ce miserable chemin. Et voilà neantmoins, quand la mort vient mettre fin à nos travaux, quand elle nous tend les bras pour nous tirer au port, quand après tant de dangereux passages et de fa-scheuses hostelleries elle nous veut mener à nostre vrai domicile, au lieu de nous resjouir, de reprendre coeur à la veuë de nostre terre, de chanter en approchant de nostre bien-heureux sejour, nous reprendrions, qui nous voudroit croire, nostre besongne, nous reguinderions la voile au vent, et rebrousserions volontiers nostre chemin.[4]

In the opening sentence, the countess used an indirect personal pronoun in the first clause instead of the second, reversing the use of this construc-tion in the French, since this resulted in more idiomatic English. She fol-lowed the parallelism and conciseness of the original, making it even more concise where possible. For instance, she omitted the relative clause and reduced a doublet to a single term in "qui sommes en ce monde attachez et liez à un perpetuel ouvrage." She again reduced a doublet to a single term in "la fin et le bout," translating it as "the ende." In the phrase "vrai port," she dropped the adjective "vrai." In the clause beginning "un voyage facheux, par gelées et par chaleurs extremes," she turned the noun "brigandages" (robberies) into an adjective modifying "deserts" (theevish deserts), applied the adjective "roide" (steep) to "rocks" instead of "mountains," and used "high" for "mountains," thereby modifying all the nouns with adjectives and increasing the parallelism. Moreover, she dropped the preposition "par," repeated six times to achieve parallelism in the original, making the sentence less repetitious and more concise, although she lost the rhetorical effect of Mornay's repetition.

On the other hand, the countess sometimes added words and phrases to clarify a passage. Occasionally, she expanded a single term into a doublet; for instance, "vrai domicile" became "true home and resting place." She occasionally added a phrase to make the meaning more specific; toward the end of this passage, she added "at the ende of our labour." More significantly, she at times expanded a metaphor that appears in the original; for example, in translating "en faisant nostre besongne" as "in weaving at this web," she continued the metaphor of Penelope's web hinted at in the original.

Let us compare Aggas' translation of this passage with that of the countess:

It is a straunge matter wherat I cannot sufficientlye mervaile, to beholde howe the labourer to the end to cease from his labours dooth even in manner hasten the course of the Sun. The Mariner for the attaining unto the desired Haven, saileth forwarde amaine, and from as farre as he can espye the coste, to shoute out for joy. And the Pilgrime or travayler, to take no rest before his jorney be ended. And yet that man in the meane time beeing bound to perpetuall laboure, tossed with continuall tempestes, and tyered with many rough and miery pathes: is neverthelesse unwilling to looke uppon or come neere to the ende of his jorney: sorowfull to see the Haven of his assured rest: and with horror and feare to draw towarde his lodging and peaceable dwelling place.

Our life resembleth a right Penelopes web, which still must be woven and woven again: a Sea habandoned to all windes, which sometime inwardly sometime outwardly tormenteth it: and a troublesome path, through frost and extreme heate: over steepie mountaines and hollow valleyes, among deserts and theevish places.

This is the communication that we doo use, beeing at our woork, pulling at our Ore, and passing through this miserable path and rough way. And yet when death commeth to finish our labours, when she stretcheth foorth her arme to helpe us into the Haven, and when after so many passages and troublesome hostryes, she seeketh to bring us into our true habitation: into a place of comforte and joy, where wee should take harte at the viewe of our lande, and drawing towarde our happy dwelling place, should sing and rejoyce: we would if we might have our owne willes, begin our woork again: returne our Sailes into the winde, and voluntarily retire back into our jorney.[5]

Aggas is a very literal translator who renders the French almost word by word, yet he is not as successful as the countess in capturing the style of the original, nor is he as accurate or concise. In the first sentence, he has lost the periodicity of Mornay's style: whereas Mornay has a series of three clauses, each beginning with "que" and ending with a colon, leading up to "et que nous cependant" (where the contrast begins between our attitude toward death and the three attitudes he has just described), Aggas fragments the development into separate sentences. He comes out saying, it is "a straunge matter" that the laborer is eager to see the day come to an end so he can rest. Then he makes a simple declarative observation about the mariner, and his statement about the pilgrim is not clearly linked to what precedes since the only verb is the infinitive. In this series of sentences, he has lost even the literal meaning.

Aggas often introduces empty phrases, such as "to the ende," and "a right." The added verb "to beholde" in the first sentence is not needed to convey the meaning. The phrase "ainsi en devisons nous," translated concisely and idiomatically by the countess as "and so we terme it," is translated wordily and awkwardly by Aggas as "this is the communication that we doo use." He used several doublets for single terms: "pellerins" became "Pilgrime or travayler"; "voyons" became "looke uppon or come neere to"; "ce miserable chemin" became "this miserable path and rough way"; and "chanter" became "sing and rejoyce."

Occasionally, Aggas made a phrase more concise: he translated "et que nous cependant qui sommes en ce monde attachez et liez à un perpetuel ouvrage" as "and yet that man in the meane time beeing bound to perpetuall laboure," using a present participle instead of the relative clause and substituting a single term for the doublet. Since the countess also dropped the relative clause and used a single term for a doublet in this sentence, she may have been influenced here by Aggas' translation. Similarly, at the close of this sentence, both translators rendered "la fin et le bout" as "the ende," and the countess again may have been influenced by Aggas.

Aggas made a series of errors in his translation of this passage. He mistranslated "au lieu de nous resjouir" (translated correctly by Mary Sidney as "in steede of rejoycing") as "into a place of comforte and joy"; he mistranslated "par maniere de dire" (translated correctly by the countess as "as it were") as "even in manner"; and he mistranslated "qui nous

voudroit croire" (translated correctly by Sidney as "who would beleeve
it?") as "if we might have our owne willes." In addition to these errors,
Aggas also altered the tone of the work. His "and yet that man" is less
personal, and therefore less immediate, involving the reader less directly,
than Mornay's "nous," translated by the countess as "wee." Similarly,
Aggas' "tormenteth it" is less personal than Mornay's "nous," translated
by the countess as "us." Aggas also introduced absurdity into the central
personification. Death has only one arm in Aggas, whereas Mornay and
the countess have the more logical plural form. This opening selection is a
typical example of the work of both writers, so it can be seen that the
countess is by far the more accurate translator.

Another striking feature of the countess' translation is its conciseness.
Although she preserved the rhetorical ornaments of the original, such as
parallel structure and emphatic repetition, she often eliminated superfluous words. French prose tends to use more introductory phrases than English, and she eliminated a good number of those, such as "en un mot,"
"en somme," "de ce monde," "en la main," "de son gré," and "le plus
souvent." She often conveyed the same semantic meaning in a more concise syntactic structure. For instance, she compressed "la douleur poig-
nante d'une pleurisie," a noun phrase plus a prepositional phrase, into a
single noun phrase, "a pricking pleurisie." She eliminated the relative
clause in "que l'infinité d'icelles que nous endurons en ceste vie," translating it as "then the endlesse misery of our life." In "ou nager contre l'eau
avec travail et peine," she used a single adverb instead of a double prepositional phrase: "or painefully swimme against the streame." She compressed "qu'à faire le sage et à se mettre à son aise" by using one verb and a
parallel construction: "to purchase themselves wisedome and rest." The
expression "pour l'amour de l'une ou de l'autre et de leur belles illusions,"
becomes, by using one noun phrase and a parallel construction, "by the
faire illusions of the one or the other." "En vaisselle d'or et d'argent" is
compressed to "in gould and silver," eliminating "vaisselle," which is
understood by the context. Sidney shortened "si nous voulons vraiement
vivre, si nous voulons voir le jour," at the expense of losing the rhetorical
repetition: "if we wil indeed live & see the light."

Although her style is eloquent, the countess favored a plain, concise
syntax, demonstrated by her habit of reducing a doublet to a single term, as
in the following phrases:

se livre et abandonne	abandons
en sa pleine force et vigueur	growne to the highest
se lier et mettre	fetter himselfe
en vertu et titre	by vertue
plaies ou maladies	sicknesses
habituée et accroupie	an habite of crookednes
griefves et douloureuses	greevous woundes or
plaies ou maladies	sicknesses

However, occasionally, she expanded a single term into a doublet for more precision:

tout estourdi	dull heavines and astonishment
un souverain bien	the chiefe and soveraigne good
suivis	followed and attended
douleur	paine and torment
accrouppis	croked and contracted

The countess' additions usually make the work more specific and more concrete. For example, she translated "la fin de nos miseres" as "death, the end of our miseries." She added "our travaile" to "nous donnant pour tout," which became "geving us for all our travaile," and "work" was added to "la fin de chasque jour," to become "the ende of every dayes worke."

Other additions provide transition and emphasis. For example, the added phrase "at first sight" anticipates a change in the direction of the argument:

You see them appareled in purple, in scarlet, and in cloth of gould: it seemes at first sight there is no contentment in the world but theirs. But men knowe not how heavy an ounce of that vaine honor weighes, what those reverences cost them, and how dearely they pay for an ell of those rich stuffes: who knewe them well, would never buy them at the price. (p. 37)

Similarly, the added phrase "all is one to him" in the conclusion of this paragraph emphasizes the main point of the argument:

For I pray what can he feare, whose death is his hope? Thinke we to banish him his country? He knows he hath a country other-where, whence wee cannot banish him: and that all these countries are but Innes, out of which he must part at the wil of his hoste. To put him in prison? a more straite prison he cannot have, then his owne body, more filthy, more darke, more full of rackes and torments. To kill him and take him out of the worlde? that is it he hopes for: that is it with all his heart he aspires unto. By fire, by swore, by famine, by sicknesse: within three yeeres, within three dayes, within three hours, all is one to him: all is one at what gate, or at what time he passe out of this miserable life. (pp. 69–70).

Her additions also take reader response into account, setting up a dialogue between writer and reader. The addition "you will say" makes it clear that it is the response expected from the reader: "But you will say, at least so long as that fortune endured, they were at ease, and had their contentment." The added negative response provides emphasis here: "No, no, they would rather languish of the goute, the sciatica, any disease whatsoever, then dye one sweete death with the least paine possible." The countess' additions are never mere padding but always enhance the meaning or style of the original.

Sidney's most notable additions are her continuations or expansions of metaphors that appeared in the original. For instance, she translated "mille fausses et dangereuses intelligences en sa propre chair" as "a thousand treacherous and dangerous intelligences among his owne forces," continuing the military metaphor. She translated "la mort donc est l'issue de nos miseres, et l'emboucheure du port, où nous serons à couvert de tous vents," as "death then is the issue of our miseries and entraunce of the porte where we shall ride in safetie from all windes," continuing the metaphor of a journey. She rendered "il tient sa vie à ferme de lui, pour en jouir tant qu'il lui plaira," as "he holdes his life at farme, as his tenant at will, to yeeld him the profites," expanding the metaphor of landlord and tenant.

Mornay's *Discours de la vie et de la mort* is a somber, graceful meditation on the theme of death, steeped in Christian and Stoic philosophy and exhibiting the rhetorical skill of a humanist scholar. The translation of Mary Sidney, Countess of Pembroke, fully conveys its meaning as well as its style. At a time when English syntax was still in an unsettled state, the countess translated Mornay's sophisticated French prose into a smooth, idiomatic English that fully reflected its rhetorical ornaments. A comparison with Edward Aggas' translation, with its awkward phrases and excess words, shows how skillful the countess' work was. Her changes even improved the original by making it more concise, more specific, and more metaphorical. One can only regret that the countess limited herself to the silent art of translation and did not write her own meditations.

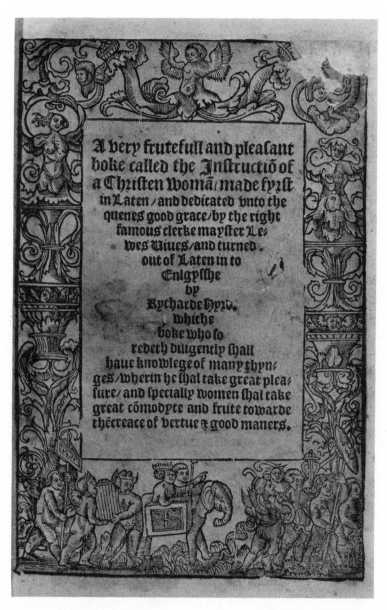

A very frutefull and pleasant
boke called the Instructiō of
a Christen Womā/made fyrst
in Laten/and dedicated vnto the
quenes good grace/by the right
famous clerke mayster Le-
wes Uiues/and turned
out of Laten in to
Englysshe
by
Rycharde Hyrd.
whiche
boke who so
redeth diligently shall
haue knowlege of many thyn-
ges/wherin he shal take great plea-
sure/ and specially women shal take
great comodyte and frute towarde
thencreace of vertue & good maners.

Title page from Juan Luis Vives, *Instruction of a Christian Woman,* trans.
Richard Hyrde (c. 1529), STC 24856.5. By permission of the Folger
Shakespeare Library.

Hans Holbein: Margaret More Roper. By permission of Lord Sackville.

¶A deuout treatise vpon the Pater noster / made fyrst in latyn by the moost famous doctour mayster Erasmus
Roterodamus / and tourned
in to englisshe by a yong
vertuous and well
lerned gentylwoman of .xix.
yere of age.

Scholarly woman as pictured on the title page of Margaret More
Roper's translation of the *Devout Treatise Upon the Pater Noster*. By
permission of the British Library.

KATHARINE PARRE

Attributed to William Scrots: Queen Catherine Parr. **By permission of the Na-**tional Portrait Gallery, London.

Unknown: Elizabeth I as Princess. By permission of Her Majesty the Queen.
Copyright reserved.

A Godly Medytacy
on of the christen sowle , concer-
ninge a loue towardes God and
hys Christe, compyled in frenche by lady
Margarete quene of Nauerre, and aptely tranflated into Englysh by the
ryght vertuouse lady Elyzabeth
doughter to our late souerayne
Kynge Henri the .viij.

Inclita filia, sereniffimi olim Anglorum
Regis Henrici octaui Elizabeta, tam Græ
cæ quam latine fœliciter in Chriſto
erudita.

Princess Elizabeth as pictured on the title page of her
translation of Marguerite de Navarre's *Godly medytacyon of the christen sowle* (1548), STC 17320. By permission of the Folger Shakespeare Library.

Unknown: "Marguerite [de Navarre] au petit chien." By permission of the
Cabinet des Estampes de la Bibliothèque Nationale.

The lattre examinacy

on of Anne Askewe, latelye mar
tyred in Smythfelde, by the wyc=
ked Synagoge of Antichrist,
with the Elucydacyon of
Johan Bale.

BIB
LIA

The veryte of the lorde endureth for euer.

Pfalme 116.

Anne Askewe ftode fast by thys veryte of
God to the ende.

I wyll poure out my fprete vpõ all flefh
(fayth God) ycur fonnes and your dough=
ters fhall prophecye. And who fo euer call
on the name of the lorde/fhall be faued.
Johel. ij.

Anne Askew on the frontispiece of Bale's edition of *The lattre examinacyon*. By permission of the Houghton Library, Harvard University.

Unknown: Lady Jane Grey. By permission of the National Portrait Gallery, London.

Mildred Cooke, Lady Burghley. By permission of the Marquess of Salisbury.

Simon de Pass: Mary Sidney, Countess of Pembroke. By permission of the National Portrait Gallery, London.

Attributed to Jan van Belcamp: Lady Anne Clifford, family historian and daughter of Lady Margaret Russell, Countess of Cumberland. Shown here is the left panel of a triptych of the Great Picture of the Clifford Family, commissioned by Lady Anne Clifford (1646). By permission of the Abbot Hall Art Gallery, Kendal, Cumbria.

Figure of Elizabeth Cary, Viscountess Falkland, from the tomb of her parents in the Parish Church of St. John Baptist, Burford, Oxfordshire. By permission of R. A. Moody.

SALVE DEVS

REX IVDÆORVM.

Containing,

1. The Paſsion of Chriſt.
2. Eues Apologie in defence of Women.
3. The Teares of the Daughters of Ieruſalem.
4. The Salutation and Sorrow of the Virgine Marie.

With diuers other things not vnfit to be read.

Written by Miſtris *Æmilia Lanyer*, Wife to Captaine *Alfonſo Lanyer* Seruant to the Kings Majeſtie.

AT LONDON
Printed by *Valentine Simmes* for *Richard Bonian*, and are
to be ſold at his Shop in Paules Churchyard, at the
Signe of the Floure de Luce and
Crowne. 1 6 1 1.

Title page of Aemilia Lanyer, *Salve Deus Rex Judaeorum* (1611), STC 15227.
By permission of the Folger Shakespeare Library.

MARGARET P. HANNAY

"Doo What Men May Sing": Mary Sidney and the Tradition of Admonitory Dedication

MARY SIDNEY, the Countess of Pembroke, was celebrated for her religious translations—of Mornay's *Discours de la vie et de la mort* and of the Psalms of David—works which are discussed in this collection, especially by Diane Bornstein and Beth Wynne Fisken. Sidney's few original works were largely confined to the margins of discourse, to the usual feminine genres of dedications and epitaphs.[1] We hear her own voice most clearly in two poems which may have been unknown to her contemporaries; they apparently never circulated and exist in one manuscript only, the 1599 presentation copy of the *Psalmes*, which never reached Queen Elizabeth.[2] Both the dedicatory poem "To the Thrice Sacred Queen Elizabeth" (or, as Waller titles it from the first line, "Even now that Care") and the accompanying epitaph, "To the Angell spirit of the most excellent Sir Philip Sidney," mourn the loss of her beloved brother who had begun the psalm translation; this effort was decorous and expected. What is surprising is the strong political statement made by the conjunction of these two poems. Apparently Mary Sidney attempted to continue not only Philip's writing but also his involvement in Protestant politics.

In "To the Angell spirit" Mary Sidney continued the partisan glorification of Sir Philip Sidney, who was not only her brother but also the hope of the more militant Protestants in England and particularly on the Continent. By 1599, Sidney had already been exalted to the position of Protestant martyr, primarily by Mary Sidney's patronage and encouragement of epitaphs. But during his life, his position in Elizabeth's court had been contradictory and frustrating. Heir to the estates of the Earl of Leicester and the Earl of Warwick, he lacked a title and land of his own. The queen alternately encouraged him with diplomatic posts and infuriated him with enforced idleness. Then, after he dared criticize her intention of marrying the Catholic Duc d'Anjou, she humiliated him by making him give way to the young Earl of Oxford, with a stinging reminder that commoners must defer to nobility.

Yet in Europe he was celebrated as the great hope of the Protestant league. As early as 1575, when Philip was just 21, the statesman Hugh Languet wrote to August of Saxony that Philip was "an Englishman of high degree. His mother is the sister of Robert, Earl of Leicester, the most powerful man at the English court." But, as James M. Osborne observes, Languet was as impressed with young Sidney's mind as with his family connections, seeing in him "the potential for a great leader of the Protestant cause, a man capable of heading a united Protestant front."[3] That opinion was generally held among European Protestants. William of Orange even offered Philip his daughter, and as dowry a position as lord of Holland and Zealand. Although Queen Elizabeth did not approve the marriage, William later called Philip "one of the ripest, and greatest Counsellors of Estate . . . that at this day lived in Europe."[4] It was only in his own country of England, and with his own queen that Sidney had little recognition, a situation the family attributed to envy at court. Hence "Angell spirit" pictures him at a heavenly court "where never envy bites" (l. 63).

Although the psalms are officially dedicated to the queen, Mary Sidney declares that they are written only for her brother:

> To thee pure sprite, to thee alones addres't
> this coupled worke, by double int'rest thine:
> First rais'de by thy blest hand, and what is mine
> inspird by thee, thy secrett power imprest.
>
> ("Angell spirit," ll. 1–4)

In a statement more accurate than most dedications, the countess acknowledges a double debt to Philip. He had begun the psalm translations before he left for the Netherlands, probably during one of the periods when he visited Mary at Wilton. When he died from wounds received at the battle of Zutphen, where he was fighting under Leicester's command in an attempt to free the Protestant Netherlands from Catholic Spain, he had translated only 43 of the 150 psalms. The countess, as she says, completed the psalms as a memorial to her brother; through him she found her voice. As Gary Waller and Beth Wynne Fisken have demonstrated, she learned her craft by following his model and by revising his drafts of the early psalms;[5] given her deprecation of her own abilities, it is probable that he had discussed the psalms with her and indicated what alterations he had planned to make. The rest of the work was her own, though inspired by him.

Had he not died and so "reft the world of all / what man could show, which we [in our imperfection] perfection call," Mary declares, then "this half maim'd peece had sorted with the best" (ll. 16–18). Her motivation in writing is clearly stated: "it hath no further scope to goe, / nor other purpose but to honor thee" (ll. 29–30). Although more than two-thirds of the psalms are hers, she takes the humble place, comparing her contribution to his work as "little streames" which "flowe to their great sea" (ll. 32–33). The next stanzas praise Philip as the "wonder of men, sole borne perfection's kinde" (l. 37), a Phoenix adorned by Heaven, fit to be adored by Earth. Her loss is such that it strikes her dumb, as it would other writers: "who knewe thee best doeth knowe / There lives no witt that may thy praise become" (ll. 48–49). Now that he is placed in heaven "among thy fellow lights," she mourns that day has been "put out, my life in darkenes cast" (ll. 57–58). As he sings with the heavenly choir in a court where he finally receives the honor he deserves, his works are, on earth, "Immortal Monuments of thy faire fame" (l. 71). Although they remain incomplete, yet "there will live thy ever praised name" (l. 77). Concluding with a prayer that he will "receive theise Hymnes" (l. 85), she signs the poem "By the Sister of that Incomparable Sidney."[6]

Although "Angell spirit" is primarily a lament for personal loss, the conjunction of this epitaph with the dedication to Elizabeth makes a powerful political statement. All eyes "which are not blindely madde," Elizabeth is told, praise Sidney's words "beyond compare" (ll. 69–70). Had he been spared to peace, he would have completed these "Immortal Monuments"—a reminder that he died in Elizabeth's service, in a war the Sidneys believed doomed by her withholding of money and supplies. In

"Angell spirit," then, the countess was reminding Elizabeth that as queen, she did not favor "the wonder of men, sole borne perfection's kinde" (l. 37) as she ought, and, by implication, that she was not fulfilling her godly duties by defending the faith as Philip had done.

The dedication is even more pointed. In the tradition of those relegated to the margins of society, she uses flattery to instruct, but "To the Thrice Sacred Queen Elizabeth" does not contain the fulsome praise of Elizabeth one would expect from the title, from her obsequious 1601 letter to the queen, and from the decorum of the cult of the *Faerie Queene*. The relatively subdued compliments of the opening stanzas flatter Elizabeth's scholarship but serve primarily as a reminder that the fate of Europe rests in her hands: she is the one "on whom in chief dependeth to dispose / what Europe acts in theise most active times" ("Even now," ll. 7–8). Like her family and like the Geneva Protestants, Mary Sidney apparently believed that Elizabeth herself was the key to the establishment of the Protestant faith, in Europe as well as England.

In stanzas 3 through 5 the countess again mourns her coauthor, Philip. The topic is deftly introduced; the Senders "which once in two, now in one Subject goe, / the poorer left, the richer reft awaye" (ll. 21–22). (Incidentally, these lines may be taken as evidence that she had worked on the psalms from the beginning; once there had been two authors, now only one.) In a most accurate metaphor, she declares that "hee did warpe, I weav'd this webb to end" (l. 27); that is, he set up the loom with the structural warp threads while she supplied the pattern of the weave. Now "I the Cloth in both our names present, / A liverie robe to be bestowed by thee" (ll. 33–34). Once again the countess is reminding the queen that Sidney died wearing her livery and that, had she chosen rightly, he would have lived to wear it in her service. Now the countess must weave a web of words to create a livery with which to adorn Elizabeth, a livery which would emphasize the queen's own position as servant to God and to the Protestant cause. The queen can then bestow this livery on others, those who serve her cause and God's.

It would not be surprising if, at the close of Elizabeth's reign, the countess believed it to be her obligation to speak out—however gently—for the Protestant cause in the tradition of her family, a tradition begun by her grandfather, Northumberland, who had been executed for his attempt to prevent Mary Tudor's Catholic rule by putting Lady Jane Grey (Mary's aunt) on the throne. The next generation of Dudleys carried on the Protestant battle. Northumberland's sons—Robert Dudley, Earl of Leicester, and Ambrose Dudley, Earl of Warwick—were the primary patrons for Protestant writings in England and advocated military intervention on the Continent in behalf of Protestants. Northumberland's daughters married men who strongly supported this cause: Mary Dudley married Henry Sidney, Lord President of the Marches of Wales and Lord Deputy of Ireland; Katherine Dudley married the Earl of Huntingdon, Lord President of the Council of the North. Only Mary Dudley Sidney produced legitimate heirs for the alliance: her son Philip Sidney married Frances Walsingham, cementing the alliance with her father, Sir Francis Walsingham, Secretary of State; and her daughter Mary Sidney married the Earl of Pembroke, who succeeded Henry Sidney as Lord President of the Marches of Wales. (For convenience I shall refer to this tightly related group as the Dudley/Sidney alliance.) Among them they controlled approximately two-thirds of the land under Elizabeth's rule.

With the Protestant Elizabeth on the throne, the Dudley/Sidney alliance had followed Castiglione's optimistic advice that the courtier should speak the truth to a ruler even when it would displease her, for good princes love good counselors.[7] But speaking the truth (as they saw it) to Elizabeth did not always have the desired result. The countess had been involved, at least indirectly, in the most famous of these attempts to influence the queen. Endeavoring to influence Elizabeth to support the Huguenots against the Valois, those great Protestant earls met at her London home, Baynard's Castle, to plan the letter dissuading Elizabeth from the marriage to the Duc d'Anjou.[8] The alliance, which chose Philip as spokesman, was working closely with the Huguenots, particularly Philippe de Mornay, Sieur du Plessis Marly. During the previous eighteen months, Mornay had been an effective ambassador to Queen Elizabeth, securing a grant from her of some eighty thousand crowns for the Huguenot cause. According to his wife, "his chief friends in England" were Sir Francis Walsingham, Secretary of State, and Philip Sidney, "the most highly accomplished gentleman in England."[9] Soon after Mornay's infant daughter had been astutely christened Elizabeth (with Sidney as godfather), he "left hurriedly," presumably because of the queen's anger at his opposition to the Anjou marriage: "M. du Plessis heartily disapproved of this marriage both on account of religion and no less for reasons of state," his wife recalls in a statement which could serve for Sidney as well. Despite the fact that "the Queen did him the honor to discuss it with him confidentially" (or perhaps because she did), Mornay departed so quickly for the Continent that he had to leave his family behind, presumably under the protection of his "chief friends in England" (p. 171). Shortly after Mornay's abrupt departure, the letter was composed which brought Philip into disfavor with Elizabeth and into retirement at Wilton with his sister Mary. The queen apparently did not appreciate Philip's blunt reminder that she was irrevocably tied to the Protestant cause: as Protestants "live by your happy government, so are they your chief, if not your sole, strength."[10] She cannot rely on Catholics, many of whom think her "an usurper" (that is, bastard), who discount her because of the pope's excommunication, and who have already risen against her in the Northern rebellion (pp. 292–93). Sidney warns that the hearts of Protestants "will be galled, if not alienated" if she takes "a Frenchman and a Papist . . . the son of a Jezebel of our age," one whose "brother made oblation of his sister's marriage, the easier to make massacres of our brethren in belief" (p. 291). Anjou himself, "having his liberty and principle estate by the Huguenot means" has shown treachery, despoiling the city of La Charitie "with fire and sword" (p. 292). Mornay himself could not have stated the Huguenot position more forcibly.

In the end, Elizabeth did not marry her "little frog," Anjou, and perhaps never meant to. Yet she never favored the members of the Dudley / Sidney alliance as she once had. Perhaps it was for personal reasons (she was violently jealous when Leicester married her cousin Lettice), or perhaps it was for political reasons (Cecil counseled moderation, urging her to stay out of the continental religious wars). Whatever the reason, even Philip's death for the cause at Zutphen and his subsequent enshrinement as a martyr could not prevail with Elizabeth when, in a space of nine years, the Dudley/Sidney alliance was destroyed; as Spenser summarized the grim situation, their "hope is failed, and come to pass [their] dread." Both Mary Sidney's father and her mother were spared grief for Philip, dying earlier that same year (1586);[11] they were soon followed by her uncles Leicester (1588), Warwick (1590), and Huntingdon (1595), all of whom died without legitimate children. Philip's father-in-law, Walsingham, died in 1590, and Mary's own husband, Pembroke, lay ill and irascible as his duties and honors in Wales were stripped away.[12] Her youngest brother, Thomas, had died in 1595, leaving only Robert who was in his tenth year as governor at Flushing, a place he said "must be the grave of my youth, and I fear of my fortune also." Recognizing his sister's plight in 1599, Robert, himself unwell, begged leave to return home because "my Lord of Pembroke's weaknesses increase . . . and my sister . . . hath now no friend to rely upon, her son being under years, but myself."[13]

With no men left in England to speak for the family, the countess was emboldened to address the queen herself, however deprecating her self-comparison with Philip. Women generally did need a "friend"—father, brother, husband, or son—to speak for them at court, but it was more common for women of the nobility to act for themselves and on behalf of others than Robert's letter would indicate. For example, Mary Sidney's own mother, Mary Dudley, acted as Queen Elizabeth's intermediary with both the Spanish ambassador Quadra and the ambassador of Emperor Ferdinand I.[14] She also interceded with the Earl of Sussex, the Lord Chamberlain, seeking better rooms for her husband at court, and with Lord Burghley requesting that her husband not be made a baron—because of financial constraints elevation to the peerage would be "utter ruwin" to the family.[15] Mary Sidney herself apparently had an effective intercessory style, for when her brother Robert's leave was delayed in 1597 she wrote a series of letters to the Lord Treasurer. Although these letters are not extant, Rowland Whyte reported to Robert, "I never reade any thing that could express an earnest desire like to this."[16] An even better indication of her persuasive powers is that the leave was granted, as was her 1601 plea to the queen that Mary's young son Philip be accepted at court. She also handled marriage negotiations for her son and Bridget, granddaughter of Lord Burghley; was involved in punishing rebels in her town of Cardiff, Wales; and negotiated with Cecil, Earl of Salisbury, for the wardship of a youth.[17]

In addition to fulfilling these business and family duties, the countess became the primary agent in the refashioning of Sidney's life into a "notable image of virtue," as was widely recognized at the time. Edmund Spenser dedicated "The Ruines of Time" (a 1591 lament for Philip) to her "as whom it most speciallie concerneth." At her request Thomas Moffet wrote *Nobilis or A View of the Life and Death of a Sidney,* a panegyric setting forth Philip's life as a model for her eldest son, William Lord Herbert; it was subsequently published to serve as an example to others as well. Furthermore, Spenser's elegy "Astrophel," published in *Colin Clouts Come Home Againe* with elegies by Bryskett, Ralegh, and Roydon, includes "The Dolefull Lay of Clorinda," once attributed to Spenser but now acknowledged to be by the countess herself. In this poem she mourns Philip, whose death was "Great losse to all that ever him did see . . . but greatest loss to me." As in "Angell spirit" she pictures him in Heaven, enjoying bliss "from jealous rancor free."[18]

The "Dolefull Lay" and "Angell spirit" are primarily personal laments, but in the dedication to Queen Elizabeth, the full intent of these epitaphs becomes clearer. Not only will Philip's memory be sustained by Mary Sidney's completion and publication of his work, but his efforts to establish a Protestant league will be carried on. If the countess is barred by her sex from political councils and from the battlefield, she will use her pen. Thus by reminding the queen of Philip's death in the first half of the dedication, Mary Sidney appears to have been continuing the family tradition of seeking to influence Elizabeth toward a more radical Protestant stance. By comparing Elizabeth to the psalmist in the second half of her dedication, she was continuing the tradition of admonitory flattery which was a standard element in the dedication of Scripture to sovereigns in both England and France.[19] Although relegated to the margins of discourse by her sex, she found a model in these vernacular translations by exiles, themselves relegated to the margins by their religion and politics; flattery is their safest weapon.[20] Using Genevan models for her choice of genre and for her trope (the David comparison), she firmly established her role as spokesperson for the Dudley/Sidney alliance and for the Protestant cause.

Two of the primary sources for the Sidneian psalms, the Geneva Bible and the Marot-Bèze psalter, were intensely political, both originating with the Protestant exiles in Geneva who had strong ties to the Dudley/Sidney alliance.[21] The Genevan community had sent their psalms to Elizabeth in celebration of her accession; two years later, when the biblical translation was complete, they dedicated it to the young queen, calling her the Zerubbabel charged with setting up the spiritual temple, and instructing her "to plant and maynetyn his holy worde to the advancement of his glorie, for your owne honour and salvation of your soule.''[22] Like the Israelites, Elizabeth is beset with enemies who ''traeterously seke to erect idolatrie and to destroy your majestie.'' Because of her birth, Elizabeth obviously had to support the Protestant cause; the Genevan exiles are not above telling her that the dissemination of Scriptures in English and the rebuilding of the Protestant church in England are necessary for the saving of her own soul as well as her kingdom. Ominously, the dedication praises the example of Asa, who enacted a law that ''whosoever wolde not seke the Lord God of Israel, shulde be slayne, whether he were smale or great, man or woman'' (p. iii). Elizabeth, early in her reign, apparently agreed with this statement of a monarch's duties, as may be deduced from her poem, ''The Doubt of Future Foes'':

> No foreign banishd wight shall anchor in this port;
> Our realm brooks not seditious sects, let them
>   elsewhere resort.
> My rusty sword through rest shall first his edge employ
> To poll their tops that seek such change or gape for
>   future joy.[23]

Yet in 1569, although Elizabeth outlined the duties of the monarch as including the salvation of her subjects' souls, she condemns both the use of force within the kingdom and ''outward wars'' as ''things unfit to be used for establishing or reforming of Christian religion,'' in direct contrast to the conviction of the more radical Protestants that force was a legitimate means of establishing the true faith.[24] They urged the Dudleys, in particular, to use the sword to defend the gospel. Lest Leicester flag in his zeal, John Feild tells him that he sins if he does not champion the gospel; similarly, Christopher Fetherstone uses his 1586 dedication of François Hotman to praise Leicester for taking arms ''in so just and holie a quarrel, as is the maintenance of his sacred religion,'' promising that God ''is on your side.'' He closes with a prayer that pictures Leicester returning home from the Netherlands received ''with such joyfull acclamations and songs of triumph, as David was by the daughters of Israel'' (in Rosenberg, pp. 250, 271). That prophesy soon became a bitter irony, for Leicester came home that year with the body of Sir Philip Sidney; there were no songs of triumph.

Mary Sidney would have been familiar with the biblical comparisons used in the Geneva dedication to justify crushing the ungodly and to warn of similar fates which would befall lax rulers.[25] Jehoshaphat, Josiah, and Hezekiah are cited as examples "to all godly rulers to reforme their countreys and to establish the worde of God with all spede, lest the wrath of the Lord fall upon them for the neglecting thereof" (p. iii). The marginalia of the Geneva version also warn what will happen to tyrants who do not support the true faith. For example, when Jezebel is killed (2 Kings 9:33), the note reads, "This he did by the mocion of the Spirit of God, that her blood shulde be shed, that had shed the blood of innocents, to be a spectacle and example of Gods judgments to all tyrants." Examples need not be multiplied, but there is another side, the promise that the people will support a godly monarch like David: "A good governour ought to be so deare to his people, that they will rather lose their lives, then ought harm shulde come to him" (2 Samuel 18:3).

Calvin's successor in Geneva, Théodore de Bèze, a close ally of the Dudleys, delineates a similar theory of conditional obedience to sovereigns in his *Droit des magistrats* (1574). Although David was chosen by God, he still had to be elected by the people before his reign, implying that the ultimate power resides in the people, not the monarch. Because David was a just monarch, the people were obligated to obey him, but David's own rebellion against the tyrant Saul had been lawful.[26] Philippe de Mornay, who was probably a close friend of Mary as well as of Philip, elaborated this principle in *Vindiciae contra tyrannos*: "The obligation between prince and people is ever reciprocal and mutual. He promises to be a just prince: they, to obey him if he is one. The people, therefore, is obligated to the prince conditionally, he to the people absolutely" (p. 191). There is "a compact . . . between the prince and the people that as long as he rules well he will be obeyed well," but the officers of the kingdom have a duty "to expel him from office forcibly" (p. 196) if he becomes a tyrant.

Addressing this same issue, Anthony Gilby, in dedicating his translation of de Bèze to the Countess of Huntingdon, Mary's aunt, makes a direct comparison between Israel and England, tracing the history from Hezekiah, who reformed religion, through Manasses who brought back idolatry, and finally to Josiah, who restored the faith. Gilby beseeches the countess "to consider the state of our time, and compare it with former times, that we may see what is like to come upon us, unles we do watch and pray."[27] Twenty-two years have not been enough to bring religion to perfection under Elizabeth, he warns, and "the horrible sinnes of former times are not yet purged with true tears of repentance" (sig. a3v). Because idolatry remains in England, particularly reverence to the eucharistic wafer, he fears that God will visit the land with plagues. Nevertheless, Elizabeth is "our Hezekias," reforming religion, however imperfectly. Because of their connections with her family, Mary Sidney must have been familiar with these works dictating the obligations of the monarch through biblical comparisons.

Although Zerubbabel, Asa, Daniel, Hezekiah, and dozens of other biblical figures were commonly used as examplars to the monarch, Mary Sidney found in David the most apt comparison; he was both persecuted by a tyrant—thereby providing an example to Protestants persecuted for their faith—and he became a lawful king—thereby providing an example to monarchs. On the one hand, the psalmist cries out for succour and/or revenge, as in Psalm 35, introduced in the Geneva by this summary: "So long as Saul was enemie to David, all that had anie authoritie under him to flatter their King (as is the course of the worlde) did also most cruelly persecute David: against whom he praieth God to pleade and to avenge his cause." On the other hand, David instructs his son and successor Solomon "how hard a thing it is to governe, and that none can do it wel, except he obey God" (1 Kings 2:3). This duality is neatly summarized by the argument introducing 2 Samuel in the Geneva Bible:

This second boke declareth the noble acts of David . . . also his great troubles and dangers, which he susteined bothe within his house and without, and treasons were wrong against him, partly by false counselors, fained friends and flatterers and partly by some of his own children and people: and how by Gods assistance he overcame all difficulties and enjoyed his kingdom in rest and peace.

By the time the countess wrote her own dedication to Elizabeth, the "Protestant David"—the David found in the commentaries of Luther, Melanchthon, Calvin, de Bèze, and Bucer—was already well established in France as a paradigm for the Reformed church.[28] In England, the David comparison was deemed particularly appropriate to Elizabeth, as Mary Sidney recognizes when she declares, "how justly square his haughty Ditties to thy glorious days," elaborating the comparison in stanza 9:

For ev'n thy Rule is painted in his Raigne:
both cleere in right: both nigh by wrong opprest:
And each at length (man crossing God in vaine)
Possest of place, and each in peace possest.
Proud Philistines did interrupt his rest,
The foes of heav'n no lesse have beene thy foes;
Hee with great conquest, thou with greater blest;
Thou sure to winn, and hee secure to lose.

Like David, Elizabeth had been menaced by an ungodly ruler; like David, she had been vindicated by God and blessed with a triumphant rule. Of course the countess does not make explicit the equation of Philistines with Catholics, but she did not need to; the text had become self-explicating. That equation was already as familiar a trope in the Protestant literature as was the comparison of the Protestant monarch (Elizabeth or Henri de Navarre) to David. For example, in his *Coronation of David* (1588), Edmund Bunny of York compared "the late unnatural practices" against Elizabeth with the various attempts on David's life, predicting that as David at last overcame his foes so Elizabeth would possess the land in peace.[29]

The countess was astute in choosing this David comparison, because Elizabeth herself had implied an identification with David in her own youthful translation of Psalm 13, appropriately a call for succor and revenge in time of affliction by "the foes of heaven." To apply the psalm to her own condition, Elizabeth needed only follow the oft reprinted advice of Athanasius, "But whosoever take this booke in his hande, he reputeth and thinketh all the wordes he readeth . . . to be as his very own wordes spoken in his owne person."[30] When her translation of the psalm was printed in 1548, John Bale's dedication interpreted it as an anti-Catholic statement:

By this do your grace unto us signifie, that the baren doctrine and good workes without faith of the hypocrites, which in their latine ceremonies serve their bellies and not Christ in gredily devouringe the patrimony of poor widows and orphanes, are both execrable in themselves, and abhominable afore God.[31]

Whether or not this reading was intended by the queen, this psalm may explain the penultimate phrase of the countess's dedication, asking that the queen may "sing what God doth"—as she had once before.

The tradition of identifying monarchs with David, the parallel between

Elizabeth's life and David's, and the queen's own early identification with David's psalms are certainly enough to account for Mary Sidney's extended analogy. However, she was probably also influenced by de Bèze's commentary on the psalms, which had virtually equated David with Henri de Navarre and the Valois with David's enemies. Both the author and the translator of that inflammatory commentary were closely tied to Mary Sidney's family; it is almost certain that she had studied the commentary.

De Bèze's connection with the Dudley/Sidney alliance may have begun prior to 1569 when the Earl of Huntingdon petitioned Queen Elizabeth for permission to sell his estates and bring ten thousand men to aid the Huguenot cause. Philip Sidney's visit to France, his experience of the St. Bartholomew massacre, and his friendship with Mornay and with their mentor Hugh Languet would have tightened that connection.[32] A further link between de Bèze and Huntingdon, to whom de Bèze dedicated his psalms and commentaries, would have been supplied by their mutual friend Anthony Gilby. De Bèze and Gilby had apparently worked together on the Genevan translations of Scripture. John Alexander has argued convincingly that the 1557 annotated psalms of the Genevan community were primarily the work of Gilby, "the most competent Hebraist of the Englishmen in Geneva," with reference to the Sternhold and Hopkins psalter (1556) and Calvin's commentaries (1557): all three works, primary sources for Mary Sidney's own psalm translations, were the simultaneous product of community effort during that period.[33] Gilby was thus well qualified by scholarship and by friendship to translate de Bèze's commentaries, just as the Sidneys translated doctrinal works of their friend Mornay in order to reach the general English populace.

In the psalter de Bèze goes beyond his 1574 treatise, *Du droit des magistrats*, which, as we have seen, used the example of David to advocate resistance against tyrants, by using David (most improbably) as an example of outright revolt. Equating Henri de Navarre with David, he proceeds to equate the Catholic Valois with David's enemies in comparisons that could not have escaped his readers.[34] For example, in the commentary for Psalm 52, Saul's massacre of the priests of Nob becomes a parallel for the St. Bartholomew massacre:

This Psalme is now also verie profitable, seeing there never want Princes, who do persecute the godlie, and specialle the pastors of the Churches, with alkinde of crueltie: and there hath bin alwaies a great number of flatterers, which have inflamed their rage with divers false accusations, a most heavie example of which wickednes more cruel than that of old, we have seen of late in the kingdom of France. (p. 117)

The first verse of Gilby's translation of this psalm could be read as a direct accusation against those in Rome who were boasting of the massacre: "But darest thou boast, even of this thy most cruel mischiefes (a valiant man forsooth! which hast slaine so manie unarmed men, not once resisting thee) howbeit notwithstanding, thou shalt never be able to destroie the assemblie of the godlie." Thus David's revolt against Saul (as de Bèze portrays it) becomes justification for the Huguenot uprising after St. Bartholomew's Eve. Edward Gosselin has argued that for de Bèze, David "elucidated the principles of resistance established in his political tracts, justified the removal of the Valois king, and displayed the nature of the holy kingship to be constituted in France by Henri de Navarre" ("Tempore Belli," p. 31). He notes that Psalm 109, David's prayer that God will crush his enemies, becomes for de Bèze virtually "a call to commit regicide and to establish the new regnum Davidicum" ("Two Views," p. 66).

As Rathmell, Waller, and others have recognized, the primary literary model for the Sidneian psalter was the French psalter of 1562, based on the fifty psalms of Clément Marot (written 1532–43) and completed by de Bèze.[35] Philip and Mary Sidney may have chosen this model for strictly literary reasons; the varied meters and rhymes employed are far superior to the thumping monotony of the English psalters, particularly the ubiquitous Sternhold and Hopkins version. But these Huguenot psalms were inherently political, even without de Bèze's 1580 commentaries. Calvin had said that singing psalms would sustain Christians in affliction; identifying their cause with that of the psalmist, his followers appropriated the psalms to their own condition, finding in them a strong—even militant— sense of identity, as Stanford Reid has demonstrated. When they went into battle, the Huguenots sang Psalm 68, "Let God arise, let his enemies be scattered." When the Prince of Condé arrived in Orleans, people sang in the streets, "If it had not been the Lord who was on our side, now may Orleans say . . . ." Martyrs in England went to the stake singing Psalm 130; in Antwerp a sermon by Dr. Hermanus was followed by psalm singing and then a riot in which the crowd demolished all the church images; in Scotland, Mary Queen of Scots was welcomed home in 1561 by crowds singing psalms under her bedroom window. About twenty years later, when the exiled John Durie returned to Edinburgh, some two thousand of his followers processed to St. Giles Church singing Psalm 124 ("Now may Israel say") and so terrified Esme Stuart, Duke of Lennox, that he fled Scotland, "more affrayed of this sight than anie thing that ever he had seen before in Scotland."[36]

Because of the importance of the Marot-Bèze psalter to the militant Protestants, those psalms aroused fierce retaliation from Catholics. Perhaps the best indicator of the inflammable material that the Sidneys were using as a model for their psalter is *Le Contrepoison des Cinquante-Deux Chansons de Clement Marot, faulsement intitlees par luy Psalmes de David,* written in 1560 by Artus Désiré. Using the same meter and tunes as the familiar psalter, Désiré parodied the words. Lest his unsubtle technique escape the readers, the dedication concludes with instruction to Henry II, telling him how to govern the kingdom, just as the Marian exiles had instructed Elizabeth:

> Notre Seigneur, qu'il vous doint telle grace
> Que vois puissiez exterminer la race
> Des Chiens mastins obstines et mauvais
> A fin que tous nous puissions vivre en paix.[37]

Like the dedication of the Geneva Bible, Désiré's dedication recommends the slaughter of the infidels—Protestants, in this case.

Although the psalms were not used as a battle cry in England until the civil war of the next century, the returning Marian exiles brought back the custom of singing psalms "after the Geneva fashion," gathering at St. Paul's cross in London, to Elizabeth's dismay.[38] These psalm-singing Protestants were a constant worry to Elizabeth, for they threatened her careful religious compromise by continuing to use every possible occasion to instruct her on the means necessary to maintain the true faith, just as the Genevan dedication on her accession had done: such pointed application of the psalms to current political issues was a very different matter from daily readings of psalms in the Book of Common Prayer.

Although Elizabeth herself had used a French psalter early in her reign,[39] Mary Sidney's gift of a psalter modeled on the Huguenot psalms could itself be interpreted as a political statement in 1599. When coupled with a lament for Sir Philip Sidney, already acknowledged as a Protestant martyr, and a dedicatory poem which began with a reference to the Continent, the political intent of her gift would be unmistakable; perhaps that is why her psalms were never delivered to the queen.

While the countess is certainly advocating neither slaughter of heretics nor regicide, unlike the more radical Huguenot works—Elizabeth is still England's David—her reference to the early adversities of Elizabeth do emphasize the prudence of a stalwart defense of the Protestant faith; like Philip's letter, Mary Sidney's dedication is a reminder that for Elizabeth the Catholics can only be the Philistines. In his peroration, which Elizabeth could not have forgotten, Philip Sidney had echoed the Genevan dedication: "You must take it for a singular honour God hath done you, to be indeed the only protector of his church." If "you make that religion, upon which you stand . . . [your] only strength" and maintain alliance with those abroad of similar faith, then "your Majesty is sure enough from your mightiest enemies." If the queen is steadfast, Sidney promises, then Protestants will continue to support her, and her reign will be glorious: "Doing as you do, you shall be, as you are, the example of princes, the ornament of this age . . . and the perfect mirror of your posterity" (in Gray, p. 303). That Elizabeth knew how to interpret such flattery is clear. During one of the early progresses, she had responded to the usual fulsome praise by saying, "I now thank you for putting me in mynd of my duety, and that should be in me."[40]

Mary Sidney's own flattering comparison of Elizabeth to David is carefully connected to her concluding prayer that the aging queen will be granted years "farre past hir living Peeres/and rivall still to Judas Faithfull King" (ll. 93–94). Like her use of the tradition of admonitory flattery and of the David comparison, this prayer for the sovereign is part of the partisan tradition. As de Bèze declares in his preface to Psalm 72, "When God does raise up such kings [as David], one must recognize that they are singular gifts of God . . . so that they may know that it is for themselves that they pray when they pray for their Lords and Magistrates" (Gilby, p. 159). This psalm is a prayer that God will teach "the king, whome thou hast appointed, the rules of right government . . . That he may justlie governe, not his people, but thine" (v. 1). If the monarch governs justly, "his memorie shal be for ever, even durable as the Sunne: and this king shall be an example of al felicitie unto al nations" (v. 17). Despite Elizabeth's negligence toward her brothers, Mary probably agreed with de Bèze's earlier conclusion that "England is the happiest [kingdom] in the world today" because the authority of the English monarch is founded on the consent of Parliament: "The happy repose the English have enjoyed . . . under the mild and beneficent government of their most gracious Queen Elizabeth, as compared with the wretched . . . condition of so many other countries, shows . . . what happiness . . . there is in moderation of royal power if it is rightly observed" (de Bèze, *Du Droit,* p. 118). But royal power can be correctly moderated only when the monarch listens to her subjects, as the countess is asking her to do.

As the last strong voice of the Dudley/Sidney alliance left in Elizabethan England, the countess not only supported the Protestant cause through her translation of a work by the Huguenot leader Mornay, and through her establishment of a hagiography which elevated her brother Philip to the status of Protestant martyr, but she also attempted to address the queen, decorously but directly. Like her psalms, Mary's dedicatory admonitions are far more subtle and literary than most of their predecessors. Nevertheless, it is clear that the countess is not merely praising Elizabeth by the David comparison; like the Genevan Protestants and like her brother Philip, she also is exhorting her to fulfill her obligations as monarch, defend the true faith, and so "doo What men may sing."

BETH WYNNE FISKEN

Mary Sidney's *Psalmes:* Education and Widsom

MARY SIDNEY's verse translations of the Psalms began as an education in how to write poetry and ended in a search for wisdom. Through close work with her brother Philip's translations as well as painstaking revision of her own efforts, she slowly gained the confidence to develop an individual style which stressed the immediacy of God's power and presence and dramatized the quandary of the psalmist seeking God's grace in adversity. Eventually Sidney's growing confidence in her work encouraged her to develop original patterns of imagery, reflecting her public experiences as lady-in-waiting at court and manager of her husband's estate as well as her individual perceptions as a woman and a mother. In doing so, she transformed her verse translations into independent poems and exercises in private meditation, teaching herself not only how to write poetry, but ultimately, how to speak to God.

Mary Sidney's process of composition revealed her dedication to the classical ideal of the education of a poet. As Gary Waller has demonstrated in his study of the extant manuscripts of her psalms, she began by revising her brother Philip Sidney's versions of Psalms 1 to 43, and then undertook the rest of the psalms, working between two copy-texts and constantly reworking and revising, at times arriving at varying independent versions of the same psalm. This process of composition, begun sometime after her brother's death in 1586, continued steadily until 1599, when the presentation copy was readied for a projected visit from Queen Elizabeth. Mary

Sidney learned first from imitating a master, her brother, and then through perseverance and laborious revision, she discovered her own style. Certainly the dazzling variety of stanzaic forms and metrical patterns she experimented with constituted a course in the discipline of suiting sound to sense that led to a technical mastery of poetic forms.[1]

The Sidneian psalms, with their inventive structure and extended imagery, were a significant departure from the unadorned literalism which was found in, for example, the prose paraphrases of the Book of Common Prayer and the Geneva Bible, or in the simple metrical psalms in common measure of the Sternhold-Hopkins psalter, a literalism which was deemed necessary for the congregational use of psalms as communal expressions of Christian devotion. Rather, the Sidneian psalms addressed a parallel tradition of reading and reciting the psalms in solitary, meditative sessions, examining the relationship between the individual spirit and God. Certainly, Mary Sidney's choice of the Psalms as the basis for her poetic endeavors reflects her intense commitment to this introspective Protestant tradition which stressed the role of the psalms as meditative paradigms; yet perhaps it also reveals a shrewd understanding on her part that religious translations were a sanctioned form of intellectual exercise for noblewomen of her time, Queen Elizabeth herself having tried her hand at them. Writing without models of serious, committed women poets for her to emulate, Mary Sidney erected her version of the Psalms on the foundations of her brother's work, plumb with the religious practices and social conventions of her time. Thus, by doubly buttressing her work, she was gradually able to build sufficient self-confidence to develop a poetic voice that would fully express the richness of her interior spiritual life.

Although Mary Sidney's poetic efforts were nourished in the security of the socially accepted forms of her time which sanctioned modest displays of scholarly attainment when subordinated to pious endeavors, she soon surpassed the conventional boundaries of mere ladylike accomplishment. Her scholarship was thorough; she consulted many available sources such as the Prayer Book Psalter to Coverdale's Great Bible of 1539, the Geneva Bible of 1560, the Bishops' Bible of 1568, and the Marot-Bèze psalter of 1562, as well as Golding's translation of Calvin's commentaries and Gilby's version of de Bèze. Mary Sidney was a learned and sensitive exegete, seeking to dramatize the predicament of the psalmist and through her reconstruction of the psalmist's voice to establish her own relationship to the spiritual issues of her time, defining her views by selecting or rejecting the glosses offered by others and then adding comparisons and elaborations unique to her. In these verse translations she discarded the literalism of her previous translations of Garnier's *Antonie* and Mornay's *Discours* in favor of a mixture of translation and interpretation which allowed for additions based on personal reflection and experience. This freer translation made her psalms exercises in the classical mode of imitation, in which Sidney strove to reconstruct the style and matter of the original within a context that would carry weight and meaning, first for her contemporary society, and ultimately, for herself as an individual. As such, her psalms are grounded in the Protestant tradition which stressed the application of the Scriptures to the situation of the individual. The psalms were interpreted simultaneously as the "emotional history of all the faithful, and . . . the particular spiritual autobiography of every particular Christian." Hence, by reworking them, Mary Sidney sought to become a "correlative type," a new David forging "a new work in the same spirit, under the impress of the same emotions."[2] Yet, for her, it was equally important that the meaning of the originals be adhered to faithfully, because to do otherwise would be to set one's own work above that of God—the very antithesis of wisdom. To personalize the meaning of the Psalms without distorting it was a delicate and demanding task, requiring both judgment and sensitivity to tone and connotation.

The Psalms were a particularly appropriate choice for models in poetic composition, as Philip Sidney himself urged in his "Defence of Poesie." The best English scholars of that time recognized that the Hebrew originals were themselves remarkable poems, and they deplored the lack of an English hymnal the equal of the French Marot-Bèze psalter at reconstructing the beauty of the originals. The complex voice of the psalmist, David's "often and free chaunging of persons," as Philip Sidney described it in his "Defence,"[3] contributed to the immediacy and intensity of the psalms as dramatizations of the conflicts of the spirit wrestling with itself in search of God. Consequently, the Psalms were thought to be a Bible in miniature, a searching "Anatomy of all the partes of the Soule," revealing "all the greefes, sorowes, feares, doutes, hopes, cares, anguishes, and finally all the trubblesome motions wherewith mennes mindes are woont to be turmoyled."[4] Therefore, the psalmist's voice subsumes all our individual voices and private concerns, and as a result, the voice of the translator becomes our voice and "translates" our hopes and desires into his or her expression of David's petitions and prayers. Not only was Mary Sidney as translator of the Psalms encouraged by her material to speak in many voices, but also to speak in her own voice when her voice was congruent with the meaning of the text. The translator, as well as the reader in private meditation, is continually urged to apply the psalms to his or her own situation for the full revelation of their meaning.[5] Not only did her material challenge Sidney to stretch her poetic repertoire to dramatize the psalmist's many personations, but also it ultimately threw her back on herself, to develop the confidence to find a poetic equivalent for her own small, personal voice, "my self, my seely self in me."[6]

By examining some of the revisions Mary Sidney made when reworking and condensing the final stanzas of seven of her brother's psalms, we can see how specific exercises in versification led to the eventual development of a style independent of her brother's influence, reflecting her own ideas, tastes, and experiences. By setting herself the task of condensing and tightening her brother's stanzas, Mary Sidney taught herself how to sharpen an image by eliminating superfluous expressions and how to dramatize rather than explain. For example, at the end of Psalm 26, she changed "That hand whose strength should help of bribes is full"[7] to "With right hands stain'd with gifts," permitting us to supply the moral connotations of "right hands." She chose to emphasize the force of the speaker's righteousness reflected in his carriage, his physical pride in standing erect and walking a straight path, in her revision of

> But in integrity
> My stepps shall guided be,
> Then me redeem Lord then be mercifull,
> Even truth that for me sayes
> My foot on justice stayes,
> And tongue is prest to publish out thy prayse
> (ll. 34–39),

to:

> But while I walk in my unspotted waies,
> Redeeme and show mee grace,
> So I in publique place,
> Sett on plaine ground, will thee Jehovah praise.
> (ll. 33–36)

Everyday routine is luminous with signs of grace if we only know how to
see them. Mary Sidney's emphasis on action rather than abstraction, her
speaker's foot "sett on plaine ground" rather than "on justice stayes,"
make the present material sphere seem laden with spiritual significance
without the need for extrapolation.

This commitment to the palpable and perceptible objects and events of
the daily routine defines the essence of the meditative self "that speaks
constantly in the presence of the supernatural, that feels the hand of the
supernatural upon himself and upon all created things."[8] There is urgent
drama in every hour of the day, as the human spirit struggles to sustain its
belief in God's grace; and it was the desolation of the soul, cut off from
God and crying for a sign of forgiveness, that most engaged Mary Sidney as
a writer.

In fact, throughout her *Psalmes,* Mary Sidney tended to view affirma-
tions of grace as precious gifts—awarded only after intense grappling and
soul searching—which are in imminent danger of loss because of the inca-
pacity to sustain faith through testing and ordeal. It is the intimate relationship between the supplicant spirit and God which is the focus of her
psalms and which is italicized by her style. God as portrayed by her psalmist's prophetic voice is familiar and plainspoken, often brusque and impa-
tient with human foibles:

> Bragg not you braggardes, you your saucy horne
> Lift not, lewd mates: no more with heav'ns scorne
> Daunce on in wordes your old repyning measure.
> (Ps. 75, ll. 10–12)

Yet, Mary Sidney's God is ever-present at the psalmist's elbow, available
to comfort as well as to discipline, and in the following memorable passage
from Psalm 50, both voices are counterpointed:

> Invoke my name, to me erect thy cries,
>   Thy praying plaints, when sorow stopps thy waie,
> I will undoe the knott that anguish tyes,
>   And thou at peace shalt glorifie my name:
> Mildly the good, God schooleth in this wise,
>   But this sharpe check doth to the godlesse frame:
> How fitts it thee my statutes to report?
> And of my covenant in thy talk to prate

Hating to live in right reformed sort,
And leaving in neglect what I relate?
(ll. 35–44)

In this dramatic monologue Sidney transformed the spare assurance of the original—"And call upon me in the time of trouble: so will I hear thee, and thou shalt praise me"[9]—into an active, sympathetic engagement with the tortured spirit of the petitioner: "I will undoe the knott that anguish tyes." The God imaged in these psalms penetrates the recesses of our souls and speaks to us in our own language to make us understand His will.

Mary Sidney not only personalized and dramatized the psalmist's relationship with God but also the internal conflicts of her speaker and, by extension, of all of us. She favored a complicated, conversational syntax studded with questions, exclamations, interruptions, and parenthetical interjections to dramatize her speaker's fits and starts of anxiety, despair, and renewed hope. At times this syntax underlines the speaker's bitterness when estranged from God and His healing grace:

Shall buried mouthes thy mercies tell?
Dust and decay
Thy truth display?
And shall thy workes of mark
Shine in the dreadfull dark?
Thy Justice where oblivions dwell?
(Ps. 88, ll. 50–54)

These headlong, tumbling questions measure the psalmist's loss of self-possession, the extent to which he is obsessed with his own suffering and self-importance, unable to wait for or even hear an answer to his complaints. At other times the speaker realizes that he has lost control and chastises himself for presumption: "What speake I? O lett me heare / What he speakes for speake he will" (Ps. 85, ll. 21–22). Often the speaker's exclamations underscore the intensity of his pleas for pardon and renewed favor: "Ah! cast me not from thee: take not againe / Thy breathing grace! againe thy comfort send me" (Ps. 51, ll. 33–34). In Psalm 62 Sidney paralleled the gradual change in her speaker's attitude from provisional to total faith in his capacity to withstand all trials, by repeating the line, "Remove I may not, move I may (l. 4), with some crucial syntactical changes: "Remove? O no: not move I may" (l. 20).

Mary Sidney's use of vigorous, colloquial language to personalize God's

voice and emphasize His nearness recreates before the reader's eye the spiritual drama of the psalmist in relation to the God who raises and crushes
him. An illusion of spontaneity is sustained by her conversational syntax
which depicts the conflicts of a mind "quailed in mind-combats mani-
fold" (Ps. 94, l. 35), continually revising and reassessing, despairing and
then disciplining itself, channeling its frustrated energies into new petitions and assertions of faith. These techniques define Mary Sidney's
style—both what she chose to preserve and stress from her sources and
models and how she chose to do so.

Not only does a characteristic style emerge from examination of Mary
Sidney's versions of the psalms, but it is also possible to sketch an outline
of her personality, temperament, tastes, and interests, particularly in those
passages in which she permitted herself greater freedom to develop or elaborate on her text, as the voice of the psalmist became distinctively her own.
Psalm 45, an epithalamium on the marriage of Solomon, is one of the
most striking examples of this fusion of translation with personal experience. In it, she drew on her own brief career as lady-in-waiting, during
which she witnessed Elizabeth's progress to Kenilworth and the ceremonial welcome to the queen and attendant ladies at Woodstock. Despite the
suggestions of Calvin and de Bèze that the lavish pomp and ceremony of
this psalm should be contemplated in light of its allegorical significance as
the prefiguration of Christ's union with the Church, Sidney chose to elaborate on the pageantry of the original as visual demonstration of the king's
power and authority, unrolling the scene as if it were occurring before her
eyes during her own time—one of the most effective ways to achieve a
composition of place to dramatize and enliven her material.[10] In her hands
Psalm 45 became an exposition of the divine rights of monarchs as well as
the duties that these rights entailed, and she emphasized in it a chain of
prerogatives and obligations issuing from God to king to his new queen
and the members of his court.

> The king is beyond other men, a reflection of God on earth:
> Fairer art thou than sonnes of mortall race:
>   Because high God hath blessed thee for ay,
> Thie lipps, as springs, doe flowe with speaking grace.
>
>   (ll. 6–8)

Sidney stressed the trappings of power in Psalm 45, not just for their
magnificence, but because they are resonant symbols in a ceremony reveal-

ing the links between God and monarch. The sceptre held in the right hand
is an emblem or "ensigne of thie kingly might, / To righteousness is linckt
with such a band, / That righteous hand still holds thie Sceptre right" (ll.
22–24). Therefore, it is a constant reminder that the king must dispense
justice as well as inspire awe and fear. The formulaic repetition of "righteous" and "righteousness" transforms this psalm into an invocation to
God to make this ideal representation of the monarchy a reality on earth.
Likewise, with her counterpoised repetition of "terror" and "mortall,"
emphasizing the two spheres linked in the image of the monarch, Sidney
created an awesome incantation of power and majesty:

> Soe that right hande of thine shall teaching tell
> Such things to thee, as well maie terror bring,
> And terror such, as never erst befell
> To mortall mindes at sight of mortall king.
>
> (ll. 13–16)

This focus on the king's terrifying power might reflect the underlying
insecurity of the Sidney's fortunes at Elizabeth's court. Mary Sidney's father was overworked as Lord President of Wales and Governor and Lord
Deputy of Ireland and consistently underpaid with insufficient allowance
for his public expenses. The family was often in financial difficulty, to the
extent that Henry Sidney was forced to refuse a peerage as too expensive
without an accompanying pension or land grant. Philip, of course, was in
brief disfavor with Elizabeth for formally protesting her marriage to the
Duc d'Alençon and d'Anjou, as was her brother, Robert, for marrying
Barbara Gamage over the queen's objections. Lurking always in the Sidney's minds, perhaps, was an uneasiness born out of the past complicity of
the families of both Mary Sidney's husband and her mother in the abortive
attempt to place Lady Jane Grey on the throne, a history that would make
them doubly vulnerable to Elizabeth's whims.

When Mary Sidney describes in Psalm 45 the position of the royal
women in the king's cortege, who "By honoring thee of thee doe honor
hold" (l. 34), she gives us a brief glimpse of the dependency of these
women on the monarch's good will. Similarly, in a vignette sketching the
situation of the queen's maids-of-honor, who "shall on her attend / With
such, to whome more favoure shall assigne / In nearer place their happie
daies to spend" (ll. 54–56), we are permitted a glance backstage at the
politics and ambition governing the hierarchy of court life. As Mary Sid-

ney knew, however, there could be unfortunate consequences to being a queen's favorite. Her mother's devotion in nursing Elizabeth through her bout with smallpox ruined her own appearance and health. At times, also, there was simply not enough "favoure" to go around at court, as was attested to by her mother's frequent petitions for less cramped quarters with adequate heating. In this psalm, there are no overt references to the potentially unpleasant consequences attendant on the subordinate position of these women, but certainly the repeated emphasis on the terror inspired by the monarch was rooted in the experiences of Mary Sidney and her family.

Sidney's verse paraphrase of Psalm 45 is a rich tapestry of interwoven privilege and obligation, as the rights and duties of the king, the noblewomen of the court, and the maids-of-honor are carefully outlined. It is the queen, however, whom the psalmist wishes to instruct by explaining her position, the homage due her by the court and other nations, as well as her corresponding duty to leave behind memories of her family and home to concentrate on producing an heir to guarantee the perpetuation of the hierarchy. Sidney's advice to the queen on how to maintain her husband's love, for example, is practical and unromantic. She should remember that:

> Soe in the king, thie king, a deere delight
>   Thie beautie shall both breed, and bredd, maintaine:
> For onlie hee on thee hath lordlie right,
>   Him onlie thou with awe must entertaine.
>   (ll. 41–44)

Beauty, fidelity, and the proper demeanor of awe are the queen's calling cards; appearance and subordination are all. This perspective on marriage recalls the Mary Sidney who conformed to the expectations of her family and the court by marrying, when she was but fifteen years old, Henry Herbert, the second Earl of Pembroke, a man twenty-five years her elder. Yet there is an ambiguity in these lines which suggests a more intimate link between the king and his new bride. If her beauty breeds in him a "deere delight," the syntax of these lines makes it equally possible to read them as saying that it is his delight in her that nourishes her beauty, a beauty based on internal contentment rather than external show. As such, the delight is mutual and reciprocal, and the gold in the "fasshion Arte divine" she wears under her clothes becomes a metaphor for the rare wealth and beauty of her soul.

There is, indeed, an "Arte divine" which fashions Psalm 45. The color and magnificence of the pageantry of the original psalm is captured so well that the procession seems to advance slowly before the reader; however, Mary Sidney was always careful to place the pomp and material splendor within the perspective of God's decrees, as but symbols of His righteousness and the ordination of His monarch over earth. This monarch's rule, reflective of God's justice, is nevertheless a rule over fallible humans, and as such requires a constant show of strength to instill a terror which then makes possible "justice, truth, and meekness." There is a tough-minded political pragmatism informing Sidney's elaboration of the following lines from the Book of Common Prayer: "Thy arrows are very sharp, and the people shall be subdued unto thee: even in the midst among the King's enemies" (p. 105). Her version of these lines gives a Machiavellian slant on how to maintain power:

> Sharpe are thie shaftes to cleave their hartes in twaine
>   Whose heads do cast thy Conquestes to withstand
> Good cause to make the meaner people faine
>   With willing hartes to undergoe thie hand.
>   (ll. 17–20)

Here is revealed an aristocratic contempt for the people's capacity for political judgment; if the masses are to be content, "with willing hartes" to be ruled, it can only be as a result of a grim demonstration of power. Sidney knew that the enemies of the state, when subjected to its will, always "frown in heart" although "they fawn in sight" (Ps. 66, l. 8).

Sidney's version of Psalm 45 is one of her most inspired imitations, as well as one of her most independent. Her emphasis is on the problem of power, how to reconcile God's mandate with the realities of an imperfect earth. She herself was no stranger to the difficulty of distinguishing between the use and abuse of power. As a result of her husband's poor health in the mid-1590s, Mary Sidney gradually undertook more and more responsibility for the management of his estate. For example, in a letter written August 3, 1602, to Sir Robert Cecil, she enclosed an exasperated, yet thoroughly practical assessment of the appropriate punishment suited to the different behavior of two rebellious bailiffs:

Now for this sedisious beggerly wretche whom it pleasd yow to bring downe under my mercy & now seemes most penetent, I must confess it were no conquest to his utter ruein & yet thinke it not fitt to take his present submission to retorne him to be disposed of according to yr will, if please yow in regard of his missery to be released of his imprisonment. The other his barbarus demeanur hath bin so odious & therein so obstinate as this hand may in no reason consent to become any meane for his release till by a more thorow fealing of his fowle offence others lykewise will be better tought by his smart . . . .[11]

The blunt self-assurance of her statement, her stern invective, reminiscent of the scornful voice of the prophet in her *Psalmes,* demonstrate a show of power esssential for a woman in her position. These lines reveal an experienced pragmatism. She remains suspicious of the seeming penitence of the first prisoner, but the appearance of reform is sufficient for her purposes. Rather, it is the obstinate unregeneracy of the second prisoner that is most threatening to peace and discipline because it poses a potentially dangerous example for others.

If publicly Mary Sidney was a tough-minded pragmatist, a firm supporter of the divine right of monarchs and the aristocratic traditions of government, we must remember that privately Mary Sidney chose to live at Wilton, in retirement from the court. Certainly she knew firsthand the sordid opportunism and factionalism that defined life at court, and it would seem that she chose to withdraw from the arena, arranging her life at Wilton so she could use her hospitality and influence to attract the fine minds of her society and through them affect the literature of her age. It was not just weariness and intellectual ambition that motivated her retirement from court, however. The privacy of her life at Wilton enabled the concentrated meditation that prepares the soul for the "searching sight" of God: "Search me, my God, and prove my hart, / Examyne me, and try my thought" (Ps. 139, ll. 85–86). The discipline of private prayer and meditation, far from the distractions and intrigues of court life, schools the soul to submit itself as naturally and unself-consciously as a child to God's examination.

One facet of this private Mary Sidney shines through in her images of birth and child care. This comparison did not originate with her, of course,[12] but Sidney invested a unique tenderness in her use of it which renders those sections of the *Psalmes* softly luminous. She never forgot the reality of the experience behind the comparison. Even in the midst of a long passage calling for the destruction of David's enemies, her tone of relentless indignation is momentarily softened by the pathos of her stillbirth comparison:

> So make them melt as the dishowsed snaile
> Or as the Embrio, whose vitall band
> Breakes er it holdes and formlesse eyes do faile
> To see the sun, though brought to lightfull land.
>   (Ps. 58, ll. 22–25)

The specific details of "vitall band" and "formlesse eyes," as well as the beautifully alliterative "lightfull land" in the explorer image, were added by Sidney to heighten the tragedy of a baby brought senseless out of the womb. As the only one of three daughters to survive past childhood, and as a mother who lost her own daughter, Katherine, at the age of three, it was perhaps impossible for her to exploit such a metaphor merely as a display of wit.

Similarly, there is an authenticity in her amplification of the standard image of God as a merciful father in Psalm 103: "Yea like as a father pitieth his own children: even so is the Lord merciful unto them that fear him" (BCP, p. 243). The father she envisions is fond of His refractory child:

> And looke how much
> The neerly touching touch
> The father feeles towards his sonne most deare,
> Affects his hart,
> At Ev'ry froward part
> Plaid by his child:
> Soe mercifull, soe mild,
> Is he to them that beare him awfull feare.
>   (ll. 57–64)

The charming and clever polyptoton, "touching touch," has an incantatory, yearning quality, capturing the tug of parental love by conjuring the image of a father holding out his arms to a toddling child.

In Psalm 139, in one of Mary Sidney's strongest, most arresting stanzas, the development of the fetus is used as an image of the conflation of spiritual and physical growth. The theme of the psalm is God's absolute knowledge of men and women. Stanza after stanza reveals yet another layer of God's penetrating understanding until the very formation of the body in the womb is laid bare to His scrutiny:

> Thou, how my back was beam-wise laid,
> And raftring of my ribbs, dost know:

> Know'st ev'ry point
> Of bone and joynt,
> How to this whole these partes did grow,
> In brave embrod'ry faire araid,
> Though wrought in shopp both dark and low.
> (ll. 50–56)

The image of the embroidery wrought in a dark shop came from suggestions made in the commentaries of Calvin and de Bèze, but the taut, tortured extension of "back was beam-wise laid" and "raftring of my ribbs" was original to Sidney. Calvin mused upon the "inconceivable skill which appears in the formation of the human body,"[13] inspiring Sidney to re-enact the stress and strain of growth. The images are ambiguous in that they suggest both the expanding pressure on the ribs and back of the mother, as well as the developing fetus. Her choice of the embroidery comparison suggests the texture of sinew and muscle, the woven skin that covers and knits "ev'ry point / of bone and joynt." The "inconceivable skill," the miraculous workings of God on earth, are described in terms of a painful distension of body and spirit, naked before God's scrutiny.

Mary Sidney's version in Psalm 51 of the psalmist's meditation on his own conception centers around the repetition of the word "cherish," chosen from Calvin's commentary. She then added a gloss from de Bèze found in *Chrestiennes Méditations* (1582)[14] in order to capture the spiritual dilemma posed by parenthood:

> My mother, loe! when I began to be,
> Conceaving me, with me did sinne conceave:
> And as with living heate she cherisht me,
> Corruption did like cherishing receave.
> (ll. 15–18)

Here the standard declaration of original sin voiced in the Book of Common Prayer, "Behold, I was shapen in wickedness: and in sin hath my mother conceived me" (p. 119), is transformed into a striking portrait of frustrated maternal energy that is not only helpless to save the child from sin, but actually generates the child's fate. The instinctive animalism of "living heate" emphasizes our sensual origins, while the alliterative connection between "conceave," "corruption," and "cherishing" underlines the irony that this physical bond between mother and child reflects the spiritual peril that is our birthright from conception.

Perhaps it was Mary Sidney's commitment to a poetry which sought to reconcile our imperfect origins with our spiritual aspirations that led her to develop a style juxtaposing a sweet lyricism celebrating the inexhaustible bounty of nature with a plain realism reminding us of our mortal roots. She gives the commonplace figure of Mother Earth some new twists:

> Earthe, greate with yong, her longing doth not lose,
>   The hopfull ploughman hopeth not in vayne . . .
> All things in breef, that life in life maintaine,
> From Earths old bowells fresh and yongly growes.
>   (Ps. 104, ll. 43–48)

The image of the earth as an aging mother, once again pregnant, underscores the miraculous renewal of spring and suggests the potential for regeneration in all of us. In Psalm 65 she chose her words carefully to convey the exuberant vitality, as well as the barren and withered source of that new life which only God can quicken. The antithetic "buried seed" and "yelding grave" epitomize the resurrection of the land:

> Thy eie from heav'n this land beholdeth,
>   Such fruitfull dewes down on it rayning,
> That, storehowse-like her lap enfoldeth
>   Assured hope of plowmans gayning.
> Thy flowing streames her drought doe temper so,
> That buried seed through yelding grave doth grow.
>   (ll. 31–36)

This cycle of birth and death can be made explicit, as in the above example, or can be merely suggested: "Even then shall swell / His blossoms fatt and faire, / When aged rinde the stock shall beare" (Ps. 92, ll. 40–42). Here the opposition of "fatt and faire" prepares the reader for the "aged rinde" that generates the flower. Similarly, in the description of Jehovah, "By whom the rayne from cloudes to dropp assign'd / Supples the clodds of sommer-scorched fields" (Ps. 147, ll. 25–26), the blunt force of "clodds" and the ominous threat of "scorched" attest to the glory of God who causes this dead land to be fertile, and yet serve as reminders that this soft abundance is ephemeral. The ample wisdom of these counterpoised images reflects, perhaps, Mary Sidney's hard-earned ability to come to terms with private sorrow. While writing these psalms, she was looking back on the deaths of her daughter, father, mother, and brothers Philip and Thomas, as well as working through the progressive decline of her husband's health—losses which were counterbalanced by the births of her children. By alternating sweetly alliterative language with the plain and vulgar diction of "fatt," "aged rinde," "bowells," "grave," and "clodds," Sidney played one vocabulary off the other to reveal the inseparability of life from death, natural beauty from aged and gnarled roots.

Throughout her *Psalmes* Mary Sidney contrasted the foolish pretensions of earthly endeavors with the wise paradoxes of heavenly wisdom. This theme is developed most clearly in her legal and business metaphors which were undoubtedly inspired by direct experience in managing her husband's estate. In her handling of this strain of imagery, the practical knowledge of the public woman was reinterpreted in light of the wisdom gleaned from private meditation, usually to emphasize the inadequacy of a merely legalistic point of view. Her comparisons continually remind us that this is how affairs are conducted on an imperfect earth, rather than in heaven. God's covenant with us is referred to as a "league" in which the land of Canaan is promised "in fee," yet we are reminded that the limited scope implied by such contractual arrangements cannot encompass the omnipotence and omnipresence of God:

> The daies bright guide, the nightes pale governesse
> Shall claime no longer lease of their enduring:
> Whome I behold as heav'nly wittnesses
> In tearmlesse turnes, my tearmlesse truth assuring.
> (Ps. 89, ll. 93–96)

"Tearmlesse" refers to both timelessness as well as freedom from restrictive legal and financial conditions. Day and night serve not as earthly witnesses to a testament of our inevitable decay, but rather as "heav'nly wittnesses" of the eternal glory of God. A lease, of course, cannot designate "tearmlesse truth," and all our contracts and stipulations only demonstrate our foolish distrust that would make conditions with that which must be unconditional.

Mary Sidney employed a major strain of antithetical repetition throughout her translation of the Psalms which contrasts the limitations of human understanding with the infinite power and wisdom of God: "O Lord, whose grace no limits comprehend; / Sweet Lord, whose mercies stand from measure free" (Ps. 51, ll. 1–2). Human arrogance "would in boundes that boundless pow'r contain" (Ps. 78, l. 128), but God always reminds us that "speciall bonds have bound" us (Ps. 145, l. 32), that we have a clearly defined position with accompanying duties outlined in the universal plan:

> All formed, framed, founded so,
>   Till ages uttmost date
> They place retaine, they order know,
>   They keepe their first estate.
>
> (Ps. 148, ll. 21–24)

The emphatic resonance of Sidney's alliteration and parallel syntax, as well as the legal, political, and class connotations of estate, would seem to suggest a confining rigor to God's arrangements on earth, but that is true only from the human perspective narrowed by a mind accustomed to operating in terms of leases and contracts. The best indication of God's grace is the free acceptance of His will; the faithful soul does not feel straitened but rather chooses freely to occupy the ordained place: "Who uncontrol'd / Sure league with him doe hold, / And doe his lawes not only understand" (Ps. 103, ll. 78–80). Once again legal imagery is used ironically to reveal its own limitations; the only genuine league is that which is "uncontrol'd." This pattern of imagery urges us to learn the distinctions between an earthly contract and our covenant with God. The one is null and void upon our death, at which time we lose all that we vainly sought to preserve as our own under its protection. The other is eternal and our only security against oblivion.

Throughout Mary Sidney's *Psalmes,* therefore, we find a sophisticated use of sacred paradox that attempts to illuminate the unknowable and yet maintain the integrity of God's mystery, to emphasize both the potential and the limit of human knowledge. Sidney chose her comparisons carefully to remind us that the soft abundance of our world can scorch and shrivel in a moment, that it is wrung from withered bowels, that the cherishing animal warmth of our mother's womb incubates the seeds of our sinfulness, and that our terms, contracts, and leases but reflect our powerlessness and the transitory nature of all earthly goods and arrangements. These paradoxes underline the folly of all human attachments and measure the vast distance between earth and heaven.

This distance is bridged in a handful of Mary Sidney's psalms where we find the peace and serenity, the simple, hopeful confidence of the soul in concert with the universe. These psalms are distinguished by a simple eloquence that is at once subdued and ecstatic:

> Looke how the sunne, soe shall his name remayne;
> As that in light, so this in glory one:
> All glories that, at this all lights shall stayne:
> Nor that shall faile, nor this be overthrowne.
> The dwellers all
> Of earthly ball
> In hym shall hold them blest:
> As one that is
> Of perfect blisse
> A patterne to the rest.
>
> (Ps. 72, ll. 71–80)

The preponderance of one-syllable words joined with the lack of qualifiers ("earthly" and "perfect" are counterpoised as the only two descriptive adjectives) create an aura in which single words are able to convey absolute meaning, reflecting the oneness of the divine spirit. There is no need here for the involved syntax, the paradoxes and wordplay that usually characterize Mary Sidney's writing. Such displays of wit are inappropriate and unnecessary in those rare moments when faith is spontaneous rather than labored. In such moments the infused state of contemplation which reveals the "single viewe of the eternall veritye"[15] supersedes the self-conscious, analytic process of meditation, as wordplay and extended comparisons can only measure the extent to which we approximate rather than know the ways of God. In this transcendent phase, reliance on the mere "Wisdom of Words" obscures the stunning simplicity of the "Word of Wisdom."[16]

It is Mary Sidney's commitment to "the wandering voices of the fallen world,"[17] however, which marks her greatest poetic achievement. Her best passages dramatize the dilemma of her speaker, who represents all of us, sinking in an apprehension of unworthiness, yet calling for a renewal of special favor from God. Her psalms are centered in the world as we know it; God speaks to us in our own words, but too often we do not hear and our pleas to Him are confused and troubled. The very effort we make to understand God's will marks our failure to do so, since such understanding must come simply and naturally without effort. Education can be inimical to wisdom and obscure the unitive way to special grace, blinding the restless spirit to the correspondences underlying diversity, the essential rightness of the way things are. However, Mary Sidney's dedication to her verse translations of the Psalms is a testimony to her faith in human effort in general and in our capacity for self-education in particular. During her many years working with the psalms, she taught herself both how to write poetry and how to speak to God. In fact, it is her insistence on the validity of applying to the psalms knowledge and understanding gained from study and personal experience that makes them exemplary models for private meditation. In the fusion of Mary Sidney's voice with that of the psalmist, the process of education and the purpose of wisdom coincide. Wisdom is gained neither by the suppression of individual energy and intelligence, nor by a vainglorious display of these qualities, but rather by an abiding appreciation that God's spirit works through individual talent which reflects the capacity of all humankind.

JON A. QUITSLUND

Spenser and the Patronesses of the *Fowre Hymnes:* "Ornaments of All True Love and Beautie"

URING the later years of Queen Elizabeth's reign, literary patronage by women took several forms which would continue to be culturally significant in the seventeenth century. An author might be a member of some noble household, either familiar as a guest or employed in the position of secretary, tutor, or chaplain. Some works of poetic craft, scholarship, or translation were set as tasks or otherwise agreed upon in advance as appropriate to the writer's station, and deserving some recognition—payment, preferment, protection, or hospitality— by the patroness to whom the book was dedicated. A writer without an established relationship to a patroness, trading perhaps on some acquaintance or family connection, might dedicate the work of "idle" hours to a noble woman in the hope of pleasing someone reputed to be generous and influential. Such patronage as resulted was, in these cases, ex post facto, but it still could affect not only the author's future career but also his choice or treatment of a subject: whether the work was worth doing and well done was more for the patroness than the reading public to decide. In an age when life was, even without the glare of modern publicity, much more public than we can easily imagine, writers were acutely conscious of their audiences, so the tastes and interests of patrons and patronesses, whether they were known to the writer directly, by reputation, or as members of their class, exercised a complex influence on the production of literature.

Edmund Spenser's relationships to the several patrons and patronesses to whom his poems are dedicated make a long story, rendered fragmentary and conjectural by the paucity of documentary evidence. The impact of patronage on his career and his creativity is difficult to estimate and best approached case by case. Spenser's career as a poet began in earnest in 1579 with *The Shepheardes Calender,* dedicated to Sir Philip Sidney not, it seems, on the basis of any prior acquaintance, but in the hope that Sidney would be pleased to have such a production associated with his name, and that the dedication would commend the book to others. Apparently this evidence of Spenser's talent secured a place in the Sidney circle for the would-be English Virgil, for whom Queen Elizabeth would be Augustus while Sidney and his uncle, the Earl of Leicester, played Pollio and Maecenas. Spenser's prestige among devout Protestants in the nobility and gentry survived his posting to Ireland and the deaths of Sidney, the Earl of Leicester, and others; his position as a poet was consolidated by the publication of three Books of *The Faerie Queene* in 1590.

Even though Spenser's title to respect as a poet was assured by 1590, he remained in need of patronage. He did not need to write to order, or in order to eat, but one can see in his several publications after 1590, with their various dedications, an anxious desire to assemble his audience and to address his readers with authority enhanced by influential and benevolent patrons. It is clear from the dedications and contents of these poems that women were a significant part of the audience. Their experience and their interests called forth or at least shaped some of his finest poetry: the wise interpreter of Spenser's career will take into account, along with inspiration and the poet's personal program, such motivations as indebtedness, friendship or admiration, a search for advantages at court, and a desire to please certain readers by responding to their expressed or unexpressed wishes. While no letters or accounts establish precisely the nature of the patronage Spenser received from the sisters to whom he dedicated the *Fowre Hymnes,* what we know of their lives and what we find in the poetry suggest that Spenser's dedication was more than convenient or conventional.

Anne Russell Dudley, Countess of Warwick, and Margaret Russell Clifford, Countess of Cumberland, are interesting in themselves and as representatives of a significant portion of the audience for Spenser's poetry.

Knowledge of their lives will deepen our understanding of Elizabethan culture and of the ways in which Spenser, as a public poet, shaped his fiction in response to the aspirations and anxieties characteristic of his time. Spenser is among the most outward-looking and self-effacing of poets, and although we can know very little about his personal life, we should recognize that it was in the experience and attitudes of other people, whether known intimately or viewed in the enchanted glass of public opinion, that he found much of his subject matter.

Spenser's poetry has been very well served by critics over the last quarter-century, but little attention has been given to its social context. Since the appearance of Rosemond Tuve's essay, " 'Spenserus,' " in 1964,[1] the cultural interests and social experience of the Elizabethan aristocracy and gentry have been studied extensively by historians. Literary scholars have been particularly interested in the circles surrounding Sir Philip Sidney and his sister, the Countess of Pembroke, but very little has been done to place Spenser and his poetry in the social milieu that constituted his first audience. Tuve was concerned, as I am, with the several allegiances and family ties which drew together Spenser and these two patronesses, Anne Russell Dudley and Margaret Russell Clifford. Tuve's emphasis fell upon the Countess of Warwick, who owned a fine manuscript of John Gower's *Confessio Amantis* in which Spenser's name is inscribed together with some apposite lines adapted from Ovid. My emphasis is on the younger sister, Margaret, Countess of Cumberland. We are fortunate to have quite a lot of information about her inner and outer life, thanks to Anne Clifford, her daughter, to whom we also owe the memorial to Spenser as "the Prince of Poets in his tyme," erected in Westminster Abbey in 1620.

Anne and Margaret were two of the three daughters of Francis Russell, the second Earl of Bedford. Less ambitious than Leicester and less powerful and energetic than Walsingham, Sir Francis was still one of the most prominent supporters of the causes to which Spenser was devoted.[2] As a young man he travelled extensively on the Continent, and he maintained friendships with Continental Reformers and refugees from Catholic persecution; his children grew up in a cosmopolitan, even bookish, household.[3] The earl's interest in learning and piety was intensified in his daughters. From Anne Clifford we learn that her mother Margaret "had no language but her own, yet was there few books of worth translated into English but she read them, whereby that excellent mind of hers was much enriched, which even by nature was endowed with the seeds of the four moral virtues."[4] This and other statements in Anne Clifford's memoir of her mother suggest that the education provided for Francis Russell's daughter was somewhat less liberal and serious than Samuel Daniel's tutoring of Anne Clifford, yet Margaret was clearly awakened to a love of much that Spenser valued. To the right side of Lady Margaret in the Clifford family portrait is a shelf bearing three large volumes, labelled, "A written hand book of Alkumiste Extraction of Distillations and excellent Medecines," "All Senekae's Workes, translated out of Latine into English," and "The Holy Bible; the Old and New Testament." In one hand Margaret holds the Psalms of David.[5]

Margaret was born July 8, 1560, the youngest of the Earl of Bedford's seven children by his first wife, Margaret St. John Gostwick. She would not have remembered her mother, who died in 1562. Francis Russell married again in 1566, but in childhood as in adult life Margaret seems to have felt much closer to her sister Anne, who was thirteen years older and is described as "a kind of mother to her and their middle sister, Elizabeth." Of Anne Russell, her niece and namesake Anne Clifford further writes that she "came to serve Queen Elizabeth when she was very young; so as she served that illustrious Queen, when she was maid, wife, and widdow, even almost from the beginning of her reign till the said Queen's death; and she was more beloved and in greater favour with the said Queen then any other lady or woman in the kingdom" (*Lives*, p. 24). Since Anne Russell married Ambrose Dudley in 1565 and remained childless, it is likely that her younger sisters were as much a part of that household as of Sir Francis Russell's.

That the young Margaret was in her father's household and yet not submissive to her parents is indicated by the romantic attachment that led to her marriage. Upon the death of Henry Clifford, the second Earl of Cumberland, in January of 1570, Francis Russell had obtained the wardship of George Clifford, then not quite eleven years old, apparently with the intention of matching the young man with his second daughter, Elizabeth. George and Margaret fell in love, however, and although her father initially disapproved and suggested another match, in 1577 they were married "with great honour and glory" and the queen in attendance.[6]

Margaret was not yet seventeen; George Clifford, near nineteen, had completed an education at Trinity College, Cambridge, which began in 1571 and led to the bachelor of arts degree in 1574 and master of arts in 1576, the year in which Spenser took his master's degree (Williamson, p. 6). Soon after the marriage, George Clifford took his young bride to his ancestral home, Skipton Castle, in the West Riding of Yorkshire. By both Margaret's own and her daughter's accounts, this introduction to married life in alien surroundings was an experience not unlike Amoret's captivity in the Castle of Busirane.[7]

Margaret Russell's character and temperament are clear from the documents preserved by her daughter. Anne Clifford describes her as "naturally of an high spirit, though she tempered it well by grace, having a very well favoured face with sweet and quick grey eyes, and of a comely personage" (*Lives*, p. 19). The countess herself reviewed her life up to the age of approximately thirty-two in a remarkable letter to Dr. John Layfield, apparently a chaplain to the family. In this passage the quality of her mind shows through some awkwardness in the syntax:

> Men commonly divide their life by sevens, observing therein their great observations, so mean I, to divide mine well known most of them to thee, four sevens, and well ca[n]tering a good part of the fifth hath my miserable self seen, still running one course with changing sometimes, comparing[,] though unfitly matching the name of a Dance[,] to the Pilgrimage of Grief, because it holds in nothing more like, for still I change and yet the Dance, or thing that makes the sound is sorrow still to me.[8]

Writing at some point between 1591 and 1595, the Countess of Cumberland recalls childhood sickliness and unhappiness, pleasure and willfulness occasioned by George Clifford's "liking" for her, a period of deep melancholia in which she was alienated from her husband and cut off from friends, and years of health in which she bore two sons, Francis in 1584 and Robert in 1585. Within the ten years beginning in 1581 she experienced both her greatest happiness and several losses. The years in which her sons were born brought the deaths of two brothers, John and Francis, and of her father. Before her daughter Anne was born on January 30, 1590, she lost her eldest son, and the second died in 1591. These deaths, together with the attractions of "a lady of quality," seem to have put an end to happiness between George Clifford and his wife, although she remained desirous of a reconciliation.[9] Lacking a male heir, the Earl of

Cumberland sought to settle his estates upon his younger brother Francis, provoking Margaret and her daughter to prolonged litigation and encouraging the highly developed sense of self and family pride we witness in their memoirs.

Margaret Russell's reflections on her experience in courtship and marriage should interest all readers of Spenser's poetry. One hesitates to call either the experience or her evaluation of it typical, yet we can plausibly seek in this testament, precisely contemporary with *The Faerie Queene*, a small-scale personal analogue to Spenser's account of a whole culture's aspirations and anxieties, its ideals and their frustration by events. Knowledge of the Countess of Cumberland's unhappy devotion to her husband, together with the fact that the Countess of Warwick had been a widow since 1590, may help us to appreciate the complex motives—not purely Spenser's own—behind the fervent idealism of the *Fowre Hymnes*.

In her autobiographical letter the countess looks back self-critically on the love in which her marriage began, and the terms of her analysis suggest that she was familiar with some of the ideas essential to Spenser's distinction between love based upon a wise choice and that grounded only in "base affections." Margaret observes: "My mind not foreseeing my own good, was not desirous I thought honour good, so rather going on the ground of common good than any particular liking, which by chance met with the like mind in him, but God that in his holy decree governs all things to that end, hee hath appointed, matched us in lawful manner in one, though our minds met not, but in contrarys and thought of discontentment" (Williamson, p. 286). She contrasts "honour" to "the ground of common good," which is a cause inferior to "any particular liking"; "common good" suggests a less than noble motive such as appetite or ambition. Her statement that "our minds met not, but in contrarys and thought of discontentment" is illuminated by these lines from Spenser's "Hymne in Honour of Beautie":

> But in your choice of Loves, this well advize,
> That likest to your selves ye them select,
> The which your forms first sourse may sympathize,
> And with like beauties parts be inly deckt:
> For if you loosely love without respect,

> It is no love, but a discordant warre,
> Whose unlike parts amongst themselves do jarre.
>   (ll. 190–96)

Spenser's contemplation of golden possibilities, coupled as it is with many expressions of frustration and wan hope, probably found responsive chords in his two virtuous, beautiful, and intelligent patronesses. Anne Clifford credits her mother with "a discerning spirit, both into the disposition of humane creatures and natural causes, and into the affairs of the world. . . . She was a lover of the study and practice of alchimy, by which she found out excellent medicines, that did much good to many" (*Lives,* p. 19). Even when limited to distillation, the art of alchemy depended upon observation of the occult sympathies between heavenly bodies and earthly phenomena. Perhaps we should read in this light Lady Anne's statement that "this noble Countess had in her the infusion from above of many excellent knowledges and virtues both Divine and humane" (*Lives,* p. 20). Consider, then, how Lady Margaret would respond to Spenser's teaching that

> Love is a celestiall harmonie,
> Of likely harts composd of starres concent,
> Which joyne together in sweete sympathie,
> To worke ech others joy and true content,
> Which they have harbourd since their first descent
> Out of their heavenly bowres, where they did see
> And know ech other here belov'd to bee.
>   (HB, ll. 197–203)

Such ideas as these, which are developed at length in the first pair of hymns, would provide both a rationale for Margaret Russell's unhappiness in her marriage and for the devotional love, anxious to rise above earthly trials to heavenly fulfillment of the soul's destiny, which Spenser represents in the second pair of hymns.

As I mentioned, in her removal to Skipton Castle in Yorkshire soon after her marriage the young Countess of Cumberland experienced something resembling Amoret's suffering at the hands of Busirane. "With what wyles I met, with what bates, with how many unknown evils!" she exclaims in her letter to Layfield. "I yet [knew] not myself, in this time, I was separated from all I knew." She found the Clifford family and her neighbors devoted to a religion contrary to her own, and her husband "not settled but carried away, with young mens opinions." Anne Clifford tells us that Margaret "grew extream sickly and discontented, and so continued for five or six years together; till at last she fell into a kind of consumption, so as many thought she would never have had any children" (*Lives*, p. 21). In her own account the countess sounds even more like Amoret led forth by Cupid (*FQ*, III.xii.19): "I with thought grew almost continually sick, looking as a ghost that wanted the soul of comfort" (Williamson, p. 286).

In the early 1580s relations between Margaret and George Clifford improved: "My Lords affections turn'd from a strange manner and carriage to much and very much love and kindness known to all and most comfortable found to mee" (Williamson, p. 286). Their happiness was vexed by the earl's absence on several privateering voyages, beginning in 1586— ventures in which Sir Walter Ralegh often took an interest. Margaret's memoir and the surviving correspondence between husband and wife make clear that she never welcomed his seafaring and was uneasy with the risks of life and fortune involved in these grand undertakings.

In this mean time my Lord grew he acquaint himself with pleasant delights of court and exchang'd his country pleasures, with new thoughts of greater worlds. So home I came alone with my two sons, to Skipton, leaving my Lord at Court, where interchangeably he lost with many goings back and forwards and turnings many for the worse, but few for the better, till we had wasted our land and substance, which in hope of better fortune of the sea, than we had of the land, he ventur'd many thousands, which we saw come empty home. (Williamson, pp. 286–87)

The earl's voyages were a claim to fame; so were his flamboyant life at court and his skill in the tiltyard, all of which led to his naming in 1590 as the queen's "peculiar Champion," succeeding Sir Henry Lee upon his retirement (Williamson, p. 67). Including the Earl of Cumberland among the knights honored with dedicatory sonnets in the 1590 *Faerie Queene*, Spenser gives his noble traits their full value, praising both his success in "late assaies" (probably an allusion to the wealth brought back from his voyage in 1589) and the promise of fruit from "The flowre of chevalry now bloosming faire" within his "corageous mind" ("To the right honourable the Earle of Cumberland"). The course of George Clifford's life and fortunes after 1590, however, tends to point the same moral as the deaths which devastated the Protestant nobility during the 1580s. "No earthly thing is sure" (*FQ*, II.ix.21.9): not the lives of defenders of the faith, and not the scapegrace George, heedless of his Una and capable of fortitude but not of wisdom. The Countesses of Warwick and Cumberland had reason to respond deeply to the ambivalence with which Spenser invests the concepts of glory, ambition, and fame.

In *Colin Clouts Come Home Againe* and elsewhere, Spenser creates an elaborate image of a circle of noble women surrounding Queen Elizabeth and embodying the virtues and cultural values affirmed in his poetry. My studies suggest that such a circle really existed, and that the Russell sisters were prominent in it and in touch with the others to whom Spenser dedicated so much of his poetry. These women formed an audience quite different from the other class of readers who mattered—university-trained young men, many of whom were fellow poets. Evidence in the historical record and the poetry suggests that Spenser shaped some of his poetry to appeal to the sometimes divergent interests of that two-fold audience. In what follows, I will even argue that without Margaret Clifford's instigation Spenser would not have written the *Fowre Hymnes*.

Spenser's relations with the Russell sisters can be understood in terms of a series of poems published between 1590 and 1596, and the *Fowre Hymnes* also are best understood in this context, as poetic responses to experience rather than expositions of doctrine. I have already remarked on the interest the two countesses, with other women of their class, could be expected to take in *The Faerie Queene*. Spenser followed Books I through III of his heroic poem by *Complaints* (1591). He dedicated the first poem in this volume, "The Ruines of Time," to Mary, Countess of Pembroke; in it he praises and mourns several noblemen who died in the 1580s—the Earls of Leicester, Warwick, and Bedford; Sir Philip Sidney; and Sir Francis Walsingham—and praises also the noble women who survived them, notably the Countesses of Warwick and Pembroke. He claims, not incidentally, that the poet's song gains immortality for the poet and his subject, while those unsinging or unsung "Die in obscure oblivion." (RT, ll. 337–64; quotation from l. 346). Spenser's earnest and artful response to the disappointment of worldly expectations transforms them into expectation of immortality in heaven (the source of both the soul and poetry) and perpetuity on earth as long as "excellent desart" is celebrated (RT, ll. 337–43).

Daphnaida, published at about the same time as *Complaints*, must also have interested the Russell sisters, who surely knew the Lady Helena, Marquess of Northampton, to whom the poem was dedicated, and Douglas Howard, whose death at eighteen Spenser mourns on behalf of her husband, Arthur Gorges. Gorges' status as an associate of Sir Walter Ralegh apparently provided the occasion for Spenser, as an aspiring member of Ralegh's circle, to offer his memorial to a young man's inconsolable suffering and the world's loss, "in her first ages spring, / . . . against all course of kinde," of a woman who had lived "on earth like Angell new divinde, / Adorn'd with wisedome and with chastitie" (ll. 239, 242, 214–15). Daphne's happiness in heaven is assured, but the poem is dominated by Alcyon's lament: "The heaviest plaint that ever I heard sound," as the narrator comments (l. 541). Sir Walter Ralegh, who in this period produced heavy plaints of his own, was surely a prominent member of the intended audience for *Daphnaida,* but Spenser cloaked his appeal to Ralegh's interest by dedicating the poem to Gorges' aunt. One is tempted to speculate that in his report of Alcyon's extravagant grief, which recent critics have tended to see as a warning against self-absorption,[10] Spenser was cloaking his feelings about Ralegh's suffering.

What would the two Russell sisters have seen in the poem? I raise the question because I believe the patronesses of the *Fowre Hymnes* were very much aware of Spenser's earlier poetry. *Daphnaida,* a minor poem among the Minor Poems and not, I suspect, one for which there was a great demand, was reprinted in the same volume with the *Fowre Hymnes* (more on this later). This fact permits a surmise that one or both of the countesses admired *Daphnaida*'s treatment of virtue, loss, and grief. Their responses must have been colored, if not determined, by knowledge of the circumstances surrounding the marriage of Douglas Howard and Arthur Gorges. It had been another love-match, but one in which the bride's father had been less understanding than Francis Russell. More selfish and passionate than any *senex* in Elizabethan comedy, Henry Howard sought to prevent the marriage, but it was favored by the girl's mother, by the queen, and by others on behalf of Gorges.[11] When the marriage was blessed with a daughter, she was christened Ambrosia with the Earl of Warwick, the Countess of Pembroke, and Lady Elizabeth Carew as godparents. To these indications that the Countess of Warwick was aware of, if not involved in, the triumph of love over aged self-will and greed, we can add the fact that

Margaret Russell and Arthur Gorges were involved simultaneously in resisting efforts to disinherit their daughters. In 1590 Thomas Howard,
Ambrosia's great-uncle, with his eye on her inheritance, charged that Ambrosia was a "changed child" and not the true issue of Arthur Gorges and
his wife. This absurd controversy was still in the air when Spenser wrote
Daphnaida and Margaret Russell, having lost her two sons, went to court
to fight George Clifford's attempt to disinherit her infant daughter Anne.
The story of the real-life Daphne and Alcyon, so charged with politics and
pathos, would have drawn public attention to Spenser's poem, and the
Russell sisters' emotional involvement must have been deeper than most.
Oram and other critics have observed that in *Daphnaida* and his later
poetry, Spenser "draws attention to the difference between his golden fictions and the brazen world of actual fact."[12] I suggest that in reading both
Daphnaida and the *Fowre Hymnes*, Spenser's contemporary audience
would have been acutely conscious of this difference.

   Colin Clouts Come Home Againe must also have interested the Russell
sisters, but for different reasons. Like *Daphnaida,* but more amply and
attractively, it is addressed to a two-fold audience: Ralegh and the other
courtiers who are Spenser's fellow poets and fellow servants of Cupid, and
Queen Elizabeth as Cynthia, together with the many "Nymphs" or "gentle maids" in her retinue.[13] Of the latter group Colin reports, "They all
. . . me graced goodly well" (l. 485) during the author's stay in London
and the introduction to the court arranged by Ralegh. While most of the
poem was written upon Spenser's return to Ireland, it was not published
until 1595, apparently during another extended visit in which he had
further occasion to cultivate a courtier's interests with admirable and influential court ladies.[14]

   The Russell sisters may have found the pastoral trappings in *Colin
Clouts Come Home Againe* vain or trivial, but I would assume their familiarity with *The Shepheardes Calender* and its championing of learning and
reformation in the church; this may have made them tolerant of Colin's
"recreative" impulse here. Both of them—Margaret with the most
reason—may have found a personal allusion in Colin's song of the river
Bregog's love for the Mulla (*Colin,* ll. 92–155). Of the Mulla we are told,
"Full faine she lov'd, and was belov'd full faine, / Of her owne brother
river, *Bregog* hight" (ll. 116–17): one might think of the love that devel-

oped between Margaret and George Clifford, raised in some respects as brother and sister. The union of Bregog and Mulla is opposed by old Mole, who watches his daughter and the attempts by "the wanton *Bregog* . . . / Him to deceive for all his watchfull ward" (ll. 135–36); this last phrase could be taken as an allusion to Francis Russell's holding of George Clifford's wardship. Such parallels are insufficient to support a conjecture that Spenser intended for such a meaning to be taken by Ralegh, by William Russell (if he was a member of the poem's Irish audience), or by anyone else. But the parallel may have seemed to Margaret, with her tender conscience and her intense feelings toward her deceitful husband, too close to be ignored.

Reading further, the countesses would have noticed the lines devoted to poets at Cynthia's court, with Arthur Gorges prominent among them (see *Colin,* ll. 384–91), and lines added in observation of the Earl of Derby's death (April 16, 1594) and his wife's mourning (see ll. 432–43). In the section devoted to Cynthia's "gentle Mayds," the Countess of Pembroke is first, and *"Theana,"* identifiable as Anne Russell, is the next praised (ll. 492–503), with due attention paid to her "carefull wydowhead" and her position of honor and intimacy with Cynthia. Next come four lines devoted to Theana's sister, "Faire *Marian,* the *Muses* onely darling"; the epithet suggests that this Russell sister (probably Margaret) had a reputation for learning and perhaps for poetry, but there is no indication that Spenser was personally acquainted with her at this time. The Marchioness of Northampton is next and *Daphnaida* is mentioned (ll. 508–15). Later Spenser gives a generous passage of praise to the three daughters of the Spencers of Althorpe (ll. 536–71). These and all the praises accorded Queen Elizabeth's "goodnesse and high grace" (l. 588) must have been admired by our two countesses.

The Russell sisters had reason to respond differently, but still favorably, to Colin's criticism of "enormities" at court which account for his return home to Ireland (see *Colin,* ll. 660–730). Colin describes a male-dominated world of dishonesty and envious striving. Pressed by Hobbinol, he allows that the court does contain "Full many persons of right worthie parts" (l. 752), but he renews his attack upon pride and envy, and adds "ydleness" and "laesie love" to the vices found at court (ll. 757–70). The satire then turns in a direction of particular interest to virtuous women.

Margaret Russell especially, lately come out of her isolation in Yorkshire to protect her interests and attempt a reconciliation with George Clifford, would have been touched personally by Colin's complaint: "Ne any there doth brave or valiant seeme, / Unlesse that some gay Mistresse badge he beares" (ll. 779–80). Experience seems to have led Margaret to a disillusionment resembling Colin's when he protests against the court's abuses of love and the profaning of "His mightie mysteries" (ll. 771–94). She might have recognized, therefore, along with the poem's most perceptive recent critic, that *Colin Clouts Come Home Againe* is "about suffering a loss that can be dignified and partly repaired by maintaining devotion to the lost object of desire."[15]

But how would a devout member of the Protestant aristocracy have responded to Colin's account of love's mysteries, which forms the climax of the poem (ll. 795–894)? The gospel for a religion of love receives compliments from Melissa, who thanks Colin on behalf of "all true lovers," concluding, "But most, all wemen are thy debtors found, / That doest their bountie still so much commend" (ll. 899–902). Spenser may have been anxious to orchestrate the responses of women among his readers, and perhaps he failed with some of them. Robert Ellrodt has joined J. W. Bennett in arguing that it was these praises "Of love and beautie" (*Colin*, l. 897), not earlier versions of the first pair of the *Fowre Hymnes*, which created the protest described in the *Hymnes'* dedicatory epistle.[16] My own studies tend to confirm their arguments.

Readers of the *Hymnes* will recall that in his dedication to the Russell sisters Spenser attributes "these former two Hymnes in the praise of Love and beautie" to "the greener times of [his] youth." He has found, he says, that they "too much pleased those of like age and disposition" and encouraged "strong passion" rather than "honest delight." For this reason, we are told, one of the sisters asked him to recall his earlier poems, but "many copies thereof were formerly scattered abroad." Which of the two had protested? In his dedication Spenser names Margaret first, a violation of protocol and a reversal of the order found in *Colin Clouts Come Home Againe;*[17] this fact and all that we know about Lady Margaret suggest that she had taken a lively and critical interest in what Spenser had written— and in what he should write. Since we have no evidence that his unpublished poems circulated widely during the 1590s, the reference to "copies

. . . scattered abroad" is probably either a fiction (one whose falsehood the lady ought not to have known) or a reference to printed copies of *Colin Clouts Come Home Againe,* in which we find lines similar to a large part of the first hymn (cf. *Colin,* ll. 839-94, and HL, ll. 57-182). Joining Bennett and Ellrodt, I think that the latter possibility is the more plausible.

What had been objectionable in *Colin Clouts Come Home Againe?* Colin's "poetic theology" may have raised some Calvinist eyebrows. In the earlier allegory of *The Shepheardes Calender,* "great *Pan*" is "The shepheards God" ("Maye," ll. 54, 113), but we hardly need the Argument to the "Maye" eclogue and a long gloss on Pan to tell us that Pan stands for Christ as worshipped by Protestants. In Spenser's later pastoral, however, the relationship between Reformed Christianity and the religious service of Love in which Colin is a priest is quite obscure. The proviso with which Colin begins his gospel—"whether rightly so, / Or through our rudenesse into errour led" (ll. 795-96)—may have intensified rather than quieted doubts. The genealogy and the power given to Love (ll. 799-810, 839-62) may have been intended to shadow forth Christ, but the signals are not clear. In *The Faerie Queene* and the *Fowre Hymnes* Spenser's syncretism does not take this form. Margaret Russell may have felt that in such a matter of faith, pastoral decorum does not excuse the appearance of heterodoxy.

The morality of love as described by Colin might also be viewed as an encouragement of such passion as Bregog shows to Mulla. Love is represented as the source of harmony in the cosmos and fertility on earth; love in man's life appears only a little more complicated. As we might expect in a poem dedicated to Sir Walter Ralegh, the masculine perspective is emphasized. Love moves the creatures "each one his like to love" by instinct, while in "man that had the sparke of reasons might," passion is reduced to choice of "the fairest in his sight," and "beautie is the bayt . . . / Beautie the burning lamp of heavens light" (ll. 863-78). Colin says nothing to show that true beauty comes from the soul, or that love is a kind of knowledge, either of the self or of a significant other. Love is dinstinguished from "disloyall lust" (ll. 889-94) and from the insincerities of love at court (ll. 775-82), but it remains in essence an impulse that Ovid would understand: seeking medicine "Of her that first did stir that mortall stownd" (l. 878). In the defense of Rosalind and prayer for her "grace" which concludes the poem's dialogue, love is devoted to "divine regard and heavenly hew" (l. 933) reminiscent of the praise of Cynthia (ll. 333–51), but Colin does not provide the justification for love or the image of its spiritual rewards that we find in *Amoretti and Epithalamion* (1595), not to mention the *Fowre Hymnes*. Colin's religion closely resembles that practiced in the Temple of Venus (*FQ*, IV. x) and epitomized in the Lucretian hymn to *alma Venus* sung there by a frustrated, earthbound lover (sts. 44–47).

Margaret Russell had learned to regret the motives that had led her into marriage with George Clifford; after much pain she had enjoyed happiness and a fruitful marriage with him, but all that was frustrated by 1591 or 1592. She may have felt, therefore, that Colin's "sacred lere" of love (l. 783) could be construed as un-Christian or impure, and also that it was neither sufficiently realistic about the dangers of passion nor sufficiently idealistic in its treatment of virtuous love.

Such an interpretation, based upon a juxtaposition of the poem and Lady Margaret's experience, is supported by consideration of the *Fowre Hymnes* in a biographical context. In the light of the background I have adduced, Spenser can be taken at his word when, in the dedication of the *Hymnes*, he refers to his resolution "at least to amend, and by way of retractation to reforme" the earlier poems which had been misinterpreted. There is a certain amount of double-talk in his reference to "these former two Hymnes" and "those two Hymnes of earthly or naturall love and beautie"; there seem to be overlapping references both to the first pair of the four now being published and to earlier poems. The effect of his comments on the "earthly or naturall" hymns is to cast doubt upon the value of all such poems—to bracket them doubly with retractions and cautions against misinterpretation. Other considerations arising from the text and context have the same effect, and I am suggesting that this is all as Spenser, with his patronesses in mind, planned it. Just as he would not have produced *Daphnaida* spontaneously—however much the poem may voice a personal grief—so he would not have written the *Fowre Hymnes* without an occasion and an audience to whom he wished to prove something. What he proves is that he too, joining the poets being sponsored by the Countess of Pembroke and noble women in her circle, could write poetry inspired by Urania, the Christian Muse, without renouncing his allegiance to the Platonic tradition represented by Ficino, Benivieni, Pico, Bembo, and Leone Ebreo.

In what spirit should the *Fowre Hymnes* be approached today by readers who wish to approximate the meaning they had for their original audience? On what basis can the four poems—two pairs—be comprehended as a structured whole? The challenge should be more manageable than that presented by Books I through IV of *The Faerie Queene,* but its complexity has given rise to controversy and uncertainty. No wonder, for beyond the questions raised by Spenser's letter of dedication, within the poems themselves lie the difficulties incidental to any serious attempt to state, and perhaps to resolve, the competing claims of secular and sacred, erotic and religious, Platonic and Christian, temporal and eternal frames of reference. We are learning to admire in Spenser's poetry not only the local and large harmonies he creates, but the subtle ways in which he admits the discord, tension, and ambivalence or contradictions that ran deep in the lives of thoughtful and passionate Elizabethans. It should be possible, then, to accommodate in our reading of the text what the context tells us of its meaning.

I believe I have established that the "former two Hymnes" to which objections were raised were not the first pair of the *Fowre Hymnes* as we have them. All four are intelligible as one poem in several parts, composed in response to the opinions and experience of his audience—his patronesses first and foremost—and composed also to contain the poet's mature reflections on the themes of love and beauty which are central to all his work. Our reading of the *Hymnes* should relate the idealism of the first pair to the two realities of a devout Elizabethan's experience (realities explored variously in Spenser's other poetry): high hopes for earthly satisfaction which are entertained in a context of frustration, and more confident hopes of eventual fulfillment in heaven. We must also give due weight to Spenser's praise of his patronesses as "ornaments of all true love and beautie, both in the one and the other kinde"—both in the joys and sufferings of marriage and in devotion to Christ and Sapience. This "both . . . and" construction, which is Spenser's most characteristic way of dealing with matters of any complexity, should be borne in mind for comparison to the "now this, *not* that" distinctions between heaven and earth with which the heavenly hymns begin and end (HHL, ll. 1–21; HHB, ll. 267–301). Each attitude is appropriate in its place; each involves a rhetorical or dramatic stance, and each contributes to a process which establishes relationships between heaven and earth.

The process involved in reading is never final; poems end by returning us to life. But reading may—as in the *Fowre Hymnes* and the *Two Cantos of Mutabilitie*—move from a position "in the middest" to contemplation of "stedfast rest" in heaven. In such cases (in contrast to all the "endings" in *The Faerie Queene* which deliberately leave us something to be desired, both in the world and in the poem), the hierarchy of the Christian universe requires a final rejection of the lower in favor of a higher truth and happiness. Spenser reminds his patronesses and the public in his dedicatory letter that the "earthly or naturall" hymns should move readers to "honest delight." As we move through the *Fowre Hymnes*, we are to learn that that delight involves aesthetic contemplation of ideals that are known to be unattainable in this life. Seen in these terms, the first pair may resemble the "self-consuming artifacts" of a later age. Much of Spenser's poetry may be read in this spirit, but the *Fowre Hymnes* are unusual in the emphasis they give to it by design.

The first two *Hymnes* have long been the focus for interest in Spenser's mature thought about love and its earthly object, beauty, which for Spenser is the physical manifestation of something ideal and immaterial. Most readers and many scholars have concerned themselves primarily with Spenser's ideas and their sources, and very little with the cultural matrix which contributed to, if it did not define, the meaning of Spenser's words. This is not the place for a full-scale interpretation, but I will end this essay with some observations on the ironies (the term is overworked and imprecise but I can do no better) that circumscribe Spenser's ideas about a love which "is Lord of truth and loialtie" (HL, l. 176; cf. HB, l. 176), which "the refyned mynd doth newly fashion / Unto a fairer forme" (HL, ll. 192–93), and about the soul's beauty, "that faire lampe, from whose celestiall ray / That light proceedes, which kindleth lovers fire" (HB, ll. 99–100).

I believe that the Platonic idealism of the first pair of hymns was sincere on Spenser's part and taken seriously by his patronesses. It is not always easy, however, to enter fully into the spirit of Spenser's seriousness. I used to read these poems as a credo, but I now consider them imaginative, even playful, in their handling of ideas and experience. The *Hymnes* together are not an anatomy of "earthly or naturall" illusions supplanted by "heavenly" certainties; I would rather see them as statements of lesser and greater beliefs. Spenser's Platonism, then, has much in common with Shelley's and Yeats's: it is not dogmatic but hortatory, and it is open to question in the light of contradictory experience even as it offers an interpretation of that experience. The "earthly or naturall" hymns themselves elaborately describe the obstacles to virtuous love and to its satisfaction in a union with beauty: experience of Love as a cruel tyrant (HL, ll. 1–18, 120–61); Jealousy and other productions of the "fayning fansie" (HL, ll. 252–72); the possibility that a beautiful soul will not achieve and preserve union with a beautiful body (HB, ll. 141–68); and failure to choose a love "The which your forms first sourse may sympathize" (HB, ll. 190–210). The poet's attitude throughout is aspiration toward the austere god of Love and the heavenly goddess of Beauty whose "dearling, [his] dear dread" (HB, ll. 281), the beloved lady, remains unresponsive to him.

The experiences of the two Russell sisters in love and marriage add emphasis to the passages describing love's obstacles: these "conventional" or "Petrarchan" passages can be seen as true to life and meaningfully related to the more "Platonic" passages. Of course the second pair of hymns, music of another kind to the ears of devout women, encourages a movement onward and upward. The figurative heaven on earth of Love's "Paradize / Of all delight" (HL, ll. 273–93) and the "heavenly beautie" which a Platonic lover creates "in his mind entyre, / The mirrour of his owne thought" (HB, ll. 222–24), yield in the second pair to higher (and more believable, in Christian terms) conceptions of both Love and Beauty. In these poems, erotic love provides the metaphors for heavenly bliss.

Yet another dimension to the situation in which Spenser embeds his amorous idealism is provided by *Daphnaida*, published in a second edition with the *Hymnes*. The two poems are one book, despite the separate title pages and dedications: the G gathering contains the last page of the *Hymnes* and the title page, dedication, and first leaf of *Daphnaida*.[19] The pagination is continuous. Similarity in stanza forms also contributes an impression of continuity if not unity to the volume: typically, the seven-line stanzas of both poems are printed four to a page. In choosing to reprint *Daphnaida*, Spenser and his publisher may have been acting on a desire to add bulk to a slim volume, but the consequences of that decision for the meaning of the *Hymnes* should still be assessed.

As noted above, *Daphnaida* treats idyllically and elegiacally a love-match threatened by parental jealousy and destroyed by death. It is a memorial to the persistence of devotion in the face of loss; it is also an extreme statement of contempt for a world rendered desolate by Daphne's death and ascent to heaven. Alcyon's lament is a mixture of willful despair and the kind of wisdom with which Spenser often responds to mutability: "For all I see is vaine and transitorie, / Ne will be helde in anie stedfast plight, / But in a moment loose their grace and glorie" (*Daph.*, ll. 495–97). Spenser's patronesses may have thought *Daphnaida* a simpler poem than it seems to us, or they may have seen its complexity more clearly, since they lived within the context of personal relationships and cutural norms which lend such a poem meaning. They would, I expect, have known how to construe the contrast between the subjective darkness of *Daphnaida* and "that soveraine light" (HHB, ll. 295) which shines throughout the *Fowre Hymnes*.

The countesses must also have known what to make of the fact that, even as *Daphnaida* was being reprinted, the once inconsolable Arthur Gorges was reporting himself "plunged over the eares by that maistering disease of affection" and contracted to marry Lady Elizabeth Clinton. As Gorges presents himself in a begging letter to Sir Robert Cecil, the gloom and desperation of Alcyon in *Daphnaida* remain, but the occasion has changed: he has spent twenty years serving the queen faithfully "without any manner of advancement or recompense," and this marriage, the *remedia amoris* of a man seeking quiet and contentment, has earned him a sojourn in the Fleet prison.[20] If the ideals of the *Fowre Hymnes* are ironically related to the actualities of love as experienced by a widow and an estranged wife, other ironies may be seen to play over the surface of the companion poem. We find in *Fowre Hymnes* and *Daphnaida* a pattern evident in the other poems considered earlier in this essay: constancy to an ideal object is articulated and held up for admiration, while loss of everything but the immortal ideal is lamented; at the same time, losses are rationalized and accepted, in the light of an eventual happiness which poetry can only anticipate.

BARBARA K. LEWALSKI

Of God and Good Women:
The Poems of Aemilia Lanyer

A volume of religious poems published in 1611, *Salve Deus Rex
Judaeorum,* was written by a gentlewoman who identified herself on her title page as "Mistris Aemilia Lanyer, Wife to Captaine Alfonso Lanyer, servant to the Kings Majestie."[1] Since published
women poets were so very rare in Elizabethan and Jacobean England, the
volume invites attention on that score alone.[2] But beyond this, it has considerable intrinsic interest as a defense and celebration of good women and
of Lanyer herself as woman poet. It has also some real, if modest, poetic
merit.

Lanyer's volume is in three parts. First, there are eleven dedications, all
to women: nine dedicatory poems to royal and noble ladies, a prose dedication to the Countess of Cumberland, and a prose epistle "To the Virtuous
Reader" which is a vigorous apologia for women's equality or superiority
to men in spiritual and moral matters—and by implication an apologia for
Lanyer herself as a religious poet. Second, the title poem on Christ's Passion and death incorporates the several subjects which are itemized on the
title page as if they were separate poems: *Salve Deus Rex Judaeorum. Containing, 1. The Passion of Christ. 2. Eves Apologie in defence of Women. 3.
The Teares of the Daughters of Jerusalem. 4. The Salutation and Sorrow of
the Virgine Marie. With divers other things not unfit to be read.* Although
the subtitle is misleading as to the contents of Lanyer's volume it properly
registers her emphasis in the title poem upon the good women associated

with the passion story. Consonant with that emphasis are the preface and coda, comprising more than a third of the poem's 1,840 lines, praising Margaret Clifford, Countess of Cumberland, as a virtuous follower of the suffering Christ. The third part of Lanyer's volume is a country-house poem in heroic couplets, "The Description of Cooke-ham," which celebrates the Countess of Cumberland's estate as a lost female paradise. This poem may or may not have been written before Jonson's "To Penshurst" (commonly thought to have inaugurated the genre in English literature) but it can certainly claim priority in publication.[3]

The volume was entered in the Stationers' Register on October 2, 1610, by the bookseller, Richard Bonian, and the poems were probably written within a year or two of this date.[4] It was issued twice in 1611, with minor changes in the imprint, and is now very rare.[5] In the British Library copy, several of the dedicatory poems and the epistle to the reader have been omitted, evidently by design, but we can only speculate as to the number of such copies issued, and the reasons for the omissions.[6]

A. L. Rowse's modern edition (1978) marshalls the known facts about Aemilia Lanyer's life, drawn chiefly from records kept by Simon Forman the astrologer, in the service of his not impossible but unproven thesis that she was the "Dark Lady" of Shakespeare's sonnets.[7] However, the possible links to Shakespeare suggested by these records are far too tenuous to support Rowse's confident identification, even if we grant his questionable assumption that the sonnets are to be read as straightforward Shakespearean autobiography.[8] The unfortunate effect of Rowse's speculation has been to deflect attention from Aemilia Lanyer as a poet and from her poems. My concern here is to examine her book in its own terms, and to assess her achievement.

First, a résumé of the little we know of Aemilia Lanyer's life. Her father was Baptista Bassano, one of the queen's Italian musicians, her mother was his "reputed wife," Margaret Johnson, and Aemilia was christened at St. Bartolph, Bishopsgate, on January 27, 1569. She had one sister, Angela. Her father died in 1576 when she was seven years old, and her mother died eleven years later. She was married in 1592 at age twenty-three to Alfonso Lanyer, one of Queen Elizabeth's (and later King James's) musicians (Rowse, *Sex and Society*, p. 102; *Dark Lady*, p. 18). Forman reports sev-

eral facts about Lanyer's early life, presumably gleaned during her visits to
him in 1597:

She hath had hard fortune in her youth. Her father died when she was young; the
wealth of her father failed before he died, and he began to be miserable in his
estate. . . . She was paramour to my old Lord Hunsdon that was Lord Chamberlain, and was maintained in great pride; being with child she was for colour
married to a minstrel [i.e., Alphonso Lanyer]. . . .

. . . She was maintained in great pomp. She is high-minded. . . . She hath
£40 a year and was wealthy to him that married her, in money and jewels. She can
hardly keep secret. She was very brave in youth. She hath many false conceptions.
She hath a son, his name is Henry. . . .

. . . She hath been much favoured of her Majesty and of many noble men,
hath had great gifts and been made much of. . . . But her husband hath dealt
hardly with her, that spent and consumed her goods.[9]

It seems clear from this that Lanyer had enjoyed some access to the life
of the court as a young girl by reason of the Hunsdon connection, and that
she had obtained an estate in money and jewels which her husband squan-
dered. The Lanyers like the Bassanos were a musical family. Alphonso
Lanyer was both a court musician and a military man: he served as gentleman volunteer on the Essex Island voyages and evidently hoped to be preferred to a knighthood (Rowse, *Dark Lady*, p. 18). Forman indicates that
when Aemilia visited him she wanted to know "whether she should be a
lady or no," and he also implies that her reduced circumstances might lead
her to questionable moral behavior: "She is now very needy, in debt and it
seems for lucre's sake will be a good fellow, for necessity doth compel. She
hath a wart or mole in the pit of the throat or near it."[10]

Alphonso Lanyer was not knighted on this voyage or in consequence of
his later military engagements, nor was he wealthy enough to buy a
knighthood from James, as so many did. In 1604 he was awarded a patent
to take revenue from the weighing of hay and grain in London, and after
his death in 1613 Aemilia was involved in several lawsuits respecting her
rights in this commission.[11] In 1617 she set up a school in St. Giles in the
Fields but was soon in litigation with her landlord about rent arrears and
repairs, during which she deposed that the death of her husband left her

poor, "he having spent a great part of her estate in the service of the late Queen in her wars of Ireland and other places." Aemelia died on April 3, 1645, at the age of 76 (Rowse, *Dark Lady,* pp. 33–34).

From her multiple dedications we can infer some facts concerning the circles she moved in—who was known to her and who was not. While these poems like most of their kind are full of hyperbole, they would not succeed in their purpose of winning favor if they were to falsify blatantly the terms of a relationship. These dedications are obviously intended to call Aemilia Lanyer to the attention of past patronesses, and perhaps to attract new ones. This strategy was common: Spenser appended to his *Faerie Queene* seventeen dedicatory sonnets honoring former and would-be patrons, while inscribing it in the first instance to Queen Elizabeth.

It is evident from these poems that Lanyer does not enjoy in the court circles of King James the associations and the favors she attracted in Elizabeth's court. The opening dedication to Queen Anne contrasts her present sorrow with an earlier, happier time, when "great *Elizaes* favour blest my youth" (l. 50). The dedications to Princess Elizabeth and to the two greatest literary patronesses of the period—Mary (Sidney) Herbert, Countess of Pembroke, and Lucy (Harrington) Russell, Countess of Bedford, do not claim personal acquaintance. And Lanyer frankly admits that she is a "stranger" to the Countess of Suffolk, Katherine (Knevet) Howard. However, other dedications attempt to renew relationships harking back to those better Elizabethan times. Lanyer addresses Lady Arabella Stuart, first cousin of James I, as "Great learned Ladie, whom I long have knowne, / And yet not knowne so much as I desired." And she addresses the Dowager Countess of Kent, Susan (Bertie) Wingfield, as "the Mistris of my youth, / The noble guide of my ungovern'd dayes," suggesting that as a young girl she had lived in the countess's household, waiting upon her. [12]

Some kind of formal patronage is implied in the dedications to Margaret (Russell) Clifford, Dowager Countess of Cumberland, and to her daughter Anne, Countess of Dorset, as well as in the praises of them incorporated in the major poems of the volume. [13] Several poets and theologians dedicated books to Margaret Clifford as patron, among them the poet Samuel Daniel who served as tutor for her daughter Anne. [14] Lanyer indicates that the countess also acted as her patron, asserting that she wrote her poems at the countess' behest, and intimating that she owes both her religious conversion and her recognition as a poet to a period of residence with the countess and her daughter at the country estate of Cookham, in Berkshire.[15] Lanyer alludes knowledgeably to the countess' domestic unhappiness with her profligate adventurer husband, George Clifford—troubles which persisted after his death in 1605, when both mother and daughter became engaged in extended litigation over the terms of his will in an effort to secure to Anne her proper inheritance.[16] At the least, Lanyer seems to have received some encouragement in learning, piety, and poetry in the bookish and cultivated household of the Countess of Cumberland. Quite possibly she was also supported by the countess in the unusual venture of offering her poems for publication.

Salve Deus Rex Judaeorum, for all its diversity of subject matter, is governed by certain unifying themes and concerns. It is set forth as a comprehensive "Book of Good Women," fusing religious devotion and feminism so as to assert the essential harmony of those two impulses. Lanyer does not imitate Boccaccio, or Christine de Pizan, or Chaucer—but she does employ several poetic genres and verse forms with considerable facility to celebrate good women.[17] Given Lanyer's questionable past, her evident concern to find patronage, and her continuing focus on women, contemporary and biblical, we might be tempted to suppose that the ostensible religious subject of the title poem, Christ's Passion, simply provides a thin veneer for a subversive feminist statement—but that conclusion would be wrongheaded. Lanyer is a woman of her times, and her imagination is governed by its terms. She appears to be sincerely, if not very profoundly, religious, and she presents Christ's Passion as the focus for all the forms of female goodness—and masculine evil—her poems treat. Her good women meditate upon and imitate this model, and as poet she interprets her experience of life in religious categories.

The first section of the book, the dedications, sets up a contemporary community of good women. Most of the dedicatees were linked through kinship or marriage with the staunchly Protestant faction of Robert Dudley, Earl of Leicester, which promoted resistance to Spain, active support of Protestantism on the Continent, continued reform in the English church, and patronage of the arts, especially Christian poetry.[18] Lanyer's dedications continually emphasize the descent of virtue in the female line, from virtuous mothers to daughters: Queen Anne and Princess Elizabeth, Margaret and Anne Clifford, Catherine and Susan Bertie, Katherine Howard and her daughters. The author positions herself among these women, describing her book as the glass which shows their several virtues, and inviting them to receive and meditate upon Christ their Bridegroom here depicted.

The extraordinary virtue and merit she discerns in these ladies also redounds upon herself as poet, justifying her in undertaking what is "seldome seene, / A Womans writing of divinest things" ("To the Queenes most Excellent Majestie," ll. 3–4). Aemilia's several apologias for her poetry excuse it as faulty and unlearned by reason of her sex, but her disclaimers seem closer to the *humilitas* topos than to genuine angst. She continually proclaims her poems worthy of attention for the virtue and divinity they manifest: the implication is that a woman poet may write worthily since all these women are seen to be so worthy.

The first dedication (in six-line pentameter stanzas rhymed *ababcc*) honors Queen Anne for embodying the qualities of Juno, Venus, Pallas, and Cynthia, and for attracting Muses and Artists to her throne. Lanyer calls the queen's particular attention to "*Eves* Apologie, / Which I have writ in honour of your sexe" (ll. 73–74), and concludes with a defense of her poems' worth as deriving from nature rather than from learning and art:

> Not that I Learning to my selfe assume,
> Or that I would compare with any man:
>> But as they are Scholers, and by Art do write,
>> So Nature yeelds my Soule a sad delight.
>
> And since all Arts at first from Nature came,
> That goodly Creature, Mother of perfection,
> Whom *Joves* almighty hand at first did frame,
> Taking both her and hers in his protection:
>> Why should not She now grace my barren Muse,
>> And in a Woman all defects excuse.
>
> (ll. 147–56)

The sonnet-like poems to Princess Elizabeth and the Lady Arabella (dedications two and four) emphasize their learning: Lanyer offers her own "first fruits of a womans wit" to Elizabeth, whose "faire eyes farre better Bookes have seene"; and she apostrophizes Arabella as "Great learned

Ladie . . . / so well accompan'ed / With *Pallas*, and the Muses."[19] The
third dedication (in seven-line pentameter stanzas rhymed *ababacc*) is
addressed "To all vertuous Ladies in generall"; it praises all who are
ladies-in-waiting to Queen Virtue, companions of the Muses, and Virgins
waiting for the Bridegroom. The fifth dedication (in the same verse form
as that to the queen) praises the Countess of Kent as the glass displaying all
virtues to the young Aemilia, and as a heroic follower of Christ even in
infancy when her staunchly Protestant mother, Catherine Bertie, Countess
of Suffolk, fled England with her family during Queen Mary's reign:[20]

> Whose Faith did undertake in Infancie,
> All dang'rous travells by devouring Seas
> To flie to Christ from vaine Idolatry,
> Not seeking there this worthlesse world to please,
>   By your most famous Mother so directed,
>   That noble Dutchesse, who liv'd unsubjected.
>
> From *Romes* ridiculous prier and tyranny,
> That mighty Monarchs kept in awfull feare;
> Leaving here her lands, her state, dignitie;
> Nay more, vouchsaft disguised weedes to weare:
>   When with Christ Jesus she did meane to goe,
>   From sweet delights to taste part of his woe.
>   (ll. 19–30)

The next dedication is given special importance by its central position,
its length (224 lines), its verse form unique in this volume (four-line pentameter stanzas rhymed *abab*), and its genre: it is a dream vision narrative
entitled "The Authors Dreame to the Ladie Marie, the Countesse Dowager of Pembroke." In it Lanyer recounts a dream visit under the conduct
of Morpheus to the Idalian groves where she finds the Countess of Pembroke enthroned in Honor's chair, crowned by eternal Fame, and receiving
tribute from various classical representatives of art, beauty, and wisdom:
the Graces, Bellona, Dictina, Aurora, Flora. Under the countess' aegis the
strife between Art and Nature is resolved, and all the company join to sing
the countess' psalm versions:

> Those holy Sonnets they did all agree,
> With this most lovely Lady here to sing;
> That by her noble breasts sweet harmony,
> Their musicke might in eares of Angels ring.

> While saints like Swans about this silver brook
> Should *Hallalu-iah* sing continually,
> Writing her praises in th'eternall booke
> Of endlesse honour, true fames memorie.
>   (ll. 121–28)

Morpheus then reveals the lady's name, indicates that she spends all her time "In virtuous studies of Divinitie," and (continuing Lanyer's argument concerning the equality or superiority of women in moral and spiritual matters) ranks the countess "far before" her brother Sir Philip Sidney "For virtue, wisedome, learning, dignity" (ll. 147, 151–52). Dismayed upon awakening from her vision, Lanyer resolves to present her own "unlearned lines" (l. 203) to that lady, expecting that she will value these "flowres that spring from virtues ground" (l. 214) even though she herself reads and writes worthier and more profound books:

> Thogh many Books she writes that are more rare,
> Yet there is hony in the meanest flowres:
>
> Which is both wholesome, and delights the taste:
> Though sugar be more finer, higher priz'd,
> Yet is the painefull Bee no whit disgrac'd,
> Nor her faire wax, or hony more despiz'd.
>   (ll. 195–200)

The poem is well conceived, well made, and charming, testifying by its length and art to the importance of the Countess of Pembroke as model for Lanyer's conception of herself as learned lady and poet.

The later dedications are again epistolary in form. That to the Countess of Bedford (in seven-line pentameter stanzas rhymed *ababbcc*) identifies Knowledge, wielded by Virtue, as the key to her heart, and emphasizes, like Jonson's epigram, her "cleare Judgement."[21] The dedication to the Countess of Cumberland—distinguished as the book's primary patron and audience by the fact that only this dedication is in prose—offers the Passion poem as a worthy text for the countess' meditations in that its subject "giveth grace to the meanest and most unworthy hand that will undertake to write thereof." Also, describing the poems as a mirror of the countess's "most worthy mind," it claims that their art can extend the life of both dedicatee and author: these poems "may remaine in the world many yeares longer than your Honour, or my selfe can live, to be a light unto those that come after."

The dedication to the Countess of Suffolk (in six-line, pentameter stanzas rhymed *ababcc*) praises her as "fountaine" of all her husband's blessings, and, with continuing emphasis upon the female community, urges the countess to guide her "noble daughters" in meditations based upon Lanyer's Passion poem (ll. 49–68). In this dedication Lanyer eschews apologies for her poetic vocation and poetic achievement, claiming that both are God-given. She was led by her birth-star "to frame this worke of grace," and is enabled to do so by God himself: "his powre hath given me powre to write, / A subject fit for you to looke upon" (ll. 7, 13–14).

The final long dedication to Anne, Countess of Dorset (116 lines, in eight-line pentameter stanzas rhymed *ababababcc*) presents her as the worthy heir to her mother's excellencies and virtues, contrasting a female succession grounded upon virtue and holiness with the male succession through aristocratic titles. In this verse epistle, uniquely, Lanyer presumes to teach proper moral attitudes and conduct to her subject, as if privileged to do so by former familiarity. Intimating (perhaps) that Anne should continue such familiarity despite the differences in their rank, and evidently alluding to the fact that Cumberland's will alienated his estates and the titles they carried from his daughter (against the terms of the entail),[22] Lanyer compares the worthlessness of aristocratic titles to the "immortall fame" which "faire virtue" wins:

> What difference was there when the world began,
> Was it not Virtue that distinguisht all?
> All sprang but from one woman and one man,
> Then how doth Gentry come to rise and fall?
> Or who is he that very rightly can
> Distinguish of his birth, or tell at all
> In what meane state his Ancestors have bin,
> Before some one of worth did honour win.
> (ll. 49–56)

She emphasizes the office of the virtuous to serve as "God's Stewards" in providing for the poor, no doubt intending some application of that stewardship to herself as she urges Anne to fulfill her role as true successor and heir to her mother's virtues:

> To you, as to Gods Steward I doe write,
> In whom the seeds of virtue have bin sowne,

> By your most worthy mother, in whose right,
> All her faire parts you challenge as your owne;
>
> .   .   .   .
>
> You are the Heire apparent of this Crowne
> Of goodnesse, bountie, grace, love, pietie,
> By birth its yours, then keepe it as your owne,
> Defend it from all base indignitie;
> The right your Mother hath to it, is knowne
> Best unto you, who reapt such fruit thereby:
>> This Monument of her faire worth retaine
>> In your pure mind, and keepe it from al staine.
>>   (ll. 57–60, 65–72)

The dedication ends by begging Anne to excuse any insufficency in her poem arising from "wants, or weakenesse of my braine" (l. 141), since her subject, Christ's Passion, is beyond any human art.

If these dedications as a group portray a contemporary community of learned and virtuous women with the poet Aemilia their associate and celebrant, the prose "Epistle to the Vertuous Reader" confirms and extends that community, offering the book "for the generall use of all virtuous Ladies and Gentlewomen of this kingdome" (sig. f3r). The epistle is a remarkable contribution to the so-called *querelle des femmes,* that ongoing controversy over women's inherent worthiness or faultiness which produced a spate of writing, serious and satiric, from the Middle Ages through the seventeenth century and beyond.[23] Lanyer first lectures those women who "forgetting they are women themselves . . . speake unadvisedly against the rest of their sexe," and she urges them to leave such "folly" to "evill disposed men." With considerable passion she denounces those men who, "forgetting they were borne of women, nourished of women, and that if it were not by the means of women, they would be quite extinguished out of the world, and a finall ende of them all, doe like Vipers deface the wombes wherein they were bred"—associating such men with those who "dishonoured Christ his Apostles and Prophets, putting them to shamefull deaths" (sig. f3r). Marshalling biblical evidence with rhetorical force and flair, she claims that God himself has affirmed women's moral and spiritual equality or superiority to men:

[God] gave power to wise and virtuous women, to bring down their pride and arrogancie. As was cruell *Cesarus* by the discreet counsell of noble *Deborah,* Judge and Prophetesse of Israel: and resolution of *Jael* wife of *Heber* the Kenite: wicked

Haman, by the divine prayers and prudent proceedings of beautiful *Hester:* blasphemous *Holofernes,* by the invincible courage, rare wisdome, and confident carriage of *Judeth:* & the unjust Judges, by the innocency of chast *Susanna:* with infinite others, which for brevitie sake I will omit. (sig. f 3v)

In clipped, forceful phrases, she cites further evidence to the same point from the singular honors accorded to women by Christ:

It pleased our Lord and Saviour Jesus Christ, without the assistance of man . . . to be begotten of a woman, borne of a woman, nourished of a woman, obedient to a woman; and that he healed women, pardoned women, comforted women: yea, even when he was in his greatest agonie and bloodie sweat, going to be crucified, and also in his last houre of his death, tooke care to dispose of a woman: after his resurrection, appeared first to a woman, sent a woman to declare his most glorious resurrection to the rest of his Disciples. Many other examples I could alleadge of divers faithfull and virtuous women, who have in all ages, not onely beene Confessors, but also indured most cruel martyrdome for their faith in Jesus Christ. (sig. f 3v)

Lanyer's long poem on Christ's Passion (in eight-line pentameter stanzas rhymed *ababababcc*) constitutes the second part of her volume. The account of the Passion emphasizes the good women who played a major role in that event, and it is presented from the vantage point of women, past and present. Not only is the Passion narrative interpreted through the sensibility of Lanyer as woman poet, it is also enclosed within descriptions of the Countess of Cumberland as exemplary image, imitator, and spouse of the suffering Saviour. As poetic interpreter, Lanyer treats her material variously, sometimes relating events, sometimes elaborating them in the style of biblical commentary, sometimes meditating upon images or scenes, often apostrophizing participants as if she herself were present with them at these events.

The conceptual scheme of this poem is of primary interest; stylistically, it is uneven. Lanyer uses rhetorical schemes—especially figures of sound, parallelism, and repetition—with considerable skill; her apostrophes often convey strength of feeling; she can describe and sometimes dramatize a scene effectively. There are few striking images or metaphors, but her allusions are usually appropriate and her language straightforward, taking on at times colloquial directness. Her greatest fault is slackness—padding lines and stanzas to fill out the metrical pattern.

The Passion poem begins with a long preface addressing the Countess of

Cumberland (sts. 1–33). The first nine stanzas propose to immortalize her in verse, and recall the solace she has found for her many sorrows in the beauties of Cookham and the love of God. Stanzas 10 to 18 comprise an embedded psalmic passage praising God as the strong support of the just and the mighty destroyer of all their enemies, with obvious (and later overt) application to the much wronged Margaret Clifford. Lanyer perhaps intends the passage as a gesture of discipleship to the Countess of Pembroke, as it echoes or paraphrases a melange of psalm texts, chiefly Psalms 18, 84, 89, and 104:[24]

> With Majestie and Honour is He clad,
> And deck'd with light, as with a garment faire;
> . . . .
> He of the watry Cloudes his Chariot frames,
> And makes his blessed Angels powrefull Spirits,
> His Ministers are fearefull fiery flames,
> Rewarding all according to their merits;
> The Righteous for an heritage he claimes,
> And registers the wrongs of humble spirits;
> > Hills melt like wax, in presence of the Lord,
> > So do all sinners, in his sight abhorr'd.
> > > (sts. 10.1–12.8)

Stanzas 19 to 33 identify the countess as one of those just who are specially beloved and protected by God, and praise her for abandoning the delights of the court to serve her heavenly king in rural retirement. This section includes a dispraise of beautiful women—Helen, Cleopatra, Rosamund, Lucretia, Matilda—whose beauty led them or their lovers to sin or ruin; by contrast, the countess' inner beauty of grace and virtue made Christ the husband of her soul, and his death "made her Dowager of all" (st. 33.1).

This statement leads into Lanyer's proper subject, the Passion (sts. 34–165). First, however, she invokes and admonishes her "lowely Muse" (sts. 34–41) for risking the fate of Icarus or Phaeton by flying so far above her "appointed straine":

> Thinke when the eye of Wisdom shall discover
> Thy weakling Muse to flie, that scarce could creepe,
> And in the Ayre above the Clowdes to hover,
> When better 'twere mued up, and fast asleepe;

> They'l thinke with *Phaeton,* thou canst ne'r recover,
> But helplesse with that poore yong Lad to weepe:
> The Little World of thy weake Wit on fire,
> Where thou wilt perish in thine owne desire.
>
> (st. 36)

But Lanyer takes courage from the story of the Widow's Mite, and the conviction that God's glory will shine the more, "the Weaker thou doest seeme to be / In Sexe, or Sence" (st. 37.1–2). Proposing like many of her contemporaries to render sacred matter "in plainest Words" so as not to distort it,[25] she prays God to "guide my Hand and Quill" (st. 41.4).

Her account of the Passion is part commentary or meditation on the biblical story and part apostrophe—a poetic figure which often intensifies emotion and creates an effect of immediacy. The first section begins with Christ's prayers and subsequent capture in the Garden of Gethsemane (sts. 42–99). Using apostrophe to poignant effect, Lanyer conveys Christ's profound isolation even from his beloved apostles:

> Sweet Lord, how couldst thou thus to flesh and blood
> Communicate thy griefe? tell of thy woes?
> Thou knew'st they had no powre to doe thee good,
> But were the cause thou must endure these blowes.
>
> (st. 48.1–4)

The emphasis throughout his section is on the sins and failures of Christ's own apostles. Peter declared that his faith would never fail, but Christ knew Peter would deny him three times. Christ implored the apostles to wait and watch with him, but they slept. The Apostle Judas proved to be "A trothlesse traytor, and a mortall foe" (st. 61.5). Peter offended Christ and the laws by drawing his sword against Christ's enemies. Turning then to the "accursed crew" of Scribes and Pharisees who apprehended Christ, Lanyer castigates them with a fine flourish of parallelism and antithesis:

> How blinde were they could not discerne the Light!
> How dull! if not to understand the truth,
> How weake! if meekenesse overcame their might;
> How stony hearted, if not mov'd to ruth:
> How void of Pitie, and how full of Spight,
> Gainst him that was the Lord of Light and Truth:
> > Here insolent Boldnesse checkt by Love and Grace,
> > Retires, and falls before our Makers face.
>
> . . . .

Here Falshood beares the shew of formall Right,
Base Treacherie hath gote a guard of men;
Tyranny attends, with all his strength and might,
To leade this siely Lamb to Lyons denne.

(sts. 64; 72.1–4)

The section ends by reverting to the disciples' failures: "Though they protest they never will forsake him, / They do like men, when dangers over-
take them" (st. 79.7–8). This formulation begins Lanyer's sharply drawn
contrast between the weak and evil men in the Passion story and the good
women who play a role in it.

The second section (sts. 80–118) focuses upon yet more wicked men,
Christ's several judges—"wicked *Caiphas*," "Proud *Pontius Pilate*,"
"scoffing Herod." It begins by describing Christ through a series of
epithets—George Herbert's technique in "Prayer I":[26]

The beauty of the World, Heavens chiefest Glory;
The mirrour of Martyrs Crowne of holy Saints;
Love of th'Almighty, blessed Angels story;
Water of Life, which none that drinks it, faints;
Guide of the Just, where all our Light we borrow;
Mercy of Mercies; Hearer of Complaints;
    Triumpher over Death; Ransomer of Sinne;
    Falsely accused; now his paines begin.

(st. 81)

The judges are characterized through striking metaphors: Caiphas'
"Owly eies are blind, and cannot see," and Pilate is a "painted wall / A
golden Sepulcher with rotten bones" (sts. 89.8; 116.1–2).

Then Lanyer addresses a lengthy apostrophe to Pilate, explicitly contrasting good women with these weak and evil men (sts. 94.5–105). Ranging herself with Pilate's wife whom she takes as the representative of
womankind, Lanyer pleads with Pilate to spare Christ, relating that plea
to a remarkable apologia pronouncing Eve guiltless of any evil intention in
the Fall:

O noble Governour, make thou yet a pause,
Doe not in innocent blood imbrue thy hands;
    But heare the words of thy most worthy wife,
    Who sends to thee, to beg her Saviours life.

.   .   .   .

> Let not us Women glory in Mens fall,
> Who had power given to over-rule us all.
>
> Till now your indiscretion sets us free,
> And makes our former fault much less appeare;
> Our Mother *Eve*, who tasted of the Tree,
> Giving to *Adam* what shee held most deare,
> Was simply good, and had no powre to see,
> The after-comming harme did not appeare:
>> The subtile Serpent that our Sex betraide,
>> Before our fall so sure a plot had laide.
>>   (sts. 94.5–96)

She presses that argument, claiming that Eve's "harmeless Heart" intended no evil at all, that her fault was only "too much love, / Which made her give this present to her Deare" (st. 101.1–2). All the guilt of the Fall belongs to Adam, who was strong, wise, and undeceived. Moreover, any faults which women might have inherited from Eve are far outweighed by the guilt and malice of men, epitomized in Pilate:

> Her weakenesse did the Serpents words obay,
> But you in malice Gods deare Sonne betray.
>
> Whom, if unjustly you condemne to die,
> Her sinne was small, to what you doe commit;
>
> . . . .
>
> Then let us have our Libertie againe,
> And challendge to your selves no Sov'raigntie;
> You came not in the world without our paine,
> Make that a barre against your crueltie;
> Your fault being greater, why should you disdaine
> Our beeing your equals, free from tyranny?
>> If one weake woman simply did offend,
>> This sinne of yours, hath no excuse, nor end.
>
> To which (poore soules) we never gave consent,
> Witnesse thy wife (O *Pilate*) speakes for all;
>>   (sts. 102.6–105.2)

The third section presents the procession to Calvary, the Crucifixion, and the Resurrection, again contrasting the responses of good women and evil men to these events (sts. 119–65). The journey scene is described with considerable dramatic effectiveness:

First went the Crier with open mouth proclayming
The heavy sentence of Iniquitie,
The Hangman next, by his base office clayming
His right in Hell, where sinners never die,
Carrying the nayles, the people still blaspheming
Their maker, using all impiety;
    The Thieves attending him on either side,
    The Serjeants watching, while the women cri'd.
                           (st. 121)

A lengthy apostrophe to the daughters of Jerusalem follows (sts. 122–26), contrasting their tears and their efforts to beseech mercy for Christ with their menfolk's cruelty:

When spightfull men with torments did oppresse
Th'afflicted body of this innocent Dove,
Poore women seeing how much they did transgresse,
By teares, by sighes, by cries intreat, nay prove,
What may be done among the thickest presse,
They labour still these tyrants hearts to move;
    In pitie and compassion to forbeare
    Their whipping, spuring, tearing of his haire.

But all in vaine, their malice hath no end,
Their hearts more hard than flint, or marble stone.
                      (sts. 125–126.2)

Then Lanyer locates herself with the mother of Jesus as observer and mourner at the crucifixion, and in an extended passage (sts. 127–42) meditates upon Mary's role in the Redemption and her exaltation as "Queene of Woman-kind:"

How canst thou choose (faire Virgin) then but mourne,
When this sweet of-spring of thy body dies,
When thy faire eies beholds his bodie torne,
The peoples fury, heares the womens cries.
                   (st. 142.1–4)

Lanyer's baroque description of the crucifixion itself is not without poetic force and religious feeling:

His joynts dis-joynted, and his legges hang downe,
His alablaster breast, his bloody side,
His members torne, and on his head a Crowne
Of sharpest Thorns, to satisfie for pride:

> Anguish and Paine doe all his Sences drowne,
> While they his holy garments do divide:
>> His bowells drie, his heart full fraught with griefe,
>> Crying to him that yeelds him no reliefe.
>>
>> (st. 146)

But the emphasis on good women continues. This icon of the Crucifixion is presented as an object of meditation to the Countess of Cumberland, who is apostrophized as "Deere Spouse of Christ" (st. 147.2), and urged to judge "if ever Lover were so true" (st. 159.3). Finally, the precious balms brought by still other good women to annoint the dead Christ are interpreted as a figure of the precious ointments "of Mercie, Charitie, and Faith" brought to the risen Christ (the Bridegroom of Canticles) "by his faithfull Wife / The Holy Church" (st. 161).

A long coda to the Countess of Cumberland (sts. 166–230), which parallels the long prologue, expatiates upon the many forms in which Christ appears to the countess as she practices the works of mercy, and portrays her in Canticles imagery as Christ's Spouse. It also proclaims her superiority to the worthy women of history. She is more noble and more faithful to her spouse than Cleopatra was, since "she flies not from him when afflictions prove" and she dies not one death for love but a thousand (st. 180). She also surpasses the famous women who fought and conquered with the sword—the Scythian women who put Darius to flight; Deborah who judged Israel; valiant Judith who defeated Holofernes—since she wages "farre greater warre . . . / Against that many headed monster Sinne" (st. 187.1–2). Hester who fasted and prayed three days so as to free her people from Haman gives way before the countess, who for "dayes, weekes, months, and yeares" has worn the sackcloth of worldly troubles (st. 190.3–4). So also Susanna's single trial of chastity is overmatched by the countess' conquest of all base affections in her own breast, And the journey of the noble Queen of Sheba to find King Solomon was but a figure of the countess' love and service to an almighty and everlasting king.

At this juncture we find a sensuous and not ineffective baroque passage (sts. 219–28) expatiating upon the sweetness of Christ's grace and love:

> Sweet holy rivers, pure celestiall springs,
> Proceeding from the fountaine of our life;
> Swift sugred currents that salvation brings,
> Cleare christall streames, purging all sinne and strife.

> Faire floods, where souls do bathe their snow-white wings,
> Before they flie to true eternall life:
>> Sweet Nectar and Ambrosia, food of Saints,
>> Which, whoso tasteth, never after faints.
>>   (st. 217)

Such sweetness "sweet'ned all the sowre of death" (st. 219.1) to the first martyrs—St. Stephen, St. Lawrence, the Apostles Andrew and Peter, and John the Baptist. The praise of these male saints as chief of the martyrs and confessors by whom "our Saviour most was honoured" (st. 229.6) provides some counterweight to the massive wickedness Lanyer lays to men's charge throughout the poem. But it is a small gesture. Lanyer concludes her poem by declaring that the Countess of Cumberland follows in the footsteps of these martyrs, folding up "all their Beauties" in her breast (st. 229.8).

The final poem, "The Description of Cooke-ham" is the gem of the volume. In 210 lines of pentameter couplets it sustains a gentle elegiac tone and contains some lovely pastoral description. The poem presumably executes the Countess of Cumberland's charge, reported in *Salve Deus* as not yet fulfilled, to write "praisefull lines of that delightfull place," the *"Paradice"* of Cookham (st. 3.5). Whether Lanyer's poem was written before or after "Penshurst," it was conceived on very different lines. It is a valediction—a farewell by the author and by the residents (the Countess of Cumberland and her daughter) to an Edenic home, perhaps in specific reference to the countess' permanent departure to those residences she would occupy as a widow.[27]

This poem also embodies but gives mythic dimension to Lanyer's dominant concerns: the Eden now lost is portrayed as a female paradise inhabited solely by women—the countess, her young virgin daughter Anne, and Aemilia Lanyer. In keeping with the Edenic myth Lanyer (who is twenty years older than Anne Clifford) describes herself as a constant participant in Anne's sports (ll. 119–21), as if they had been young girls together at Cookham. Located in Berkshire a few miles from Maidenhead, the area is still a beauty spot, with extensive frontages on the Thames, rich woodlands, lush meadows, picturesque scattered hamlets, and high hills in the west—which however do not afford a prospect into thirteen shires, as Lanyer's poem asserts.[28]

The elegiac tone is established in the opening lines, as Lanyer bids fare-

well to the place she associates with her conversion and the confirmation
of her vocation as poet:

> Farewell (sweet *Cooke-ham*) where I first obtain'd
> Grace from that Grace where perfit Grace remain'd;
> And where the Muses gave their full consent,
> I should have powre the virtuous to content:
>
> . . . .
>
> Never shall my sad eies againe behold
> Those pleasures which my thoughts did then unfold.
>
> (ll. 1–10)

She represents the countess as sharing these elegaic sentiments, and advises
her to regard those "pleasures past" as but "dimme shadowes of celestiall
pleasures."

Then begins the description of the estate, as it responds to the arrival
and departure of its mistress in terms of the seasonal round. The house
itself is barely mentioned, but the estate becomes a *locus amoenus* as each
part decks itself out in all its spring and summer loveliness for her arrival:

> The Walkes put on their summer Liveries,
> And all things else did hold like similies:
> The Trees with leaves, with fruits, with flowers clad,
> Embrac'd each other, seeming to be glad,
> Turning themselves to beauteous Canopies,
> To shade the bright Sunne from your brighter eies:
> The cristall Streames with silver spangles graced,
> While by the glorious Sunne they were embraced:
> The little Birds in chirping notes did sing,
> To entertain both You and that sweet Spring.
>
> (ll. 21–30)

Other aspects of nature contribute to the welcome with an obsequiousness
analogous to that of the Penshurst fish and game offering themselves to
capture, but Lanyer's tone carries no hint of Jonson's amused exaggera-
tion.[29] The hills descend humbly that the countess may tread on them, the
gentle winds enhance her pleasure in the woods by their "sad murmure";
the "swelling Bankes deliver'd all their pride" (their fish) upon seeing this
"Phoenix"; and the birds and animals sport before her—(only slightly
more timorous than they would have been with Eve):

> The pretty Birds would oft come to attend thee,
> Yet flie away for feare they should offend thee:

> The little creatures in the Burrough by
> Would come abroad to sport them in your eye;
> Yet fearefull of the Bowe in your faire Hand,
> Would runne away when you did make a stand.
>
> (ll. 47–52)

Like that other Eden the focus of interest in this place is a "stately Tree" (l. 53). This oak surpasses all its fellows in height and also incorporates qualities of other trees: it is straight and tall "Much like a comely Cedar" and it has outspread arms and broad leaves "like a Palme tree," veiling the sun and fanning the breezes (ll. 57, 61). Seated by this tree the countess enjoys regal honors and delights: "Hills, vales, and woods, as if on bended knee" salute her, and the prospect of "thirteene shires" (if not of all the world) is "fit to please the eyes of Kings" (ll. 68, 72). However, this tree offers no temptation, only contentment and incitement to meditate upon the creatures as they reflect their Creators' beauty, wisdom, love, and majesty. Elsewhere in the woods the countess meditates on the Scriptures, "Placing his holy Writ in some faire tree" (l. 83), and in her daily life at Cookham she follows in the spiritual footsteps of the greatest Old Testament saints:

> With *Moyses* you did mount his holy Hill,
> To know his pleasure, and performe his Will.
> With lovely *David* you did often sing,
> His holy Hymnes to Heavens Eternall King.
>
> . . . .
>
> With blessed *Joseph* you did often feed
> Your pined brethren when they stood in need.
>
> (ll. 85–92)

The next passage is a complaint that Lanyer can no longer associate with Anne Clifford, now Countess of Dorset, because "Unconstant Fortune" has placed too great a social divide between them (l. 102). While the passage gives vent to Lanyer's discontent with her station, and makes a transparent bid for further attention from Anne, it is thematically appropriate. The social constrictions attending Anne's nobility by birth and marriage are set off against the natural associations, dictated solely by virtue and pleasure, in Edenic Cookham, "Whereof depriv'd, I evermore must grieve" (l. 125).

Next, Cookham's grief at the ladies' preparations for departure is described in a notably effective passage in which pathetic fallacy fuses with the seasonal change from autumn to winter:

Me thought each thing did unto sorrow frame:
The trees that were so glorious in our view,
Forsooke both floures and fruit, when once they knew
Of your depart, their very leaves did wither,
Changing their colours as they grewe together.
But when they saw this had no powre to stay you,
They often wept, though speechlesse, could not pray you;
Letting their teares in your faire bosoms fall:

. . . .

Their frozen tops, like Ages hoarie haires,
Showes their disasters, languishing in feares:
A swarthy riveld ryne all over spread,
Their dying bodies halfe alive, halfe dead.

(ll. 132–46)

The countess' gracious leavetaking of all the beloved creatures and places on the estate culminates in the charge to Lanyer to preserve them in poetry. Then the scene declines into sentimentality as Lanyer portrays herself stealing the farewell kiss the countess bestows on the noble oak.

The final passage echoes the imagery of the opening passage, as all the beauties of the *locus amoenus* wither in desolation:

And those sweet Brookes that ranne so faire and cleare,
With griefe and trouble wrinckled did appeare.
Those pretty Birds that wonted were to sing,
Now neither sing, nor chirp, nor use their wing;
But with their tender feet on some bare spray,
Warble forth sorrow, and their owne dismay.

. . . .

Each arbour, banke, each seate, each stately tree,
Lookes bare and desolate now for want of thee;
Turning greene tresses into frostie gray,
While in cold griefe they wither all away.
The Sunne grew weake, his beames no comfort gave,
While all greene things did make the earth their grave:
Each brier, each bramble, when you went away,
Caught fast your clothes, thinking to make you stay:
Delightful Eccho wonted to reply
To our last words, did for now sorrow die:
The house cast off each garment that might grace it,
Putting on Dust and Cobwebs to deface it.
All desolation then there did appeare,
When you were going whom they held so deare.

(ll. 183–294)

In sharpest contrast to Jonson's "Penshurst" which celebrates a quasi-Edenic place whose beauty and harmony are centered in and preserved by its lord who "dwells" permanently within it, Lanyer's country-house poem portrays the destruction of an idyllic place when its lady departs. Cookham takes on the appearance of a ravaged Eden after the first human couple is expelled. But here it is a female pair—or rather trio—who depart: the countess called away by her "occasions"; the virgin daughter to her marriage; Lanyer to social decline. Offering her poem as "This last farewell to *Cooke-ham*" (l. 205) Lanyer suggests strongly that none of them will return to this happy garden state, in which women lived without mates, but found contentment and delight in nature, God, and female companionship. Though of uneven quality, "The Description of Cooke-ham" is an attractive poem presenting a sustained imaginative vision.

Until we can learn more about Lanyer's life we will be unable to answer most of the questions her book so insistently provokes: What influences and circumstances led her to write—and especially to publish—poetry? What poetic models did she look to? How much patronage did she in fact enjoy and from whom? Was "Penshurst" written before "Cooke-ham" or did Lanyer invent the English country-house poem? How important was religion and religious devotion to her? How was her book received? Did she write anything else? And especially, how ought we to account for the strong feminism which pervades every part of her book?

Despite its artistic flaws, Lanyer's volume is worthy of attention for the charm of the "Cooke-ham" poem and for its quite remarkable feminist conceptual frame. The patronage poems present a female lineage of virtue from mother to daughter, a community of good women extending from Catherine Bertie, Protestant fugitive in Mary Tudor's reign, to the young Anne Clifford, heir to the "Crowne / Of goodness, bountie, grace, love, pietie" long worn by her mother, the Countess of Cumberland. The Passion poem extends this community back to biblical times, portraying women as Christ's truest apostles and followers. In the "Cooke-ham" poem a female Eden suffers a new Fall when the structures of a male social order force its women inhabitants to abandon it. In sum, the fundamental Christian myths—Eden, the Passion, the Community of Saints—are here revised, with women at their center.

SANDRA K. FISCHER

Elizabeth Cary and Tyranny, Domestic and Religious

L ADY ELIZABETH TANFIELD CARY, Viscountess Falkland (1585–
1639), was the chiefly self-educated daughter and heiress of a
genteel Renaissance family.[1] She has been remembered primarily
for her Catholic polemics, manifested most boldly in a translation, published in Douay in 1630, of Cardinal Perron's answer to criticism of his
works by James I; for her temerity and conviction Lady Cary found her
book confiscated and publicly burned. This was not, moreover, her first
receipt of closed-minded and tyrannical oppression: if the Renaissance
changed women, it may have been, as Joan Kelly-Gadol suggests, to a dual
dependence on favor from husband *and* ruler.[2] Indeed, Lady Cary's life
speaks as a series of conflicts between the ideal and the real: personally,
religiously, politically, and artistically. Her biographers have not been
blind to this conflict and the way Lady Cary met it. Lady Georgiana Fullerton finds her plight both typical of women and exemplary, prefacing her
biography with the heartening comparison of our own "hardships resembling those she underwent" and the encomium, "as a generous, courageous, noble-hearted woman, who fought a good fight, kept the faith, and
continued it to the end, she may well be honoured and admired, and her
example offered to the imitation of all who suffer for justice' sake"
(pp. vii–viii).

So voracious a reader in her youth that she bribed the servants for more
candles to use surreptitiously in her bedroom for night study, Elizabeth

Tanfield was most attracted to the writings of the church fathers and the lives of saints. Consequently, at the age of nineteen, she privately and intellectually converted to Catholicism:[3] a happy change for her conscience and temperament, but an unfortunate choice for domestic expediency. She had already, at fifteen, been contracted in marriage to a knight's son of a strong anti-Catholic predisposition. Because the marriage was arranged primarily to consolidate Tanfield money with Cary prestige, Sir Henry Cary left his young wife first in the care of her family and then of his mother.[4] Thus it was rather easy for Elizabeth to conceal her new religion, a deception she continued for twenty years. Her parents innocently assisted in the ruse by having letters to her husband written by another in Elizabeth's name; when he finally saw a letter of his wife's own composition, he was flabbergasted by her erudition and style and insisted that it was a forgery.

Lady Cary attempted to be a dutiful wife inasmuch as it was compatible with her beliefs: she gave birth to eleven children, followed her husband to Ireland, and dedicated an early play she wrote to him. Moreover, the concept of conjugal duty was consistent with her religious ideals of humility and self-effacement. She advised her eldest daughter, Anne, "Whenever conscience and reason will permit it, always prefer the will of another to your own" (Fullerton, pp. 25–26), and she attempted to conform to this credo herself. The entire marriage could have been a battle of wills on many fronts, but Lady Cary consistently bowed to her husband's wishes, which often necessitated altering her character and disposition. Although she preferred study to nursery, she handled all the domestic tasks, including rearing of the children; she loathed horses but learned to ride because it pleased her husband; she cared little for clothing and appearance yet dressed up according to her husband's preferences. As Fullerton reports, "Her women were fain to walk round the room after her, pinning on her things . . . whilst she was thinking seriously on some other business, and it was always her custom to write or to read whilst they curled her hair" (p. 28).

Despite the efforts of Lady Cary to be a proper wife in all external matters, when Sir Henry discovered her religious conversion, in 1626, he sent his wife into isolation and near-destitution. His intent, according to Fullerton, was to "starve his wife into submission" (p. 66). Her father followed suit by disinheriting his daughter, and the king had her imprisoned in her rooms for six weeks, hoping to force her to recant. Sir Henry wrote letters to the king disclaiming his wife, and all her friends abandoned her in the face of scandal.[5] After nearly starving to death for her religious beliefs, Lady Cary boldly brought her case before the Privy Council, which in 1627 ruled that Sir Henry must support her with an allowance of £500 per annum. He was remiss in doing so even after the order, revealing his qualities of pride and bigotry, but Lady Cary, reluctant to displease her husband further, did not complain to the council a second time. In politics Lord Falkland was similarly tyrannical, demanding that all priests be banished from Ireland in direct opposition to crown orders and good sense. Eventually Queen Henrietta Maria, because of her own Catholic background, interceded to promote nuptial reconciliation between the Carys. In 1633 the whole family was reunited in a single household, but a few weeks later Sir Henry broke his leg in a fall from his horse: it gangrened, was amputated, and he bled to death. Before he died he allegedly asked to see a priest.

Even in the face of such domestic and economic disaster, Lady Cary persevered in her love of letters. In addition to her Perron translation, she undertook lives of three saintes in verse, hymns to the Virgin Mary, a history of Edward II (erroneously attributed to her husband, who would certainly not have been capable of the praise of the pope that it contains),[6] and two plays, one now lost and the other remarkable for being the first extant original English tragedy by a woman, *The Tragedie of Mariam, the Faire Queene of Jewry* (1613). This play is even more remarkable in the plight of its heroine, who, like Lady Cary, must come to terms with domestic and political tyranny in the form of her husband Herod, tyrant par excellence.

Although the minimal criticism focused on this play has judged Elizabeth Cary's sentiments as in part rebellious,[7] it is more accurate to say that she is interested, here and elsewhere, in how a woman handles tyranny and maintains her own integrity. Mariam's actions are for the most part sympathetic, although her end is tragic; her problems are lack of agency and situations offering only Hobson's choices. In "The History of . . . King Edward the Second," Cary swings the focus to his queen, whose actions, in a predicament similar to Mariam's, she disdains: "Certainly this man was infinitely tyrannical and vicious, deserving more than could be laid upon him; yet it had been much more to the Queen's reputation and honour, if she had given him a fair and legal trial . . ." (*Harleian Miscellany*, I, 89). She seems to have consciously chosen for artistic expression historical women who also faced tyranny with a clear conscience, yet who found their choices for solution similarly ambiguous.

Lady Cary's tendency to choose well-known stories from prominent sources indicates one of the circumlocutious devices of the genres of marginality: in a simple retelling of the facts, the author is not obliged to accept responsibility for what may be considered rebellious notions. She may, in her verse or prose reinterpretation of history, test the responses of characters in plights similar to her own; she may discernibly call for restitution against domestic and religious tyranny; but the composition remains distanced from reality, as Annis Pratt suggests, an ideal "in itself merely rhetorical, an artifact or idea rather than an action." Such marginal genres as religious writings, translations, and closet drama in a sense afford vicarious action: the writing itself, whether or not disseminated and read, becomes a philosophically justified enactment of the author's life. She may speak with liberty and impunity of an ancient queen of Judea and the archetypal dramatic tyrant, or of the wife of a medieval English king—but the subject is ever herself. A woman writer may establish her own realistic precedent in art; she may create her own role models. Judith Fetterley insists that all literature and literary criticism are by nature political; indeed, Cary's writings primitively and innocently work toward "revision"—that is, examining the stereotypes, redefining feminine identity, and locating an authentic voice outside the male tradition.[8] The voice of silence thus speaks through historical reinterpretation.[9]

Lady Cary, as a writer and a recusant, of necessity found herself confronted with other paradoxes, which involved establishing a maverick self-image and retaining an apparently perverse personal integrity against the conflicting voices of authority. Even with the accomplished, wily, and intelligent Elizabeth on the throne, and a few other women prominent in Tudor society as literati, there must have been an inherent tension then, as now, in being a "smart woman." As a child Cary was both encouraged and dissuaded from learning; she could privately stretch her accomplishments to the limits of her potential but then must publicly conceal the extent of her "unladylike" abilities. One is reminded of the wide-ranging humanistic education of the daughters of Thomas More, and the paradox of these talents being put to use only as dinner entertainment for household guests. Moreover, as a Catholic, Cary revered all authority and believed in self-effacement, always, for instance, kneeling when in the presence of her mother.

Yet this same woman stressed internal consistency: she must be true to her talents and beliefs. Thus, as a writer, she found in the world of letters an acceptable arena of action. According to Edward Hyde, Earl of Clarendon, she had a "most masculine understanding" and, although she probably did not expect a wide readership for any of her works, could not allow the constrictions to silence her. The life of the mind could be chronicled creatively: she, like other Renaissance women writers, "apparently believed that [her] writings would be useful records of experience available nowhere else."[10] In religious terms the same paradox expressed itself in her life, for to be true to her religion and its authority, she must flout civil authority. Although recusants in late Tudor England were increasingly being persecuted for their practice, Lady Cary consistently risked such punishment by attending private masses.[11]

Although isolated intellectually, spiritually, and physically from her husband and alienated from her king, Lady Cary continued private and social inquiry into her favorite subjects. We may have this artistic perseverance to account for the publication of *Mariam*. The poet John Davies, Elizabeth Cary's childhood writing master, was also well-acquainted with Philip Sidney's sister, Mary Herbert, Countess of Pembroke, herself a published dramatic translator who encouraged her coterie to write philosophical closet drama like *The Tragedie of Mariam*.[12] Although Cary's daughter asserts the standard noble excuse for publication of the play, that it was stolen away and entered illegally in the register, it appeared in print shortly after Davies had published complimentary verses to his literary women acquaintances, lauding the dramatic ability of Lady Falkland. He dedicates "The Muse's Sacrifice, Or Divine Meditations" of 1612 to the "most noble, and no lesse deservedly-renowned Ladyes, as well Darlings, as Patronesses, of the *Muses; LUCY, Countess of Bedford;* MARY, Countesse-Dowager of Pembroke; and ELIZABETH, *Lady Cary,* (Wife of Sr. *Henry Cary:*) Glories of Women." Davies manifests special delight at the talents of Lady Falkland because he had been her tutor, and he encourages her to give credit to womanhood by publishing her plays:

> CARY (*of whom* Minerva *stands in feare,*
>   *lest she, from her, should get* ARTS Regencie)
> *Of* ART *so moves the great-all-moving* Spheare,
>   *that ev'ry* Orbe *of* Science *moves thereby.*
>
> *Thou mak'st* Melpomen *proud, and my* Heart *great*
>   *of such* a Pupill, *who, in* Buskin *fine,*
> *With* Feete *of* State, *dost make thy* Muse *to mete*
>   *the* Scenes *of* Syracuse *and* Palestine.
>
> Art, Language; *yea; abstruse and holy* Tongues
>   *thy* Wit *and* Grace *acquir'd thy* Fame *to raise;*
> *And still to fill thine* owne, *and* others' Songs;
>   thine, *with thy* Parts, *and* others, *with thy* praise.
>
> *Such nervy* Limbes *of* Art, *and* Straines *of* Wit
>   Times *past ne'er knew the weaker* Sexe *to have;*
> *And* Times *tc come, will hardly credit it,*
>   *if thus thou give thy* Workes *both* Birth *and* Grave.
>
> *Yee Heav'nly* Trinary, *that swayes the State*
>   *of* ARTS *whole* Monarchie, *and* WITS Empire,
> *Live long your* Likes *(unlike) to animate*
>   *(for all* Times *light) to blow at your* Arts Fire.[13]

One may wonder at the inclusion of Lady Falkland's name alongside the more famous Countesses of Bedford and Pembroke, particularly because Elizabeth Cary typically had little money or favor to bestow upon struggling poets.[14] She was, however, quite renowned as a hostess and leader of intellectual coteries, no matter how mean her surroundings and scarce her funds. By age four she had mastered five languages; she adored the theater and was well pleased when Sir Henry himself appeared in a masque at court in 1612. After his death she pursued intellectual stimulation with great vigor, being particularly fond of Oxford men and "freedom of conversation." Dr. Laud found her Catholic arguments so convincing and influential that he recommended her banishment from London and the court (Fullerton, pp. 6, 32, 143, 167).

One mark of Elizabeth Cary's contemporary position as a learned and influential lady is the number of works dedicated to her or mentioning her. These include John Marston's *Works:* "To the Right Honourable, the Lady

Elizabeth Carey, Viscountess Falkland . . . because your Honour is well acquainted with the Muses"; the 1614 edition of *England's Helicon*, published by Richard More: "TO THE TRULY VERTUOUS AND Honourable Lady, the Lady ELIZABETH CARIE"; lines by a Mr. Clayton, on her prolific output, in *In Laudem nobilissimae Heroinae* . . . ; and by a Father Leander, praising her learning and quality of mind (Fullerton, pp. 115–18). To express her religious philosophy she chose primarily to translate Catholic treatises from the Continent; but for private concerns her subject was tyranny, protected under the cloak of true historical source.

One final biographical instance completes the pattern of Lady Cary's battle against religious and political tyranny. After the death of Sir Henry, their son Lucius became Lord Falkland; he was alone among the Cary children in remaining Protestant rather than converting to Catholicism. Fearing that her younger sons, Patrick and Placid, would be subverted by Lucius and a morally dubious acquaintance of his, a Mr. Chillingworth, Lady Cary first removed her sons to Catholic boarding houses "in obscure parts of London" with the intent of eventually sending them to seminaries in France. Lucius assiduously set out to find his brothers; when he failed, he had his mother called before the Privy Council for interrogation. She would not reveal their whereabouts, answering truthfully about her intentions, and thus was briefly imprisoned in the Tower for defiance. When the Chief Justice released Lady Cary, she continued undaunted with her plan, managing to sneak her sons out of the country: Placid became a monk in Paris, and Patrick went to Rome with the intention of becoming a priest, although he later decided that his primary duty was to produce a proper—that is, Catholic—heir (Fullerton, pp. 243–51).

As Murdock summarizes the pattern of Lady Cary's life, "She was caught in one of the central dilemmas of her time, between intellectual conviction and expediency, between loyalty to an ideal and loyalty to her husband, between the pursuit of Heaven and the race for favor with the King" (p. 17). This also perfectly describes the position of Mariam at the opening of Cary's play. Although Cary is predictably faithful (according to our theory of marginal intent) to her source in the *Antiquities* of Josephus,[15] she makes several artistic alterations in focus and emphasis that help to reveal her main concerns. First, she chooses Mariam, the wronged wife, over king, husband, and tyrant Herod as her tragic focal point. Additionally, she augments the depiction of other women in the history and shows them as defined solely in relation to men: as wives, widows, sisters, former wives, mothers-in-law, maidens, whores. As Simone de Beauvoir suggests, women's social value and extent of power as well as their identities derive from these relationships.[16] The men, in turn, become foils, alternatives for the judging of women and the treatment of wives, with Constabarus and Herod at opposite ends of the spectrum.[17] Mariam's primary foil is Salome, who may have some feminist principles but no moral sense. Finally, Lady Cary hints, by the end of the play, at a continuum linking the martyrdom of Mariam and the sacrifice of Christ, adumbrating a comparable release from tyranny and the old law in these symbolic deaths (see Beilin, "Elizabeth Cary," p. 60).

While Mariam exhibits defiance on two primary levels—political and domestic—Cary adds a persistent undertone of moral difference as well. From the beginning of the play Mariam is nearly alone in possessing scruples in her society—and indeed this must be as Lady Cary herself felt in her religious conversion and subsequent alienation. It is noteworthy in this regard that Herod can be nothing less, in stage tradition and in symbol, than tyranny personified: certainly Lady Cary was familiar with Hamlet's admonition to the players to avoid passionate rantings in the Herodian vein (*Hamlet*, III.ii.8–15), and she found she could easily use the religious implications of the literary Herod as "the tyrant ogre . . . , the usurper from whom the world is now to be saved," and "the extreme symbol of the misgoverning, tenacious ego" who "has brought mankind to the nadir of spiritual abasement."[18] The spiritual, moral, or religious level is of greatest interest to the playwright: Mariam would have no tragedy were she not in inner conflict over duties of the conscience and duties of the world.

The play opens with a striking soliloquy illustrative of this conflict. Mariam is above all (and despite minor flaws of overconfidence and pride) a woman of scrupulous conscience and rigorous self-examination. Upon hearing rumors of Herod's demise, the heroine wants to exult at the death of personal and social tyranny, but while she hated her husband's hypocrisy, she finds herself guilty of the same crime:

> When *Herod* liv'd, that now is done to death,
> Oft have I wisht that I from him were free:
> Oft have I wisht that he might lose his breath,
> Oft have I wisht his Carkas dead to see. . . .

Hate hid his true affection from my sight,
And kept my heart from paying him his debt. . . .
For hee by barring me from libertie,
To shunne my ranging, taught me first to range.
But yet too chast a Scholler was my hart,
To learne to love another then my Lord.
(ll. 17–20, 22–23, 27–30)

What crime has this woman committed? Cumulative anaphora reveals her justified attitude toward husband and tyrant, but now she chastises herself for mental disobedience. Although his treatment of her—murdering her brother and grandfather, usurping the throne, leaving a command for her execution if he fails to return from battle, exhibiting extreme jealousy, and doting on her image of beauty rather than her spiritual or intellectual excellence—legitimizes her response, she has not been unfaithful; yet still she feels guilty. Such meticulous moral logic sets the tone for the entire play.

Indeed, all the characters project guilt upon Mariam as the plot unfolds, and in self-examination she must concur by realizing that reputation is as important as actual innocence.[19] Her error was to alienate husband and king; thus, while her conscience is clear, Mariam is guilty of political and marital inexpediency. Her dilemma lies in how to reconcile promptings of the heart with public forms and duties. Mariam knows morally what constitutes right action, yet she does not understand the misinterpretation of her pure motives through the spectacles of will, jealousy, and ambition.

The play advances primarily through Senecan confrontational dialogue: Mariam is first joined by her mother, Alexandra, who understands political expediency to the extent that it eclipses morality. She would betray her own daughter to save herself. Salome, sister of Herod, next enters, suspicious of political plotting between the queen and her mother. She will actually plan and enact a poisoning ruse to indict Mariam of the very crimes of which she herself is guilty. Just as survival motivates Alexandra, so Salome is driven by an individualistic will that overtops morality. These powerful exchanges between the foremost women in the society of the play are remarkable in that they fail to offer a "counter-universe" to the male-oriented and dominated order (de Beauvoir, pp. 542–43). Their invectives do not afford the progression discernible in Shakespearean plays, for instance, where Carole McKewin finds scenes between women alone offering the opportunity for "self-expression, adjustment to social codes, release, relief, rebellion, and transformation."[20] Instead, each woman postures against the representation of tyranny in her own way and alone.

At the midpoint of the play, reports of the death of tyranny have filtered through the whole society, causing a realignment of personal possibilities: Pheroras may marry the servant Graphina, Doris must plot to institute her son as heir by killing Mariam's children, Constabarus may release the sons of Babus from hiding, and Salome must jockey for power to fulfill her concupiscent will. However, as we have begun to suspect, the announcement comes that Herod still lives, and a new realignment begins. Mariam fatally decides to quit a life of hypocrisy: she will abstain from the bed of Herod, forcing congruency between thought and action. She realizes how easy it would be to dissemble and ensure her political position, but instead she trusts her innocence and good character to speak for themselves:

> I know I could inchaine him with a smile:
> And lead him captive with a gentle word,
> I scorne my looke should ever man beguile,
> Or other speech, then meaning to afford. . . .
> Oh what a shelter is mine innocence, . . .
> Gainst all mishaps it is my faire defence, . . .
> Mine innocence is hope enough for mee.
> (ll. 1166–69, 1174, 1176, 1183)

Sohemus, keeper of Mariam and counselor to Herod, has been charged to murder the queen if Herod dies away from Palestine. He, however, has been moved by Mariam's modesty, chastity, purity of heart, and mistreatment at the tyrant's hands. He knows that he is in danger because he failed to complete his commission, but he would gladly die to save the good queen. This decision writes both their death warrants, for Herod believes that Mariam must have engaged in "criminal conversation" for Sohemus to be so swayed. Simultaneously the Butler brings in the poisoned cup sent by Salome, which is supposed to be a love potion concocted by Mariam for Herod. Both the Butler and Sohemus are thus effective agents in the doom of Mariam, yet both betrayers are repentent immediately before their deaths, reformed by recognition of Mariam's goodness.

Only a willful misreading of instances such as this could allow the critical observation that Cary "has a low opinion of women in general."[21] Comments upon which this judgment may be based are directed against

Salome in order to enhance the portrayal of Mariam and to underscore the
perverse irony of her execution. The sons of Babus, for example, meet their
deaths with equanimity, claiming that they are happy to die because it will
free them from women. But their comments stem from the experience of
their only true friend, Constabarus, who, even while he inductively curses
all women because of Salome's actions, reiterates that Mariam is the sole
redemption of her sex:

> But no farewell to any female wight.
> You wavering crue: my curse to you I leave,
> You had but one to give you any grace:
> And you your selves will Mariams life bereave,
> Your common-wealth doth innocencie chase.
> (ll. 1578–82)

Imagistically, Salome is, based on Matthew 23:27,

> a painted sepulcher,
> That is both faire, and vilely foule at once:
> Though on her out-side graces garnish her,
> Her mind is fild with worse then rotten bones.
> And ever readie lifted is her hand,
> To aime destruction at a husbands throat: . . .
> Her mouth though serpent-like it never hisses,
> Yet like a Serpent, poysons where it kisses.
> (ll. 880–89)

Mariam, however, is exempt from this portrayal. Part of her tragedy is her
lack of whitewash: the beauty of Mariam is an indication of spiritual
purity and innocence.

From the point of Herod's return the play turns symbolically religious,
casting over the sacrifice of Mariam a Christ-like aura. She becomes a
combined symbol of scapegoat and sacrificial lamb whose death will
cleanse the kingdom of tyrannical misjudgment as it also releases the heroine from her insoluble dilemma. Herod vacillates in Pilate-like fashion
through an entire scene in giving the command for her execution. Should
he behead her? No weapon would consent to pierce her lovely skin. Should
he drown her? Rivers would change course to save her. Should he burn her?
Fire would be unable to harm the very origin of passion. Even though
Herod typically employs hyperbole regarding Mariam—indeed, his only
redeeming quality is his love for her, and it is excessive, possessive, and

uxorious—his uncertainty indicates the religious symbolism of the final portion of the play. "[A]nd *Hebrew* why," he asks himself, "Seaze you with Lyons pawes the fairest lam / Of all the flocke?" (ll. 1512–14).

As the Nuntio brings report of Mariam's death, the religious effect of her sacrifice makes itself known. Her last message to Herod is that in three days he will pray for her resurrection. Herod recognizes his tyrannical error and repents for the slaughter of innocence not in three days, but in three minutes. Mariam's individual sacrifice has a profound social effect: it prepares the way for the death of all tyranny. Herod laments through all of Act V for his misguided actions, comparing Mariam's death to the archetypal murder:

> Retire thy selfe vile monster, worse then hee
> That staind the virgin earth with brothers blood,
> Still in some vault or denne inclosed bee,
> Where with thy teares thou maist beget a flood,
> Which flood in time may drowne thee: happie day.
> (ll. 2191–95)

This flood of tears will baptise the kingdom to open the way for a new order. The redemption of humanity by Christ's sacrifice becomes equivalent to the redemption of womanhood by Mariam's sacrifice.

Although Lady Cary inserts this hint of hope at the end of the tragedy with the seeds of conversion of the tyrant, the play is remarkable in its avoidance of feminist propositions, especially considering the proliferation of broadsides of the Swetnam and Munda variety at this time, both attacking and defending the female sex.[22] Mariam experiences tragic anagnorisis because she cannot facilely dismiss duties to husband and state: all personal decisions have public ramifications. The antifeminist viewpoint, even to the extent of misogyny, is given free and vituperative voice in the complaints of Constabarus against Salome; but Mariam stands in example to explode the stereotype. Cary speaks for a quiet feminism that recognizes the many contradictory roles of the intelligent, educated, noble Renaissance wife and mother. Choric commentary in *The Tragedie of Mariam* is conventionally traditional, almost reactionary in its observations, and certainly not to be heard as the voice of the playwright. The Chorus is effective, however, in symbolically pinpointing the dilemma of a woman of independent thought who also believes unerringly in the Catholic ideals. While Mariam tentatively chooses to trust in her virtues and defy the convention, the Chorus speaks to her as conservative conscience: a woman must be willing to dedicate her mind as well as her body to her husband. It is Mariam's decision not to submit with mind *or* body that instigates her peripety.

Like Cary, Mariam is unsuccessful in escaping the tragedy of personal and political tyranny; however, her death asserts the integrity of her conscience and apotheosizes her as a victim whose suffering and sacrifice affect the tyrant and open the way for change. This was perhaps more than Lady Falkland could hope for personally, and she used the marginal genre as a forum for the philosophical investigation of the subject closest to her heart. Mariam's dilemma is no less ambiguous and her end indeed tragic, but she exhibits the same strength of character and dedication to ideals in the face of conflicting duties that Elizabeth Cary herself attempted in her recusant position. She and her husband were apparently reconciled at his deathbed, and among his private papers was found a copy of her Perron translation (Fullerton, p. 136). Her domestic vigilance, similarly, brought her a final victory, for of her eight surviving children, six found vocations in the Catholic church, including all four of her daughters.

GARY F. WALLER

Struggling into Discourse: The Emergence of Renaissance Women's Writing

I write as a man and also a would-be feminist. I write also as a reader of Renaissance texts, specifically by and about Renaissance women writers, and of the silence created by the lack of those texts. Ten years ago to have made any of these claims preliminary to writing an essay on Renaissance women writers would have seemed strange. To read any text then would not have seemed as problematic as today it does—except that then there were seemingly no Renaissance women writers apart perhaps from the Countess of Pembroke as a translator, Queen Elizabeth herself, and a handful of others who barely seemed worth mentioning in, say, C. S. Lewis' Oxford *History*. On that matter, a lot has changed in the last decade or so: we now have editions of the Countess of Pembroke's poetry and prose writings, of Lady Mary Wroth and Aemilia Lanyer, studies of women translators, many critical essays, and a number of useful anthologies.

But the real difference is not the fine historical research on what women writers there were and which we have, but rather the theoretical revolution which literary studies is going through—and, in particular of course, the rise of feminist criticism. Moreover, this particular kind of feminist criticism is not only determined to discover, revive, and publish writing by Renaissance women, but also to raise questions related to women's own discourse, the linguistic and discursive structures of women's writing, and even the gender-specific nature of our own scholarly or critical discourse. And (in both cases) we must look most particularly at the gaps, silences, and margins of the subject—as we know, among the most important work on women's writing today is that which focuses less on what is seemingly "there" in a text than what is *not* there: not so much on what women's writings "say" so much as what they did or could not say, and why.

Another relevant aspect of recent criticism relates to the opening sentence of this essay. Increasingly, we have come to acknowledge that the critic or historian is accountable for and implicated in his or her own readings. The reader, and critic, also write in history, and, specifically, in his or her own history. That is why my position as a reader of the writings of Renaissance women must be acknowledged as, necessarily, culture-specific and gender-specific. I cannot pretend to be neutral or universal in my questions: as Althusser puts it, no readings are innocent—we are required to say what readings we are guilty of. But more, I can't pretend, as Jonathan Culler confidently claims, to read as a woman. As Elaine Showalter argued recently, there is a crucial distinction between reading as a woman on the one hand, and reading as a man *and* a feminist on the other. No reading is privileged: just as a man must be willing to acknowledge and explore the masculinist bias of his own reading system, so we must also raise the question of how many women readers have found themselves spoken by a male-centered discourse, under the assumption that there is a gender-neutral discourse. It may be there is, but the question of its existence needs to be raised.[1]

There is a revealing scene in Jean-Luc Godard's film, *Une Femme Mariée*, in which the heroine, Charlotte, stands in front of a mirror. She compares her reflection to what we are told are and what she accepts as "the ideal breasts of Venus de Milo." In doing so she accepts her insertion into a discursive structure already and seemingly always in place—a concept of woman given by our culture, an apparently natural language of sexuality and sexual difference which provides her with a passport to visibility not only to men but to herself.[2] The scene is a vivid reminder of the ways in which women within our culture have been placed as empty signs within male-created patterns of discourse, and this also introduces my consideration of the struggles women, women writers, and scholars of women's writing (including feminist critics) have to locate themselves within discourse. In particular, this introduces the focus of my paper which is the insertion into the dominant forms of discourse of the writings of Renaissance women; they, after all, lived (albeit indirectly) under the shadow of the Venus de Milo.

The state of scholarship and criticism of Renaissance women's writing is subject no less than Charlotte to residual, and seemingly natural, assumptions and limitations. This, I suggest, is even true of feminist criticism, which has—at least in its dominant Anglo-American form—in the last twenty years been mainly concerned with the analysis (often with attendant praxis) of fictional representations of women, in both men's and women's writing, and has concentrated on reviving lost or undervalued writer's images of women, gender stereotypes, and so forth. Ann Kaplan, for instance, defines feminist criticism as "part of a general interest in researching subject areas that have mainly been considered hitherto from a male point of view."[3] One might add, as Julia Kristeva and others have suggested, that it is perfectly conceivable that such criticism could be written by men, but I leave aside the arguments for and against the biographical phallacy to concentrate on two different points. One is what would traditionally be called the subject or area of my paper: what happens, I want to ask, when there is a lack of material which can be considered from the feminist point of view as I have just defined it? If we consider, say, the poetry written between 1500 and 1650 by English Renaissance women— and only to limited extent is it less true of the Continent—the amount of published or unpublished women's poetry is small indeed. There have survived perhaps half a dozen substantial collections of poetry, plus a fair number of incidental or occasional poems and all these poets worked, seemingly without seriously questioning, within male-created and dominated literary modes of production, genre, and assumptions. The second and connected concern is, I will argue, that our modern dominant, seemingly natural, methods of studying, enjoying, and even reviving (or exhuming) the participants in this particular "obstacle race," to use Germaine Greer's term,[4] are as limiting and as phallocentric as the categories within which Godard's Charlotte gazes at the reflection of her own breasts. In what follows I will explore these methodological considerations in relation to some of the women writers of the sixteenth and seventeenth centuries.

Introducing their recent anthology of French feminist writing, Elaine

Marks and Isabelle de Courtivron remark that "feminist discourse has always picked up the terms of anti-feminist discourse and been determined by it."[5] Within Anglo-American criticism, at least until recently, the dominant critical modes have been positivist historicism and New Critical formalism. Despite its questioning of so many of the received categories of literary discussion, most work on Renaissance women writers has grown up and remains within these dominant critical paradigms which are, I suggest, inherently limiting, even antithetical, to its interests. Briefly, both historical scholarship and formalism have produced a discourse that locates both the critic and the literary "object" within structures that render authorship, text, reading, and history nonproblematic; that is, they assume that the text is a "reflection" or "expression" of its author or its society, that the text can be correlated with an apparently unproblematic, given reality "outside" the text, and, most importantly, that the reader of such texts should concentrate on the patient annotation of what is, seemingly, "there" on the page or, in some cases, of course, in the manuscript. The commitment of the historian or critic within *his* or *her* history is also not seen as problematic, it being assumed that it is the reader's role to be as objective as possible and let the "text" speak "for itself."

The phrases just used are, given the recent history of theory and criticism, increasingly difficult to use without unease. All these supposedly natural assumptions are limiting to the development of an adequate criticism of Renaissance women poets, and not only from a feminist viewpoint. There are, interestingly, some signs of a revisionist women's historicism in general Renaissance studies in which the place of the historian is foregrounded. Joan Kelly-Gadol, for instance, has queried whether the model of Renaissance history we have inherited from Burckhardt actually fits women's (as opposed to men's) history. She argues that there was no renaissance for women—at least not during the Renaissance. On the contrary, she claims, there was a marked restriction of the scope and powers of women. In her work can be seen the seeds of an alternative view of social and cultural history that has its equivalent in some areas of later literary history, where women writers are treated as a separate tradition or subculture within a large male-dominated cultural system.[6] Within Anglo-American literary criticism, however, the question of a revisionist literary history of women's writing, especially in the pre–1800 period, has barely been broached. It is now, when our residual critical categories are being called so radically into question—by poststructuralism, deconstructionism, semiotics, and by a revisionist cultural history—that it would indeed be unfortunate if work on Renaissance women's writing should be held back and neutralized by its remaining ties to an archaic paradigm. In what follows, I suggest some of the ways more vital work might be pursued. Work on women's writing, in any period, must grapple with the methodological revolution now going on, and, in dealing with Renaissance women in particular, simply to acknowledge there is relatively little material on which to work is to be limited by a positivism that feminist critics, at the very least, should be roused to see as imposed by a dominant intellectual paradigm that is suspiciously male-oriented. Our cultural history is full of occasions when seemingly natural or commonsense assumptions have hidden very partial and very real relations of power. In arguing in this way, I would add, I am offering an act of contrition for some of my own, albeit enthusiastic and well-intentioned earlier work in the area, and I hope that others will join in the debate I intend to open up.

Let us start with an obvious and much analysed topic: the representations or images of women in men's and women's writing, and the presentation of women in Petrarchanism. Even with such a plenitude as afforded by Petrarch, Sidney, Spenser, Shakespeare, Donne, and all their lesser ephebes, and while we can undoubtedly "explore the ways in which sexual bias and/or stereotyped formulations in society become codified in literary texts,"[7] our empiricist methodology—the postivist insistence on observing and analyzing what is given or apparently there in the text—ends in an impasse and an acceptance of discursive limitations which quietly oppress or marginalize our concerns to examine and perhaps challenge the dominant categories not only of our literature but of our history.

It certainly seems easy to categorize the recognizable features of the Petrarchan mistress. She is the alluring, the unappproachable, the inexpressible being who yet draws her lover into the confusion of words, the icy fire, and so forth. Yet, as most commentators recognize, in describing her we are thus depicting her entirely as the product of the poet-lover's shifting desires and projections. The Petrarchan love poem is a theater of desire—one in which men have the active roles and the women are assigned silent, iconic functions, and are notable primarily for their absence in the script. The declared focus of *Astrophel and Stella* is a woman, for example, but the focus is upon her only as the inspirer of the male character's complex feelings. He is the poet or lover; she the subject of his anguish, attempted manipulation, and struggles of conscience.

So much is commonplace enough, but what we should also note is that this level of empirical analysis radically limits what we can say about what Sidney coincidentally terms the "absent presence" of the woman in the Petrarchan scheme. Some years ago, before I had even started to examine the theoretical basis on which I taught Petrarchan poetry, I was puzzled by one of my brightest women students asking what Stella might reply to Astrophel's earnest, but self-regarding, pleas for favor. Even if her response was not in the poem, what might she say? Was her silence the repression of the poet? Or the dominant male character? The structure of discourse in which he or the absent she or we ourselves struggled to intervene? Such are the questions that my student, without being able to articulate them any more than I could then, was in effect voicing.[8] The insistence that we analyze what is in the words of the text, the valorization of the perceivable, the pictorial, "images" of women (and indeed the formalist shibboleth of "image" generally) are all indications of how a dominant, seemingly natural, vocabulary may act to censor or limit discussion. No less than with Godard's Charlotte accepting her society's definition of her femininity, to accept the formalist limitation of "image" is to accept not only certain methodological restrictions, but more—it is to accept that "woman" is there, given, an object unquestioned in the text. It is a critical—but more, a cultural, and even perhaps gender-specific—discourse, that a text (like a body) contains a plenitude of meaning, open for analysis and inspection, ready for consumption, and requiring control and mastery. Thus if we simply list the usual Petrarchan characteristics, and speak, for instance, of the alluring unapproachability of the icy fire of passion, then we are locating ourselves within a discourse in which woman is interpolated as a focus of gaze, as the object of mens' obsessions and insecurities, simply by virtue of her gender-role. Such a placing of the woman has achieved tangible form and apparent "natural"-ness within our cultural history in novels, poems, paintings, films, and ordinary, seemingly innocent, language. Woman is the forbidden, the alluring, the mysterious, and her acceptance of that subject role is her passport to speech and praxis within a male-dominated world.

Such a subjection is ironically borne out by the majority of scholarly and critical work by women scholars on Renaissance poetry—as unquestioning of methodology as that by men. I think, for instance, of the patient and incisive scholarship of Mary Ellen Lamb or Josephine Roberts on the Sidney women poets, the important editions of Renaissance tracts by and about women by my friend and colleague, the late Diane Bornstein, and even the potentially methodologically more advanced work by Ann Rosalind Jones on French women writers.[9] Even more interesting are doctoral dissertations by women, written unquestioningly within the dominant historicist formalist structures and coming to such conclusions as that men poets were starting to write love poems from the viewpoint of women personae, providing them with a feminine psychology, which was, it is argued, characterized by such features as self-disparagement, delicate sensibility, engaging sympathy, and so forth.[10] One looks closely for signs of such criticism wrestling, even unconsciously, with the received categories—not merely literary, but psychological and cultural—and the vocal absence of any such struggle is often a tribute in itself to a discourse that for so long has dominated scholarly practice that it seems natural, given, universal even, or especially, to those who are most intimately its victims. Ideology, as Althusser has taught us, is located not so much in ideas as in our unconscious assumptions about our daily (and scholarly) lives.

What different questions might we then ask? What, if anything, can we learn from the postpositivist critical paradigms that have become so powerful recently? From Derrida or Foucault, Althusser or Kristeva, Lacan or Barthes, or those others who have brought fear or excitement to criticism in the past two decades? I suggest there are, indeed, some especially crucial lessons.

The first lesson, which grows directly out of my brief survey of Petrarchanism, is Michel Foucault's conception of discourse as the subject of power. As the struggles and, even more clearly the blindness, of women critics show, certainly with more excuse than men, it is not men and women who make their history as free agents, but the discourses which speak through them. As Foucault puts it in *The Order of Things,* we are spoken by and in "the fundamental codes of a culture—those governing its language, its schemes of perception, its exchanges, its techniques, its values, the hierarchy of its practices." In that convenient Lacanian formulation, we do not speak, we are spoken—or we are speakings. In what has become a key strategy, even a commonplace, of the *nouvelle critique*, Foucault raises the question of how the excluded or marginalized voices of a culture can be heard within the seemingly replete language constituted by specific discursive practices, as those voices struggle against the power of a dominant system which tries to organize all a society's cultural activity. Above all, what power seeks to control is discourse since it is there that "reality" is defined by the society; further it is only through discourse that a society's speaking subjects may enter and participate in it.[11] So how do oppositional forces speak when the dominant language refuses them words? How are the voices of silence heard? And above all, in what ways might they be heard today?

The English Renaissance women poets whose writings have descended to us exemplify such considerations in part in the ways—like the images of women in Petrarchanism—women were and have become fixed within an alien but familiar language. No less than Astrophel's Stella or Drayton's Idea, they are fixed as "images," objects of gaze and analysis, within languages they did not invent and do not control. One might say, indeed, that the Petrarchan mistress is less the subject of eroticization than she is of power. Ironically, criticism which focuses, with whatever good intentions, on the "image" of women in Petrarchanism without asking what is *not* there, not in the text, and why, is no less perpetuating women as objects of circulation and exchange than the poetry it observes. Think, for instance, of the process by which Philip and Robert Sidney's sister, Mary Sidney, Countess of Pembroke (I describe her in that way deliberately, since it was a dual appellation and subjection she accepted unquestioningly) and other women writers generally were largely confined—to religious writing and to translation. Note also the uncanny intensity with which the traditional humility topos is incessantly used by them to apologize for entering a male domain, as by Anne Bradstreet whose poems were published without her knowledge and with repeated apologies for entering the "public view" when they were merely the "ill-formed offspring" of a "feeble brain."[12]

The period's most substantial woman writer, Mary Sidney, is then a particularly interesting example. She was certainly not silenced, but her life and writing make very explicit that her brother's power, example and literary ideals were at the center of her literary and personal life. Her *Psalmes* completed his versifications; what little original lyric poetry she

wrote was dedicated directly to him or written to fulfill his ideals for
Elizabethan poetry. She wrote no prose romance; she edited his *Arcadia*.
She wrote no original drama; following Philip's exhortation, she translated Robert Garnier's closet-drama *Antoinie*. Instead of composing a
heroic poem, she translated one of Petrarch's *Trionfi;* instead of writing an
original devotional treatise, she translated *Discours de la vie et de la mort*
by her brother's friend, Philippe de Mornay. She gives us, indeed, the most
substantial set of texts by a woman writer in the period and she has become
rightly the subject of some of the best scholarship on Renaissance women
poets in the past twenty years, including most recently the useful edition of
the *Discours* edited by Diane Bornstein.[13]

But, as any survey of her writings shows, her work is interesting as much
for its absences, what she did not write, as for its palpable achievements.
Her work, however, is representative. What stands out with all the women
poets of the period—for instance, the other major English woman poet
before the Civil War, Mary Sidney's niece Mary, Lady Wroth—are the
structures of power within the language these women use and that create
them as subjects, denying them any owned discourse. A very condition of
their ability to write is their acceptance of constraints which deny them
authentic speech. Repression, as such, is not only located in social systems,
but very specifically in language, which provided the women poets only
gaps, silences, and the role of the other, within male discourse. "The relations of power are perhaps among the most hidden things in the social
body" writes Foucault, and it is in language, or more precisely in the gaps
and silences in language, that the operations of power can be seen most
intensely.[14]

More obviously with women writers than with men—though a comparative case can be made for the writings of working-class men or, as the
essays in this volume make clear, certain religious minorities—we can see
how wider cultural power relations are inscribed in the gaps and absences
of texts, not merely in what pretends to be in them. The voices of opposition or counterdominance are heard only as murmurs against the discourse
of power which attempts, by the subjection of language, to suppress its
loud silences. How does one speak more eloquently of such silences? How
might *we*? With Renaissance women poets, it is difficult to raise directly
the much-discussed question of whether there is a distinctive woman's

language except as the significant gaps in man's. But we can perhaps put it this way: what is the status of woman within the dominant vocabulary, syntax, rhetoric, of Renaissance poetry? In what ways, in its absences, in the ways their texts are not only silent but are unable to speak, do the writings of women call attention to gender-specific items? The seemingly replete words—*les mots pleins,* according to Marks and Cortivron (p. 163)—are man's, creating and manipulating the woman as object or, where she is permitted speech, controlling her as subject to a male (though seemingly God-given) discourse; otherwise she is relegated to the blanks and margins of the discourse. In 1630, as Bob Hodge and David Aers point out, the courtesy writer Robert Cleaver voiced his culture's subjection of woman's language: "As the echo answereth but one word for many, which are spoken to her; so a woman's answer should be in a word."[15] That is not exclusively a Renaissance phenomenon, of course. Within our culture woman's speech has long had to struggle within what has passed for public language but which has in fact been created and controlled by man. The commonality that defined the language of the Petrarchan sonnet sequence, for instance, was the creation of the male-dominated court; even when, as in Elizabethan England, the highest rung of that system was occupied by a woman, the language of the court poet was that of a discourse that elevated the woman only to subjugate her and imprison her in her apparent autonomy. To enter history an oppressed or underprivileged class can speak only through or against the dominant discourse and disrupt only by its negation or subdued silences—but we can say that such silence finally does speak (even if it is not acknowledged as having been said by being stated within the privileged monumentality of a text), and it is the critic's responsibility to make those silences speak.

Let me illustrate these rather cryptic theoretical assertions by another example—by glancing at Mary Wroth's *Pamphilia to Amphilanthus,* a collection of Petrarchan sonnets appended to her Arcadian romance *Urania* (1620) and purportedly written by her long-suffering heroine to her fickle male lover.[16] Like the romance, the poems are dominated by betrayal, deception, broken promises, and erotic frustration: we are in the familiar Petrarchan world of plaint and paradox, sophisticated but generalized emotion, rhetorical smoothness occasionally counterpointed by the mild disruption of question, ejaculation, despair, or joy. We can, once again,

explain away her poetry empirically as a minor, belated, variant of Petrarchan love-poetry pointing out, as Josephine Roberts and I have done,
that Mary Wroth writes not only in the shadow of her uncle's *Astrophel
and Stella* but also as an anxious ephebe of her father, Robert, whose
collection of Petrarchan love-poetry has only recently come to our attention.[17] But we might ask further questions: what difference does the author's gender make to her sequence? Or is the woman as positioned subject
rendered so controlled that we hear only the dominant discourse, speaking
without interruption, through her? Even reasonably sensitive positivist
historical scholarship will not take us very far toward answers. Wroth is
writing within a genre entirely structured by male categories—by the dis-
tancing of the erotic by logic, by the fixing of the female as a body which is
the subject of power, requiring her passivity as the object of anguish or
manipulation. Do we see any signs at all of what Lilian Robinson and Elise
Vogel have termed the "necessary psychic distortion and alienation" that
occurs when a woman writer represses her gender-specific desires to
write?[18]

We do see something of the sort in a process of displacement, transferred
and projected upon a subject the dominant discourse afforded Lady
Wroth—the Jacobean court. In both *Urania* and *Pamphilia* there emerges
a deep disillusion with court civilization that is unusual for its wholesale
and helpless passivity, reminiscent of the ultimate helplessness of the central female characters in Webster's court tragedies.[19] Often this disillusion
emerges in the commonplace *otium* of the pastoral desire to escape from
the court to the country, but inevitably the country, too, is fundamentally
deceptive. The all-encompassing melancholy of Wroth's poems seems to
grow from wider cultural disillusion than the Petrarchan convention affords. In her poems, the woman is happiest alone, even in her abandon-
ment; love's only constancy is its changeableness, which is presented not as
a theological or psychological observation, but as growing from love's
location within discourse as an activity for men, a passivity for women.
Whereas a courtier-lover, like the fickle Amphilanthus, has the autonomy
of constant adventure—martial, erotic, and linguistic—Pamphilia must
wait, abandoned and insecure, the more threatened she is, the more faithful. She is, as one poem puts it, "married to sorrow," bound in her passive
helplessness. Whenever she acts or speaks she is, in a word that recurs
through both the romance and the poetry, "molested."[20]

Part of the frustration that emerges from *Pamphilia to Amphilanthus* may be read, therefore, as a frustration at the subjection to a language which emphasizes the woman's role as empty, passive, helpless, and yet which insists that Lady Wroth, as a woman and a woman in court, write within linguistic and social structures that do not permit her to transcend that role. The Platonic-Petrarchan metaphors which dominate the sequence at once create a place within the discourse of love and exclude her from the production of authentic speech. Pamphilia projects Amphilanthus as presence, herself only as an absence—as lack, incompleteness, and finally, as silence, waiting to be completed. She transfers her alienation upon the object that is afforded her by her society's seemingly public discourse—the court. Indeed, she can speak only with the language of the alien and oppressor, and her speech is unusually charged with a rejection and frustration that goes beyond the courtly Petrarchan situation, but which cannot name the cause or the solution of its fragmentation.

One distinctive note that erupts through most Renaissance poetry, men's and women's, is the fragile anxiety of the individual speaking voice, struggling to find within the inherited discourse a space for the increasing self-consciousness of ego-psychology, the ego of Cartesian philosophy or of Donne's poetry. Indeed, we can see the whole Petrarchan lyric tradition anticipating what Foucault speaks of in *The History of Sexuality:* the development of detailed techniques within the confessional or daily self-examination to form a representation in speech and thought of sexual pleasure.[21] In this way, sexuality becomes an object to be examined, supervised, confessed, and transformed into discourse. Petrarchan poetry, I think we can argue, is part of this "will to hear the other speak the truth of his sex."[22] But what about the truth of *her* sex? Is there any sense of the truth of woman's sexuality having become part of discourse in the Renaissance?

One important aspect of poststructuralism, seen in particular among recent French feminist writers, has been the suspicion of a male-dominated discourse of sexuality and a questioning of how it has, through Western history, failed to answer to woman's sexuality. Such writers as Luce Irigaray and Hélène Cixous have raised radical questions about the relationship between the female body as it interiorizes and understands itself as language.[23] As we sense the gaps and frustrations in Wroth's jagged, disruptive text, can we sense the silent inexpressibility of woman's sexuality, never put into words since there are, as yet, no words for it? It is necessary, I think, to root such remarks as Irigaray's that "woman's desire does not speak the same language as man's desire" very firmly within history. It may be true that "it has been covered over by the same logic that has dominated the West since the Greeks," but we need to focus more closely on the exact process of historical production that fought within and against woman's speech.[24] As I have noted, the logic of love-poetry in the Renaissance is that of the gaze, the discrimination of form and the rendering open and passive of the beautiful object—the woman perceived as territory. She is in Donne's words, a "kingdom" desired and conquered by another body and by another language which conveys its conquest in metaphors of dominance. In Donne's comic blazon, "To His Mistress Going to Bed," for instance, the woman is characterized by the male subject's admiration of the inviting convexity of the hills and valleys he creates in her, and by his invasive insertions and intrusions into her passageways and hidden recesses, all laid open, admired, and eventually "covered" by the active male organ and ego.[25] Within such a language situation, the woman can speak only as a blank space, a hole in discourse, or—as a passive recipient of the male organ of speech/sex—within the man's language.

The erotic poetry of the Renaissance, by both men and women, then, does afford us the possibility of speculation on the mode of absence by which women writers express themselves. Their voices may indeed be heard within the silent murmuring of discourse or, to use a phrase of Derrida's, "active and stirring," the result of an effaced but real struggle, "inscribed in white ink, an invisible drawing covered over in the palimpsest."[26] I want now to turn to another area of language which connects us with the main emphasis of the essays in this collection, one in which, especially in the seventeenth century, Renaissance women were by contrast encouraged to write—and that is in the expression of devotional or pietistic sentiments. In France, one thinks of Marguerite de Navarre, in England (again) the Countess of Pembroke, Aemilia Lanyer, and (if we go outside poetry) the large number of pious, highly educated women who translated or wrote devotional or theological works. In England during the first sixty years of the seventeenth century there is an increasing division between the spheres of public discourse and that of private experience, and it is the latter—in domestic poetry like Anne Bradstreet's and, especially, in devotional poetry, that women find a permitted linguistic space. The Puritan emphasis on the women as the helpmeet in marriage and the insistence on domesticity as a proper, semiautonomous, realm of activity seem to most of us today a little too reminiscent of Phyllis Shaffley and the resistance to women's rights. But in the seventeenth century it is arguable that such developments marked, despite their intentions perhaps, a real breakthrough. What we can observe in Bradstreet's poetry, for instance, is something akin to what commentators on many Shakespeare plays—the history plays in particular—point to as the silent or marginalized power of women, standing for an area of experience which is denied or distorted by the rough, exploitative, largely male, public world. However marginalized and trivialized (and therefore permitted to women) it represents a breach, a contradition, that opens a space for struggle and opposition. Within the early seventeenth century the blank space which is Woman is filled increasingly by what Man relegates as merely private: she is created as helpmeet, wife, domestic subordinate, and thus in some classes acquires a degree of what, to adapt a term of Althusser, we might call "relative autonomy." In doing so, she acquires a subversive potential within the dominant discourses of that age.

The methodology by which we are able to write a history of eloquent silence or of woman's struggle into discourse (or that of any marginal culture) is complex and only starting to be explored. One way is, as here, by attempting to look forward to periods when what is only half articulated or, indeed, silent in an early period, is on the point of finding articulation—when language is becoming available to fill in those gaps, as it were. If we look fifty or so years ahead from Mary Sidney's and Mary Wroth's time, we can see the developments in this one area which at once affords women a permitted space within discourse. At the same time, paradoxically, religious writing offers counterdominant potential, and here again a brief reference to Mary Sidney is useful. There is, for instance, some interesting analysis still to be done on the adaptions, changes, and omissions made by the countess to the psalms she versified. As I have shown elsewhere, there are times when the exigencies of form or the resources of the Elizabethan lyric tradition meant that she made distinctive changes to what contemporary commentators might have regarded as her original—often by making a communal lyric more the utterance of an

individual voice, or by elaborating upon the courtly finery or ritual in ways
that remind the reader of the atmosphere of the Elizabethan court.[27] When
we read these poems, in short, we look not only to the ways Mary Sidney
tried to be faithful to her task and articulate what was "there" in her text;
we must also pay attention to the dislocations and gaps in her writing, to
the *silences* (what she chose not to say) and the *absences* (what she could
not say). As is always the case with historical criticism, later readers who
approach texts from the past with their own questions and concerns are
often in position to articulate what neither she nor her writing were able to
put into words. As with so much writing by women in this period, it is the
struggle from *silence*—a struggle that often ends in *absence*—that is most
characteristic. In future studies, I hope to take up the distinction between
silence and absence that I have introduced here, a distinction that seems to
me to be crucial for our understanding of women writers in this period.

But however fascinating her work is for us here, both in terms of what
the works articulate and the methodology by which we can investigate
them, something more directly relevant can be seen when we look beyond
the confines of class, family, and dominant literary modes that defined a
Mary Sidney. To do so we must glance ahead of her more than fifty years.
The dominant discourse of the mid-seventeenth century, valorized in Cartesian dualism, the growth of positivist science and the Royal Society, is
that of clarity, rationalism, the given world of "facts and events, of business and leisure."[28] Even from within the limitations of conventional literary history, we can note homologous shifts: the lyric poem, always potentially subsersive of discursive domination, virtually disappears or is
marginalized in such forms as the Methodist hymn; the dominant literary
mode becomes, despite Swift and, later, Sterne, the classic illusionism of
bourgeois realism and the categories of male rationalism. Yet in the middle
three decades of the seventeenth century, disrupting and allowing us to
deconstruct this seemingly universal movement from ambiguity and anxiety to clarity and rationalism, occurred not only a major, short-lived and
perhaps premature, political revolution, but also an incipient linguistic
revolution. If focussed, as revolutions so often do, not only on political
power but also on sexuality, on religion, and on the place permitted to
women. Of the "29 sects here living in London," to use the title of an
anonymous (and hostile) pamphlet of 1642, most were castigated as in-

dulging in free love, speaking out of turn and in strange tongues, and encouraging the unseemingly display and power of women.[29] While there is no woman writer, even among the sects, whom we could classify as a "feminist" in the sense of articulating a conscious political program, nonetheless, by an examination of the activities and, interestingly enough, the poetry of the women of the Civil War sects, we can see the spasmodic eruption of a genuine feminine discourse.

The exaltation of family life by seventeenth-century Protestantism did not consciously call into question the patriarchal structure or the marginalization of woman's speech or writing, yet among the more independent sects in mid-century, there were trends which, as Keith Thomas has shown, did radically put into question certain key aspects of the residual model of discourse.[30] Within certain sects, aspiring members of a congregation, men and women alike, had to provide proof of regeneration, and it was in fact easier for women than men to gain acceptance. While "after the Fall . . . the Man was to rule over his Wife," after "restoration by Christ . . . they are helpmeets, Man and Woman, as they were before the Fall" and, moreover, the spiritual injunction that women should keep silence, refer to "local and temporary conditions which have now passed away," among the Society of Friends, at least. As Thomas comments, "Christ was one in male and female alike" (pp. 47, 48). One result was the large number of women preachers, prophets, and writers, including at least two poets whose work has come down to us, Anne Wentworth and Anna Trapnell, neither of whose work would be noted in a conventional literary history. Trapnell's work, in particular, represents an especially interesting refusal to enter the dominant public discourse of poetry—she condemns herself to marginality by the distinctive voice of her work, which is that of ecstasy, seeming incoherence, and (a common charge against women writers generally at the time) apparent madness.[31]

Here I think we start to see more clearly something of the relationship of the repressed voices of women in relation to the increasingly dominant discourse of rationalist Cartesian Europe. In short, this is a way we can make silence speak. As Foucault has shown, societies define as mad or irrational what challenges the dominant definition of rationality, and throughout the Middle Ages and Renaissance, there is a close association between sorcery, hysteria, and madness, and the disruptive potential of women.[32] Trapnell's poetry is, by the increasingly dominant neoclassical standards of seventeenth-century poetry, irrational and ludicrously indecorous. But it may also be seen as idiomatic, informal, and struggling to give voice to emotions which were able to be articulated because they were socially marginal, largely irrelevant to and scorned by the hegemonous social forces. On the fringes of society, Trapnell was able to give voice in however inchoate and incomplete a way, to experiences that writers like Mary Sidney and Mary Wroth, more closely tied to the dominant structures of their age, were not.

It is not too far, I think, from these observations to what Julia Kristeva speaks of as the presymbolic or semiotic nature of woman's speech.[33] Kristeva sees poetry as opening a "deep fissure between the thetic and those practices and impulses" which threaten its dominance. She sees, for instance, the production of sounds, rhythms, vocal gestures, fantasy, musicality, and the babble of madness as the realm of woman, the Other, the presymbolic.[34] Even if we are skeptical about her concept of the Other, nonetheless her categories have real point here. If the discourse of seventeenth-century poetry is becoming increasingly dominated by a positivist insistence on clarity and rationality, by the Royal Society's ideal of one word for each object, then it is perhaps in the prophetic ravings of an Anna Trapnell—or, equally interesting, the socially peripheral visions of a Thomas Traherne—that we can see emerging what Kristeva calls "the space occupied by poetry,"[35] which by the mid-seventeenth century has been linguistically and socially rendered marginal in both men's and women's writing. In part because it has been rendered irrelevant, branded even as madness, it can, paradoxically, emerge. And because that newly opened space in the social textuality of the period is occupied by both men and women, we can start to hear the authentic voice of woman's discourse emerging.

Once again, I say "we"; though we will all ask slightly different questions of this past which we have largely lost, nonetheless, we can ask them because of the categories and structures of "our" discourses, not "theirs." If, as Kristeva argues, poetry and madness have been seen as one of the strategies of opposition within Western culture, perhaps here, in the mid-seventeenth century sects where women occupied an unusually and temporarily powerful role, we can see the beginnings (or is it the momentary flicker?) of ways women did not have to succumb to the regimentation of the symbolic as a condition of speech. We can see that what Kristeva calls the "spasmodic force" of woman could emerge precisely because it embodied a socially irrelevant and ludicrously marginal activity. Insofar as she has a specificity of her own, as Kristeva argues, a woman's truth lies in her being the force of rejection, of fierce marginality. She finds her specificity in "asociality, in the violation of communal conventions" (in Feral, pp. 10, 11). Kristeva's remarks are born out, perhaps for the first time in English literary history, and not again perhaps until the nineteenth century, by the incoherent, disruptive, and distintegrative verse of Anna Trapnell. Within the discourse of Rennaissance and, even more so, of neoclassical poetry, such writing is undecipherable, unstable, and incoherent, verging on but never quite engulfed by the silence to which its society tried to reduce it. Like much avant-garde writing, it resists or undermines closure and seems to combine or confuse traditional forms. It allows us to look forward to greater articulation in the future, but also to look back to the pre-emergent, to women like the Countess of Pembroke or Lady Wroth who were struggling (even more obscurely) into owned discourse.

This is, then, one powerful way by which we can start to share our readings of women's writing in the Renaissance. There is, to return to my opening, enormous value in the patient scholarly work done by such scholars as Diane Bornstein, Josephine Roberts, or Mary Lamb—the careful editing and explicating of texts and contexts, which must be done before a meaningful answer can be given to the kind of questions I am raising. But such work must remain merely preliminary, and its methodological limitations—not merely partaking of an outdated critical stance but also blind to its own place in history—can too easily prevent us from going further and asking the more important questions. They will take us into the necessarily speculative but, I believe, crucial areas of criticism, out of antiquarianism or pseudo-objective (and masculinist) discourse into a history in which we, too, are implicated. I think we are, indeed, able to see in the study of Renaissance women's writings something of what Annabel Patterson noted when she remarked in 1980 that "at last the theorists" have got into Renaissance studies.[36] It is one way we can not only help create a new paradigm for literary studies but also struggle against many of the wider repressive structures of our culture, including the one—to return to my starting point—that holds Godard's Charlotte, as it has held so many of her ancestors (not least the women writers of the Renaissance) to a mirror-image created to silence or marginalize her. Readers will perhaps note the deliberate overuse of "we" in this paragraph, and perhaps elsewhere. Now it is time to break down the "we." There are, undoubtedly, claims and questions "we" twentieth-century readers have the opportunity to put to "our" pasts. But there are other gender-specific and class-specific questions that each "I" finds him/herself able to ask as "owned." The kind of study I have sketched here thus becomes a way to enable me, as a man, not to pretend to read women's writing as a woman but, I hope, as a man aware of and sensitive to what it is like to read and be read, to write and be written, as a woman.

Notes

Introduction

Throughout this volume, the original Tudor spellings have been maintained, except that the use of "j," "v," and "s" is modernized.

1. Margaret L. King, "Book-Lined Cells: Women and Humanism in the Early Italian Renaissance," in *Beyond Their Sex*, ed. Patricia H. Labalme (New York: New York Univ. Press, 1980), p. 76.

2. Virginia Woolf, "Professions for Women," in *The Death of a Moth and Other Essays* (New York: Harcourt, Brace and Co., 1942), pp. 237–42; Patricia H. Labalme, "Women's Roles in Early Modern Venice: An Exceptional Case," in *Beyond Their Sex*, pp. 143, 129. The Woolf essays mentioned are now conveniently collected in Virginia Woolf, *Women and Writing*, ed. Michèle Barrett (New York: Harcourt Brace Jovanovich, 1980).

3. Harington, cited in H.T.R., "Lady Mary Sydney and Her Writings," *The Gentleman's Magazine*, 24 (1845), 366. Yet Sir John Harington sent manuscript copies of four of the psalms to Lucy, Countess of Bedford (Sidney's cousin), praising Mary Sidney in the accompanying letter (Dec. 29, 1600) as "the mirroir of our age" for "Poesie." See Petyt MSS. 538, 431, fol. 284–86. Marie de France cited in Joan M. Ferrante, "The French Courtly Poet: Marie de France," in *Medieval Women Writers*, ed. Katharina M. Wilson (Athens: Univ. of Georgia Press, 1984), p. 64.

4. Notebook in British Library, Addl. ms. 4244; Joan Goulianos, ed., *By a Woman Writt* (New York: Bobbs-Merrill, 1973), pp. 72–73.

5. Meg Bogin, *The Women Troubadours* (New York: W. W. Norton & Co., 1976), p. 160.

6. Suzanne W. Hull, *Chaste, Silent & Obedient* (San Marino, Calif.: Huntington Library, 1982), p. 142.

7. Christine de Pizan, *The Book of the City of Ladies*, trans. Earl Jeffrey Richards (New York: Persea Books, 1982), I.10.57, p. 30; Anne Cooke Bacon, trans. *Sermons Concerning the Predestination and Election of God* (London, c. 1570), sigs. A4r–v.

8. Lord Edward Denny to Lady Mary Wroth, Salisbury MSS. 130/118–119, Feb. 26, 1621/22. The correspondence between Wroth and Denny is printed in Josephine A. Roberts, ed., *The Poems of Lady Mary Wroth* (Baton Rouge: Louisiana State Univ. Press, 1983), pp. 237–41.

9. See Eileen Power, *Medieval English Nunneries* (Cambridge: Cambridge Univ. Press, 1922). Power's work in nunnery records is the basis for Nicholas Orme, *English Schools in the Middle Ages* (London: Methuen and Co., 1973), pp. 52–55. Until recently, it was common to seek the voice of secular English women in the "woman's song," which may well be part of the antifeminist tradition. The songs are male interpretations of a woman's feelings, particularly those songs which present her pleasure in sex, "pleasure with no attendant complications or responsibilities," thereby embodying "a fantasy which is male as well as aristocratic." See John F. Plummer, ed., *Vox Feminae* (Kalamazoo, Mich.: Medieval Institute Publications, 1981), p. 140. Chaucer's Wife of Bath has also frequently been presented as a spokesperson for the medieval woman although she is a male satire on women, part of the antifeminist tradition which presents women as lustful, greedy, manipulative, and deceitful.

10. Maureen Fries, "The 'Other' Voice: Woman's Song, its Satire and its Transcendence in Late Medieval British Literature," in *Vox Feminae*, p. 157; Bogin, p. 13. Christine de Pizan concluded the *City of Ladies* by warning women to flee the deceptive snares of courtly love: "Under these smiles are hidden deadly and painful poisons." Therefore, "Be well-informed in all things and cautious in defending your honor and chastity against your enemies!" (III.xix.6, pp. 256–57).

11. Joan Kelly-Gadol reopened this question in "Did Women Have a Renaissance?" in *Becoming Visible*, ed. Renate Bridenthal and Claudia Koonz (Boston: Houghton Mifflin, 1977), pp. 137–64; William Harrison, *The Description of England*, ed. George Edelen (Ithaca, N.Y.: Cornell Univ. Press, 1968), p. 228, cited in Hull, pp. 2–3. Retha M. Warnicke suggests that Harrison "greatly overestimated" the linguistic abilities of both sexes; see *Women of the English Renaissance and Reformation* (Westport, Conn.: Greenwood Press, 1983), p. 132.

12. David Cressy, "Literacy in Pre-industrial England," in *Societas, A Review of Social History*, 4 (Summer 1974), 229–40, cited in Hull, p. 4; Martin Billingsley, *The pen's excellencie or the secretaries delighte* (1618), sig. B4v.

13. John Florio, trans., Montaigne's *Essayes* (London, 1603), sig. A2r.

14. See particularly the recent work of Mary Ellen Lamb: "The Myth of the Countess of Pembroke: The Dramatic Circle," *Yearbook of English Studies*, 11 (1981), 194–202, and "The Countess of Pembroke's Patronage," *English Literary Renaissance*, 12 (1982), 162–79.

15. Woolf, "Women and Fiction," in *Women and Writing*, p. 43.

Some Sad Sentence: Vives' *Instruction of a Christian Woman*

1. Carlos G. Noreña, in *Juan Luis Vives* (The Hague: Martinus Nijhoff, 1970), p. 304, lists thirty-one editions in his appendix, but he leaves out five of the English editions included in the *Revised STC*. Ruth Kelso lists thirty-four sixteenth-century editions in her bibliography to *Doctrine for the Lady of the Renaissance* (Urbana: Univ. of Illinois Press, 1956), pp. 421–22, but the *Revised STC* includes two English editions she does not note. When she adds in her text that *The Instruction* went through "something over forty editions and translations before the end of the sixteenth century" (p. 72), she probably provides the best estimate. The Latin edition, which first appeared in 1523, was translated into Dutch, French, German, Italian, Spanish, and English.

2. See Diane Valeri Bayne's "*The Instruction of a Christian Woman*: Richard Hyrde and the Thomas More Circle," *Moreana*, 45 (1975), 6–8, for a discussion of this possibility and its complications.

3. Foster Watson called it the "leading theoretical manual on women's education of the sixteenth century" in his influential book, *Vives and the Renascence Education of Women*

(London: Edward Arnold, 1912), p. 21. Others who refer to it as an educational manual include Diane Bornstein, ed., *Distaves and Dames: Renaissance Treatises for and About Women* (Delmar, N.Y.: Scholars' Facsimiles, 1978), p. xviii; and Constance Jordan, "Feminism and the Humanists: The Case of Sir Thomas Elyot's *Defence of Good Women*," *Renaissance Quarterly*, 36 (1983), 188.

4. I will quote throughout from the facsimile of a 1529 English edition in Diane Bornstein's collection, *Distaves and Dames*, sig. B1r. I have expanded abbreviations, modernized *i, j, u,* and *v,* and eliminated the virgules that appear so often in this early edition. The text has no commas, so occasionally I have provided them when they help for reading and when a virgule appears in that position.

5. Gloria Kaufman, "Juan Luis Vives on the Education of Women," *Signs,* 3 (1977–78), p. 894. Kelso, *Doctrine,* p. 38, also refers to *The Instruction* as a conductbook. Pearl Hogrefe, in *The Sir Thomas More Circle* (Urbana: Univ. of Illinois Press, 1959), pp. 201–50, suggests the association between education and conduct for women by discussing Vives' *Instruction* and other works in a chapter called, "Education of women: love, marriage."

6. See the introduction to *Sir Nicholas Bacon's Great House Sententiae,* ed. and trans. Elizabeth McCutcheon, in *English Literary Renaissance,* Suppl., No. 3 (Amherst: Univ. of Massachusetts Press, 1977). I am also grateful to Professor McCutcheon for her generous help on this essay.

7. *De Tradendis Disciplinis* is translated by Foster Watson in *Vives: On Education* (Cambridge: Cambridge Univ. Press, 1913). The plans of study are translated by Watson in his *Renascence Education,* pp. 137–50 and 241–50. Both these works of Vives' were published in 1523 under the titles *De Ratione Studii Puerilis.*

On the differences in educational approaches for men and women, see Kaufman, p. 895; Bayne, pp. 13–14; William Harrison Woodward, *Studies in Education during the Age of the Renaissance, 1400–1600* (1906; rpt. New York: Columbia Univ. Press, 1967), pp. 180–210; Norma McMullen, "The Education of English Gentlewomen 1540–1640," *History of Education,* 6 (1977), 87–101; and Hilda Smith, "Feminism in Seventeenth-Century England," Diss. Univ. of Chicago 1975, who remarks, "What was education for men was simply not education for women. For instance even when men and women read a work—in moral philosophy or a guide to household management—they read it for different reasons. The man to learn the precepts of proper governing and the wife to learn obedience and her sphere in the household hierarchy. . . . The purpose of education in a very real sense was to train them how to be properly different from one another—not to present them with a body of knowledge the understanding of which would make them either socially or intellectually compatible" (p. 58).

8. Bayne, p. 8, and *Revised STC* 24856–24863.

9. The word is unfortunate because there was no "feminist" movement during the Renaissance against which men were reacting. On the contrary, women's advocates were reacting against what we term "antifeminist" attitudes about women, so it was they who were on the defensive. Those we call antifeminists were actually more "antiwoman" in their perspective. The word "feminist" is even more problematic when it is used by moderns to describe attitudes in earlier times. Works by Christine de Pizan may, I think, be accurately described as feminist, but I cannot agree with Constance Jordan that most humanist treatises "are dedicated to establishing an equality between the sexes," p. 182. For that reason, I find the term "feminist" as applied to them misleading. So does Linda Woodbridge in *Women and the English Renaissance* (Urbana: Univ. of Illinois Press, 1984), pp. 2–3, 16, 18, 168, and throughout her excellent study of the Renaissance debate.

10. I discuss this probability briefly in "Refashioning the Shrew," *Shakespeare Studies,* 17 (1984), forthcoming.

11. Woodward discusses Erasmus' views, for example, in *Desiderius Erasmus Concern-*

ing the Aim and Method of Education (1904; rpt. New York: Columbia Univ. Press, 1964), esp. pp. 148–53. See also J. K. Sowards, "Erasmus and the Education of Women," *Sixteenth Century Journal*, 13 (1982), 77–89.

12. John Milton, *Paradise Lost* in *Complete Poems and Major Prose*, ed. Merritt Y. Hughes (Indianapolis: Odyssey Press, 1957), IV, 297–98.

13. Watson, *Renascence Education*, pp. 204–05.

14. C. S. Lewis, *English Literature in the Sixteenth Century excluding drama* (Oxford: Oxford Univ. Press, 1973), pp. 28–29.

15. Fifteen pages in chapter 9 for the maid and five in chapter 8 for the wife.

16. See Mary E. Hazard, "Renaissance Aesthetic Values: 'Example,' for Example," *The Art Quarterly*, 2 (1979), 24–26; Ronald B. McKerrow, *Printers & Publishers' Devices in England & Scotland, 1485–1640* (London: The Bibliographical Society, 1913), fig. 80. Of course that sacrificial figure may be interpreted as imitating Christ, but as the following discussion makes clear, the emphasis on chastity suggests that through it women might gain not only religious salvation, but a version of secular salvation as well. The figure of Lucrece was clearly not meant to be interpreted ironically, but it seems very likely to me that Shakespeare's heroines do serve as ironic comments on the values of their time. There is not much that is conventional about Shakespeare's treatment of chastity.

17. Richard Hooker, *Of the Laws of Ecclesiastical Polity: Book V*, Vol. II of *The Folger Library Edition of the Works of Richard Hooker*, ed. W. Speed Hill (Cambridge, Mass.: Belknap Press, 1977), p. 401.

18. On the emphasis on chastity for women, see Joan Kelly-Gadol, "Did Women Have a Renaissance?" in *Becoming Visible*, ed. Renate Bridenthal and Claudia Koonz (Boston: Houghton Mifflin, 1977), pp. 139–64; Margaret L. King, "Book-Lined Cells: Women and Humanism in the Early Italian Renaissance," in *Beyond Their Sex*, ed. Patricia H. Labalme (New York: New York Univ. Press, 1980), pp. 66–90; Keith Thomas, "The Double Standard," *Journal of the History of Ideas*, 20 (1959), 195–216; and Virginia Woolf, *Three Guineas* (New York: Harcourt, Brace, 1938), chapter 2, n. 38, pp. 166–69.

19. *Instruction*, sig. S3v; and Watson, *Renascence Education*, p. 206.

20. Woodward, *Vittorino da Feltre and Other Humanist Educators* (Cambridge: Cambridge Univ. Press, 1905), pp. 119–20 (the tract was *De Studiis et Literis*); Janis Butler Holm, "Thomas Salter's *The Mirrhor of Modestie*: A Translation of Bruto's *La Institutione di Una Fanciulla Nata Nobilmente*," *The Library*, 5 (1983), 53–57.

21. Joel B. Altman, *The Tudor Play of Mind: Rhetorical Inquiry and the Development of Elizabethan Drama* (Berkeley: Univ. of California Press, 1978), p. 2; Pearl Hogrefe, *Tudor Women* (Ames: Iowa State Univ. Press, 1975), p. 101.

22. William Bercher, *The Nobility of Women*, ed. R. Warwick Bond (London: Roxburghe Club, 1904), pp. 152–53. George B. Parks attributes this work to a William Barker in "William Barker, Tudor Translator," *Papers of the Bibliographical Society of America*, 51 (1957): 126–40.

23. Carolly Erickson, *The First Elizabeth* (New York: Summit Books, 1983), p. 134, citing John Nichols, *The Progresses and Public Processions of Queen Elizabeth* (1823; rpt. New York: AMS Press, 1969), I, 9–10.

Margaret More Roper's Personal Expression in the *Devout Treatise Upon the Pater Noster*

1. The woodcut, found in *A Devout Treatise Upon the Pater Noster* (London: T. Berthelet, 1526?), STC 10477, is listed in Edward Hodnett, *English Woodcuts, 1480–1534* (London: The Bibliographical Society, 1935), No. 2012, p. 397. The woodcut is reproduced in *Moreana*, 9 (1966), 65. Although the STC says "1526?" J. A. Gee argues convincingly for a 1524 printing in "Margaret Roper's English Version of Erasmus' *Precatio Do-*

minica and the Apprenticeship behind Early Tudor Translation," *Review of English Studies*, 13 (1937), 257–71.

2. Thomas Stapleton, *The Life and Illustrious Martyrdom of Sir Thomas More* (1588), trans. Philip E. Hallett (New York: Benziger Brothers, 1928); rpt., E. E. Reynolds, ed. (New York: Fordham Univ. Press, 1966), pp. 103, 106. Cited hereafter in text as Stapleton.

3. See, for example, Joan Goulianos, ed., *By a Woman Writt* (New York: Bobbs-Merrill, 1973); or Mary R. Mahl and Helene Koon, eds., *The Female Spectator: English Women Writers Before 1800* (Bloomington: Indiana Univ. Press, 1977). Francis L. Utley refers to Margaret once and that fleetingly in *The Crooked Rib* (New York: Octagon Books, 1970), p. 84.

4. Unfortunately, Margaret's work has been lost; for her father's treatise, *Remember the Last Thynges* (unfinished), c. 1522, see *The Works . . . in the English Tonge*, ed. William Rastell (London, 1557), STC 18076. (Cited hereafter as Thomas More, E.W.) For an excellent discussion on the work, see Alistair Fox, *Thomas More: History and Providence* (New Haven: Yale Univ. Press, 1983), pp. 100–107.

5. Retha M. Warnicke, *Women of the English Renaissance and Reformation* (Westport, Conn.: Greenwood Press, 1983), p. 23. See also E. E. Reynolds' comments in the preface to the biography, *Margaret Roper* (New York: P. J. Kennedy & Sons, 1960), p. lx.

6. Robert Bolt, *A Man for All Seasons* (New York: Random House, 1960), p. xii; Betty Travitsky, ed., *Paradise of Women* (Westport, Conn.: Greenwood Press, 1981).

7. Marie-Claire Robineau, Gertrude-Joseph Donnelly, Germain Marc'hadour, and E. E. Reynolds, "Correspondence entre Erasmus et Margaret Roper," *Moreana*, 12 (1966), 29–46. Quotation on p. 44.

8. See Stapleton's discussion in *The Life of Thomas More*, Chap. 16, and Walter Gordon, "Tragic Perspective in Thomas More's Dialogue with Margaret in the Tower," *Cithara*, 17, No. 2 (1978), 3–12.

9. William Rastell, Sir Thomas More's nephew who published and printed More's *English Works* (see "Rastell," *DNB*, XVI, 748), identifies Alice Alington clearly as "wyfe to Syr Gyles Alington knighte, and daughter to Syr Thomas Mores seconde and last wyfe." Thomas More, E.W., p. 1433.

10. *The Correspondence of Sir Thomas More*, ed. Elizabeth F. Rogers (Freeport: Books for Libraries Press, 1947; rpt. 1970), No. 205, "Alice Alington to Margaret Roper," lines 14–16, p. 512.

11. The Act of Succession required of civil and ecclesiastical officers declared not only that Anne Boleyn was the legitimate queen and that her children would be "lawful heirs," but also indicated that no foreign ecclesiastical power had the right to interfere with England's decisions regarding the question of succession. Anyone who in word, writing, print, or deed "slandered . . . the said lawful matrimony" was considered guilty of "treason." *English Historical Documents, 1485–1558*, ed. A. R. Meyers (London: Eyre and Spottiswoode Ltd., 1969), V, 447–51. The act under which More and Fisher ultimately were executed was an addition (26 Henry VIII, c. 13) to an existing "Law of Treason." See *English Historical Documents*, pp. 475–77. On this matter see also A. F. Pollard, *Henry VIII* (New York: Harper Torchbooks, 1966), p. 265.

12. Thomas More refutes both Tyndale and Barnes, a follower of Luther, in his *Confutation of Tyndale's Answer*. See particularly Book VIII of the *Confutation*, in Vol. VIII of *The Complete Works of St. Thomas More*, ed. L. Schuster et al. (New Haven: Yale Univ. Press, 1973), Part ii, pp. 831–992; and in the same volume, James Lusardi, "The Career of Robert Barnes," Part iii, pp. 1365–1415.

13. Thomas More, E.W., p. 1434. The quotation is also found in Rogers, p. 514, preceding letter no. 206. Unfortunately, the quotation in this edition contains several errors.

14. Judith P. Jones, *Thomas More* (Boston: Twayne Publishers, 1979), p. 115; R. W.

Chambers, "The Continuity of English Prose," in Elsie V. Hitchcock, ed., *Harpsfield's Life of More, Early English Text Society* 186, p. clxii. J. A. Guy and Louis Martz attribute the work to Thomas More, although Martz concedes that the composition was planned by both of them. See J. A. Guy, *The Public Career of Sir Thomas More* (New Haven: Yale Univ. Press, 1980), p. 23n, and Louis Martz, "The Art of Improvisation," in *A Dialogue of Comfort*, Vol. XII of *Complete Works*, p. lxi.

15. Desiderius Erasmus, *Precatio Dominica Digesta in Septem Partes, Juxta Septem Dies, Opera Omnia*, ed. Jean Le Clerc (Leiden, 1703), V, 1218–28 (hereafter cited in the text); Tertullian, *De Oratione*, found in *Patrologiae Latina (PL)*, I, 1149–96 as *De Oratione Liber*, trans. Sister Emily Joseph Daly as "Prayer," in *Tertullian: Disciplinary, Moral and Ascetic Works* (New York: Fathers of the Church, Inc., 1958), pp. 151–88 (whether *De Oratione* was known to Erasmus is debatable; although Tertullian's *Opera* was edited by Erasmus' friend Rhenanus and printed by Froben in Basle in 1521, the *De Oratione* is not included in that edition of the works; Cyprian, *De Oratione Dominica*, found in *PL*, IV, 520–37 and *Corpus Scriptorum Ecclesiasticorum Latinorum (CSEL)*, Book I, Vol. III (1868), pp. 265–94, trans. Roy J. Deferrari as "The Lord's Prayer," in *Saint Cyprian: Treatises* (New York: Fathers of the Church, Inc., 1958), pp. 123–59; *Cyprianus: Opera . . . Atq[ue] haec omnia nobis praestitit ingenti labore suo Erasmus roterodamus . . . [1521]*. The 1520 edition was revised by Erasmus. For Sermo Sextus, *De Oratione Dominca*, see pp. 231–45.

16. See also "Letter to Ulrich Hutten," *Opus Epistolarum*, ed. P. S. Allen et al. (Oxford: Oxford Univ. Press, 1906–58), IV, No. 999, p. 18n. The particular passage can be found in *Thasci Caecili Cypriani Epistvlae*, ed. G. Hartel, *CSEL*, Epistvla XXX (1871), p. 551.

17. Cyprian's *De Oratione Dominica* is divided into thirty-six sections: parts 1 through 8, introduction to the Lord's Prayer; 9 through 27, commentary on the particular phrases of the Lord's Prayer; and 28 through 36, discussions on effective prayer.

18. Richard L. DeMolen, Introd., *A Devout Treatise*, in *Erasmus of Rotterdam* (New York: Twayne Publishers, 1971), p. 94. Both St. Cyprian and Erasmus refer to the ungracious Jews who spurned God's son. See Erasmus, *Precatio Dominica*, 1220D and St. Cyprian, *De Dominica Oratione*, section 10. In his work *Inquisitio De Fidei* (1524), a dialogue on the Apostle's Creed, Erasmus several times does asknowledge St. Cyprian as the source for his ideas.

19. See for example, William G. Crane, *Wit and Rhetoric in the Renaissance* (New York: Columbia Univ. Press, 1937), p. 71, and Virginia W. Callahan, "The *De Copia*: The Bounteous Horn," in *Essays on the Works of Erasmus*, ed. Richard L. DeMolen (New Haven: Yale Univ. Press, 1978), p. 104. Donald King and H. David Rix, eds., in the introduction to Erasmus, *On Copia of Words and Ideas* (Milwaukee: Marquette Univ. Press, 1963), charitably point out "there is no mention of Quintilian in the dedicatory epistle to Colet. . . . But of course, Erasmus is not the only great writer to be silent about sources" (p. 3).

20. See Charles Whibley, "Translators," *The Cambridge History of English Literature*, ed. A. W. Ward and A. R. Waller (New York: G. P. Putnam's Sons, 1910), IV, 28.

21. Martin Luther, *Ain betbüchlin* (Wittenberg, 1522). For a translation by Martin H. Bertram, see Luther's *Personal Prayer Book*, found in Luther's *Devotional Writings*, ed. Gustav K. Wieneke; Vol. XLIII of *Luther's Works*, gen. ed. H. T. Lehmann (Philadelphia: Fortress Press, 1968), pp. 3–45. Nine editions of the *Personal Prayer Book* appeared in 1522 (p. 7).

22. By the end of 1521, Venice, Naples, and London had had ceremonial sessions for the burning of Luther's books. See Carl S. Meyer, "Henry VIII Burns Luther's Books, 12 May 1521," *Journal of Ecclesiastical History*, 9 (1958), 180.

23. E. E. Reynolds, *Thomas More and Erasmus* (New York: Fordham Univ. Press,

1965), p. 192. For Erasmus' early reactions to Luther, see Preserved Smith, *Erasmus: A Study of His Life, Ideals and Place in History* (New York: Harper Brothers, 1923; rpt. New York: Dover Publications, 1962), pp. 209–29. As late as January 1523 Erasmus advised Pope Adrian VI that the reasons for reaction and rebellion within the church "must before all else be healed. . . ." See Reynolds, *Thomas More*, pp. 190–91.

24. Erasmus, *De immensa dei misericordia* (1523), trans. Gentien Hervet as "A sermon of the excedynge great mercy of god. . . ." (1526?), STC 10474. For a discussion on this translation, see J. A. Gee, "Hervet's English Translation, with its Appended Glossary of Erasmus' De Immensa Dei Misericordia," *Philological Quarterly*, 15 (1936), 136–52. For a modern translation and a good concise introduction to the work, see *The Essential Erasmus*, trans. and ed. John P. Dolan (New York: Mentor Books, 1964), pp. 222–70. J. A. Gee, in his "Tindale and the 1553 English *Enchiridion* of Erasmus," *PMLA*, 49 (1934), 460–71, argues that the English translation of the *Enchiridion*, published in 1533 (STC 10479), was translated by Tyndale in the early 1520s.

25. Although Pollard STC catalogue dates the *Devout Treatise* as "1526?," Richard Hyrde in his prefatory letter to the work mentions the "laboure that I have had with it about the printing," and concludes the preface with the words, "At Chelcheth / the yere of our lorde god / a thousande fyve hundred xxiiii. The first day of Octobre."

26. See Frederick S. Siebert, *Freedom of the Press in England, 1476–1776* (Urbana: Univ. of Illinois Press, 1965), pp. 41–43, and Arthur W. Reed, "The Regulations of the Book Trade before the Proclamation of 1538," *Transactions of the Bibliographical Society*, 15 (1918), 157–71; *English Historical Documents, 1327–1485*, IV, 855–57.

27. See for example, J. J. Scarisbrick, *Henry VIII* (Berkeley: Univ. of California Press, 1968), pp. 111ff.; John Bowle, *Henry VIII* (Boston: Little, Brown and Co., 1964), p. 91; John M. Headley, Introd., *Responsio ad Lutherum, Complete Works*, Vol. V, Part ii, pp. 719–21.

28. Jones, p. 28. On More's anti-heresy activities, see also G. R. Elton, *Reform and Reformation: England, 1509–1558* (Cambridge: Harvard Univ. Press, 1977), pp. 75–78, and Guy, pp. 103–05.

29. The records covering the years 1520 to 1538 were kept by Richard Foxford and are preserved in the Records Department at Somerset House, London. This information is found in Siebert, p. 43.

30. Harpsfield, pp. 84–87. See also R. W. Chambers, *Thomas More* (London: J. Cape Ltd., 1935), pp. 32–33 and 186–87.

31. *A Devout Treatise Upon the Pater Noster*, tourned into Englishe by a yong gentylwoman (London: T. Berthelet, 1526?).

32. See, for example, the letter to John Botzheim, Jan. 30, 1523, in Allen, I, No. 1, and the letter to William Budé, c. Sept. 1521, Allen, IV, No. 1233. On the letter to Budé, see also J. K. Sowards, "Erasmus and the Education of Women," *Sixteenth Century Journal*, 13 (1982), 82–83.

33. Erasmus, *De Ratione Studii*, IV and IX, found in *Desiderius Erasmus Concerning the Aim and Method of Education*, ed. and trans. William H. Woodward (New York: Bureau of Publications, 1904), pp. 165, 172–73; Allen, V, No. 140, and VIII, No. 2211.

34. N. Pocock, ed., *Records of the Reformation: The Divorce*, 2 vols. (Oxford: Clarendon Press, 1852), Vol. I (1527–33), p. 88. Hyrde seems to have more than the usual variation in the spelling of his name: Hyrde, Hyde, Hart, Hirtius, Hirte. See also Diane Valeri Bayne, "The *Instruction of a Christian Woman*: Richard Hyrde and the Thomas More Circle," *Moreana*, 45 (1975), 5–15.

35. See Richard Hyrde's prefatory letter in DeMolen, *Erasmus of Rotterdam*, p. 101. Cited hereafter as Hyrde. Hyrde's significant preface can also be found in Foster Watson, *Vives and the Renascence Education of Women* (New York: Longmans and Green, 1912), pp. 159–73.

36. See Margaret's translation in DeMolen's *Erasmus of Rotterdam*, p. 105. DeMolen has expanded certain contractions, such as "ye," "yt" and "pte." in his reprint. All quotations are taken from this edition. Page references will be worked into the text. The translation is also available in *Moreana* 7–13.

37. See Dionysius, Carthusianus, *The mirroure of golde for the synfull soule*, trans. Margaret Countess of Richmond, 1522, STC 6895. See also Travitsky, pp. 70 and 272. For a brief discussion of the mystical treatise, see Joseph B. Collins, *Christian Mysticism in the Elizabethan Age* (Baltimore: Johns Hopkins Univ. Press, 1940), p. 83n. For excellent studies on sixteenth-century translations, see T. Savory, *The Art of Translation* (Boston: The Writer, Inc., 1968); F. R. Amos, *Early Theories of Translation* (New York: Octagon Books, 1973); F. O. Mattheissen, *Translation: An Elizabethan Art* (New York: Octagon Books, 1965), p. 228. For thorough, concise discussion of Elizabethan translations, see Whibley, "Translators," 1–28.

38. See Gee, "Margaret Roper's English Version," pp. 257–71. For Margaret's experience in English composition, see Carole Weinberg, "Thomas More and the Use of English," *Moreana*, 59 (1978), 21–30 and Chambers, pp. xlv–clxxiv.

39. *De Copia* had gone through 85 editions by 1536, *On Copia*, ed. King and Rix, Book I, Chap. 8, pp. 16–17.

40. In the sixteenth century Margaret could use "imbecilite" for "imbecilitatem," since the meaning of the English word was similar to its Latin equivalent, i.e., weakness, feebleness in a physical sense. Not until the seventeenth century did the word begin to focus on the sense of mental weakness, or wanting of mental power. See "imbecilite," *MED*, VI, 87 (Ann Arbor: Univ. of Michigan Press, 1968) and "imbecility," *OED*, V, 55–56 (Oxford: Clarendon Press, 1933).

Patronage and Piety: The Influence of Catherine Parr

This study was supported by a grant from the Penrose Fund of the American Philosophical Society.

1. The seminal study concerning patronage by women during the mid-Tudor period is James K. McConica's *English Humanists and Reformation Politics under Henry VIII and Edward VI* (Oxford: Clarendon Press, 1965), Chap. 7. Focusing on the role played by Catherine Parr during the final years of Henry VIII's reign (1543–47), he documents the preservation of the Erasmian fusion of evangelical piety and humanism. Especially valuable is the account of the queen's commitment to education in bringing humanist scholars such as John Cheke, Roger Ascham, and Anthony Cooke to court as princely tutors. McConica rightly defines the humanistic piety of Catherine Parr as a continuation of noncontroversial traditions established at court by Margaret Beaufort and Catherine of Aragon. The present study breaks new ground, however, by demonstrating Catherine Parr's influence on Protestant aristocratic women and the shift to a new policy of patronizing the translation and publication of devotional texts for a mixed audience of aristocratic and ordinary readers by Protestant women associated with Henry VIII's last queen.

Betty Travitsky includes excerpts from the writings of Catherine Parr in her anthology, *The Paradise of Women* (Westport, Conn: Greenwood Press, 1981). These texts and introductions are a helpful starting point for the study of Tudor women authors. Roland H. Bainton's *Women of the Reformation: In France and England* (Minneapolis: Augsburg Publishing House, 1973), and Pearl Hogrefe's *Women of Action in Tudor England* (Ames: Iowa State Univ. Press, 1977) contain brief lives of prominent women mentioned in this essay. Hogrefe's *Tudor Women* (Ames: Iowa State Univ. Press, 1975) should be checked against the original sources.

Useful background information is contained in the following studies: Suzanne W. Hull's valuable survey, *Chaste, Silent & Obedient* (San Marino, Calif.: Huntington Library, 1982); Myra Reynolds, *The Learned Lady in England 1650-1760* (Boston: Houghton Mifflin, 1920); Ruth Kelso, *Doctrine for the Lady of the Renaissance* (Urbana: Univ. of Illinois Press, 1956); J. R. Brink, ed., *Female Scholars* (Montreal: Eden Press Women's Publications, 1980); Marlene Springer, ed., *What Manner of Woman: Essays on English and American Life and Literature* (New York: New York Univ. Press, 1977).

Unless otherwise noted, London is the place of publication of works cited herein. The modern use of i/j, u/v, s, and w has been followed; contractions are expanded. The British Library is abbreviated as BL.

2. John Foxe, *Acts and Monuments*, ed. S. R. Cattley, 4th ed., rev. and enlarged by J. Pratt, 8 vols. (The Religious Tract Society, 1877), V, 52, 58, 60, 137, 402, 553-61. Compare his treatment of Catherine Howard as an instrument of reaction against Protestantism (V, 402). The printer John Day issued the *Book of Martyrs* in 1563.

3. See John Aylmer's *Harborowe* [Harbor] *for Faithfull and Trewe Subjectes* (J. Day, 1559): "Was not Quene Anne the mother of this blessed woman, the chief, first, and only cause of banyshing the beast of Rome, with all his beggerly baggage?" (sig. B4v).

4. François Lambert, *Summe of Christianitie*, trans. Tristram Revel (1536).

5. Anne Askew, *Examinations*, ed. John Bale, 2 vols. (Wesel, 1546-47), II, sigs. F3r-v, I, sig. I1v. Included in Bale's *Select Works*, ed. Henry Christmas, Parker Society, Vol. XXXVI (Cambridge: Cambridge Univ. Press, 1849). For discussion of the Anne Askew affair, see McConica, pp. 222-24, 226-27; John N. King, *English Reformation Literature: The Tudor Origins of the Protestant Tradition* (Princeton: Princeton Univ. Press, 1982), pp. 71-75, 79; and Elaine Beilin's essay in this collection.

6. Hugh Latimer, *Selected Sermons*, ed. A. G. Chester (Charlottesville, Va.: Univ. Press of Virginia for Folger Shakespeare Library, 1968), pp. 127-28; preface to Luke in Desiderius Erasmus, *Paraphrases of the New Testament*, trans. Nicholas Udall et al., 2 vols. (1548-49), sigs. A1v-2r. See also Udall's preface to John, which praises her "for composyng and setting foorth many goodly psalmes and diverse other contemplative meditacions" (sig. AAa2r).

7. *Tudor Royal Proclamations*, ed. Paul L. Hughes and James F. Larkin, 3 vols. (New Haven: Yale Univ. Press, 1964-69), No. 272. See Foxe, V, 557.

8. William P. Haugaard ignores the testimony of Foxe and Anne Askew in questioning whether such a group existed before the reign of Edward VI in "Katherine Parr: The Religious Convictions of a Renaissance Queen," *Renaissance Quarterly*, 22 (1969), 350.

9. Quoted from the text in *The Monument of Matrones*, ed. Thomas Bentley (H. Denham, 1582), sig. L5r. See C. Fenno Hoffman, Jr., "Catherine Parr as a Woman of Letters," *Huntington Library Quarterly*, 23 (1959-60), 355. On the relationship to à Kempis, see F. P. Tudor, "Changing Private Belief and Practice in English Devotional Literature, c. 1475-1550," Ph.D. thesis, Oxford University, 1985. She argues convincingly that many copies of Catherine's prayer book were purchased for devotional use at court.

10. On the significance of the *Paraphrases*, see John N. Wall, Jr., "Godly and Fruitful Lessons," in *The Godly Kingdom of Tudor England: Great Books of the English Reformation*, ed. John Booty (Wilton, Conn.: Morehouse-Barlow Co., Inc., 1981), pp. 73-85. See also Wall's facsimile reproduction of *The First Tome or Volume of the Paraphrase of Erasmus upon the New Testamente*, with an introduction (Delmar, N.Y.: Scholars' Facsimiles and Reprints, 1975).

11. Bodleian Library, MS Cherry 36, dated Dec. 30, 1544. Edited and discussed in Renja Salminen's critical text of *Le Miroir* in *Dissertationes Humanarum Litterarum*, No. 22 of *Annales Academiae Scientiarum Fennicae* (Helsinki, 1979). See Anne Prescott's essay in this collection.

12. St. Augustine, *The Twelfe Steppes of Abuses* (1550), sig. A3r. See also Askew, *Examinations*, II, sig. B3r; Foxe, III, 705; and King, pp. 72-73.

13. Lynne's translation of Luther's *A Frutefull and Godly Exposition of the Kyngdom of Christ* (1548), sig. A3r; Bullinger, *Absoluta de Christi Domini et catholicae eius Ecclesiae Sacramentis* (1551), sig. *4r.

14. Letters 4-6 in *Epistolae Tigurinae*, ed. Hastings Robinson, Parker Society, Vol. LIV (Cambridge: Cambridge Univ. Press, 1848); ed. and trans. Robinson in *Original Letters Relative to the English Reformation*, 2 vols. in 1, Parker Society, Vol. LIII (Cambridge: Cambridge Univ. Press, 1846–47).

15. Thomas Becon, *The Floure* [Flower] *of Godlye Prayers* (1551), as quoted from the complete *Worckes*, 3 vols. (1560–64), II, sig. 3E4v.

16. Nicolas Denisot, *Annae, Margaritae, Janae, sororum virginum heroidum Anglarum in mortem divae Margaritae Valesiae, Navarrorum reginae, Hecatodistichon* (Paris, 1550).

17. Erasmus, *Christian Humanism and the Reformation: Selected Writings*, ed. John C. Olin (New York: Harper and Row, 1965), p. 97.

18. Andrew Maunsell includes the following item in his *Catalogue of English Printed Bookes* (1595), Part i, sig. H1r: "Lady Eliz. *Fane* her certaine psalmes of godly meditation in number 21. with a 102. proverbs. printed by Rob. Crowley: 1550. in 8."

19. Franklin B. Williams, "The Literary Patronesses of Renaissance England," *Notes and Queries*, 207 (1962), 366.

20. Thomas Wilson, *Vita et obitus duorum fratrum Suffolciensium* (1551).

21. Trans. Joannes Epinus, *A Very Fruitful Exposition upon the .XV. Psalme* [i.e., Psalm 15], trans. Lesse (c. 1548), sigs. A5v–6r.

22. Olde, preface to 1 and 2 Peter, in Erasmus, *Paraphrases*, II, *1v; Hugh Latimer *Seven Sermons* (1572), sigs. A4v, ¶2r, published as part two of *Frutefull Sermons*, ed. A. Bernher (1571).

23. See Jennifer Loach, "Pamphlets and Politics, 1553-8," *Bulletin of the Institute of Historical Research*, 48 (1975), 31–44; and J. W. Martin, "The Marian Regime's Failure to Understand the Importance of Printing," *Huntington Library Quarterly*, 44 (1980–81), 231–47.

24. Queen Elizabeth, *Poems*, ed. Leicester Bradner (Providence: Brown Univ. Press, 1964), p. 3.

25. Thomas Deloney, *The Great Troubles of the Dutches of Suffolke* in his *Strange Histories* (1602); Thomas Drue, *The Life of the Dutches of Suffolke* (1631).

26. On the Knox relationship, see Patrick Collinson, "The Role of Women in the English Reformation illustrated by the Life and Friendships of Anne Locke," *Studies in Church History*, 2 (1965), 261, 266–67.

The Pearl of the Valois and Elizabeth I: Marguerite de Navarre's *Miroir* and Tudor England

1. For Marguerite's life and friendships, see Pierre Jourda, *Marguerite d'Angoulême* (Paris: Champion, 1930), Vol. I, and his *Répertoire analytique et chronologique de la correspondance de Marguerite d'Angoulême* (Paris: Champion, 1930), Vol. I. All in-text references to Jourda are to *Marguerite*.

2. Pierre de Ronsard, *Oeuvres*, ed. Gustave Cohen (Paris: Gallimard, 1950), I, 605, from Marguerite's *Tombeau* (1551).

3. *Letters and Papers, Foreign and Domestic, of the Reign of Henry VIII, 1509–1547*, ed. James Gairdner, and R. H. Brodie (21 vols., London, 1862–1910), henceforth cited as *L&P*; numbers, unless otherwise identified, refer to items. For these particular contacts see, e.g., III, p. 310, 912; VI, 692; VII, 958; IX, 378. For Marguerite's compliments to Anne Boleyn and concern for Anne of Cleves, see Jourda, *Répertoire*, 569, 882. In February 1542 Marguerite told Ambassador Paget she had to love Henry because she had almost been his

stepmother or wife (*L&P*, XVII, 128). Marguerite's tone is hard to judge; Henry had recently executed Catherine Howard. On marriage negotiations concerning Marguerite and England see also Jourda, *Marguerite*, pp. 12–16.

4. *The Mirror of the Sinful Soul*, photographic facsimile ed. Percy Ames (London, 1897). Elizabeth's own title is "The glasse of the synnefull soule." My quotations from Elizabeth come from the Ames edition; I have normalized i and j and expanded some contractions. For additional bibliographical information see Ruth Hughey, "A Note on Queen Elizabeth's 'Godly Meditation,' " *The Library*, 4th ser., 15 (1935), 237–40. Hughey identifies and describes later printed editions of the translation; she is wrong, however, to call Marguerite a "Protestant queen."

I had hoped to make use of Renja Salminen's 1979 dissertation, *Marguerite de Navarre*, a critical edition of *Le miroir* followed by Elizabeth's *Glasse of the synnefull soule* (*Dissertations Humanarum Litterarum*, No. 22 of *Annales Academiae Scientiarum Fennicae*), Helsinki (1979), but I have been unable to see it.

5. Sidney Lee, *The French Renaissance in England* (Oxford: Oxford Univ. Press, 1910), p. 129. There has been little work on Marguerite and England. A. H. Upham, *The French Influence in English Literature* (New York: Columbia Univ. Press, 1908), argues plausibly that Marguerite was a useful model for Mary Sidney, Countess of Pembroke (although the Renaissance had many such patronesses). Recently, Hugh Richmond, *Puritans and Libertines: Anglo-French Literary Relations in the Reformation* (Berkeley: Univ. of California Press, 1981), has argued sometimes intriguingly for Marguerite's influence—through her court at Nérac and her *Heptaméron*—on the tone of English culture and especially on Shakespeare. All three books are very inaccurate, and should be used only after careful checking and with some skepticism as to their claims. Furthermore, Richmond is wrong to say (pp. 10 and 24) that there was talk of marriage between Marguerite and Henry VIII around 1530 (Marguerite had a husband), and the poem he quotes by Ronsard (p. 266) is not, as he says, about Marguerite but about her niece. Lee and Richmond think Elizabeth's translation reflects Anne Boleyn's affection for Marguerite, but this may be to take Anne's cordiality as queen too seriously. Marguerite was at first unhappy over the divorce and for a while refused to see Anne (Jourda, *Marguerite*, p. 172; *L&P*, VI, 134). What Anne privately thought of Marguerite we do not know. Nor do we know if Elizabeth knew her mother's opinion.

6. Marguerite d'Angoulême, reine de Navarre, *Le Miroir de l'âme pécheresse*, ed. Joseph L. Allaire (Munich: Wilhelm Fink, 1972), Humanistische Bibliothek, II, no. 10; the introduction discusses the date of composition and the possible reasons for the condemnation, which include Marguerite's use of a French Bible. See also Jourda, *Marguerite*, pp. 178–80.

7. On Marguerite's religion see especially Lucien Febvre, *Amour sacré, amour profane: autour de l'Heptaméron* (Paris: Gallimard, 1944), and Simone Glasson's introduction to her edition of Marguerite's *Prisons* (Geneva: Droz, 1978), which has an excellent bibliography. H. Heller, "Marguerite de Navarre and the Reformers of Meaux," *Bibliothèque d'humanisme et renaissance*, 33 (1971), 271–310, traces the sources of some of the queen's ideas and mannerisms. There is some interesting material on her relationship with Calvin in Charmarie J. Blaisdell, "Calvin's Letters to Women: The Courting of Ladies in High Places," *Sixteenth Century Journal*, 13, No. 3 (1982), 67–84.

8. Thus even in 1542 the English ambassador William Paget could write Henry that François had at least discussed the possibility of breaking with Rome, although he had asked Paget to keep the conversation secret. (*L&P*, XVII, 200). Such interviews, however intended, kept English hopes alive for a surprisingly long time.

9. J. E. Neale, *Queen Elizabeth* (New York: Harcourt Brace, 1934), pp. 14–15; at least he did give Elizabeth's translation a look, if with an unsympathetic eye, for he quotes some heated lines. Like Ames, Neale suspects a connection between Marguerite's *Miroir* and *The mirroure of golde for the synfull soule* by Elizabeth's great-grandmother, Margaret Beau-

fort, but in fact the golden mirror was not by Margaret but only translated from Denis de Leeuwis's *Speculum aureum animae peccatricis*. Mirrors were common in titles; see Jourda, *Marguerite*, pp. 355–56. For de Leeuwis, see James K. McConica, *English Humanists and Reformation Politics under Henry VIII and Edward VI* (Oxford: Oxford Univ. Press, 1965), p. 55.

10. Anthony Martienssen, *Queen Katherine Parr* (London and New York: McGraw-Hill, 1973), p. 189; Alison Plowden, *The Young Elizabeth* (New York: Stein and Day, 1971), p. 77 (Plowden is very useful on Elizabeth's education, although she may assume too much about Elizabeth's devotion to Henry); Carolly Erickson, *The First Elizabeth* (New York: Summit Books, 1983), p. 57.

11. Paul Johnson, *Elizabeth I: A Study in Power and Intellect* (London: Weidenfeld and Nicolson, 1974), p. 21; McConica, p. 231 (his suggestion, p. 8, that Anne Boleyn acquired Elizabeth's copy when she lived in France is chronologically impossible); J. J. Scarisbrick, *Henry VIII* (Berkeley: Univ. of California Press, 1968), p. 457.

12. There has not been much extended criticism of the *Miroir*. Febvre says, perhaps rightly, that it is too long (p. 59), but the very reiterations to some ears might develop a cumulative power. For some sympathetic general comments on Marguerite's poetry, see I. D. McFarlane, *A Literary History of France: Renaissance France* (London: Benn, 1974), pp. 125–28. I have been unable to consult R. M. Bernardo's 1979 dissertation, "The Problem of Perspective in the *Miroir de l'âme pécheresse*, the *Prisons* and the *Heptaméron* of Marguerite de Navarre" (DAI 40:2087A).

13. For evidence that Marguerite used this translation, see Allaire's introduction to the *Miroir*, pp. 19–22.

14. A parallel usefully pointed out by McConica, pp. 8 and 231. Marguerite's position vis à vis the Catholic church was more ambiguous than Catherine's, however, and it seems to me that the the latter's *Lamentacion of a sinner* (1547), although hardly Calvinist, is more militant in tone than the *Miroir*.

15. *L&P*, IV, 2068. There are many more references to Marguerite in the state papers than I can cite in this article; they offer evidence for her character and her relationship to the English that has never been examined in full (Jourda being, of course, more interested in their indications of Marguerite's whereabouts and activities). It should also be stressed that for the most part the English dealt with her at or near the French court. Some who comment on her influence in England write as though she spent most of her time ruling her court at Nérac. She did not, and it is precisely her role at the French court that attracted English attention during her lifetime. Only in later years was she often remembered writing religious verse and witty stories near the Pyrenees. Except for the *Miroir* and its companion religious poems and some plays (one farce is mentioned in *L&P*, XVII, 128, Feb. 26, 1542), she had in 1544 no great literary reputation; she was a patron, a moderate Reformer, and a politician.

16. *L&P*, XV, 223; XVII, 148. Norfolk's conversation with Marguerite in June 1533 (*L&P*, VI, 692) offers a fascinating insight into her teasing, complex character and her modus operandi. I think that she was flirting a little with the man even while using her seeming candor to shape his perceptions. She loves Henry as a brother, she says, so she gives Norfolk some political advice and while she's at it puts a few knifestrokes in the back of her enemy Montmorency—suggesting that he is untrustworthy, that he admires Charles V, and that he makes trouble between the dauphin and the king (her examples include sexual escapades described with lively dialogue). As for the queen (Charles V's daughter, Eleanor), her brother has not slept with her for seven months. Why not? Because "when he doth lie with her, he cannot sleep." "Madam, what should be the cause?" Why, says Marguerite of her own sister-in-law, "She is very hot in bed and desireth to be too much embraced." And then, reports Norfolk, "she fell upon a great laughter." Norfolk must have been amused, notorious womanizer that he was. He must also have been interested to hear that the

conservative Professor Béda was banished (perhaps one reason, as I have mentioned, the Sorbonne censured her book a few months later) and that his writings doubtless contained "shameful railings against the kings of England and of France." More gossip. More on Montmorency. A few words on the Imperial reaction to Henry's divorce. "My opinion is," concludes Norfolk, "that she is your good and sure friend." Yes, but one misses in Norfolk's dispatch any awareness of what Marguerite stood to gain from all this charm and frankness. On occasion Marguerite did find English envoys disagreeable, as see her comments on Bonnet, *L&P*, XV, 223.

17. *L&P*, XVII, 128; XX, ii, 1024. Jourda, *Marguerite*, pp. 271–72, understandably finds the conversation a puzzle. I suspect Marguerite had a personality that led her insensibly into tune with the minds of those she liked or whose opinion she valued. She may well have believed most of what Paget thought he heard while she was speaking to him—and she may also have warmed to the nuns she knew and even to the Bishop of Rome when he cultivated her friendship. Paget quarreled with her briefly in the spring of 1545, but in the years before Elizabeth's translation he seems to have elicited from her a great deal of gossip and news, although when reading of this subtle pair's conversations it is hard to judge who was manipulating whom.

18. *L&P*, XIV, i, 369, a letter from Thomas Broke of Calais to Cromwell writing on behalf of Hambert, "late of Tournay." No. 370 is "a small taste" of the "great secrets" he is offering Cromwell. Jourda, *Marguerite*, p. 235, mentions this letter but assumes, incorrectly, that it was Marguerite who had the copy sent to Henry.

19. For the English Bible affair, see *L&P*, XIV, i, 37, 371 (the French government devoted considerable effort to soothing Henry); Jourda's "Tableau chronologique des publications de Marguerite de Navarre," *Revue du seizième siècle*, 12 (1925), 209–55, does not specify a month for the 1539 edition, but the title page says 1539, suggesting a date after Easter and thus too late for Hambert. All in-text references are to this 1539 edition.

20. On such language applied to God, see William Kerrigan, "The Fearful Accomodations of John Donne," *English Literary Renaissance* 4 (1974), 337–63. Kerrigan associates an increased verbal and "devotional anthropomorphism" especially with Luther.

21. Elizabeth gets into real trouble on two occasions toward the end of her work, confused by either the French or the line of thought. She somewhat garbles Marguerite's description of God loving himself from within the loved mortal and, interestingly, she stumbles over a hard passage on God as fire (*Miroir*, ll. 1302–10; 1356–62).

22. Particularly helpful for setting Bale's edition in context are McConica; Leslie P. Fairfield, *John Bale: Mythmaker for the English Reformation* (West Lafayette, Ind.: Purdue Univ. Press, 1976); and John N. King, *English Reformation Literature: The Tudor Origins of the Protestant Tradition* (Princeton: Princeton Univ. Press, 1982). Fairfield does not, however, discuss Bale's edition of Elizabeth. King gives a stirring defense of Bale's racy polemical style, and although he does not treat the *Godly medytacyon* in any detail, his comments on Protestant propaganda, patronage, and the cultivation of Elizabeth are enlightening.

23. On Bale's miscalculations concerning Paget, see King, p. 112. Bale's was not the last edition of Elizabeth's translation; see Hughey for some Elizabethan editions.

24. The volume is described by Henri Chamard in his introduction to Joachim du Bellay's *Oeuvres poétiques* (Paris, 1934), Vol. IV, and by Clément Jugé, *Nicolas Denisot* (Paris, 1907). See also Jourda, *Marguerite*, pp. 341ff. I have not seen a copy. Chamard prints the Latin distichs as footnotes to du Bellay's translation, pp. 57–84, and it is this text (the most readily available nowadays) which I quote and to which my numbers refer.

25. Distich 86: "Who will not wonder at her mirror in which the true image of God is given refracted" (not, interestingly, "reflected"; du Bellay translates "refracta" as "reverberée"). Strictly, Marguerite's "mirror" is for the soul, but *speculum* and "mirror" were often used with just this ambiguity in works with titles like Marguerite's.

26. On Denisot see Jugé and, more recently, the fascinating article in the *Dictionnaire de biographie française*, ed. R. d'Amat et R. Limouzin-Lamothe (Paris, 1933–); Jugé describes Denisot's extraordinary career in detail. There seems little doubt that he later was a spy, and a good one, smuggling out the plans for Calais's fortifications while posing as a tutor to the English governor's children. Exactly what he did at Somerset House is unclear. Writing soon afterwards, Nicholas Wotton referred to his "falsifying papers" and warned the English at Calais not to trust him. Jugé reprints Wotton's urgent warnings (the summaries in the *Calendar of State Papers* misread "Denisot" as "Devisat").

27. In following Edward Seymour's ups and downs I have relied on the *DNB;* Wilbur K. Jordan, *Edward VI: The Young King* (Cambridge: Harvard Univ. Press, 1968), and *Edward VI: The Threshold of Power* (Cambridge: Harvard Univ. Press, 1970); and Barrett L. Beer, *Northumberland* (Kent, Oh.: The Kent State Univ. Press, 1973), which is particularly helpful in describing the festivities in 1550 and 1551 celebrating Anglo-French friendship. King's *English Reformation Literature* is very useful on Seymour as a Protestant patron of learning and on his efforts during and after his fall to appear pious (that this was good for his "image" need not mean he was insincere). King's sympathy for Seymour is a good antidote to the extreme dyspepsia of M. L. Bush's *The Government Policy of Protector Somerset* (Montreal: McGill-Queens Univ. Press, 1975).

28. Ronsard, I, 592. The 1551 *Tombeau* is quite rare; I read the copy belonging to the Houghton Library, Harvard University.

29. Quoted in William P. Haugaard's remarkable interesting essay, "Elizabeth Tudor's *Book of Devotions*: A Neglected Clue to the Queen's Life and Character," *Sixteenth Century Journal*, 12, No. 2 (1981), 79–106. Haugaard does not discuss the *Miroir* or Elizabeth's translation.

30. Haugaard, p. 84.

Anne Askew's Self-Portrait in the *Examinations*

1. Immediately after her death, Askew proved her value to the Protestant cause. John Bale claimed a thousand converts were made, and even discounting for propaganda, we may suppose that many were swayed by her faith and fortitude. A Latin epitaph for her rejoiced that her truth was not shaken by fetters and that eternal life crowned her ashes. Askew's reputation lived on in the seventeenth century. In "An Essay to Revive the Ancient Education of Gentlewomen" (1673), Bathsua Makin attributed the English Reformation itself to women, particularly like Anne Askew, "a person famous for learning and piety, who so seasoned the Queen and ladies of the Court, by her precepts and examples, and after sealed her profession with her blood, that the seed of reformation seemed to be sowed by her hand." See *The Female Spectator* ed. Mary Mahl and Helene Koon (Bloomington: Indiana Univ. Press, 1977), p. 134. The legend continues, enshrined in two novels, Anne Manning's *The Lincolnshire Tragedy: Passages in the Life of the Faire Gospeller, Mistress Anne Askew* (London, 1866; New York, 1867), and Alison Macleod's *The Heretic* (Boston: Houghton Mifflin, 1966). Both books reflect the power of Askew's writing to spark the sympathy and admiration of her readers, for both quote at length from the *Examinations* and find in them the imaginative source of Askew's character.

2. *The first examinacyon of Anne Askewe, lately martyred in Smythfelde, by the Romysh popes upholders, with the Elucydacyon of Johan Bale* (Wesel, 1546); quote from Bale's preface "to the Christen readers," p. 9v. All further references to this work appear in the text and are designated as "I." *The lattre examinacion of the worthye servaunt of God mastres Anne Askewe* (Wesel, 1547). All further references to this work appear in the text as "II." All quotations are given with modernized j, u, v, and s. The two works are commonly known as the *Examinations*. John Foxe, *Actes and Monuments of these latter and perillous dayes touching matters of the Church* . . . (London, 1563), sig. PPiii.

3. Educators like Thomas More and Juan Luis Vives actively supported the education of women as a means of increasing their virtue, but they strictly defined that virtue in private and domestic terms. A woman versed in Scripture, Latin, and philosophy would become chaste, obedient, modest, and pious, and so a better companion for her husband, and a better mother to her children. On Vives, see Valerie Wayne's essay in this collection. Margaret More Roper seems to have fulfilled all the humanists' best hopes; see Rita Verbrugge's essay in this collection.

4. In *British Autobiography in the Seventeenth Century* (London: Routledge and Kegan Paul; New York: Columbia Univ. Press, 1969), Paul Delaney studies both secular and religious autobiography, proposing that the latter may have had its roots in Scripture (the Psalms, St. Paul), Augustine's *Confessions,* and the medieval *exemplum.* He notes, however, that "religious autobiographies were not commonly written in Britain until more than a hundred years after Henry's break with the Pope" (p. 33). In general, "autobiographers seem to have been moved to write especially in response to the challenge to their faith of religious oppression or persecution" (p. 38). In *John Bale: Mythmaker for the English Reformation* (West Lafayette, Ind.: Purdue Univ. Press, 1976), Leslie P. Fairfield calls *The vocacyon of John Bale* a "fragment of autobiography" in which, describing only the years 1552 to 1553, "Bale casts himself as a Protestant saint . . . [drawing] on his own experience for examples of good and evil" (p. 141). Fairfield speculates that Bale was encouraged to write his own work because he "had seen how successful Anne Askew's accounts of her examinations had been" (p. 142).

5. Fairfield argues for the pivotal position of Bale in changing the English conception of sainthood. In the case of Askew's *Examinations,* "the main point of Bale's commentary was to show that Anne Askew's faith had been biblical and her martyrdom valid, and therefore that her judges and interrogators had been agents of the devil" (p. 132). In *English Reformation Literature: The Tudor Origins of the Protestant Tradition* (Princeton: Princeton Univ. Press, 1982), John King shows how "Bale designed the text as virulent anti-government propaganda," using Askew's words as ammunition against the Catholic establishment (p. 72).

6. The two examinations were published separately at Wesel in 1546 and 1547 with Bale's elucidation. Four editions combining the two examinations were printed in England during Edward VI's reign, three of which omitted Bale's commentary. Fairfield speculates that there might therefore have been a total of 3,500 copies in circulation (p. 135). The examinations also appeared in Foxe's *Actes and Monuments* without Bale's commentary.

7. Writing about the religiosity of the thirteenth-century nuns of Helfta, Caroline Walker Bynum shows, "First, the mystical union these women achieved, which was sometimes expressed in visions of themselves as priests, enabled them to serve as counselors, mediators, and channels to the sacraments—roles which the thirteenth-century church in some ways increasingly denied to women and to laity. Second, the eucharistic piety that is so pronounced at Helfta, particularly in the form of the cult of the sacred heart, expressed the same need for direct contact with God and direct authorization to act as mediators to others. . . . [W]omen who grew up in monasteries were less likely to be influenced by the contemporary stereotype of women as morally and intellectually inferior. Such women were more likely to see themselves as functioning with a full range of male and female, governing and comforting roles, paralleling the full range of the operations of God." See *Jesus as Mother: Studies in the Spirituality of the High Middle Ages* (Berkeley: Univ. of California Press, 1982), pp. 184–85. Deep religiosity, whether in the thirteenth-century cloistered Catholic or the sixteenth-century Protestant martyr, may indeed have modified women's internalization of narrow definitions of their sex.

8. Helen White, *Tudor Books of Saints and Martyrs* (Madison: Univ. of Wisconsin Press, 1963), p. 12.

9. A. G. Dickens notes that before she came to London, Askew may have known the Nottinghamshire Reformer, John Lascelles, who had become a sewer of the king's chamber

and "the leading spirit" of a Reformist group at court. See *Lollards and Protestants in the Diocese of York 1509–1558* (London: Oxford Univ. Press, 1959), pp. 33–34.

10. Derek Wilson, *A Tudor Tapestry: Men, Women, and Society in Reformation England* (Pittsburgh: Univ. of Pittsburgh Press, 1973), p. 188.

11. John Lascelles, with whom Askew was burned, wrote a letter from prison wholly concerned with his sacramentarian beliefs. See Foxe, *Actes and Monuments*, sigs. PPiiiv–PPiiiiv.

12. With considerably more color, Bale says of Rich, "Without all dyscressyon, honestye, or manhode, he casteth of hys gowne, and taketh here upon hym the most vyle offyce of an hangeman and pulleth at the racke most vyllanouslye" (II, p. 45v).

13. This stanza is, of course, based upon Ephesians 6:11ff.

Lady Jane Grey: Protestant Queen and Martyr

I would like to thank Dennis Moore, Judith Aiken, Janis Butler Holm, Howard Solomon, and Stanley Rolnick for their helpful suggestions. Earlier versions of this paper were presented at the Sixteenth Congress on Medieval Studies, Western Michigan University, 1981, and the Eighth Conference on Patristic, Mediaeval, and Renaissance Studies, Villanova University, 1983.

1. Thomas Decker and John Webster, *The Famous History of Sir Thomas Wyatt* in *The Dramatic Works of John Webster*, ed. William Hazlitt (London: John Russell Smith, 1897), I, see for example, pp. 8, 10, 36, 39, 55, 57, 60. Seventeenth-century historians who developed this view include Bishop Gilbert Burnet, *History of the Reformation of the Church of England* (1681; new edn., Oxford: Oxford Univ. Press, 1829), II, 469, and Peter Heylin, *The History of the Reformation of the Church of England* (London: H. Twyford, J. Place, T. Basset, W. Palmer, 1670), p. 148. Lady Jane Grey was the darling of Victorians. See, for example, George Howard, *Lady Jane Grey and Her Times* (London: Sherwood, Neely, and Jones, 1822); David W. Bartlett, *The Life of Lady Jane Grey* (Philadelphia: Porter and Coates, 1886); and Richard Davey, *The Nine Days' Queen* (London: Methuen and Co., Ltd., 1909). For more recent interpretations, see David Mathew, *Lady Jane Grey: The Setting of the Reign* (London: Eyre Methuen, 1972), and Barrett L. Beer, *Northumberland* (Kent, Oh.: The Kent State Univ. Press, 1973). Roland Bainton includes a brief sketch of Jane Grey in *Women of the Reformation: In France and England* (Boston: Beacon Press, 1975), pp. 181–90.

2. Hester Chapman, *Lady Jane Grey* (London: Jonathan Cape, 1962), p. 56.

3. On educating daughters, see, for example, Frances Murray, "Feminine Spirituality in the More Household," *Moreana*, 27, 28 (1970), 92–102; M. J. Tucker, "The Child as Beginning and End: Fifteenth and Sixteenth Century English Childhood," in Lloyd DeMause, ed., *The History of Childhood* (New York: Harper-Torchbook, 1975), pp. 229–58; and Pearl Hogrefe, *Tudor Women* (Ames: Iowa State Univ. Press, 1975), p. 5. Nicholas Harris Nicholas points out that it is questionable whether she had any real proficiency in languages other than Greek, Latin, and French in *The Literary Remains of Lady Jane Grey: With a Memoir of Her Life* (London: Harding, Triphook, and Pepard, 1825), pp. xii–xiii. See also, Josephine Kamm, *Hope Deferred: Girls' Education in English History* (London: Methuen and Co., Ltd., 1976), p. 39.

4. William Haugaard, "Katherine Parr: The Religious Convictions of a Renaissance Queen," *Renaissance Quarterly*, 22 (1969), 355. On Parr's influence, see John King's essay in this collection.

5. Ascham's description of Lady Jane Grey in *The Scholemaster* is consistent with his earlier accounts of the meeting. Writing to John Sturm in December 1550 he calls Lady Jane one of the two most learned ladies in England (the other was Mildred Cooke Cecil,

daughter of Anthony Cooke and wife to William Cecil). He recounts finding Jane reading Plato, adding that she was "so thoroughly understanding it that she caused me the greatest astonishment." In a letter to Jane herself written in January 1551 he tells her that of all his travels and all the variety of experience he has had, "nothing has caused me so much wonder" as the visit to Bradgate. Roger Ascham, *The Whole Works*, ed. J. A. Giles (London: J. R. Smith, 1865; new edn., New York: AMS Press, 1965), I, Part i, pp. lxxi, lxxiv–lxxvi.

6. Roger Ascham, *The Schoolmaster*, [*sic*], ed. Lawrence V. Ryan (Ithaca: Cornell Univ. Press, 1976), pp. 35–36.

7. *The Acts and Monuments of John Foxe*, ed. Rev. George Townsend (rpt. New York: AMS Press, 1976), VIII, 700 (unless otherwise indicated, all quotes by Jane Grey will be cited in text by volume number and page number of this edition); John Aylmer, *An Harborowe for Faithfull and Trewe Subjects* (London: j. Daye, 1559), STC 1005.

8. The traditional explanation has always been that the whole plot was developed by Northumberland. A recent exponent of this perspective is Beer, pp. 148–49. Wilbur K. Jordan, *Edward VI: The Threshold of Power* (Cambridge: Harvard Univ. Press, 1970), p. 517, however, argues that Edward originated the idea of a changed succession and convinced Northumberland to go along with it. See also G. R. Elton, *Reform and Reformation: England, 1509–1558* (Cambridge: Harvard Univ. Press, 1977), pp. 374–75, and Mathew, pp. 135–36, for an appraisal of the evidence.

9. The 1554 edition of Jane Grey's writings, *Here in this booke ye have a godly epistle made by a faithful Christian* (STC 5153) states that Jane herself wrote the account of the Feckenham debate, but this seems highly unlikely, and Foxe does not mention it. Sixteenth-century editions of her work include *Here in this booke* (1554), which includes the debate with Feckenham, her letter to her sister Katherine, and her scaffold speech. Her letter to her sister was also published as "An Exhortation written by the Lady Jane, the night before shee suffered" in Otto Werdmuller, *A Most fruitefull, pithe, and learned treatise, how a Christian man ought to behave himself in the daunger of death*, trans. Miles Coverdale (Antwerp, 1555; London, 1579), STC 25251 and 25253. Thomas Bentley, ed., *Monument of Matrones* (London: H. Denham, 1582), STC 1892–94, contains the debate, her prayer, and her letter to Katherine. *The Life, death, and actions of the most chast, and religious lady Jane Grey* (London: Printed for G. Eld, 1615), STC 7281, contains all of her writings including a longer scaffold speech, though the meaning is unchanged. Except for this, the differences between the editions are minimal. I have chosen to use Foxe, since it was best known in its time; see VI, 415–525.

Lady Jane Grey's writings are also collected with a long biographical introduction in Nicolas, *The Literary Remains of Lady Jane Grey*.

10. See, for example, not only the account in Foxe, but also the references to Lady Jane Grey in Aylmer and in *Holinshed's Chronicles*, ed. Henry Ellis (London: J. Johnson, etc., 1808; rpt. New York: AMS Press, 1965), IV, 22; John N. King, *English Reformation Literature: The Tudor Origins of the Protestant Tradition* (Princeton: Princeton Univ. Press, 1982), p. 419.

11. *The Accession, Coronation, and Marriage of Mary Tudor as Related in Four Manuscripts of the Escorial*, trans. and pub. by C. V. Malfatti (Barcelona, 1956), p. 72.

12. Ruth Hughey, "A Ballad of Lady Jane Grey," *Times Literary Supplement* (Dec. 7, 1933), p. 878. On the impact of Foxe, see William Haller, *The Elect Nation: The Meaning and Relevance of Foxe's Book of Martyrs* (New York: Harper and Row, 1963), p. 14, and D. M. Loades, *The Oxford Martyrs* (New York: Stein and Day, 1970), p. 30.

13. See, for example, Steven May's unpublished paper, "Tudor 'Tower Verse': The Poetics of Imprisonment," pp. 2–4. I wish to thank Professor May for generously sharing his work with me while in manuscript. On More, see Elizabeth F. Rogers, ed., *The Correspondence of Sir Thomas More* (Princeton: Princeton Univ. Press, 1947), pp. 502, 507–08,

564; Louis L. Martz and Frank Manley, eds., *The Complete Works of St. Thomas More* (New Haven: Yale Univ. Press, 1976), XII, see especially, pp. lix, lxv, cii, cvi–cvii. I am indebted to Anne Lake Prescott for her help with the works of Thomas More.

14. Catherine Parr describes herself as a "wretche and of my self always redy and prone to evyll" in her *Prayers or Medytacions,* cited in Haugaard, p. 355. Lady Jane Grey's extravagance of language and wit are also reminiscent of the earlier martyr Anne Askew, see Foxe, V, 548–51.

15. Nicolas does not accept this, however; see pp. lxxvi–lxxvii. King suggests that simply referring to Harding as "a friend" works to universalize the letter (p. 420).

16. *The Chronicle of Queen Jane by a Resident in the Tower of London,* ed. John Gough Nichols (Camden Soc., 1850; rpt. New York: AMS Press, 1968), p. 25.

17. See, for example, William Tyndale, *Doctrinal Treatises,* ed. Henry Walter (Cambridge: Cambridge Univ. Press, 1848); Simon Fish, *A Supplication of the Beggars* (London, 1529), STC 10883; Robert Barnes, *A Supplication Unto Henry VIII* (2nd edn., London: J. Bydell, 1534), STC 1470. See also, A. G. Dickens, *The English Reformation* (New York: Schocken Books, 1964); James Edward McGoldrick, *Luther's English Connection* (Milwaukee: Northwestern Publishing House, 1979); William A. Clebsch, *England's Earliest Protestants* (New Haven: Yale Univ. Press, 1964).

18. Foxe, VI, 422; for an account of Katherine Grey's life, see Hester Chapman, *Two Tudor Portraits* (Boston: Little, Brown and Co., 1960), pp. 149–238.

19. Foxe, VI, 424. Though Lady Jane Grey's speech in some ways follows the formula of scaffold speeches given in the sixteenth century, it is also both individual and passionately sincere. For a discussion of scaffold speeches, see Lacey Baldwin Smith, "English Treason Trials and Confessions in the Sixteenth Century," *Journal of the History of Ideas,* 25 (October 1954), 471–98.

The Cooke Sisters: Attitudes toward Learned Women in the Renaissance

1. Joan Kelly-Gadol, "Did Women Have a Renaissance?" in *Becoming Visible,* ed. Renate Bridenthal and Claudia Koonz (Boston: Houghton Mifflin, 1977), pp. 137–64. See also Susan Groag Bell, "Christine de Pizan (1364–1430): Humanism and the Problem of a Studious Woman," *Feminist Studies,* 3 (1976), 173–84; Gloria Kaufman, "Juan Luis Vives on the Education of Women," *Signs,* 3 (1977–78), 891–96.

2. Gary F. Waller, "Struggling into Discourse: The Emergence of Renaissance Women's Writing," in this collection; Suzanne W. Hull, *Chaste, Silent & Obedient* (San Marino, Calif.: Huntington Library, 1982).

3. Nicholas Udall, trans., Desiderius Erasmus, *Paraphrases of the New Testament,* 2 vols. (London, 1548–49), dedication.

4. Letter to Johann Strum in 1550, in Roger Ascham, *The Whole Works,* ed. J. A. Giles (1865; rpt. New York: AMS Press, 1965), I, lxx–lxxi; on Mildred, see also Pearl Hogrefe, *Women of Action in Tudor England* (Ames: Iowa State Univ. Press, 1977), p. 5, and Arthur Collins, ed., *Life of Burghley* (London, 1732), p. 6; *Life of Burghley* also included in Francis Peck, *Desiderata Curiosae* (London, 1779), pp. 1–49.

5. Ruth Hughey, "Lady Anne Bacon's Translations," *Review of English Studies,* 10 (1934), 211. On Margaret, see George Ballard, *Memoirs of British Ladies* (London, 1775), pp. 146–47, where he mentions rumor of a sixth daughter and cites a poem written on the marriage of the fifth daughter; "but after all, *quaere,* whether she was not a natural daughter," he inquires. Often only the four eldest are mentioned; see, for example, Charles Gerbier, *Elogium Heroinum: or, The Praise of Worthy Women* (London, 1651), sig. C11r.

6. See Patricia Gartenberg and Nena Thames Whittemore, "A Checklist of English

Women in Print, 1475–1640," *Bulletin of Bibliography,* 34 (1977), 1–13. More variety of kinds of written work by women began to appear in the early 1600s.

7. John E. Booty, *John Jewel as Apologist of the Church of England,* (London: SPCK, 1963), p. 6; for general discussion see also W. M. Southgate, *John Jewel and the Problem of Doctrinal Authority* (Cambridge: Harvard Univ. Press, 1962).

8. C. S. Lewis, *English Literature in the Sixteenth Century excluding drama* (Oxford: Clarendon Press, 1954, 1965), p. 307.

9. Elizabeth Cooke Hoby, *A Way of Reconciliation* (London, 1605), sigs. O3r–v; Roland Bainton, *Women of the Reformation in France and England* (Minneapolis: Augsburg Publishing House, 1973), p. 162.

10. Letter by De Silva, *Calendar of State Papers, Spanish, 1558–1567,* pp. 520, 580; cited by Conyers Read, *Mr. Secretary Cecil and Queen Elizabeth* (London: Cape, 1955), pp. 35, 336.

11. Letter from John Jewel to Peter Martyr, quoted by Sidney Lee, "Sir Anthony Cooke," *DNB,* IV, 1001.

12. "Nicholas Bacon," *DNB,* I, 839.

13. Anne Cooke Bacon, *Sermons Concerning the Predestination and Election of God* (London, c. 1570), sigs. A4r–v.

14. Richard Hyrde, ded. of Desiderius Erasmus, *Devout Treatise Upon the Pater Noster,* trans. Margaret Roper (London, c. 1526), sig. A2r.

15. Vives, *Instruction of a Christian Woman* (London, 1585), sig. E2r. I chose the 1585 edition because it was contemporary with some of the work of the Cookes. On Vives, see Valerie Wayne's essay in this collection. For an excellent discussion of the attitudes of the church fathers toward women, see Rosemary Radford Ruether, "Misogynism and Virginal Feminism in the Fathers of the Church," in *Religion and Sexism,* ed. Ruether (New York: Simon and Schuster, 1974), pp. 150–83.

16. For a fascinating discussion of the relationship between education and the assumption of power in the Renaissance, see Walter J. Ong, "Latin Language Study as a Renaissance Puberty Rite," *Studies in Philology,* 56 (1959), 106–24.

17. Elizabeth Jocelyn, *Mothers legacie* (London, 1624), sig. a1v; the editor's dedicatory epistle is called the "Approbation," implying need for public approval for this work. This "Approbation" makes clear that the work was not intended for publication by the author, but was found among her papers after her death. For a discussion of this and other works, see Joan Larsen Klein, "Women and Marriage in Renaissance England: Male Perspectives," *Topic: 36: The Elizabethan Woman* (Fall 1982), pp. 20–37.

18. Margaret Tyler, trans., *Mirrour of Princely Deedes and Knighthood* (London, c. 1578), sig. A4v.

19. John Florio, trans., Montaigne's *Essayes* (London, 1603), sig. A2r.

20. The term "hatchet" was used as a transitive verb meaning "to cut with a hatchet"; in fact, Florio's passage was used as a source for the meaning of this word in the *OED,* V, 116.

21. "M.C. to the Ladie A.B.," in *An Apologie or answere in defence of the Church of Englande,* trans. Anne Bacon (London, 1564), n.s. The first edition of 1562 did not contain this prefatory material.

22. Nicholas Breton, "An Olde Mans Lesson and a Young Mans Love," *The Works in Verse and Prose of Nicholas Breton,* comp. Alexander B. Grosart (1879; rpt., New York: AMS Press, 1966), II, 14.

23. John Harington, commentary to Book 37 of Ariosto's *Orlando Furioso,* 1591; (facs. ed., New York: Da Capo Press, 1970), p. 314.

24. Latin verse and translation reproduced in Ballard, pp. 142, 143.

25. *Historical Manuscript Commission Report on the Manuscripts of the Marquis of*

Salisbury Preserved at Hatfield House (London: His Majesty's Stationery Office, 1892–1904), IV, 460–61; IX, 384; X, 52.

26. In James Spedding, *Letters and Life of Francis Bacon* (London: Longman, Green, and Co., 1890), pp. 40–42, 113, 115.

27. Trans. by Ballard, p. 128; discussed by Hogrefe, pp. 29–30.

The Style of the Countess of Pembroke's Translation of Philippe de Mornay's *Discours de la vie et de la mort*

This essay revises and supplements the introduction to Diane Bornstein's *The Countess of Pembroke's Translation of Philippe de Mornay's Discourse of Life and Death* (Detroit: Medieval and Renaissance Monographs, 1983).

1. Nancy Lee Beaty, *The Craft of Dying* (New Haven: Yale Univ. Press, 1970), p. 82. On the Dudley/Sidney alliance, see Hannay's essay in this collection.

2. Gary F. Waller, *Mary Sidney, Countess of Pembroke: A Critical Study of Her Writings and Literary Milieu* (Salzburg: Univ. of Salzburg, 1979), p. 132; Charlotte de Mornay, *A Huguenot Family in the XVI Century: The Memoirs of Philippe de Mornay, Sieur du Plessis Marly, Written by his Wife*, trans. Lucy Crump (London: George Routledge and Sons, Ltd., 1926), p. 169; Philippe de Mornay, *A Woorke Concerning the Trewnesse of the Christian Religion*, trans. Sir Philip Sidney and Arthur Golding (London, 1587).

3. *The Countess of Pembroke's Translation of Philippe de Mornay's Discourse of Life and Death*, ed. Diane Bornstein (Detroit: Medieval and Renaissance Monographs, 1983), pp. 26–27. All references to the countess' translation are from this edition.

4. Philippe de Mornay, *Il Discours de la Vie et de la Mort di Philippe du Plessis-Mornay*, ed. Mario Richter (Milan: Etrice vita e pensiero, 1964), pp. 41–43. I am quoting from Richter's critical edition, but I have also consulted the original French edition, the *Excellent discours de la vie et de la mort* (Geneva, 1576).

5. Edward Aggas, trans., *The Defence of Death* (London, 1576), sigs. A5r–v.

"Doo What Men May Sing": Mary Sidney and the Tradition of Admonitory Dedication

1. For a discussion of the question of authorship, see Gary F. Waller, *Mary Sidney, Countess of Pembroke: A Critical Study of Her Writings and Literary Milieu* (Salzburg: Univ. of Salzburg, 1979), particularly pp. 257–76. On epitaphs as an appropriate feminine genre, see Mary Ellen Lamb's essay in this collection.

2. Mary Sidney Herbert, "Even now that Care" and "To the Angell spirit of the most excellent Sir Philip Sidney," in Gary F. Waller, ed., *The Triumph of Death and Other Unpublished and Uncollected Poems by Mary Sidney, Countess of Pembroke (1561–1621)* (Salzburg: Univ. of Salzburg, 1977), pp. 88–95. On the manuscripts see Waller, *Triumph*, p. 189; J. C. A. Rathmell, Introd., *The Psalms of Sir Philip Sidney and the Countess of Pembroke* (Garden City, N. Y.: Anchor Books, 1963), pp. xxvii, 357. The manuscript, owned by B. E. Juel-Jensen, is labeled "J" by William Ringler in *The Poems of Sir Philip Sidney* (Oxford: Oxford Univ. Press, 1962). It apparently is derived from "A," the Penshurst manuscript, although "A" is missing several pages, including these poems. It may be the presentation copy prepared for the planned 1599 visit of Queen Elizabeth to Wilton. (See Ringler, p. 547.) Although that visit was apparently cancelled, Elizabeth did visit Penshurst on Nov. 3, 1599 during one of Robert's brief visits to England. See letter from Rowland Whyte to Sir Robert Sidney, De L'Isle MSS. U1475 C12/179. However, Pem-

broke was dying and the countess was apparently with him at Wilton rather than with her brother Robert and the queen.

3. James M. Osborne, *Young Philip Sidney 1572–1577* (New Haven: Yale Univ. Press, 1972), pp. 287, 389.

4. Sir Fulke Greville, *Life of Sir Philip Sidney* (1562; rpt. Oxford: Clarendon Press, 1907), p. 27. Philip was 26 at this time.

5. Sir Philip Sidney's *Arcadia*, the most popular prose fiction for two centuries, was dedicated "To My Dear Lady and Sister the Countess of Pembroke," and written "only for you, only to you. . . . Your dear self can best witness the manner, being done in loose sheets of paper, most of it in your presence, the rest by sheets sent unto you as fast as they were done." *The Countess of Pembroke's Arcadia*, ed. Jean Robertson (Oxford: Clarendon Press, 1973), p. 3. Philip's psalms may have been written in the same way. On Mary Sidney's developing poetic ability, see Waller, *Mary Sidney*, pp. 152–256; Fisken, "Education and Wisdom," in this collection.

6. She identified herself as Sidney's sister on other occasions. See, for example, the furious postscript of her letter to Sir Julius Caesar (British Library, Addl. MSS. 12,503, f. 152) which concludes, "It is the Sister of Sir Philip Sidney who yow are to right and who will worthely deserve the same." Although she married one of the wealthiest English earls and was mother to William, Earl of Pembroke, and Philip, Earl of Montgomery, she continued to identify herself as a Sidney, using the Sidney porcupine as her crest, rather than the Herbert lions.

7. Castiglione, *The Book of the Courtier*, trans. Charles S. Singleton (Garden City, N.Y.: Anchor Books, 1959), pp. 293ff.

8. Osborne, p. 503. That famous tennis court quarrel with the Earl of Oxford was connected with this same struggle. See Greville, pp. 63–69. For arguments that the marriage would protect Protestants, see the letter from the Earl of Sussex to the Queen, Aug. 28, 1578, in Edmund Lodge, ed., *Illustrations of British History, Biography and Manners* (London: John Chidley, 1838), II, 109–16.

9. Charlotte de Mornay, *A Huguenot Family in the XVI Century: The Memoirs of Philippe de Mornay, Sieur du Plessis Marly, Written by his Wife*, trans. Lucy Crump (London: George Routledge and Sons, Ltd., 1926), p. 168.

10. Letter to Queen Elizabeth, in William Gray, ed., *The Miscellaneous Works of Sir Philip Sidney* (Boston: T.O.H.P. Burnham, 1860), p. 291. Elizabeth called Anjou her "frog"; he responded with a golden brooch which incorporated his portrait on a frog; Carolly Erickson, *The First Elizabeth* (New York: Summit Books, 1983), p. 304. On the use of frog imagery by those opposed to the marriage, see Doris Adler, "Imaginary Toads in Real Gardens," *English Literary Renaissance*, 11 (1981), 236–60.

11. Edmund Spenser, "The Ruines of Time," in *Spenser: Poetical Works*, ed. J. C. Smith and E. de Sélincourt (London: Oxford Univ. Press, 1912), p. 273, l. 113; Henry Sidney died May 5; Mary Dudley Sidney, Aug. 11; Philip, Oct. 11—surely a catastrophic year for Mary Sidney.

12. See, for example, Pembroke's correspondence with Cecil from 1598–1600 on his duties in Wales. Particularly telling are the letters of June 26, 1598, in Edward Salisbury, ed., HMC *Calendar of the Manuscripts of the Most Honorable the Marquesse of Salisbury* (London: His Majesty's Stationery Office, 1883–1923), VIII, 233, with a subsequent apology on July 16, p. 264; and Sept. 18, p. 352. On Apr. 4, 1600, Pembroke was so distressed that he wrote to the queen herself; X, 98–99.

13. Robert Sidney to the Earl of Essex, May 24, 1597, Salisbury MSS, VII, 210–11; Robert Sidney to Robert Cecil, Apr. 26, 1599, Salisbury MSS, IX, 141–42.

14. Pearl Hogrefe, *Women of Action in Tudor England* (Ames: Iowa State Univ. Press, 1977), p. 108.

15. Frances Berkeley Young, *Mary Sidney: Countess of Pembroke* (London: David Nutt, 1912), pp. 14, 19. See also her letters to Molineaux about their treatment at court (De L'Isle MSS. U1475 C7/6 and C7/7) and her correspondence with Sussex printed in Young, pp. 16–20.

16. Rowland Whyte to Robert Sidney, Jan. 14, 1597/8, in De L'Isle MSS. U1475 C12/121.

17. Letters from Mary Sidney printed in Young, pp. 64, 97, 107. See also Margaret Hannay, "Unpublished Letters of Mary Sidney, Countess of Pembroke," *Spenser Studies*, forthcoming.

18. "The Dolefull Lay," in Waller, *Triumph*, p. 179; on the question of authorship, see Waller, *Mary Sidney*, p. 266.

19. Eleanor Rosenberg, *Leicester: Patron of Letters* (New York: Octagon Books, 1976), p. 208.

20. One of the earliest models she would have known is Coverdale's flattery of Henry VIII, which compares him to Josias, Josaphat, and Hezekiah, using the examples of Moses, Jeremiah, and even Christ himself to demonstrate that none "could stand against the godly obedience of his prince, except he would be at defiance with God." Nevertheless, Coverdale manages to slip in the example of Nathan, who, although he reverenced King David, "spared not to rebuke him, and that right sharply, when he fell from the word of God to adultery and manslaughter." Miles Coverdale, "Dedication and Prologue to the Translation of the Bible," in *Remains of Bishop Coverdale*, ed. George Pearson (Cambridge: Cambridge Univ. Press, 1846), pp. 7–8. Tavener also flatters Henry by comparing him to Ezachias (Hezekiah) establishing the true religion before praying that Henry, like Solomon, will seek wisdom. *An Epitome of the Psalmes*, trans. A. Tavener (1539), STC 2748.

21. One indication of this connection is the extensive list of works, and particularly translations, dedicated to members of the alliance. Leicester's patronage, revealed by dedications such as Golding's translations of Calvin's commentaries on Daniel (1570) and of de Bèze's *Book of Christian Question* (1572), is discussed at length by Rosenberg. Other members of the family received similar dedications. For example, Theophile de Banos dedicated his posthumous publication of Ramus's *Commentaries* to Sir Philip Sidney (1576). Throughout the 1570s and early 1580s John Feild dedicated to Huntingdon and Leicester several translations from de Bèze, Mornay, and Olevain. De Bèze's dedication of his commentary on the Psalms to Huntingdon and Gilbys' dedication of his translation of that commentary to the Countess of Huntingdon are also indicative. (See note 27.)

22. *The Bible and Holy Scriptures* (Geneva, 1560); also available in facsimile reprint (Madison: Univ. of Wisconsin Press, 1969), p. ii. References in text are from this edition.

23. Queen Elizabeth, "The Doubt of Future Foes" in *The Poems of Queen Elizabeth*, ed. Leicester Bradner (Providence: Brown Univ. Press, 1964), p. 4.

24. Queen Elizabeth, "The State of the Nation" (1569), in *The Public Speaking of Queen Elizabeth: Selections from her official addresses*, ed. George P. Rice, Jr. (New York: Columbia Univ. Press, 1951), p. 131. For example, the 1569 version of Sternhold and Hopkins includes "A prayer for the whole state of Christes Church" which implores that "the Quenes majestie and all her counselers" will "execute their office, that thy Religion may be purely maynteined, manners reformed, and sin punished." *The Whole Book of Psalmes collected into English meter by Thomas Sternold, J. Hopkins, and others* (Geneva: J. Crespin, 1569), STC 2440a.

Several members of the Dudley alliance did use violent means. In addition to Leicester's campaign in the Netherlands were the attempts by Henry Sidney, Pembroke, and particularly Huntingdon to crush Catholicism in their jurisdictions. Huntingdon found two ways to make saints in York—by establishing an outstanding educational program for Protestant youth and by offering Catholics the opportunity for martyrdom. The most famous of these martyrs is St. Margaret of York, a housewife who was crushed to death for harboring a Jesuit.

25. Note that such actions were also in accordance with the argument of *Vindiciae contra tyrannos*, which holds both the ruler and the nobility responsible for maintaining the faith both in their own and in other lands. The nobility are "obligated not only to perform their own duties, but also to hold the prince to his." *Vindiciae contra tyrannos* (Basel, 1579), rpt. in *Constitutionalism and Resistance in the Sixteenth Century*, ed. Julian H. Franklin (New York: Pegasus, 1969), p. 193. Franklin argues convincingly that the anonymous tract is by Mornay, probably with the assistance of Hugh Languet; both men were close friends of Sir Philip Sidney.

26. Théodore de Bèze, *Du droit des magistrats* (Heidelberg?, 1574), in Franklin, p. 118.

27. Théodore de Bèze, *The Psalmes of David, truly opened and explaned by paraphrasis, according to the right sense of everie Psalme*, trans. Anthonie Gilbie (1581), sig. a3v. STC 2034. The dedication is dated 1579. Because de Bèze had dedicated his 1580 psalms and commentaries to Huntingdon, his friend Gilby's English translation the following year was dedicated to Katherine Dudley, Countess of Huntingdon, as "appropriate." It is unclear whether she knew no Latin, or whether she was particularly interested in promoting Protestant education in the vernacular, as her work in York would suggest.

28. Edward A. Gosselin, "Two Views of the Evangelical David: Lefevre D'Etaples and Theodore Beza," in *The David Myth in Western Literature*, ed. Raymond Frontain and Jan Wojcik (West Lafayette, Ind.: Purdue Univ. Press, 1980), p. 193n. 27.

29. Cited in Claire Cross, *The Puritan Earl: The Life of Henry Hastings, Third Earl of Huntington* (New York: Macmillan, 1966), p. 267.

30. M. Parker, *The Whole Psalter translated into English metre*; setting by T. Tallis (1567), STC 2729.

31. Dedication of Margaret d' Angoulême, reine de Navarre, in *A godly medytacyon of the christen sowle*, trans. from the French by Elizabeth (1548). STC 17320. It is almost certain that Mary knew of the psalm, because it prefaced the elaborately bound translation Elizabeth had presented to Queen Catherine Parr; since Anne Parr, sister to Queen Catherine, was Henry Herbert's mother, it would be probable that a family tradition had preserved memory of the psalm, even apart from Bale's printed copy. On Bale's use of this psalm, see Anne Prescott's essay in this collection.

32. "Théodore de Bèze," *DNB*, IX, 126–28. See Osborne for accounts of Sidney's presence at the massacre and of his friendship with Languet and Mornay.

33. John Alexander, Introd., Geneva Bible facsimile, p. 10. See also David Daiches, *The King James Version of the English Bible* (Chicago: Univ. of Chicago Press, 1941), pp. 179, 180.

34. Edward A. Gosselin, "David in Tempore Belli," *Sixteenth Century Journal*, 7 (1976), 40.

35. Rathmell, p. vii; Waller, *Mary Sidney*, p. 159; Ringler, p. 505.

36. W. Stanford Reid, "The Battle Hymns of the Lord: Calvinist Psalmody of the Sixteenth Century," *Sixteenth Century Essays and Studies*, 2 (1971), 43–53.

37. Artus Désiré, *Le Contrepoison des Cinquante-Deux Chansons de Clement Marot* (1560; facs. rpt. Geneva: Librairie Droz S.A., 1977), dedication. For a similar French satire, see Lodge, II, 456–58 which parodies the catechism in a dialogue between Pantalon and Zani. See also O. Douen, *Clement Marot et Le Psautier Huguenot* (Paris, 1878; rpt., B. de Graaf, 1967). This pseudo-psalter was only one of Désiré's "odieux libelles," as Douen labeled them; he also wrote *La Singerie des huguenots* accusing them of ribaldry and fornication "suyant la nature des marmots et guenons, qui sont les plus luxurieuses bestes de tout le monde." De Bèze took the works seriously enough to satirize him in the *Comedie du pape malade*, wherein Satan embraces Désiré as his dear friend who has done him great service.

38. Reid, pp. 52–53. Elizabeth may have been more pleased by the singing of Psalm 124 to celebrate the defeat of the Spanish armada (p. 50).

39. Queen Elizabeth, "Written in her French Psalter," in *Poems*, p. 4.

40. Cited in James Garrison, *Dryden and the Panegyric* (Berkeley: Univ. of California Press, 1975), p. 20. Garrison argues that "the Renaissance found a serious purpose behind the panegyric: instruction of the monarch" (p. 20).

Mary Sidney's *Psalmes:* Education and Wisdom

1. For a complete discussion of Mary Sidney's manuscripts, as well as speculation that she revised some psalms as late as 1611, after publication of the King James Version, see Gary F. Waller, *Mary Sidney, Countess of Pembroke: A Critical Study of Her Writings and Literary Milieu* (Salzburg: Univ. of Salzburg, 1979), pp. 152–78. For further discussion of the variety of stanzaic and metrical forms in Mary Sidney's *Psalmes*, see pp. 190–203.

2. Barbara K. Lewalski, *Protestant Poetics and the Seventeenth-Century Religious Lyric* (Princeton: Princeton Univ. Press, 1979), pp. 234, 245. See, in particular, her discussion of the Sidneian psalms as "re-revelations."

3. Philip Sidney, "Defence of Poesie," in *The Prose Works of Sir Philip Sidney*, ed. Albert Feuillerat (Cambridge: Cambridge Univ. Press, 1962), III, 7.

4. Jean Calvin, *Psalmes of David and Others*, trans. Arthur Golding (London, 1571). David was assumed to prefigure Christ and to be dimly aware of his antecedent role. As such he spoke in the person of Christ as well as himself, and ultimately, as a representative voice for the congregation of the Church.

5. For detailed discussion of the multiple voices of the psalmist, as well as the conflation of translator with psalmist, see Lewalski, pp. 39–53 and 231–50.

6. Mary Sidney, "Psalm 104," in *The Psalms of Sir Philip Sidney and the Countess of Pembroke*, ed. J. C. A. Rathmell (New York: New York Univ. Press, 1963), p. 244, l. 101. All other references to Mary Sidney's psalms will come from this edition and will be indicated in the text by psalm and line numbers.

7. Philip Sidney, "Psalm 26," in *The Poems of Sir Philip Sidney*, ed. William A. Ringler, Jr. (Oxford: Clarendon Press, 1962), l. 33. All other references to Philip Sidney's psalms will come from this edition and will be indicated by psalm and line numbers in the text.

8. Louis Martz, *Poetry of Meditation* (New Haven: Yale Univ. Press, 1954), p. 324.

9. Miles Coverdale, ed., *The Prayer Book Version from the Great Bible 1539–41*, in *Our Prayer Book Psalter*, ed. Ernest Clapton (London: Society for Promoting Christian Knowledge, 1934), p. 117. All other references to this version of the psalms will come from this edition and will be indicated by page number and the abbreviation BCP for Book of Common Prayer in the text.

10. A technique of concrete visualization of a scene to enable extended meditation on its significance. See Martz, pp. 27–30.

11. Salisbury MSS, Cecil Papers, holograph, as quoted in Frances Berkeley Young, *Mary Sidney: Countess of Pembroke* (London: David Nutt, 1912), p. 97.

12. For example, Philip Sidney used it in his dedication included in the 1590 *Arcadia*, in which he referred to his work as "a baby I could well find in my harte, to cast out in some desert of forgetfulness" and a fetus that "if it had not ben in some way delivered, would have growen a monster." Feuillerat, I, 3.

13. Jean Calvin, *Commentary on the Book of Psalms*, trans. Rev. James Anderson (Edinburgh, 1846), V, 215.

14. Text estab. by Mario Richter (Geneva: Droz, 1964), p. 74. "Deslors mon Dieu, que ceste povre creature fut conceuë, la corruption y estoit attachee: deslors, di-je, que ma mere

m'ayant conçeu m'eschauffa en son ventre, le vice y estoit au dedans de moy comme la racine . . ." Also, trans. I. Stubbs (London: Christopher Barker, 1582).

15. Luis de la Puente, *Meditations upon the Mysteries of our Holie Faith* . . . , trans. John Heigham (St. Omer, 1619), I, 29, as quoted in Martz, p. 16.

16. These terms were used to distinguish the Anglican style of preaching with its emphasis on wit, classical allusions, and extended comparisons, from the Puritan style, which concentrated on the Scriptures without elaboration.

17. David Kalstone, Introd., *The Selected Poetry and Prose of Sidney* (New York: Signet, 1970), p. xxx. Although Kalstone is referring to the flexibility of Philip Sidney's poetic voice in *Astrophel and Stella*, these words also apply to Mary Sidney's *Psalmes* which dramatize the same sort of perplexed, divided sensibility on the part of the religious soul seeking union with God as that of the lover portrayed in *Astrophel and Stella*.

Spenser and the Patronesses of the *Fowre Hymnes:* "Ornaments of All True Love and Beautie"

This essay revises and supplements a paper presented in Kalamazoo, Michigan, in 1982, and published as delivered, with supporting documentation, in *Spenser at Kalamazoo 1982*, ed. Russell J. Meyer (Clarion, Pa.: Clarion State College, 1982), pp. 54–70, published here by permission; in the same collection, see John Webster's prepared response, "Two by Two or One by Four: The Structural Dilemma of Spenser's *Fowre Hymnes*," pp. 71–80.

1. First published in a festschrift for A. S. P. Woodhouse, and reprinted in *Essays by Rosemond Tuve: Spenser, Herbert, Milton*, ed. Thomas P. Roche, Jr. (Princeton: Princeton Univ. Press, 1970), pp. 139–63.

2. For Wallace T. MacCaffrey, "Place and Patronage in Elizabethan Politics," in *Elizabethan Government and Society*, ed. S. T. Bindoff (London: Athlone Press, 1961), pp. 101–02, Bedford exemplifies a political type "new to the English scene": the "man of conviction, for whom office or influence meant the chance to advance an ideal." Cf. Patrick Collinson, *The Elizabethan Puritan Movement* (Berkeley: Univ. of California Press, 1967), pp. 31, 52–53.

3. See Muriel St. Clare Byrne and Gladys Scott Thomson, " 'My Lord's Books': The Library of Francis, Second Earl of Bedford, in 1584," *Review of English Studies*, 7 (1931), 385–405.

4. Anne Clifford, *Lives of Lady Anne Clifford . . . and of Her Parents, . . .* ed. J. P. Gilson (London: Roxburghe Club, 1916), p. 19. Family history was a genre thought appropriate for women writers of the sixteenth and seventeenth centuries; see Natalie Zemon Davis, "Gender and Genre: Women as Historical Writers, 1400–1820," in *Beyond Their Sex*, ed. Patricia H. Labalme (New York: New York Univ. Press, 1980), pp. 153–82, and pp. 161–67 in particular. Davis finds no examples of memoirs concerned with the lives and characters of women.

5. Thomas Dunham Whitaker, *The History . . . of Craven*, ed. A. W. Morant (Leeds & London, 1878), p. 340. Many books, each meticulously titled, are featured in the Clifford family picture: details are given in Whitaker, pp. 339, 349–52; see also Martin Holmes, *Proud Northern Lady: Lady Anne Clifford, 1590–1676* (London: Phillimore, 1975), pp. 133–41.

6. On the same occasion George's sister Frances wed Philip Wharton, Baron Wharton. See Clifford, *Lives*, pp. 6–7, and George C. Williamson, *George, Third Earl of Cumberland (1558–1605): His Life and His Voyages* (Cambridge: Cambridge Univ. Press, 1920), pp. 11–12, 286. According to Peter Laslett's data, they were married much earlier than

most Elizabethans; see *The World We Have Lost*, 2nd ed. (New York: Scribner's, 1973), pp. 84–112.

7. See cantos xi-xii in Book III of *The Faerie Queene*. For this poem, I cite the edition of A. C. Hamilton (London: Longmans, 1977). All other poems cited are from *Spenser's Minor Poems*, ed. Ernest de Sélincourt (Oxford: Clarendon Press, 1910, 1960), and are abbreviated in parenthetical references in the text as follows: for the *Fowre Hymnes*, HHB for "An Hymn of Heavenlie Beautie," HHL for "An Hymn of Heavenlie Love," HB for "An Hymne in Honour of Beautie," and HL for "An Hymne in Honour of Love"; for others frequently cited, RT for "The Ruines of Time," *Colin* for *Colin Clouts Come Home Againe, Daph.* for *Daphnaida.*

8. Williamson, p. 285. Brackets indicate my emendations; at some points it seems that either Williamson's text or his transcription is faulty. Perhaps "The Pilgrimage of Grief" was a musical composition; the end of the sentence is perfectly iambic and may be a quotation from verse: "for still I change . . . ."

9. The quoted phrase is Anne Clifford's; she records that her mother was blessed "with extream love and affection of her husband, which lasted about nine or ten years toward her, and but little more" (*Lives*, pp. 7, 21).

10. See /William Oram, "*Daphnaida* and Spenser's Later Poetry," *Spenser Studies*, 2 (1981), 141–58; Duncan Harris and Nancy L. Steffen, "The Other Side of the Garden: An Interpretive Comparison of Chaucer's *Book of the Duchess* and Spenser's *Daphnaida*," *Journal of Medieval and Renaissance Studies*, 8 (1978), 17–36; Donald Cheney, "Spenser's Fortieth Birthday and Related Fictions," *Spenser Studies*, 4 (1983), 9–12. Both Oram and Cheney consider the possibility that Spenser himself had been widowed recently.

11. These and other facts are presented by Helen Estabrook Sandison, "Arthur Gorges, Spenser's Alcyon and Ralegh's Friend," *PMLA*, 43 (1928), 645–74, summarized in the Variorum *Minor Poems*, I, 434–35.

12. Oram, p. 152; cf. Cheney's article.

13. See *Colin Clouts Come Home Againe*, ll. 456–583. Another audience of shepherd swains and lasses in Ireland figures in the poem but is irrelevant to my purposes here.

14. Alexander C. Judson, *The Life of Edmund Spenser* (Baltimore: Johns Hopkins Univ. Press, 1945), pp. 177–78.

15. Thomas R. Edwards, *Imagination and Power: A Study of Poetry on Public Themes* (London: Oxford Univ. Press, 1971), p. 59.

16. Josephine Waters Bennett, "The Theme of Spenser's *Fowre Hymnes*," *Studies in Philology*, 28 (1931), 53–57; Robert Ellrodt, *Neoplatonism in the Poetry of Spenser* (Geneva: Droz, 1960), pp. 21–22, 124–29.

17. Also, the Countess of Warwick is addressed as "Marie," not Anne, an anomaly that has never been explained: either the poet or his printer made an error, or Marie was a "middle" name in use among the countess's intimates. In what may be an analogous instance, Jane Sibella Morrison (daughter of Sir Richard and Bridget Morrison, later the wife of Edward Russell and of Arthur, Lord Grey) is addressed as "Lady Sibill": see G[eorge] E[dward] C[okayne], *The Complete Peerage* . . . , rev. edn. by Vicary Gibbs et al. (London: St. Catherine Press, 1910–59), II, 76.

18. Since this essay was written, I have profited from reading Mary I. Oates, "*Fowre Hymnes*: Retractations of Paradise," *Spenser Studies*, 4 (1983), 143–69. Oates applies ideas from modern developmental psychology to a reading of the *Hymnes* as a series of lyrics: her argument tends to confirm what I have gathered from historical and biographical evidence, and sheds light, incidentally, on Margaret Russell's development in love and Christian devotion.

19. The book is thus very different from *Complaints*, which "has the appearance of a collection of pamphlets rather than of a single volume." See Harold Stein, *Studies in Spenser's Complaints* (New York: Oxford Univ. Press, 1934), pp. 5–9.

20. Sandison, p. 659; Historical Manuscripts Commission, *Calendar of Manuscripts . . . Preserved at Hatfield House*, VI, 481; *The Poems of Sir Arthur Gorges*, ed. Helen Estabrook Sandison (Oxford: Clarendon Press, 1953), p. xxi. The date of Gorges' letter to Cecil—Nov. 18, 1596—suggests that his commitment to marry Lady Elizabeth and his disfavor at court were virtually simultaneous with the publication of *Fowre Hymnes* and *Daphnaida* (Spenser's dedication of the former is dated Sept. 1, 1596).

Of God and Good Women: The Poems of Aemilia Lanyer

Research for this paper was supported by a Guggenheim Fellowship in 1980–81.

1. All citations are from the Huntington Library copy of the first issue (STC 15227) with the imprint in four lines, "AT LONDON / Printed by *Valentine Simmes* for *Richard Bonian* and / are to be sold at his Shop in Paules Church- / yard. *Anno* 1611." The STC lists only this single copy of the first issue, with imprint in four lines. At the end of the book, in a postscript addressed "To the doubtfull Reader" Lanyer explains the origin of the title in a dream many years before the book itself was conceived:

> Gentle Reader, if thou desire to be resolved, why I give this Title, *Salve Deus Rex Judaeorum*, know for certaine, that it was delivered unto me in sleepe many yeares before I had any intent to write in this maner, and was quite out of my memory, untill I had written the Passion of Christ, when immediately it came into my remembrance, what I had dreamed long before; and thinking it a significant token, that I was appointed to performe this Worke, I gave the very same words I received in sleepe as the fittest Title I could devise for this Booke.

2. The Countess of Pembroke's poetic translation of Robert Garnier's classical drama appeared in 1595 as *The Tragedie of Antonie*, her pastoral dialogue in honor of Queen Elizabeth was published in Davison's *Poetical Rhapsody* in 1602, and (if it was hers) "The Dolefull Lay of Clorinda" appeared as part of Spenser's elegy for Sidney, "Astrophel," in *Colin Clouts Come Home Againe*, 1595. But her terza rima translation of Petrarch's "Triumph of Death" was published for the first time in 1912, and the Sidney-Pembroke version of the Psalms circulated only in manuscript and was not published for over two centuries. Queen Elizabeth's metrical translation of Psalm 13 [14] appeared in her translation of Marguerite de Navarre's *Godly medytacyon of the christen sowle*, edited by John Bale in 1548, but her other poetic translations and poems remained in manuscript. Other aristocratic women—Lucy, Countess of Bedford for one—evidently wrote poetry for private circulation (as did their male counterparts) but very little seems to have survived. The only other women who published substantial original poetry (besides Lanyer) in the Elizabethan-Jacobean period are Elizabeth Cary, Lady Falkland, whose verse drama, *The Tragedie of Mariam, the Fairie Queene of Jewry* appeared in 1613, and Lady Mary Wroth, niece of Sir Philip Sidney and the Countess of Pembroke, whose pastoral sonnet sequence with interspersed songs, "Pamphilia to Amphilanthus," appeared as part of her unfinished Arcadian romance, *The Countesse of Montgomeries Urania* in 1621.

3. From internal evidence it is clear that Jonson's "Penshurst" was written sometime before the death of Prince Henry in 1612 (l. 77), but it was first published in the folio of 1616. Lanyer's poem was written sometime after Anne Clifford's marriage to Richard Sackville on Feb. 25, 1609 (she is referred to as Dorset, the title her husband inherited two days after the marriage) and before the volume was registered with the Stationer on Oct. 2, 1610. If Jonson's poem was written first Lanyer might have seen it in manuscript, but there are no obvious allusions.

4. Since the Passion poem contains an apology for the author's delay in fulfilling the Countess of Cumberland's charge to write about Cookham, it was evidently written before the Cookham poem. Since it alludes to the countess as a widow, it was clearly written

sometime after the death of George Clifford, Earl of Cumberland, on Oct. 30, 1605. The several dedications were probably written shortly before publication; the Countess of Dorset's marriage date supplies a *terminus post quem* for the dedication to her.

5. The STC (1976) lists eight copies, only one of the rare first issue, and seven with the imprint in five lines, "AT LONDON/ Printed by *Valentine Simmes* for *Richard Bonian,* and are/ to be sold at his Shop in Paules Churchyard, at the/ Signe of the Floure de Luce and/ Crowne, 1611" (STC 15227.5).

6. The British Library copy may be a unique book prepared for the Countess of Cumberland or the Countess of Dorest, or it may possibly represent a special issue. It omits the dedication to Arabella Stuart (probably because she had been taken into custody in March 1611 and sent to the Tower). It also omits the dedications to the Countesses of Kent, Pembroke, and Suffolk—perhaps so as to identify the volume yet more closely with the Countess of Cumberland and her daughter, and to present it only to the obvious court partrons: the queen, the Princess Elizabeth, and the Countess of Bedford who was the queen's most influential lady-in-waiting and the most important Jacobean literary patroness. The epistle "To the Virtuous Reader" is also omitted, possibly because its strong feminist tone would offend the audience for whom this version was prepared. The front matter is not reset: signature *c* is eliminated as are all but the final leaf of signature *d* (d4, the Bedford dedication), and signature *f* (all but the first seven stanzas of the Dorset dedication and the epistle to the reader). The final sheets are shifted so that the dedications appear in the following order: the Queen, Princess Elizabeth, All Virtuous Ladies, the Countess of Bedford, the Countess of Dorset, the Countess of Cumberland.

7. A. L. Rowse, ed., *The Poems of Shakespeare's Dark Lady: Salve Deus Rex Judaeorum by Emilia Lanier* (London: Jonathan Cape, 1978). The edition is based on the Bodleian copy, complete except for the Cookham poem, which is supplied from the British Library copy. Rowse urges his thesis in an edition of Shakespeare's sonnets and also in *Sex and Society in Shakespeare's Age: Simon Forman the Astrologer* (New York: Scribner's, 1974).

8. Rowse notes that Shakespeare's landlady also visited Forman; that in 1592, as a girl of seventeen, Lanyer had an illigitimate son by Lord Hunsdon, the Lord Chamberlain, later patron of the company of players with whom Shakespeare was associated; and that Lanyer, as an Italian beauty from a family of court musicians, with some literary talent and a questionable moral character, fits the general description Shakespeare gives to the "Dark Lady" in the sonnets.

9. Forman records that Lanyer visited him on May 17, June 3, and June 16, 1597, and the three passages quoted are from his notes on these three occasions, respectively. Cited in Rowse, *Dark Lady,* pp. 11–12.

10. From Forman's record on June 16, 1597, cited in Rowse, *Dark Lady,* p. 12. Forman follows up his speculation about her loose morals with an account of his efforts to seduce her, and he implies some success in that endeavor—but it is hard to know how far to believe this self-styled Casanova in such matters.

11. *Calendar of State Papers, Domestic, 1634–35,* pp. 516–17.

12. Princess Elizabeth was later Elizabeth of Bohemia, the Winter Queen. Lanyer honors her primarily as namesake of the great Queen Elizabeth.

The Countess of Pembroke, sister of Sir Philip Sidney and Sir Robert Sidney of Penshurst, wife of Henry Herbert, third Earl of Pembroke, extended hospitality and patronage at her Wilton estate to many writers—such as Nicholas Breton, Samuel Daniel, Abraham Fraunce, Gervase Babington, Thomas Moffatt—and received dedications from many others—Michael Drayton, Thomas Nashe, Henry Lok, Nathaniel Baxter, Edmund Spenser. Lucy, Countess of Bedford, was patron and friend to Donne and Jonson, among many others. Franklin B. Williams, Jr.'s *Index of Dedications and Commendatory Verses in English Books Before 1641* (London: Bibliographical Society, 1962) lists more dedications and praises addressed to these two noblewomen than to any other patronesses except members of the royal family.

Katherine, Countess of Suffolk, was wife to the wealthy and ambitious Lord Admiral and Lord Chamberlain of the Household, Thomas Howard, whose manor, Audley End, was said to have been built with a foundation of Spanish gold. She alone seems out of place in Lanyer's company of good women, though she and her husband were not yet notorious for the rapacity which was to lead in 1618 to their disgrace and imprisonment for extortion and embezzlement.

Arabella Stuart was a constant focus for political intrigue during the final years of Elizabeth's reign and the early years of James, because of her strong title to the throne derived from Margaret, eldest sister of Henry VIII. Forbidden to marry without the king's permission, she did so secretly in July 1610 to William Seymour, grandson of Catherine Grey—an alliance which strengthened her title. When the marriage became known, she was taken into custody on Mar. 3, 1611, and after an abortive attempt to escape in June 1611 was lodged in the Tower.

Susan Bertie's first husband was Reynold Grey of Wrest, de jure Earl of Kent, who died in 1573. In 1581 she married Sir John Wingfield of Withcall, a member of the Leicester-Sidney faction (knighted by Leicester at Zutphen, one of the twelve honor guard at Sidney's funeral, and a participant in the Cadiz expeditions). Lanyer's residence with the countess may or may not have taken place before the countess' second marriage, but clearly antedates Lanyer's own marriage in 1592. Lanyer is probably being ingenuous when she disclaims (ll. 43–48) any thought of "former gaine" or "future profit" from the countess.

13. Margaret Clifford, third and last daughter of Francis Russell, second Earl of Bedford, married George Clifford, third Earl of Cumberland in 1577. Their only surviving child, Anne, married Richard Sackville, Earl of Dorset in 1609, was widowed in 1624, and in 1630 remarried Philip Herbert, younger son of Mary, Countess of Pembroke, and then Earl of Pembroke and Montgomery. See George C. Williamson's biographies, *Lady Anne Clifford, Countess of Dorset, Pembroke and Montgomery. 1590–1676,* (Kendal: Titus Wilson and Son, 1922), and by the same author, *George, Third Earl of Cumberland (1558–1605): His Life and His Voyages* (Cambridge: Cambridge Univ. Press, 1920).

14. There are dedications to Margaret, Countess of Cumberland, by Robert Greene, Thomas Lodge, Samuel Daniel, Henry Lok, Edmund Spenser, Samuel Hieron, Henry Peacham, William Perkins, Richard Greenham, and Peter Muffett, among others. See Williams, *Index*. On her connection with Edmund Spenser, see Jon Quitslund's essay in this collection.

15. Cookham, a manor belonging to the crown from before the Norman Conquest until 1818, was annexed to Windsor Castle in 1540. It was evidently granted or leased to the Cliffords and occupied by Margaret, Countess of Cumberland, at some periods during her estrangement from her husband in the years before his death in 1605. The countess may have spent some time there during the early months of her widowhood, before the journey she and her daughter made in 1607 to visit the Cumberland and Westmorland estates. In 1608 they took up residence at Lady Clifford's own house at Austin Friars. Anne Clifford's diary records a visit to Cookham in 1603, but unfortunately there are no entries from 1603 to 1616; see *The Diary of the Lady Anne Clifford*, ed. V. Sackville-West (London, 1923), p. 15. It is not clear just when or for how long Lanyer was at Cookham.

16. George Clifford, noted Elizabethan seaman, explorer and adventurer, and womanizer was for several years virtually separated from his wife (*Diary of Anne Clifford*, pp. 10–15), though he begged forgiveness and reconciled with her on his deathbed. He left a will bequeathing to his brother, Sir Francis Clifford, the new Earl of Cumberland, his northern estates (with a reversion to the Lady Anne in the event of the failure of male heirs). In doing so he ignored a deed executed in the reign of Edward II entailing the estates upon his child regardless of sex. Margaret Clifford and later Anne herself engaged in continual litigation and court appeals to secure her right to these estates, but they only redounded to her in 1643, at the death of her cousin Henry Clifford, son to Sir Francis. Williamson, *Lady Anne Clifford*, pp. 25–55.

17. Lanyer may or may not have known or known about Boccaccio's *De claris mulieri-bus,* Chaucer's *Legend of Good Women,* or Christine de Pizan's *Book of the City of Ladies,* published in 1521 in an English translation by Brian Anslay. But Anne Clifford might have directed her to Chaucer: much later in her life (1649), Anne declared Chaucer to be a favorite poet and a great consolation to her in trouble (Harley MS. 7001, f. 212).

18. I am indebted to my colleague David Sacks for this observation and for working out the geneologies supporting it.

19. These poems are in 14 lines, divided into two stanzas. That to Princess Elizabeth is rhymed *ababacc, dededff;* that to Arabella Stuart, *ababbcc, dedeeff.*

20. The dedication "To the Ladie Susan, Countesse Dowager of Kent, and daughter to the Duchesse of Suffolke," associates her at the outset with her famous mother whose flight and wanderings with her family in Europe—as recorded by her husband Richard Bertie—was incorporated in Foxe's *Book of Martyrs.* Catherine married Richard Bertie in 1553, after the death of her first husband Charles Brandon, Earl of Suffolk; Susan was born in 1554, only a few months before the flight. Susan herself accompanied her second husband, Sir John Wingfield, on his military expeditions and was imprisoned with him briefly in Breda after the fall of Gertruydenburg.

21. Cf. Jonson, "Epigram 76," in *The Complete Poetry of Ben Jonson,* ed. W. B. Hunter (New York: Norton, 1968), p. 32, which ascribes to her "a learned, and a manly soule."

22. See note 16 above. Anne Clifford could not have inherited her father's earldom, but she could and eventually did inherit titles which pertained to the estates: Baronesse Clifford, Westmorland, and Vessey, Lady of the Honor of Skipton in Craven, High Sheriffesse of the County of Westmorland.

23. For an account of and bibliography pertaining to this controversy through 1568 see Francis L. Utley, *The Crooked Rib* (New York: Octagon Books, 1970), and for discussion and listing of later titles see Suzanne W. Hull, *Chaste, Silent & Obedient* (San Marino, Calif.: Huntington Library, 1982).

24. Cf. Psalm 104 to Lanyer's passage:
   2. Who coverest thyself with light as with a garment: who stretchest out the heavens like a curtain:
   3. Who layeth the beams of his chambers in the waters: who maketh the clouds his charriot: who walketh upon the wings of the wind.
   4. Who maketh his angells spitits; his ministers a flaming fire.
   32. He looketh on the earth, and it trembleth: he toucheth the hills, and they smoke.

25. See the discussion of this concern in Barbara K. Lewalski, *Protestant Poetics and the Seventeenth-Century Religious Lyric,* (Princeton: Princeton Univ. Press, 1979), pp. 3–13, 213–50.

26. Cf. George Herbert, "Prayer I," in *The Works of George Herbert,* ed. F. E. Hutchinson (Oxford: Clarendon Press, 1941), p. 51:
   "Prayer the Churches banquet, Angels age,
   Gods breath in man returning to his birth,
   The soul in paraphrase, heart in pilgrimage,
   The Christian plummet sounding heav'n and earth . . ." (ll. 1–4)

27. See note 15. The valedictory mode of this poem suggests a permanent rather than a seasonal departure, probably related to the move the countess would have to make from the major Clifford properties to her own estates or to dower residences after she was widowed in 1605.

28. *The Victoria History of Berkshire,* ed. P. H. Ditchfield and William Page, 4 vols. (London: A. Constable, 1906–24), III, 124–25.

29. Cf. Jonson, "To Penshurst," in *Complete Poetry,* pp. 78–79, ll. 29–38:
   The painted partrich lyes in every field,
     And, for thy messe, is willing to be kill'd.

And if the high swolne *Medway* faile thy dish,
Thou hast thy ponds, that pay thee tribute fish,
Fat, aged carps, that runne into thy net.
And pikes, now weary their owne kinde to eat,
As loth, the second draught, or cast to stay,
Officiously, at first, themselves betray.
Bright eeles, that emulate them, and leape on land,
Before the fisher, or into his hand.

Elizabeth Cary and Tyranny, Domestic and Religious

1. She was the daughter of Lawrence Tanfield, Chief Baron of the Exchequer, and Elizabeth Symondes Tanfield. Elizabeth was, of course, a popular first name for women in England during the Renaissance, and Cary (also Carey, Carye, and Carie) was a common surname. It is thus crucial to identify this author precisely, using both maiden name and title. Arthur Cyril Dunstan, for instance, in *Examination of two English Dramas* (Konigsberg: Hartungsche Buchdruckerei, 1908), p. 10, erroneously attributes *The Tragedie of Mariam* to Elizabeth Spencer Carey, Second Lady Hunsdon, who was a great patroness and a kinswoman of Edmund Spenser, who dedicated introductory sonnets to *The Faerie Queene* to her. Her daughter was Elizabeth Carey Berkeley. Elizabeth Tanfield Cary, Viscountess Falkland, dedicated *Mariam* to Elizabeth Bland Cary, who was married to Philip, Henry Cary's brother. They may also have had a sister named Elizabeth Carye Savell, who was married to John Savell in Herts on Nov. 20, 1586. Elizabeth Tanfield Cary's husband, Henry (Harry) Cary (1576–1633) was Comptroller of the Royal Household in 1617. In 1620 he was named Viscount Falkland and appointed Lord Deputy of Ireland in 1622. He had attended Oxford and fought valiantly in France and the Low Countries. He is not to be be confused with Henry Carey, Lord Hunsdon, cousin of the queen and her household chamberlin, who fought famously on the Scottish border, and who is also included by Spenser in a second round of dedicatory sonnets. The issue is confused by the fact that Elizabeth Tanfield Cary reportedly had a cousin named William Spencer, from whom she borrowed money. See Alexander C. Judson, "The Life of Edmund Spenser," in *The Works of Edmund Spenser* (Variorum), ed. Edwin Greenlaw et al. (Baltimore: Johns Hopkins Univ. Press, 1955), pp. 1–2, 142–43; the entries for "Cary, Sir Henry" and "Elizabeth Cary, Lady Falkland" in the *DNB*; Betty Travitsky, ed., *The Paradise of Women* (Westport, Conn.: Greenwood Press, 1981), pp. 209–12; Nancy Cotton Pearse, "Elizabeth Cary, Renaissance Playwright," *Texas Studies in Literature and Language*, 18 (1977), 601–08; and two prominent biographies, upon which I draw extensively in my summary of her life: Kenneth B. Murdock, *The Sun at Noon: Three Biographical Sketches* (New York: Macmillan, 1939), pp. 1–38, and Lady Georgiana Fullerton, *The Life of Elisabeth Lady Falkland 1585–1639* (London: Burns and Oates, 1883). The latter was found in the archives of the Benedictine Convent in Cambray, probably written by Lady Cary's eldest daughter Anne, who later became Dame Clementina. The manuscript was revised by son Patrick Cary and published in 1861. Lady Fullerton bases her account on that revision.

2. Joan Kelly-Gadol, "Did Women Have a Renaissance?" in *Becoming Visible*, ed. Renate Bridenthal and Claudia Koonz (Boston: Houghton Mifflin, 1977), p. 161.

3. Accounts of the date of conversion vary, but by this time she was questioning both Hooker and Calvin. In 1621 she was a practicing Catholic, although she did not publicly convert until 1626.

4. According to Fullerton, "She had no beauty to recommend her beyond a very fair complexion, and her heart and mind were under lock and key, so to speak, in his presence. . . . She had a dowry that suited his decayed fortunes, and that was all he cared

for" (p. 12). Murdock describes her as having "a good complexion, and [being] very fair, but short and fat" (p. 8). We may have a tyrannical Mrs. Cary, mother of Henry, to thank for Elizabeth's artistry, for when she locked the young woman in her room and took away her books—study being an unladylike activity in her judgment—Elizabeth had no recourse but to write.

5. According to Fullerton, "Her husband allowed her nothing. Her mother turned her out of her house in London, where she had lived since her return from Ireland. Both bitterly reproached her for her change of religion, and told her that her misfortunes were owing to herself, and that she deserved all she suffered" (p. 94). Moreover, her husband wrote, "I care not whether such a prodigal impostor as I know her to be, is constrained to eat husks with pigs or to live on alms. As to her protestation to be ready to conform herself to my will, where her conscience might not be touched, I only wish she had a will to fulfill any duty, or a conscience to be touched" (p. 103).

6. [Elizabeth Tanfield Cary?] "The History of the most unfortunate Prince, King Edward the Second" in *The Harleian Miscellany* (1808; rpt. New York: AMS Press, 1965), I, 74. This manuscript was discovered among the papers of Sir Henry Cary and not published until 1680.

7. Suggested in Elaine Beilin, "Elizabeth Cary and *The Tragedie of Mariam*," *Papers on Language and Literature*, 16 (1980), 46-47.

8. Annis Pratt, *Archetypal Patterns in Women's Fiction* (Bloomington: Indiana Univ. Press, 1981), p. 177 (here she suggests that escapes into imagination for women are "for the purpose of personal transformation," not simply artistic achievement); Judith Fetterley, *The Resisting Reader: A Feminist Approach to American Fiction* (Bloomington: Indiana Univ. Press, 1978), pp. xi, xix-xxiv.

9. In *Mariam* Cary has Herod's admirable brother, Pheroras, say, "Silence is a signe of discontent" (l. 587) in a woman.

10. Murdock, pp. 6-13. See also *The Female Spectator*, ed. Mary R. Mahl and Helene Koon (Bloomington: Indiana Univ. Press, 1977), p. 3.

11. See, e.g., accounts in William Raleigh Trimble, *The Catholic Laity in Elizabethan England 1558-1603* (Cambridge, Mass.: Belknap Press, 1964).

12. Mahl and Koon (p. 101) suggest that *Mariam* is modeled on Mary Sidney's translation of Garnier's *Tragedie of Antonie*.

13. In *The Complete Works of John Davies of Herford*, ed. Alexander B. Grosart (New York: AMS Press, 1967), II, 4-5.

14. Lady Cary was notorious for not having a head for figures. As Murdock notes, she preferred the abstract to the concrete (pp. 6, 20). Although she initially had some means, being the Tanfield heir, she lost her inheritance partly through financial irresponsibility, her father's reaction to her prodigality, and the following necessity: "Upon my lord's going into Ireland I was drawn, by seeing his difficulties, to offer my jointure into his hands, that he might sell or mortgage it for his supply, which accordingly was done" (Fullerton, p. 89).

15. She probably read this in Hebrew. See Elizabeth (Tanfield) Cary Falkland, *The Tragedy of Mariam*, ed. A. C. Dunstan (1613; Malone Society Reprints, Oxford: Horace Hart for the University Press, 1914), p. xiii. This is the only edition of the complete play currently available, except for excerpts and microfilm reproductions of the original quarto edition. All subsequent line numbers refer to this edition.

16. Simone de Beauvoir, *The Second Sex*, trans. and ed. H. M. Parshley (New York: Knopf, 1952), p. 155.

17. See William Whiston, trans., *The Works of Flavius Josephus* (London: Chatto and Windus, n.d.), Vol. I, *Antiquities*, Book XV, Chapter 6, for the actions of Herod and the Mariam story.

18. Joseph Campbell, *The Hero with a Thousand Faces*, 2nd ed. (1968; rpt. Princeton: Princeton Univ. Press, 1973), pp. 308, 349.

19. Lady Cary had engraved in the wedding ring of her daughter, "Be and seem." Fullerton, p. 26.

20. Carole McKewin, "Counsels of Gall and Grace: Intimate Conversations between Women in Shakespeare's Plays," in *The Woman's Part: Feminist Criticism of Shakespeare*, ed. Carolyn Ruth Swift Lenz, Gayle Greene, Carol Thomas Neely (Urbana: Univ. of Illinois Press, 1980), p. 129.

21. Maurice J. Valency, *The Tragedies of Herod & Mariamne* (1940; rpt. New York: AMS Press, 1966), p. 90.

22. A popular debate on the nature of women in an extension of the *querelle des femmes* was initiated by Joseph Swetnam's *The Arraignment of Lewde, Idle, Froward, and Unconstant Women* (1615). Answers included Constantia Munda's *Worming of a madde Dogge* (1617), Ester Sowernam's *Ester hath hang'd Haman* (1617), and Rachel Speght's *A Mouzell for Melastomus* (1617); but Jane Anger's *Her Protection for Women*, a pamphlet of similar ilk, had appeared in 1589.

Struggling Into Discourse: The Emergence of Renaissance Women Writers

1. For a useful critique of Althusserianism, see Tony Bennett, *Formalism and Marxism* (London: Methuen, 1979), pp. 127–76; for the controversy between Culler and Showalter, see Elaine Showalter, "Critical Cross-Dressing: Male Feminists and The Woman of the Year," *Raritan*, 3, No. 2 (Fall 1983), 130–49.

2. For a forceful reading of the film in this light see [Laura Mulvey and] Colin MacCabe, *Godard: Images, Sounds, Politics* (Bloomington, Ind.: Univ. of Indiana Press, 1980), p. 91.

3. Ann Kaplan, "Feminist Criticism: A Survey with Analysis of Methodological Problems," *University of Michigan Papers in Women's Studies*, 1 (1976), 1.

4. Germaine Greer, *The Obstacle Race: The Fortunes of Women Painters and their Work* (London: Secker & Warburg, 1979).

5. Elaine Marks and Isabelle de Courtivron, eds., *New French Feminisms: An Anthology* (Amherst: Univ. of Massachusetts Press, 1979), p. 6.

6. Joan Kelly-Gadol, "The Social Relation of the Sexes: Methodological Implications of Women's History," *Signs*, 1 (1976), 811; "Did Women Have a Renaissance?" in Renate Bridenthal and Claudia Koonz, eds., *Becoming Visible* (Boston: Houghton Mifflin, 1977), pp. 139–64; and "Notes on Women in the Renaissance and Renaissance Historiography," in Marylyn Arthur et. al., eds., *Conceptual Frameworks for Studying Women's History* (Bronxville: Sarah Lawrence College, 1975); Elaine Showalter, "Literary Criticism," *Signs*, 1 (1975), 444–46.

7. Annette Kolodny, "Some Notes on Defining a Feminist Criticism," *Critical Inquiry*, 2 (1975), 75.

8. Sir Philip Sidney, "Astrophil and Stella," 106, in William A. Ringler, Jr., ed., *The Poems of Sir Philip Sidney* (Oxford: Oxford Univ. Press, 1962), p. 235. I owe the initial stimulus to work in this area to Margaret A. McLaren (Witten-Hannah), whose work on Lady Wroth may be found in an important unpublished diss., University of Auckland, 1979, "A Study of Lady Mary Wroth's *The Countesse of Mountogomerie's Urania*." See the mention in *Sidney Newsletter*, 1, No. 1 (1980), p. 36. My discussion of Elizabethan and Cavalier lyrics in this paper also owes much to the stimulation of my colleague and collaborator, Kathleen McCormick-Leighty, who rescued some of the thinking here, in its late stages, from culture-specific but culpable sexism.

9. See, e.g., Mary E. Lamb, "Three Unpublished Holograph Poems in the Bright Manuscript: A New Poet in the Sidney Circle," *Review of English Studies* (forthcoming, 1985); Josephine R. Roberts, "Lady Mary Wroth's Sonnets: A Labyrinth of the Mind," *Journal of*

Women's Studies in Literature, 1 (1979), 319-29; Diane Bornstein ed., *Distaves and Dames: Renaissance Treatises for and About Women* (New York: Scholar's Facsimiles, 1978); Ann Rosalind Jones, "Assimilation with a Difference: Renaissance Woman Poets and Literary Influence," *Yale French Studies*, 62 (1981) 135-53.

10. E.g., Barbara B. J. Bloy, " 'Woman's Exercise': Studies in the Female Personae of Elizabethan Miscellanies," Diss. University of Tennessee 1977.

11. Michel Foucault, *The Order of Things*, (New York: Vintage Books, 1973), pp. xx-xxii; "The Discourse on Language," *The Archeology of Knowledge*, trans. A. M. Sheridan Smith (New York: Harper, 1972), p. 216.

12. Jeannine Hensley, ed., *The Works of Anne Bradstreet* (Cambridge: Harvard Univ. Press, 1967), p. 221.

13. For Mary Sidney's work, see Gary F. Waller, ed., *The Triumph of Death and Other Unpublished and Uncollected Poems* (Salzburg: Univ. of Salzburg, 1977), and Waller, *Mary Sidney, Countess of Pembroke: A Critical Study of Her Writings and Literary Milieu* (Salzburg: Univ. of Salzburg, 1979). In addition to the editions and studies listed in the latter study, see Diane Bornstein, ed., *The Countess of Pembroke's Translation of Philippe de Mornay's Discourse of Life and Death* (Detroit: Medieval and Renaissance Monographs, 1983).

14. Michel Foucault, "The History of Sexuality: Interview," trans. Geoff Bennington, *Oxford Literary Review*, 4, No. 2 (1980), 10.

15. Bob Hodge and David Aers, " 'Rational Burning': Milton on Sex and Marriage," *Milton Studies*, 13 (1979), 6.

16. *Lady Mary Wroth, Pamphilia to Amphilanthus*, ed. Gary F. Waller (Salzburg: Univ. of Salzburg, 1977). For a complete edition of Lady Wroth's poems, see Josephine A. Roberts, ed., *The Poems of Lady Mary Wroth* (Baton Rouge: Louisiana State Univ. Press, 1983).

17. See Josephine Roberts, " 'The Anxiety of Influence': A Comparative View of the Poetry of Sir Robert Sidney and Lady Mary Wroth," *Sidney Newsletter*, 1, No. 1 (1980), 345. For Robert Sidney, see, e.g., Gary F. Waller, "The 'Sad Pilgrim': The Poetry of Robert Sidney," *Dalhousie Review*, 55 (1975-76), 689-705.

18. Lilian Robinson and Elise Vogel, "Modernism and History," in Susan Kippelman-Cornillon, ed., *Images of Women in Fiction: Feminist Perspectives* (Bowling Green: The Popular Press, 1972), p. 288.

19. Angela Carter, *The Sadeian Woman* (London: Virago, 1979), p. 18, makes the point that the myths by which relationships between the sexes are described are inevitably paradigmatic of a society's general social relations.

20. Mary Wroth, *The Countesse of Montgomeries Urania* (London, 1622), p. 409.

21. Michel Foucault, *The History of Sexuality*, trans. Robert Hurley (Harmondsworth: Penguin Books, 1976), I, 59.

22. Foucault, "The History of Sexuality: Interview," *Oxford Literary Review*, 4, No. 2 (1980), 3-4.

23. For useful surveys, see Josette Feral, "Antigone or *The Irony of the Tribe*," *Diacritics*, 8 (Sept. 1978), 2-14, and Verena Conley, "Missexual Misstery," *Diacritics*, 7 (June 1977), 70-82.

24. Luce Irigaray, "This Sex Which Is Not One," in *New French Feminisms*, p. 100, 101.

25. John Donne, "Elegy 19: To His Mistress Going to Bed," in *The Complete English Poems*, ed. A. J. Smith (Harmondsworth: Penguin Books, 1971), pp. 124-26.

26. Jacques Derrida, "White Mythology: Metaphor in the Text of Philosophy," *New Literary History*, 6 (1974), 71.

27. Waller, *Mary Sidney*, pp. 220-25. See also Beth Wynne Fisken's essay in this collection.

28. Francis Barker, "The Tremulous Private Body," in Francis Barker et al., *1642: Literature and Power in the Seventeenth Century* (Colchester: Univ. of Essex, 1980), p. 2.

29. *A Discovery of 29 Sects here in London* (London, 1642), p. 4.

30. Keith Thomas, "Women and the Civil War Sects," *Past and Present*, 13 (1958), 42–62.

31. For Anna Trapnell, see *The Cry of a Stone* . . . *uttered in prayers and spiritual songs* (London, 1654), *A Legacy for Saints* (London, 1654), and the material cited by Thomas, p. 59n. 48. On seventeenth-century women's writing, for two interesting essays from viewpoints similar to my own, see Sandra Findley and Elaine Hoby, "Seventeenth Century Women's Autobiography," and Christine Berg and Philippa Berry, "Spiritual Whoredom: An Essay on Female Prophets in the Seventeenth Century," in Barker, pp. 11–36, 37–54.

32. Michel Foucault, *Madness and Civilization*, trans. Alan Sheridan (New York: Pantheon Books, 1965).

33. See, e.g., Julia Kristeva, "Women Can Never Be Defined," in *New French Feminisms*, pp. 140–41; Ann Rosalind Jones, "Writing the Body: Toward an Understanding of L'Ecriture Feminisme" *Feminist Studies*, 7 (1981), 247–63. I owe Ann Jones thanks for clarifying this and other parts of the essay.

34. Allen White, *Exposition and Critique of Julia Kristeva* (Birmingham: Centre for Contemporary Cultural Studies Occasional Stencilled Paper, General Series, No. 49), p. 3; Kristeva, p. 137.

35. Feral, pp. 10, 11, quoting Kristeva, *Polylogues* (Paris: Seuil, 1977), p. 79.

36. Annabel Patterson, "Recent Studies in the English Renaissance," *Studies in English Literature*, 20 (1980), 153.

Selected Bibliography

The most complete sources for these listings are Merry E. Wiesner, *Women in the Sixteenth Century: A Bibliography* (St. Louis: Center for Reformation Research, 1983), and the bibliographic essays by Elizabeth H. Hageman, "Recent Studies in Women Writers of Tudor England. Part I: Women Writers, 1485–1603, Excluding Mary Sidney, Countess of Pembroke," *English Literary Renaissance*, 14 (1984), 409–26, and by Josephine R. Roberts, "Recent Studies in Women Writers of Tudor England. Part II: Mary Sidney, Countess of Pembroke," *English Literary Renaissance*, 14 (1984), 426–39. Elizabeth Hageman's "Recent Studies in Women Writers of Seventeenth-Century England," forthcoming in *English Literary Renaissance*, is also useful. A few of the book-length studies are listed here to give a context for our own work.

The first step toward a study of women writers is to make the texts themselves available. General anthologies were a most useful beginning and still have enormous value as texts for survey courses, such as Joan Goulianos, ed., *By a Woman Writt: Literature from Six Centuries By and About Women* (New York: Bobbs-Merrill, 1973), and Louise Bernikow, ed., *The World Split Open: Four Centuries of Women Poets in England and America, 1552–1950* (New York: Vintage Books, 1974). More specialized anthologies, which generally include biographical material and some critical discussion, include Meg Bogin, *The Women Troubadours* (New York: W. W. Norton and Co., 1976); Mary R. Mahl and Helene Koon, eds., *The Female Spectator: English Women Writers Before 1800* (Bloomington: Indiana Univ. Press, 1977); Betty Travitsky, ed., *The Paradise of Women: Writings by Englishwomen of the Renaissance* (Westport, Conn.: Greenwood Press, 1981); John F. Plummer, ed., *Vox Feminae: Studies in Medieval Woman's Songs* (Kalamazoo, Mich.: Medieval Institute Publications, 1981); Margaret L. King and Albert Rabil, Jr., eds., *Her Immaculate Hand: Selected Works by and*

About the Women Humanists of Quattrocento Italy (Binghamton, N.Y.: Medieval and Renaissance Texts and Studies, 1983); Katharina M. Wilson, ed., *Medieval Women Writers* (Athens: Univ. of Georgia Press, 1984). Wilson is currently editing a sequel, *Renaissance Women Writers.*

Biographical/critical studies follow a similar pattern of grouping together women who were associated or at least were writing in the same time or place: Eileen Power, *Medieval English Nunneries* (Cambridge: Cambridge Univ. Press, 1922); Pearl Hogrefe, *Tudor Women: Commoners and Queens* (Ames: Iowa State Univ. Press, 1975), and *Women of Action in Tudor England* (Ames: Iowa State Univ. Press, 1977); Roland Bainton, *Women of the Reformation: In France and England* (Minneapolis: Augsburg Publishing House, 1973); J. R. Brink, *Female Scholars: A Tradition of Learned Women Before 1800* (Montreal: Eden Press Women's Publications, 1980); Patricia H. Labalme, ed., *Beyond Their Sex: Learned Women of the European Past* (New York: New York Univ. Press, 1980); and Peter Dronke, *Women Writers of the Middle Ages: A Critical Study of Texts from Perpetua (203) to Marguerite Porete (1310)* (Cambridge: Cambridge Univ. Press, 1984).

The writings of some of the more significant individual women have been recently reissued in modern editions, including works by Christine de Pizan, Julian of Norwich, Jane Anger, Queen Elizabeth, Louise Labé, Marguerite de Navarre, Vittoria Colonna, Lady Margaret Dakins Hoby, St. Theresa, Mary Sidney, and Mary Wroth. Critical studies of these writings which began in the late nineteenth-century and then languished are once again beginning to emerge in various literary journals.

A closely related topic is the controversy over women in medieval and Renaissance texts. Antifeminist writings were earlier analyzed by Louis B. Wright, in "The Popular Controversy over Women" in *Middle-Class Culture in Elizabethan England* (Chapel Hill: Univ. of North Carolina Press, 1935); by Francis L. Utley, *The Crooked Rib: An Analytical Index to the Argument About Women in English and Scots Literature to the End of the Year 1568* (Ohio: Ohio State Univ. Press, 1944; rpt. New York: Octagon, 1970); and by Carroll Camden in *The Elizabethan Woman* (New York: Elsevier, 1952). More recent studies include Katharine Rogers, *The Troublesome Helpmate: A History of Misogyny in Literature* (Seattle: Univ. of Washington Press, 1966); Vern Bullough, *The Subordinate Sex: A History of Attitudes toward Women* (Urbana: Univ. of Illinois Press, 1973); and Linda Woodbridge, *Women and the English Renaissance: Literature and the Nature of Womankind, 1540–1620* (Urbana: Univ. of Illinois Press, 1984). Ian Maclean extended the discussion to include scholasticism and medicine in *The Renaissance Notion of Woman: A Study in the Fortunes of Scholasticism and Medical Science in European Intellectual Life* (Cambridge: Cambridge Univ. Press, 1980).

Books written for Renaissance women are the subject of Ruth Kelso, *Doctrine for the Lady of the Renaissance* (Urbana: Univ. of Illinois Press, 1956); Suzanne

W. Hull, *Chaste, Silent & Obedient: English Books for Women 1475–1640* (San Marino, Calif.: Huntington Library, 1982); and of Diane Bornstein, *The Lady in the Tower: Medieval Courtesy Literature for Women* (Hamden, Conn.: Archon Books, 1983). Specifically medical matters are treated by Audrey Eccles in *Obstetrics and Gynaecology in Tudor and Stuart England* (Kent, Oh.: Kent State Univ. Press, 1982).

General surveys of women's education and roles include Douglas Radcliff-Umstead, ed., *The Roles and Images of Women in the Middle Ages and Renaissance* (Pittsburgh: Univ. of Pittsburgh Publication on the Middle Ages and Renaissance, 1975); Eileen Power, *Medieval Women*, ed. M. M. Postan (Cambridge: Cambridge Univ. Press, 1975); Susan Mosher Stuard, ed., *Women in Medieval Society* (Philadelphia: Univ. of Pennsylvania Press, 1976); Phyllis Stock, *Better Than Rubies: A History of Women's Education* (New York: G. P. Putnam's Sons, 1978); Frances and Joseph Gies, *Women in the Middle Ages* (New York: Thomas Y. Crownwell Co., 1978); and Retha M. Warnicke, *Women of the English Renaissance and Reformation* (Westport, Conn.: Greenwood Press, 1983).

Index

Actes and Monuments (Book of Martyrs) (Foxe), 45–46, 51, 98

Aggas, Edward: tr. Discours de la vie et de la mort, 127–28, 130–31

Apologia Ecclesiae Anglicanae (Jewel; tr. A. Bacon), 117–18

Apology for the Church of England, 117–18

Aragon, Catherine of, 15, 18

Ascham, Roger (The Scholemaster), 52, 59, 95

Askew, Anne (see also Examinations of Anne Askew), 77–91; and defense at Lincoln, 82–83; on divorce, 82; early life of, 77–78, 82; interrogated about Catherine Parr's circle, 45; as Protestant martyr, 80–81, 270n. 1; and motives for writing, 83–84; personality of, 79–80; rhetorical art of, 82, 85, 86–87, 88, 89; on women's biblical discourse, 85; mentioned, 11, 57

Bacon, Anne. See Cooke, Anne

Bacon, Nicholas, 111

Bale, John: and Examinations of Anne Askew, 11, 78, 80–81, 85–86, 88–91; publishes A Godly medytacyon of the christen sowle, 72–73; and Catherine Parr's circle, 51; as religious historian, 271n. 5

Barker, William, 27–28

Bartlett, Thomas, 37

Becon, Thomas, 53

Bentley, Thomas (The Monument of Matrones), 4

Bercher (Barker), William (The Nobility of Women), 27–28

Berthelet (Bartlett), Thomas, 37

Bible: archetypes for rulers, 50–51, 156–60, 164–65; archetypes for women, 52, 212–13; political interpretations and uses of, 19, 45–46, 82, 157–58, 161–63, 175. Cited: Acts of the Apostles 17, 87; 2 Corinthians 12, 80; Proverbs 19, 87; Psalm 45, 172–75; Revelation 12, 52

Billingsley, Martin (The pen's excellencie), 8

Boleyn, Anne, 44, 208

Bonner, Bishop, 82–83, 87–88

Book of Common Prayer, 177–78

Book of Martyrs, 45–46, 51, 98

Brandon, Catherine, 55–59

Breton, Nicholas ("An Olde Mans Lesson"), 118–19

Cary, Elizabeth (Viscountess Falkland), 225–37; early life of, 225–26; conversion to Catholicism of, 226–27; marriage of, 226–27; description of, 287n. 4; literary career of, 227, 228–31; in po-

Contributors

ELAINE BEILIN received her doctorate from Princeton University and has taught at Mount Holyoke College and Boston University. She has just completed a book, *Redeeming Eve: Women Writers of the English Renaissance*.

DIANE BORNSTEIN, Professor of English Literature at City University of New York, was well known for her work on Renaissance women, including *Ideals for Women in the Works of Christine de Pizan, The Lady in the Tower: Medieval Courtesy Literature for Women*, and her edition of the Countess of Pembroke's translation of Philippe de Mornay's *Discours de la vie et de la mort*. Diane died suddenly in February 1984.

SANDRA K. FISCHER, Assistant Professor of English Literature at the State University of New York at Albany, is the author of articles on Crashaw and St. Theresa, George Eliot, the genre of economic drama, and of a book entitled *Econolingua: A Glossary of Coins and Economic Language in Renaissance Drama*. She is also Associate Editor of *Theatre Survey*.

BETH WYNNE FISKEN recently completed her doctoral work at Rutgers University where she now teaches. Her essay in this collection amplifies ideas initially developed in portions of her dissertation, "The Education of Mary Sidney." She has also published several articles on Mary Wilkins Freeman.

MARGARET PATTERSON HANNAY, Assistant Professor of English Literature at Siena College, has written numerous articles on Spenser, Philip Sidney, Mary Sidney, Milton, and various modern authors, and is currently completing a literary biography of the Countess of Pembroke. She is also the author of *C. S. Lewis* and editor of *As Her Whimsey Took Her: Critical Essays on the Work of Dorothy L. Sayers*.

JOHN N. KING, Professor of English Literature at Bates College, is the author of *English Reformation Literature: The Tudor Origins of the Protestant Tradi-*

tion, as well as of numerous articles and reviews published in *Renaissance Quarterly, English Literary Renaissance, Modern Philology,* and other journals. He has held long-term NEH Visiting Fellowships at Brown University and the Huntington Library.

MARY ELLEN LAMB, Associate Professor of English Literature at Southern Illinois University, has published articles on the Countess of Pembroke, Sidney manuscripts, and Shakespeare, in such journals as *English Literary Renaissance, Shakespeare Survey,* and *Review of English Studies.*

CAROLE LEVIN, Coordinator of Women's Studies and Assistant Professor of History at the State University of New York at New Paltz, has published articles on the changing image of King John in the English Renaissance and on Tudor presentations of women and queenship in such journals as *Sixteenth Century Journal, Journal of the Rocky Mountain Medieval and Renaissance Association,* and the *International Journal of Women's Studies.*

BARBARA KIEFER LEWALSKI is William R. Kenan Professor of English Literature at Harvard University. Her recent books include studies of Milton's *Paradise Regained,* Donne's *Anniversaries,* and Protestant Poetics. Her *Paradise Lost and the Rhetoric of Literary Forms* will be published in 1985.

ANNE LAKE PRESCOTT, Associate Professor of English Literature at Barnard College and Columbia University, is the author of *French Poets and the English Renaissance.* Together with A. Kent Hieatt and Charles Hieatt she is working on a book exploring the impact of du Bellay and Spenser on Shakespeare's sonnets, and over the next few years she also hopes to do a book on Rabelais and Renaissance England.

JON A. QUITSLUND is Associate Professor and Chairman of the English department at The George Washington University. He holds his Ph.D. from Princeton University; it was there, at the suggestion of Thomas Roche, that he first became interested in the circumstances surrounding Spenser's *Fowre Hymnes.*

RITA VERBRUGGE received her Ph.D. in 1984 from the University of Michigan and is currently teaching at Calvin College.

GARY F. WALLER is Professor of Literary Studies and Head of the Department of English at Carnegie Mellon University. He is the author of *The Strong Necessity of Time, Mary Sidney, Countess of Pembroke,* and many other Renaissance studies, including the forthcoming *English Poetry of the Sixteenth Century.* He has also published on contemporary American literature, including *Dreaming America,* and has published a volume of poetry, *Impossible Futures, Indelible Pasts.*

VALERIE WAYNE, Assistant Professor of English Literature at the University of Hawaii, has published essays and reviews on the shrew character, on feminist criticism of Shakespeare, and on Christine de Pizan. She is currently at work on an edition of Edmund Tilney's *Flower of Friendshippe.*